T0214092

Communications
in Computer and Information Science 1270

Commenced Publication in 2007
Founding and Former Series Editors:
Simone Diniz Junqueira Barbosa, Phoebe Chen, Alfredo Cuzzocrea,
Xiaoyong Du, Orhun Kara, Ting Liu, Krishna M. Sivalingam,
Dominik Ślęzak, Takashi Washio, Xiaokang Yang, and Junsong Yuan

Mirella Cacace · Raija Halonen ·
Hongxiu Li · Thao Phuong Orrensalo ·
Chenglong Li · Gunilla Widén ·
Reima Suomi (Eds.)

Well-Being in the Information Society

Fruits of Respect

8th International Conference, WIS 2020
Turku, Finland, August 26–27, 2020
Proceedings

 Springer

Editors
Mirella Cacace ⓘ
Catholic University of Applied Sciences
Freiburg, Germany

Hongxiu Li ⓘ
Tampere University
Tampere, Finland

Chenglong Li ⓘ
University of Turku
Turku, Finland

Reima Suomi ⓘ
University of Turku
Turku, Finland

Raija Halonen ⓘ
University of Oulu
Oulu, Finland

Thao Phuong Orrensalo ⓘ
Åbo Akademi University
Turku, Finland

Gunilla Widén ⓘ
Åbo Akademi University
Turku, Finland

ISSN 1865-0929   ISSN 1865-0937 (electronic)
Communications in Computer and Information Science
ISBN 978-3-030-57846-6   ISBN 978-3-030-57847-3 (eBook)
https://doi.org/10.1007/978-3-030-57847-3

This Springer imprint is published by the registered company Springer Nature Switzerland AG
The registered company address is: Gewerbestrasse 11, 6330 Cham, Switzerland

Preface

The first international conference on Well-being in the Information Society (WIS) was introduced in 2006. The current conference (WIS 2020) is already the 8th biannual implementation of the series. WIS 2020 was organized by University of Turku in cooperation with Åbo Akademi University, Tampere University, Turku University of Applied Sciences, and the Finnish National Institute for Health and Welfare. WIS 2020 was implemented under the topic "Fruits of Respect" in Turku, August 2020. Along with years passing and new smart technology developed, the role of respect and related values deserve special attention when designing new applications and solutions for individuals and organizations. With this topic we wanted to emphasize respect, especially from its human, concerning, and encouraging nature, and see its importance when building an information society.

Due to the special times of the COVID-19 pandemic, the conference was arranged predominately online.

The submitted papers consisted of academic contributions on the topics of intersection of health, ICT, and fruits of respect as seen from different directions and contexts. The number of submissions remained smaller than during the previous WIS implementations, which we interpreted as due to the difficult situation globally at the time and related restrictions that were constantly changing and frequently updated internationally. However, thanks to the international reviewers, we were able to accept 19 papers to be presented at the conference and to be included in the conference program. We are grateful for the efforts of the reviewers in identifying relevant and topical research papers for WIS 2020.

The proceedings are structured in four sections as follows:

I. Improving Quality and Containing Cost in Health Care and Care for the Elderly by Using Information Technology

Part I of this collection reflects ethical considerations in the use of information and communication technology (ICT) in health care and care for the elderly. Essentially, this part asks how health care processes can be improved by using ICT to benefit health care consumers, and what the implications are.

In their contribution, Nilmini Wickramasinghe and Rima Gibbings point out that coordination and integration of services are essential for delivering high-quality care in the US health care system. Digitalization offers opportunities for improved scheduling and tracking, but achieving these objectives is impossible without involving the patient. Understanding patients' needs is of particular interest for providing access to vulnerable populations, such as the elderly or lower socio-economic groups.

As Sio Lai Karppinen, Jori Karppinen, and Raija Halonen point out, in particular the needs of the elderly tend to be neglected when it comes to the design of services. This is a major conceptual shortcoming, as this population group is receiving the bulk of care provided by the health care system. Not only is the number of elderly people growing, but also the incidence of dementia. In their contribution, the authors study non-pharmacologic solutions to support people suffering from dementia and their caretakers.

The elderly and their special needs are also the focus of the contribution by Konsta Rantakangas and Raija Halonen. By reviewing the state-of-the-art literature, the authors start by identifying several special characteristics of the elderly caused by high age or diagnosed reasons such as memory-related diseases. Core recommendation will need to search for ways to let the elderly participate in the development, which is crucial to mitigate the challenges they face when using web-based services.

The issue of participation and consumer involvement is also highly salient when the users are the main sources of data generation themselves, i.e., in the case of self-collected devices. Looking at occupational programs and health insurers, Stefan Stepanovic shows the crucial importance of motivating users in order to obtain complete and reliable data. Gamification and financial incentives may be useful instruments in the short run, but they are rarely sustainable. With his contribution, the author identifies the main motivational incentives potentially leading to the development of effective digital programs.

The collection of data and knowledge generation are not an end in itself, they are subordinate to other objectives, such as improving processes and outcomes. However, orientation in the 'data jungle' becomes increasingly difficult the more information is available. To minimize information losses, it is of particular importance to agree on common terms and expressions. By studying the multiple understandings of private health records through a systematic literature review, Jani Koskinen and Minna Rantanen show how far we are away from such a common understanding. According to these authors, a clear and systematic structure is necessary, and discourses about core ideas in health care are essential to benefit from technical innovation.

Public health systems, in particular, are held accountable to use funds from collective, tax-funded sources prudently. Therefore, when aiming at improving the value of health care, cost considerations must apply. According to Olli Sjöblom, Sonja Turnbull-Smith, Heikki Minn, and Jani Keyriläinen, the objects of saving costs and achieving high-quality care are not necessarily mutually exclusive; it is possible to align these concepts. Taking the example of radiotherapy, the authors show how providers have focused on reducing costs by applying methods that do not cause adverse effects on health-care quality to achieve value-based outcomes.

II. Collecting the Fruits of Respect in Entrepreneurship and Management of Organizations

Part II discusses the sub-theme of the conferences in three papers:

The contribution by Mari Hartemo and Mika Suutari was motivated by a 'democratic deficit' and the imperative of participative leadership in a university setting. By applying the theoretical framework of the International Association of Public Participation (inform, consult, involve, collaborate, and empower) they seek to explore the potential of digitalization to improve participation of employees. As this seems to be a quite frequently encountered deficit, their results might be of value for other organizations as well.

Quitting smoking greatly reduces the risk of developing smoking-related diseases. In her contribution, Chenglong Li focuses on smoking cessation with regards to online health communities. These combine internet-based smoking-cessation interventions with the feedback of users. As a novel approach, the contribution explores the various consequences of user satisfaction with online health communities from a social support perspective. The findings provide some important practical implications for management. Accordingly, service providers should promote knowledge sharing and recommendation by enhancing users' satisfaction with smoking cessation. Furthermore, they should focus on strategies to promote the sharing of emotional and esteem support among users.

Thao Orrensalo and Shahrokh Nikou investigate how trust and respect impact entrepreneurs' information-seeking behavior. The results show that trust and respect are two fundamental aspects influencing entrepreneurs' preference for information sources. Furthermore, the findings show that both trust and respect act as a predominant factor for entrepreneurs to build and advance their relationships. With this only scarcely researched theme, the authors are paving the way to entrepreneurship for further information-seeking behavior studies.

III. Friend or Foe: Society in the Area of Tension Between Free Data Movement and Data Protection

Part III shows that developers and policy makers have to consider and balance the information requirements of the population, their reservations, and data protection needs.

Accuracy and data collection abilities are growing in Internet of Things (IoT) solutions. This brings a tension between the desire to benefit from the collected data and privacy protection. As legal constraints have their limits, Mikko Vermanen, Jani Koskinen, and Ville Harkke are seeking to provide guidance on how data collection, processing, and distribution can be conducted in an ethically sustainable manner. In order to foster accountability of data distributors, the authors suggest a 'decision tree' relating the data distribution to technical objects, environment, and individuals. This is providing sufficient knowledge and clear guidelines to address the ethical issues properly.

Hanna Kirjavainen and Harri Jalonen investigate in the social media posts of socially withdrawn young persons on an internet forum. Their aim is to find out what challenges are preventing socially withdrawn youths from participation and inclusion, and what would motivate them to 'join in.' Problems with mental health, social anxieties, and frustration towards society were identified as the main reasons for social withdrawal, indicating that the participants do not feel like their skills and persona is appreciated by society.

Based on the technology affordance theory, the contribution by Ting Long seeks to understand how social media affords each particular need of travelers at different stages of the travel processes. The author conducted 21 interviews to explore the relationship between travelers' activities and the technology capabilities of social media in the tourism context. His research contributes to the literature on affordances of social media used during the entire process of travel and offers practical implications for managing social media in tourism.

As the importance of data is growing, so does the role of data economy ecosystems. The analysis by Minna Rantanen and Jani Koskinen shows that individuals should be respected as active members of data economy ecosystems by providing tools and information through transparent, honest, and secure practices. The authors conclude that transparency seems to be the prime enabler of value congruence and thus also the fundamental basis for respecting individuals.

Blockchain is a recent development in technology, which allows a cryptographically secured, decentralized, and distributed storage of data. As Sami Hyrynsalmi, Sonja M. Hyrynsalmi, and Kai K. Kimppa point out, while this technology has potentially a remarkable power to shape the modern digital societies, its usage provokes several ethical questions. Based on a systematic literature study, the authors show that a deep understanding of relevant ethical concerns is required when using this technology.

IV. Bridging the Digital Divide: Strengthening (Health-) Literacy and Supporting Trainings in Information Society

Part IV introduces five papers pointing out challenges related to the digital divide:

In order to bridge the digital divide, a reflection of the principles and definitions guiding the research on this subject is required. A major issue here is to understand what distinguishes digital natives from digital immigrants. By referring to the educational context, Milla Aavakare and Shahrokh Nikou criticize that this distinction currently is bound solely to the age factor. As this distinction is falling short, their study aims to look beyond age as a divider. Their results show that digital literacy and technology acceptance is a competence that depends on the access, frequency of use, and the ability to use digital technologies. In conclusion, the interactions of individuals with digital technologies should be used for classification instead.

The study by Brita Somerkoski, Päivi Granö, and Teija Koskela investigates how international students are reflecting on the physical and psychological dimensions of learning environments. The qualitative research design examined 20 training portfolios that the trainees used during the practical training in their homeland in the Southern African region. As a result, the trainees successfully managed strategies such as self-reporting, discussions in groups, learning cafés, and teamwork. Regarding the physical learning environment, the scarcity of materials in their homeland made some of them replace technical devices with other learning materials in order to bridge the digital divide.

As the population is ageing, immigrants will be an important source of labor in the future. The contribution by Saaga Somerkoski assesses the attitudes among Finnish second grade students towards immigrants in a region where the number of immigrants currently is one of the lowest in Finland. Attitudes were mixed, with the immigration of children and workers being regarded more positively compared to unemployed migrants and refugees. No respondent reported about immigration as a positive phenomenon. These results are quite remarkable given the problem of a quickly ageing population also in that region.

In a quantitative survey, the study by Ágústa Pálsdóttir collected information about satisfaction with a new technology that was implemented nationwide in Iceland. The new health information and communication technology includes information about health history and healthy lifestyle of the user. In order to investigate acceptance of the technology, the author questioned people aged between 18 and 60 years in an online survey, and individuals 60 years and older by telephone. The results show that it is of the utmost importance to accompany the introduction of new health information and communication technology by trainings as well as proper technical support.

As a major effort to make use of information technology in health care thereby bridging the digital divide, Heini Utunen presents the World Health Organization's (WHO) ePROTECT. The project is an occupational health and safety online briefing for the Ebola Virus. The program has become a key resource in battling the disease at the frontline in different professional roles in various organizations. Broad access is secured via an open-source online platform adjusted for low-bandwidths, and applications with mobile and download capabilities.

We want to express our deepest gratitude to our organizing institutions that have constantly supported us with the conference in several ways. We also want to thank the Finnish Foundation for Economic Education for financial support, all the authors for contributions, and all the reviewers for their quality assured work. Our conference management group, with the addition of our editor group consisting of Katja Heikki-nen, Jukka Kärkkäinen, Marja Rautajoki, Sanna Salanterä, Brita Somerkoski, and Tapio Vepsäläinen, also deserves a big thanks. The conference program, in addition to the academic papers, was enriched by keynotes by Tobias Mettler and Liisa-Maria Voipio-Pulkki. Finally, we are grateful to Springer for again accepting our proceedings for publication, and especially to editorial director Aliaksandr Birukou who has always encouraged us during the process. As has been the case since WIS 2006, the organizers look forward to the next biannual WIS in 2022 with a fresh subtopic and a lot of interesting contributions and people from all around the world.

July 2020

Mirella Cacace
Raija Halonen
Hongxiu Li
Thao Phuong Orrensalo
Chenglong Li
Gunilla Widén
Reima Suomi

Organization

Organizing Committee

Suomi, Reima (Conference Chair)	University of Turku, Finland
Li, Chenglong (Organizing Committee chair)	University of Turku, Finland
Cacace, Mirella (Program Co-chair)	Catholic University of Applied Sciences Freiburg, Germany
Halonen, Raija (Program Co-chair)	University of Oulu, Finland
Heikkinen, Katja	Turku University of Applied Science, Finland
Kärkkäinen, Jukka	The National Institute for Health and Welfare, Finland
Li, Hongxiu	Tampere University, Finland
Rautajoki, Marja	University of Turku, Finland
Salanterä, Sanna	University of Turku, Finland
Somerkoski, Brita	University of Turku, Finland
Vepsäläinen, Tapio	University of Turku, Finland
Widén, Gunilla	Åbo Akademi University, Finland

Program Committee

Ahonen, Pia	Turku University of Applied Sciences, Finland
Aromaa, Minna	City of Turku, Finland
Cabral, Regis	Funding for European Projects, Sweden
Carmichael, Laurence	The University of the West of England, UK
Cellary, Wojceich	Poznan University of Economics, Poland
Eriksson-Backa, Kristina	Åbo Akademi University, Finland
Eskola, Eeva-Liisa	Åbo Akademi University, Finland
Gan, Chunmei	Sun Yat-Sen University, China
Gea-Sànchez, Montserrat	University of Turku, Finland
Hansen, Preben	Stockholm University, Sweden
Heikkinen, Katja	Turku University of Applied Sciences, Finland
Hupli, Maija	University of Turku, Finland
Hyrkkänen, Ursula	Turku University of Applied Sciences, Finland
Kangasniemi, Mari	University of Turku, Finland
Karukivi, Max	University of Turku, Finland
Kini, Ranjan	Indiana University Northwest, USA
Klein, Stefan	University of Muenster, Germany
Kokol, Peter	University of Maribor, Slovenia
Lamersdorf, Winfried	University of Hamburg, Germany

Li, Xiaodong	Tampere University, Finland
Liu, Yong	Aalto University, Finland
Mandl, Thomas	University of Hildesheim, Germany
Mari, Lahti	Turku University of Applied Sciences, Finland
Mononen, Jukka	Oulu University, Finland
Oduor, Michael	Oulu University, Finland
Pakarinen, Anni	University of Turku, Finland
Palsdottir, Agusta	University of Iceland, Iceland
Pelander, Tiina	Turku University of Applied Sciences, Finland
Peltonen, Laura-Maria	University of Turku, Finland
Päivärinta, Tero	Oulu University, Finland
Raitoharju, Reetta	Turku University of Applied Sciences, Finland
Rasmussen, Niels Kristian	Ostfold County Council, Denmark
Ryjov, Alexander	Moscow State University, Russia
Salman, Iflaah	University of Oulu, Finland
Scott, Philip	University of Portsmouth, UK
Sheerin, Fintan	University of Dublin, Ireland
Sjöblom, Olli	University of Turku, Finland
Somerkoski, Brita	University of Turku, Finland
Stolt, Minna	University of Turku, Finland
Suhonen, Riitta	University of Turku, Finland
Teixeira, Jose	Åbo Akademi University, Finland
Usman-Langrial, Sitwat	Sur University College, Oman
Virtanen, Heli	University of Turku, Finland
Wang, Ping	Central China Normal University, China
Wells, George	Rhodes University, South Africa
Widén, Gunilla	Åbo Akademi University, Finland
Womser-Hacker, Christa	Universitt Hildesheim, Germany
Wrycka, Stanislaw	University of Gdansk, Poland
Xi, Nannan	Tampere University, Finland

Contents

Improving Quality and Containing Cost in Health Care and Care for the Elderly by Using Information Technology

Understanding the Difficulties of People with Dementia and Their Caretakers in Finland

Sio Lai Karppinen$^{(\boxtimes)}$, Jori Karppinen, and Raija Halonen

Faculty of ITEE, M3S, University of Oulu, Oulu, Finland
ssiolai@gmail.com, jori.karppinen@gmail.com,
raija.halonen@oulu.fi

Abstract. The number of people with memory issues—and especially with dementia—is a growing challenge that raises both economic and psychological issues worldwide, and most healthcare systems currently emphasise pharmaceutical solutions to managing the everyday lives of dementia patients and their families. This study sought to determine the real issues experienced by people with dementia and their caretakers and the solutions they use. The study was carried out in Finland, and data was collected by online interviews due to the pandemic. The results showed that most elderly enjoyed music, stories and especially from interaction with other people. Many also suffered from too little physical activity, and some from sleeping disorders, leading to problematic behaviour. As the social meetings designed for the patients and their caretakers were arranged in different locations, there were also issues with getting there. The results were to be applied when building the non-pharmaceutical solution.

Keywords: Dementia · Alzheimer's disease · ICT technologies · Elderly healthcare · Caregiver · Family caregivers · Technological innovations · Remote home care · Personalised · Serious game · Gamification · E-Health

1 Introduction

The purpose of this study was to find knowledge about the current problems and non-pharmaceutical solutions of people suffering from dementia, and of their caregivers in Finland. This research study was based on a request by a local association in Finland for seeking a solution to maintain relationships between dementia patients, their spouses and caretakers. Based on the findings, an innovative Serious Games package was to be created and the impact of using this artefact on dementia patients and their caretakers to be studied.

There are approximately 50 million people worldwide diagnosed with dementia and the number of dementia cases is increasing year by year all over the world. In 2050 there will be 152 million people impacted by dementia [1].

The main reasons for adopting non-pharmaceutical interventions are to minimize the drug–drug interactions and their side effects for using medicine on patients as well as overcoming limitations in pharmaceutical solutions for intervention [2].

© Springer Nature Switzerland AG 2020
M. Cacace et al. (Eds.): WIS 2020, CCIS 1270, pp. 3–23, 2020.
https://doi.org/10.1007/978-3-030-57847-3_1

In this study, we were looking for the most important issues which disturb the patient community's life. Moreover, we wanted to know what the current solutions are and which activities are organized for them in Finland. Based on the findings, an innovative serious games package will be created and the impact of using this artifact on dementia patients and their caretakers will be studied. The initiatives of this research project was to find out the elements for building an artefact to be developed in the future. The aim in creating this artefact was to offer healthier and better care, and to enhance the quality of life.

2 Earlier Knowledge

2.1 Current Challenges for the World, Dementia Patients and Caretakers

Alzheimer's Disease International, a non-profit organisation, has estimated that the global costs of dementia in 2015 were US$818 billion [3], and the average cost of taking care of a dementia patient is around 81% higher than patients with other conditions, such as heart disease, cancer or stroke [4, 5]. These costs can be separated into direct costs, including in-patient treatment, institutional care, nursing homes, community care, specialist visits, family support organisations, medications and research and development institutes [6], and indirect costs to society for taking care of patients, including costs for family caretakers and unpaid research work. According to a study in Switzerland, direct costs represent 55.7% of the total costs of dementia and indirect costs represent 44% [6]. Another study found similar proportions of indirect costs for mild (42%) and severe (43%) dementia patients [7]. The indirect costs of supporting this community must therefore not be ignored [6, 8].

The indirect costs of taking care of people with dementia can be categorised into two types: financial costs and mental costs. The changes of behaviour on dementia patients will request caregivers to spend more time and additional resources to prepare the physical and mental challenges which are caused by the illness [9]. To give better care to their life partner who had been diagnosed with dementia, family caretakers might need to reduce their working hours or even resign from their regular jobs [8, 10–12]. The costs of informal family caregivers could be considered to equate to the salaries they would otherwise earn in the job market or the societal costs of paying a nurse or caretaker. The estimated amount of informal service offered weekly to a dementia patient at home is around 50 h [6], and caretakers' quality of life and social activities might also be affected, rescheduled or reduced, depending on the level of dependency of the patients. These changes can be very challenging and cause depression problems in caretakers [13–16].

The enormous toll of dementia is not only financial, but also mental, both for those with dementia and their caretakers. Previous studies have shown that commonly experienced symptoms in this community include communication [17–19], emotional [20], behavioural [21–23], wandering [24–27] and comprehension [6, 17, 28–30] problems. Current medical treatments for dementia patients can slow the progress of dementia and improve mental health and behaviour, but pharmaceutical approaches are more focused on reducing symptoms than improving their quality of life.

Even though the lifespan of people with dementia is idiosyncratic, the average lifespan for people diagnosed with dementia is around 4 years—although some can live 20 years or more after being diagnosed [31]. As there is no medical cure and some patients' symptoms cannot be improved by pharmaceuticals [1], some patients and their caretakers might live with the symptoms for many years. Therefore, besides the financial and medical aspects, enhancing the quality of life of this group should be studied.

2.2 Importance of Non-pharmaceutical Therapies

Overuse of pharmaceutical treatment is said to create negative side effects on the patients and will reduce their joy of living [32]. Adopting non-pharmaceutical methods on people with dementia has potential to improve their quality of life and reduce their emotional and depression problems [33, 34]. Instead of relying purely on drug therapy, complimenting it with non-pharmaceutical treatment could reduce efficacy gaps and minimise the problems caused by maladaptive behaviour [16, 34, 35], thus increasing patients' self-confidence and decreasing their caretakers' burdens. Reducing the use of drugs can also lower the chance of side effects [36, 37].

Non-pharmaceutical treatment is more effective in early-stage than in late-stage dementia patients. Although early-stage dementia patients will start to have difficulties with concentration or finding words or may experience changes in personality or behaviour, many can still take care of themselves independently and participate in social activities. Early-stage patients can therefore participate more and have more interaction using non-pharmaceutical treatment than patients at other stages [38].

Furthermore, the early stages of dementia can last for years. As non-pharmaceutical treatment can benefit patients by ameliorating symptoms and improving behaviour, it may also extend the length of the early stage. Annual per-person net costs for taking care of early-stage (mild), middle-stage (moderate) and late-stage (severe) dementia patients in Germany have been calculated to be approximately €15,000, €32,000 and €42,000, respectively [39]; as noted above, the indirect costs are only slightly less, and non-pharmaceutical treatment can be considered part of both [6–8]. Therefore, the contribution of non-pharmaceutical programmes is essential and irreplaceable. Since independence limitations, wandering problems, communication issues and inappropriate behaviour become more serious as the disease progresses from the mild stage to the severe stage, extending the length of each stage could contribute to reducing the overall financial burden on society and improving the patients'—and their caretakers'—quality of life. Therefore, the contribution of non-pharmaceutical programs for this community is essential and irreplaceable.

As a summary, one can conclude that considering the independence, wandering problem, communication skills and altering behaviour, changes in a patient are typically greater while the illness transforms from mild to a more severe stage. Extending the length of different stages in dementia has a potential contribution to reducing the overall financial burden of the illness for the whole society, and improving the quality of life for patients' and their caretakers.

2.3 Importance of Personalization Information in the Therapies

Psychosocial interventions can have more beneficial effects than drugs, especially among those who suffer from the psycho-behavioural symptoms of dementia. Furthermore, while interacting with patients it is better for conversation experience if the topics are focused on their personal backgrounds and interests [1]. One of the three most important elements for developing efficient interventions in behavioural therapy is to include users' personal preferences [40]. The Health Foundation, an independent UK charity [51], contends that person-centred care is more efficient and can enhance service quality in patient treatment as it increases a patient's willingness to participate in medical care, which can reduce the use and costs of emergency hospital services [42].

Furthermore, "Tailored Activities Program" which considers patients' backgrounds and interests as one of its components, can improve dementia patients' behaviours, including 'shadowing, agitation, argumentation, and repetitive questioning' [43]. Thus, integrating personalised information and interests into a treatment programme can enhance its effectiveness [1, 40–42].

Some dementia symptoms can be improved if the topics of discussions are related to personal preferences, as patients are more interested in speaking about topics related to their own life stories or memories [44]. When patients are more interested in participating in treatment, their self-confidence increases [44], improving their behaviour and health outcomes [41]. Topics with personalised content and preferences, such as pictures, music and videos, can stimulate the brain more than the same topics with more general content [44]. Person-centred care services can thus offer a better quality of life to people with dementia [30].

2.4 How Technologies Benefit Healthcare Industry

Studies have shown that improving the quality of caring services is important to study both 'care processes' – which indicates the way a service is organised – and 'staff interactions with patients as well as their families, referring to human interactions [42]. Therefore, using interactive mobile applications in dementia patients' psychosocial treatments instead of only shifting its burden from caretakers to patients' families and close friends, technology can allow more people to participate into the programs/activities, enhancing communication and connections between distant relatives and people with dementia [46].

Another important aspect is to consider how people with dementia can benefit from technology, as far as Serious Games are concerned. Instead of aiming for pure entertainment, a Serious Game is for slowing down the progress of the illness on a patient by maintaining their skills, abilities or/and behaviour by using this application. A study showed that the top five aspects of applying a Serious Game in health care are "education, exergaming, cognitive rehabilitation, psychology, and physical rehabilitation" [29]. Here, for this Serious Game authors are gamifying the personal memories of their participating patients, in a manner respectful to them. While the outcome of this application is targeted to be fun and catchy, it is aiming at becoming a research prototype to a therapeutic e-Health application for further research. In this research, the patient's personal multimedia content - in form of image, video and audio files – will be gamified into this application. Based on metadata analysis performed on the content level in application logic, the game engine is generating a unique, custom puzzle for the patients to play, containing their very own personalised memories.

2.5 Importance of this Study in Finland

According to data reported by Statistics Finland, the proportion of people with dementia in Finland was the highest in the European Union (EU) in 2016 [42]. In 2017, 20% of stated causes of death for people over 65 in Finland were dementia and Alzheimer's disease [47], and, in 2018, 19% of deaths for people over 65 in Finland were caused by dementia—more than 10,000 people—and 33% of people aged over 85 died due to dementia and Alzheimer's disease [48].

The total number of people who died from dementia and Alzheimer's disease in Finland in 2016 was 9,200, which rose to 10,120 in 2018 [49, 50]. Similarly, deaths caused by dementia and Alzheimer's disease increased 47.1% from 2008 to 2018 [51]. Therefore, the number of deaths from dementia and Alzheimer's disease in Finland has increased around 10% every two years and 50% over ten years. Moreover, dementia and Alzheimer's disease were the only causes of death that increased after 2008 [51].

The proportion of people aged 65 and over in the population is expected to rise from 19.9% in 2015 to 26% by 2030 and 29% by 2060 [52]. The trend in all European countries is for elderly people to want to be cared for at home [53], but resources and funding will probably not increase sufficiently to satisfy the service needs of seniors with dementia in Finland. The average total direct and indirect costs of caring for one dementia patient was around €36,000 euro per year in 2008 in Northern Europe [54], and, in the United States, the average total Medicare payment for a person with dementia over five years was almost twice that of a heart disease or cancer patient [55]. Thus, new or different methods or technologies that offer better and more cost effective services for caring for this group may relieve part of the financial burden on the country.

3 Research Approach

This qualitative study used interviews to gather up-to-date information from current staff who were working for the Alzheimer's Association and the Alzheimer Society of Finland, to understand the present situation of dementia patients and their caretakers.

3.1 Qualitative Research

Qualitative research is a useful method for collecting information on new topics or achieving a deeper understanding of a community, especially when the data is related to experiences, feelings and interactions within society. Responses can be unique and are more accurate when recorded verbally than categorically, as unique answers might not have been allowed for in existing assessments but are especially important when developing a new and innovative artefact [56]. Furthermore, individual interview is a usual way to collect data in health and social research study as it can prove the research group an in-deep knowledge in the area [57].

In qualitative studies, informants can be invited, such as by personal meetings, email contacts and public announcements. In general, qualitative research focuses on understanding phenomena instead of seeking representative samples, and it allows for more informants to be invited after the data collection has started [58].

3.2 Application of the Research Method

Participants

The criteria for choosing participants are relevant to their answers, and the informants in this research needed to have prior experience of caring for patients with dementia. In this study, authors discovered the contacts of potential respondents online from websites of two different memory illness supporting organisations in Finland: Alzheimer's Association and Alzheimer Society of Finland. Invitations were sent by email that asked recipients to answer the questions independently online.

Questionnaire

Questions for the interview were designed based on Stone's criteria: appropriate, intelligible, unambiguous, unbiased, omnicompetent, piloted and ethical [56]. The lengths, wordings, grammar and order of the questions were also important aspects of the design of the questionnaire [59–61].

Since the aim of this study was to understand the difficulties of people with dementia and their caretakers in Finland. Three main research questions were addressed: (1) What activities were arranged by the memory illness supporting organisations in Finland (2) What psychosocial challenges the people with dementia and their caretakers are facing? (3) Can activities reduce negative impacts by dementia symptoms in view of the respondents?

Interview's Design and Setup

Pilot tests were conducted during the development of the questionnaire and before starting the actual interviews. The objective for pilot tests in questionnaire design is to tap the experience and knowledge of people with similar interests and backgrounds to enhance the accuracy of the questions; to help determine what kinds of questions should be presented, the structure of the questionnaire and the format used; to avoid misinterpretation of the questions [61, 62]; and to ensure the interviewees will not experience difficulties or uncomfortable feelings when answering the questions [46]. Researchers can also get a better estimate of the time to complete the questionnaire to ensure that interviewees do not become exhausted [46]. Finally, pilot tests can uncover hidden problems, offering the researchers a chance to improve the instrument. When problems are found, the researchers must consider the necessity of modifying the instrument and how to do so [62, 63].

For this study, authors had invited a former occupational therapist to design the questionnaire before issuing it out to the targeted interviewees. In order to minimize and avoid uncomfortable feelings of the interviewees, all the questions in the questionnaire were cautiously selected and written. Furthermore, the length, words and sequence of questions were carefully considered [61]. Upon the readiness of the steps above, authors had invited two nurses to answer the questionnaire as a test. This was to ensure the interview could run smoothly, ensuring its quality and suitability for the study. After the test, some changes were made following the pilot, and questions were added to enhance the value of the research.

Methods

As the purpose of this study was to collect up-to-date information about current methods from professional caretakers, conducting a one-to-one interview was considered the most suitable method. The invitations for the interviews were sent by email, but, at the time of the study, a global pandemic was still ongoing, and no face-to-face interviews were possible. The interviews were therefore conducted online between the 3rd and 17th of April 2020, and analysis was conducted thereafter.

In consideration of cost and efficiency in creating the questionnaire and distributing it to targeted interviewees, the authors chose a readily available survey engine offered by Google. Results of the questionnaire were saved in Google's online storage and only authorised people were able to access and download the data.

After collection, the data was organised, summarised, categorised and reviewed. This study follows Braun and Clarke's [64] six-step framework for conducting thematic analysis: familiarisation with the data collected from the interviews; generating initial codes; categorising the data into potential themes; reviewing, defining and naming the themes; reporting the findings; and analysing them based on the initial research questions. The responses were transcribed and are summarised below.

4   Results

4.1   Profile of Participants

For this study, the authors sent invitations to around 70 contacts by email. In total, 16 participants completed the interview with full response data. All of the respondents had been working within activity-organising networks for dementia patients, either at the Alzheimer's Association or the Alzheimer Society of Finland. Six participants had worked with dementia patients for 20 or more years, two for 11–19 years and seven for 1–10 years. All of the participants had working experience with dementia patients, and only one did not specify the length of that experience.

The respondents described their educational and occupational histories to support the reliability and validity of their responses. To further assist the research, the interviewees also shared links and references online and traditional publications with more information on the topic of this research. Almost 70% (11 participants) of the respondents were interested in the progress of the research and further cooperation or participation in follow-up interviews and provided their email addresses for future correspondence.

4.2   Results

Out of 16 interviews with professionals of memory care, the following results were recorded in tabular and textual formats for each of the questions presented subchapters.

4.2.1   Please Describe Psychosocial Problems Faced by Memory Patients, Their Caretakers and Family Members?

In Table 1 below, psychological issues recognised by interviewees are presented. The generality of each psychosocial problem is identified by the total number of occurrences mentioned by memory care professionals in their interviews. Moreover, in order to recognise the significance of a single psychosocial problem for patients, their caretakers and family members, a percentage for weighted significance to each problem is calculated based on a number of occurrence proportional to its highest value. In comparison, the highest value of occurrence will always be assigned with 100% and other psychosocial issues a percentage relative to it.

Table 1. Psychosocial issues as faced by memory patients, their caretakers and family members

Psychosocial problems		Number of occurrence	Weighted significance
Emotional	Patient's depression/anxiety/emotional/mental problems	10	100%
	Sleeping/resting/tiredness on patient	8	80%
	Loss of friendship/social relationships/connections, feeling of loneliness/isolation from others	6	60%
	Experienced shame on illness	5	50%
	Sleeping/resting/tiredness on family member	3	30%
Independence	Family member adapting to new roles a patient used to take care of before and feeling challenged by the new responsibilities	7	70%
	Family members's depression/worry/sorrow/mental load over the patient	3	30%
	Lack of initiativeness to function/operate as per situation	2	20%
	Difficulty to join social events due to unavailability of suitable transportation/social support permitting to use it	1	10%
Comprehension	Patient's worry over illness and loss of their skills/ability/accuracy to operate	2	20%
	Incapability to receive up-to-date information from society, e.g. news and instructions provided only on the Internet instead of over traditional channels	1	10%

(continued)

Table 1. (*continued*)

Psychosocial problems		Number of occurrence	Weighted significance
	Problems due to a patient not being able to recognise family members or close relatives	1	10%
Behavioural	Family members needing to adapt to changed behaviour or personality of a patient, e.g. aggressiveness	9	90%
	Lack of diagnosis/care/information/on memory illness yielding to misinterpretation and misunderstanding by others	1	10%
Wandering	Loss of direction/wandering outside a safe distance from caretakers/family	2	20%
Communication	Incapability to follow conversations due to illness	1	10%
Confusion	Illusions/Hallusinations	1	10%

Furthermore, the same principle with the weighted significance and number of occurrence is applied to all the resulting Tables 2, 3, 4, 5 and 6 in below.

4.2.2 What Type of Activities Can Improve or Reduce Psychosocial Problems?

In Table 2 below, activities found as useful by specialists of dementia care for improving or reducing psychosocial problems are presented. Patients with diagnosed memory disorders require a variety of different activities to better cope with the illness. The content and arrangement of these activities are depending on the patient's level of illness and psychosocial challenges discovered.

Table 2. Activities found by respondents as useful for improving or reducing psychosocial problems

Activities useful for psychosocial issues		Number of occurrence	Weighted significance
Hobbies and exercises	Continuing the same hobbies and exercises as before the illness and as long as possible	10	100%

(continued)

Table 2. (*continued*)

Activities useful for psychosocial issues		Number of occurrence	Weighted significance
Daily routines	Support in maintaining the daily routines the same as before the illness and as long as possible	6	60%
Rehabitation	Activeness on chords and activities (preferrably outdoors) at times awake to help issues with sleeplessness	6	60%
	Listening to patients and caretakers for their worries	6	60%
	Friendship companions for patients and their caretakers	4	40%
	Discussions on pleasant memories as an exercise	4	40%
	Support on independent completion of personal chords by patients, whereas possible	3	30%
	Emphasis on arts, music and culture therapies for exercising the memory	3	30%
	Being present to the patients and considering their needs individually	2	20%
	Joint group activities mixed with memory patients and memory healthy people	2	20%
	Tolerance to patient's memory issues and incapabilities to remember	1	10%

(*continued*)

Table 2. (*continued*)

Activities useful for psychosocial issues		Number of occurrence	Weighted significance
Transportation support	Transportation services for patients and their caretakers	3	30%
Care substitution	Support on caretakers/relatives in management and duties of their own life	3	30%
	Volunteer service for taking care of the patients as substitutes of their caretakers	2	20%
Financial support	Programs for financial support of patients and their caretakers	1	10%

4.2.3 What Type of Activities Do Memory Patients Enjoy the Most?

Concerning all the activities arranged for the memory patients, in the interviews the specialists of dementia care were queried about their popularity. The specialists were requested to estimate what type activities are most enjoyed by the memory patients. Patients with a diagnosed memory disorder require a variety of different activities for their better well-being. In the Table 3 below, the results on activities most popular among memory patients are presented, based on the observations by specialists.

Table 3. Activities enjoyed the most by memory patients as per the observations by specialists

Activities most enjoyed by memory patients		Number of occurrence	Weighted significance
Activity Description	Listening to music	13	100,0%
	Social gatherings/Getting to know new people/Conversations	12	92,3%
	Puzzles, quizzes and games providing a sufficient level of challenge (not overly difficult) for memory rehabitation and entertainment	11	84,6%

(*continued*)

Table 3. (*continued*)

Activities most enjoyed by memory patients		Number of occurrence	Weighted significance
	Outdoor exercising	8	61,5%
	Memorising personal details/items, locations, events and history experienced	7	53,8%
	Getting to exercise own dear hobby	7	53,8%
	Singing together	6	46,2%
	Indoor exercising	6	46,2%
	Field trips out to learn new things	5	38,5%
	Arts, painting and drawing	4	30,8%
	Daily routines	3	23,1%
	Activities personalised for the patient in question	1	7,7%
	Variety of activities arranged for the patient	1	7,7%
	Touches and sweeps	1	7,7%
	Using a Memoera device for playing	1	7,7%

4.2.4 What Type of Activities Do Caretakers and Family Members of Memory Patients Enjoy the Most?

Another very important aspect in treatment of memory patients are the caretakers and family members who occasionally are constituting of the same people. Occasionally, these people of highest importance as for the treatment are required to provide constant, round the clock support to a memory patient. Due to this, their both physical and mental capacities are challenged, which requires assistance from the society as well as memory support organisations involved in order to release them from stress, refresh them and not leave them in sole responsibility for treatments and care of a patient. In Table 4, based on the observations by the memory specialists, the activities enjoyed the most by caretakers and family members are listed.

Table 4. Activities most enjoyed by caretakers and family members of patients as per the specialists

Activities most enjoyed by caretakers and family members of a patient		Number of occurrence	Weighted significance
Activity description	Field trips/refreshing time out	10	100%
	Social gatherings, interactions and conversations/confidential conversations	10	100%
	Group time together with other patients and their caretakers/family members in peer groups	7	70%
	Volunteer service for taking care of the patients as substitutes of their caretakers/family members and provide them with time for chords and refreshing hobbies of their own	5	50%
	Outdooring/events in nature	4	40%
	Visits/lectures by specialists	3	30%
	Seasonal dinners together with fellow caretakers	1	10%

4.2.5 Describe Activities Your Organization is Arranging for Memory Patients?

Until this point of the interviews, the specialists of memory care have thoroughly identified psychosocial issues experienced by the patients with their caretakers and family members, as well as the activities which are able to help their lives.

In order to respond to the social-economical requirements and demands the patients have by providing them with a respective service, the memory specialists are listing the activities currently served by their home organisations. A lack of correspondence of the service to the demand in the market would leave a gap for the Serious Game application to fill in and by this complete the pool of treatments required.

In Table 5 activities arranged for the memory patients by their supporting organisations are listed.

Table 5. Activities arranged for the memory patients by their supporting organisations

Activities arranged for the memory patients by their supporting organisations		Number of occurrence	Weighted significance
Activity description	Social gatherings and conversations with patients, their caretakers/family members, volunteers and visiting specialists (upon needs)	25	100%
	Conversations in peer groups	18	72%
	Memory rehearsals, exercises, puzzles, quizzes and games for performing individually/in groups	15	60%
	Field trips	13	52%
	Music as listened and sang	12	48%
	Creation of supportive material and applications	11	44%
	Outdoor exercising	10	40%
	Indoor exercising	9	36%
	Educational events/public lectures for information sharing	9	36%
	Arts, handcrafts and poetry oriented events	8	32%
	Seasonal celebration/events/dinners	6	24%
	Visits by doctors of medicine specialised in memory issues	2	8%
	Appointments with psychotherapists	2	8%
	Friendship service by home visits/phone calls	2	8%
	Visits by legal attorneys specialised in legal aid	1	4%
	Models and practices for individual guidance	1	4%

4.2.6 Which Activities of Yours Make it Possible for Caretakers or Family Members to Participate Together with Their Memory Patient?

Finding pleasure from learning, doing and enjoying the time together is one of the most crucial activities in coping together through the daily life.

Similarly, recognising gaps in service offering leaves a room and possibility for the Serious Game application to either support the existing activities or provide new possibilities for both the memory patient with one's caretaker and family members to learn and get entertained while helping to battle against the progress of the illness.

In Table 6, joint activities arranged for the memory patient with their caretakers and family members by the supporting organisations are listed.

Table 6. Joint activities arranged for the memory patient with their caretakers and family members by the supporting organisations

Joint activities arranged for memory patients with by their caretakers and family members by supporting organisations		Number of occurrence	Weighted significance
Activity description	Social gatherings and conversations with patients, their caretakers/family members, volunteers and visiting specialists (upon needs)	10	100%
	Memory rehearsals, exercises, puzzles, quizzes and games for performing individually/in groups	10	100%
	Conversations in peer groups	6	60%
	Music as listened and sang/Touch as a method of comfort	4	40%
	Outdoor exercising	4	40%
	Indoor exercising	4	40%
	Field trips	3	30%
	Arts, handcrafts and poetry oriented events	3	30%
	Educational events/public lectures for information sharing	2	20%
	Friendship service by home visits/phone calls	2	20%

(*continued*)

Table 6. (*continued*)

Joint activities arranged for memory patients with by their caretakers and family members by supporting organisations		Number of occurrence	Weighted significance
	Creation of supportive material and applications	1	10%
	Seasonal celebration/events/dinners	1	10%
	Visits by doctors of medicine specialised in memory issues	1	10%
	Appointments with psychotherapist	1	10%
	Visits by legal attorneys specialised in legal aid	1	10%
	Models and practices for individual guidance	1	10%

The informants explained that music and touch were important when dealing with patients, as was using several modes of interaction. When asked about the nature of the activities the caretakers enjoyed, they highlighted those that were performed among everyday tasks, sometimes offering example highlights.

Related to psychological problems in their daily work, the informants mentioned behaviour issues that they felt could be reduced by treating the patient individually and being present in her or his life. Interestingly, one respondent suggested that patients should be kept active when awake to avoid issues with sleeping during the daytime and then being awake at night.

Local organisations may offer peer groups, memory cafes and meetings for hobby crafts for the patients in which caretakers can also participate or take a break from caring. Some peer groups are arranged separately for patients, family members and other caretakers to allow confidence and discretion in discussions and to avoid hurting anybody's feelings. However, many patients and their caretakers face huge barriers to participating in available activities because they lack support, including a lack of public transport or a car.

Brain training was described in several responses. The greater the skills to manage daily tasks, the longer a family member can continue as the caretaker, and the most important objective in daily activities is encouraging the patients to be as independent as possible, such as by choosing and eating their own meals. In daily activities, tasks are broken down, and the patient receives encouragement and guidance, and brain activity is encouraged by urging patients to remember, do physical exercise, sing and engage in quizzes and word games.

5   Discussion

Dementia is an increasing problem globally that results in huge economic and human losses [3] and has prompted a lot of research as nations seek to reduce its burden [6–8]. The current study interviewed 16 respondents who reported their views and experiences of working with dementia patients and their caretakers. Most of the issues and challenges they reported were related to patients who suffered from behavioural changes that presented as problematic situations and feelings, but the respondents did not consider these to be the primary issue, but rather symptoms of the main disease, dementia, which needed to be managed with care.

The most important need was to reduce brain-related symptoms that prevented the patients from remembering or comprehending everyday moments. Efforts to reduce these symptoms included singing, telling stories, seeking memories and interacting in safe settings, which required time from the caretakers. Earlier studies have revealed how informal caretakers, such as family members, often need to reduce their working hours to spend more time with the person with dementia [8, 10–12].

Interestingly, the informants mentioned that the different locations of the patients and the services, such as meetings and supportive activities, created challenges if transportation was not available. This is a significant issue that could be addressed with new services, but it is an encouraging finding as it offers a potential step forward for dementia patients.

Moreover, the interviews based on specialist opinions insighted the authors with on usefulness and entertainment the games, puzzles and quizzes provide for memory patients on daily basis. At current, as per the response data, there are indications on social demand and acceptance for this gaming to get digitalised, by an example of Memoera, which paths the way for further development of the Serious Game application. In this, specific carefulness in design of the user interaction, experience and interfaces is required to be paid attention to due to the acknowledge difficulty for memory patients in learning and adopting the use of new technologies.

6   Conclusions and Limitation

This study had certain limitations. First, due to time constraints and available networks, only the people who worked at or with the Alzheimer's Association and the Alzheimer Society of Finland were involved. Other professionals, such as memory disorder therapists and nurses, who might also have valuable opinions, were not invited to participate. These missing participants might have had different opinions that could have expanded the information on this topic. Second, due to COVID-19 and social distancing recommendations, the interviews could only be conducted online, so some information, which might have been elicited in a face-to-face interview, could be missing. Finally, this study was focused on the Finnish context and therefore may not be generalisable to other cultural contexts.

The next phase of the research is a design science research project. The authors are in a process of developing a Serious Game application to reduce the symptoms of people with dementia and thus to enhance their quality of life in the future. As for further research and development of this as a prototyping game artefact and due to encouraging results on culture of gaming being strong within the memory training communities across the country, digitalisation of this gaming is considered as welcome.

Importantly, another supporting factor for continuation of research and development on the application is observed in popularity of sessions for memorising locations, events, personal history and past of the patient, in form of a guided exercise. In addition to personalised sessions, these exercises, similarly as gaming, are commonly taking place in collaborative, social formats together with their fellow patients and their caretakers. Thus, this setting and regular arrangement would welcome a Serious Game prototype to be further tested in a field trial type of setup in the patient communities. While one of the major psychosocial issues recognised is concerning the loss of friendship and social relationships due to illness, a field trial on the gamified application in social context of a group would give the research an interesting angle of assessment. Confirmation on whether a Serious Game of this type could be of assistance in preventing social isolation or not is yet remaining to be further researched and analysed.

Moreover, as a research approach further, more focus will be considered in directing the Serious Game application and its customised content to inclusion on past locations places and events personal to the patient. This has the potential to assist memory organisations in their constant requirement to develop content for their daily and weekly exercises with patients.

References

1. World Alzheimer Report (2018). https://www.alz.co.uk/research/WorldAlzheimerReport2018.pdf Accessed 20 Apr 2020
2. Kraft, E., Marti, M., Werner, S., Sommer, H.: Cost of dementia in Switzerland. Swiss Med. Wkly. **140**, w13093 (2010)
3. Prince, M., Wimo, A., Guerchet, M., Ali, G.C., Wu, Y.-T., Prina, M.: The World Alzheimer Report 2015, The Global Impact of Dementia: An analysis of prevalence, incidence, cost and trends. Alzheimer's Disease International. https://www.alz.co.uk/research/WorldAlzheimerReport2015.pdf Accessed 20 Apr 2020
4. Gina, K.: Costs for dementia care far exceeding other diseases. The New York Times (2015). https://www.nytimes.com/2015/10/27/health/costs-for-dementia-care-far-exceeding-other-diseases-study-finds.html. Accessed 20 Apr 2020
5. Boseley, S.: Dementia research funding to more than double to £66 m by 2015. The Guardian. London (2012). https://www.theguardian.com/society/2012/mar/26/dementia-research-funding-to-double. Accessed 20 Apr 2020
6. Thomassen, H.E., Farshchian, B.A.: A technology-enhanced service for person-centered dementia care: preliminary results from a field trial. In: Proceedings of the Ninth ACM International Conference on Pervasive Technologies Related to Assistive Environments, 29 June–1 July, Corfu Island, p. 52. Association for Computing Machinery (Ed.), Greece (2016)
7. Leicht, H., et al.: AgeCoDe study group: Net costs of dementia by disease stage. Acta Psychiatry Scand **124**(5), 384–395 (2011)
8. Beach, S.R., Schulz, R., Yee, J.L., Jackson, S.: Negative and positive health effects of caring for a disabled spouse: longitudinal findings from the caregiver health effects study. Psychol. Aging **15**(2), 259–271 (2000)
9. Douglas, S., James, I., Ballard, C.: Non-pharmacological interventions in dementia. Adv. Psychiatry Treat. **10**, 171–179 (2004)

10. Prince, M.: Care arrangements for people with dementia in developing Countries. Int. J. Geriatr. Psychiatry **19**(2), 170–177 (2004)
11. Papastavrou, E., Kalokerinou, A., Papacostas, S.S., Tsangari, H., Sourtzi, P.: Caring for a relative with dementia: family caregiver burden. J. Adv. Nurs. **58**(5), 446–457 (2007)
12. Colucci, L., Bosco, M., Fasanaro, A.M., Gaeta, G.L., Ricci, G., Amenta, F.: Alzheimer's disease costs: what we know and what we should take into account. J. Alzheimer Dis. **42**(4), 1311–1324 (2014)
13. Carroll, L.: Alzheimer's extracts a high price on caregivers, too. Today (2013). http://www. today.com/health/alzheimers-extracts-high-price-caregivers-too-8C11070658. Accessed 20 Apr 2020
14. Cohen-Mansfield, J., Lipson, S., Werner, P., Billig, N., Taylor, L., Woosley, R.: Withdrawal of haloperidol, thioridazine, and lorazepam in the nursing home: a controlled, double-blind study. Arch. Intern. Med. **159**, 1733–1740 (1999)
15. Yamaguchi, H., Maki, Y., Yamagami, T.: Overview of non-pharmacological intervention for dementia and principles of brain-activating rehabilitation. Psychogeriatrics **10**(4), 206–213 (2010)
16. Cohen-Mansfield, J., Lipson, S., Werner, P., Billig, N., Taylor, L., Woosley, R.: Withdrawal of halo-peridol, thioridazine, and lorazepam in the nursing home. Arch. Intern. Med. **159**(15), 1733–1740 (1999)
17. Bayles, K.A., Tomoeda, C.K., Trosset, M.W.: Relation of linguistic communication abilities of Alzheimer's patients to stage of disease. Brain Lang. **42**(4), 454–472 (1992)
18. Honig, L.S., Mayeux, R.: Natural history of Alzheimer's disease. Aging Clin. Exp. Res. **13**(3), 171–182 (2001)
19. Magai, C., Cohen, C., Gomberg, D., Malatesta, C., Culver, C.: Emotional expression during mid- to late-stage dementia. Int. Psychogeriatr. **8**(3), 383–395 (1996)
20. Finkel, S.: Behavioral and psychological symptoms of dementia: a current focus for clinicians, researchers, and caregivers. J. Clin. Psychiatry **62**(Suppl 21), 3–6 (1998)
21. Cipriani, G., Vedovello, M., Nuti, A., Di Fiorino., M.: Aggressive behavior in patients with dementia: correlates and management. Geriatr. Gerontol. Int. **11**(4), 408–413 (2011)
22. Teri, L., Truax, P., Logsdon, R., Uomoto, J., Zarit, S., Vitaliano, P.P.: Assessment of behavioral problems in dementia: the revised memory and behavior problems checklist. Psychol. Aging **7**, 622–631 (1992)
23. Robinson, L., et al.: Effectiveness and acceptability of non-pharmacological interventions to reduce wandering in dementia: a systematic review. Int. J. Geriatr. Psychiatry **22**, 9–22 (2007)
24. Cipriani, G., Lucetti, C., Nuti, A., Danti, S.: Wandering and dementia. Psychogeriatrics **14**(2), 135–142 (2014)
25. Hope, R.A., Fairburn, C.G.: The nature of wandering in dementia—a community based study. Int. J. Geriatr. Psychiatry **5**, 239–245 (1990)
26. Yong, T.K., Young, S.Y., Koo, M.S.: Wandering in Dementia. Dement. Neurocognitive Disord. **14**(3), 99–105 (2015)
27. Jefferies, E., Patterson, K., Jones, R.W., Lambon Ralph, M.A.: Comprehension of concrete and abstract words in semantic dementia. Neuropsychology **23**(4), 492–499 (2009)
28. de Carvalho, I.A., Mansur, L.L.: Validation of ASHA FACS-functional assessment of communication skills for Alzheimer disease population. Alzheimer Dis. Assoc. Disord. **22**(4), 375–381 (2008)
29. Korhonen, T., Halonen, R.: Serious games in healthcare: results form a systematic mapping study. In: 30th Bled eConference: Digital Transformation - From Connecting Things to Transforming Our Lives, pp. 349–368 (2017)
30. Kim, S., Park, M.: Effectiveness of person-centered care on people with dementia: a systematic review and meta-analysis. Clin. Interv. Aging **2017**(12), 381–397 (2017)

31. Dementia statistics: numbers of people with dementia. https://www.alz.co.uk/research/statis tics. Accessed 20 Apr 2020
32. Ballard, C., et al.: Can psychiatric liaison reduce neuroleptic use and reduce health service utilization for dementia patients residing in care facilities. Int. J. Geriatr. Psychiatry **17**(2), 140–145 (2002)
33. Brooker, D.J., Woolley, R.J., Lee, D.: Enriching opportunities for people living with dementia in nursing homes: an evaluation of a multi-level activity-based model of care. Aging Mental Health **11**(4), 361–370 (2007)
34. Fraker, J., Kales, H.C., Blazek, M., Kavanagh, J., Gitli, L.N.: The role of the occupational therapist in the management of neuropsychiatric symptoms of dementia in clinical settings. Occup. Ther. Health Care **28**(1), 4–20 (2014)
35. Burgener, S.C., Buettner, L.L., Beattie, E., Rose, K.M.: Effectiveness of community-based, nonpharmacological interventions for early-stage dementia: conclusions and recommendations. J. Gerontol. Nurs. **35**(3), 50–57 (2009)
36. Schneider, L.S.: Meta-analysis of controlled pharmacologic trials. Int. Psychogeriatr. **3**(Suppl 8), 375–379 (1996)
37. Takeda, M., Tanaka, T., Okochi, M., Kazui, H.: Non-pharmacological intervention for dementia patients. Psychiatry Clin. Neurosci. **66**(1), 1–7 (2012)
38. Ku, L.J.E., Pai, M.C., Shih, P.Y.: Economic impact of dementia by disease severity: exploring the relationship between stage of dementia and cost of care in Taiwan. PLoS ONE **11**(2), 1–12 (2016)
39. Dubale, T.: Dementia in the elderly: epidemiology and care perspectives in Finland (2016). https://www.theseus.fi/bitstream/handle/10024/108005/End%20Final.pdf2% 281%29.pdf?sequence=2&isAllowed=y. Accessed 20 Apr 2020
40. Manthorpe, J., Samsi, K.: Person-centered dementia care: current perspectives. Clin. Interv. Aging **11**, 1733–1740 (2016)
41. De Silva, D.: Helping People Help Themselves. The Health Foundation, London (2011). https://www.health.org.uk/sites/default/files/HelpingPeopleHelpThemselves.pdf. Accessed Jan 2020
42. Hogan, D.B., et al.: Diagnosis and treatment of dementia, 5: nonpharmacologic and pharmacologic therapy for mild to moderate dementia. CMAJ **179**(10), 1019–1026 (2008)
43. Cohen-Mansfield, J.: Nonpharmacologic interventions for inappropriate behaviors in dementia: a review, summary, and critique. Am. J. Geriatr. Psychiatry Fall **9**(4), 361–381 (2001)
44. Pinto-Bruno, Á.C., García-Casal, J.A., Csipke, E., Jenaro-Río, C., Franco-Martín, M.: ICT-based applications to improve social health and social participation in older adults with dementia. A systematic literature review. Aging Mental Health **21**(1), 58–65 (2017). http://dx.doi.org/10.1080/13607863.2016.1262818
45. Ryan, F., Coughlan, M., Cronin, P.: Interviewing in qualitative research: one-to-one interview. Int. J. Ther. Rehabil. **16**(6), 309–314 (2009)
46. Czaja, R.: Questionnaire pretesting comes of age. Market. Bull. **9**, 52–66 (1998)
47. Every fifth person aged over 65 died of dementia and Alzheimer's disease (2018). http://www.stat.fi/til/ksyyt/2017/ksyyt_2017_2018-12-17_kat_003_en.html. Accessed 20 Apr 2020
48. Causes of death in 2018 (2019). http://www.stat.fi/til/ksyyt/2018/ksyyt_2018_2019-12-16_kat_001_en.html. Accessed 20 Apr 2020
49. Deaths from dementia and Alzheimer's disease are increasing (2017). http://www.stat.fi/til/ksyyt/2016/ksyyt_2016_2017-12-29_kat_003_en.html. Accessed 20 Apr 2020
50. Finland's Elderly Care Crisis (2017). https://newsnowfinland.fi/editors-pick/finlands-elderly-care-crisis. Accessed 20 Apr 2020

51. One in three persons aged 85 or over died of dementia and Alzheimer's disease (2019). http://www.stat.fi/til/ksyyt/2018/ksyyt_2018_2019-12-16_kat_003_en.html. Accessed 20 Apr 2020

52. Memory disorders (2019). https://thl.fi/en/web/chronic-diseases/memory-disorders. Accessed 20 Apr 2020

53. Share of young people in the population is in danger of diminishing further (2015). http://www.stat.fi/til/vaenn/2015/vaenn_2015_2015-10-30_tie_001_en.html. Accessed 20 Apr 2020

54. Kolata, G.: Costs for Dementia Care Far Exceeding Other Diseases. The New York Times (2015). https://www.nytimes.com/2015/10/27/health/costs-for-dementia-care-far-exceeding-other-diseases-study-finds.html. Accessed 20 Apr 2020

55. Merriam, S.B.: Introduction to qualitative research. In: Merriam, S.B., & Associates (eds.) Qualitative research in practice: Examples for discussion and analysis. Jossey-Bass, San Francisco, CA (2002). http://stu.westga.edu/~bthibau1/MEDT%208484-%20Baylen/introduction_to_qualitative_research/introduction_to_qualitative_research.pdf. Accessed 20 Apr 2020

56. Stone, D.H.: Design a questionnaire. Br. Med. J. **307**(6914), 1264–1266 (1993)

57. Moyle, W., Jones, C., Sung, B.: Telepresence robots: encouraging interactive communication between family carers and people with dementia. Australas. J. Ageing **39**(1), e127–e133 (2019)

58. Ratislavová, K., Ratislav, J.: Asynchronous email interview as a qualitative research method in the humanities. Hum. Aff. **24**(4), 452–460 (2014)

59. Brace, I.: Questionnaire Design: How To Plan, Structure and Write Survey Material for Effective Market Research. Kogan Page Publisher. London (2004)

60. Yasuda, K., Kuwabara, K., Kuwahara, N., Abe, S., Tetsutani, N.: Effectiveness of personalised reminiscence photo videos for individuals with dementia. Neuropsychol. Rehabil. **19**(4), 603–619 (2009)

61. Lietz, P.: Research into questionnaire design – a summary of the literature. Int. J. Mark. Res. **52**(2), 249–272 (2010)

62. Nanda, T., Gupta, H., Kharub, M., Singh, N.: Diagnostics for pretesting questionnaires: a comparative analysis. Int. J. Technol. Policy Manage. **13**(1), 67–79 (2013)

63. deLeeuw, E., deHeer, W.: Trends in household survey nonresponse: a longitudinal and international comparison. In: Groves, R., Dillman, D., Eltinge, J., Little, R., (eds.) Survey Non-Response, pp. 41–54. Wiley, New York (2002)

64. Braun, V., Clarke, V.: Using thematic analysis in psychology. Qual. Res. Psychol. **3**(2), 77–101 (2006)

What is a PHR? Definitions of Personal Health Record (PHR) Used in Literature—A Systematic Literature Review

Jani Koskinen[✉] and Minna M. Rantanen

Turku School of Economics, University of Turku, Turku, Finland
{jasiko,minna.m.rantanen}@utu.fi

Abstract. The purpose of this article is to clarify how term personal health record (PHR) is defined and used in literature. A systematic literature review was conducted to find out what are used as definitions for personal health record. We found and screened in total 1,781 articles published in years 2000–2017. Four databases chosen in review were ScienceDirect, IEEEXplore, Proguest and Pubmed. After criteria screening 1,234 articles were taken under further analysis. Most of the articles did not have any definition for term "personal health record" (n = 1,001; 81%). Only 233 (19%) articles included some kind of definition of the term. Few definitions were found that are constantly used in the field of medical informatics. However, those definitions are in contradiction between others and overall discourse in field. Thus, we need clear and systematic structure for different PHRs and proposal for hierarchy is presented in this article.

Keywords: Personal health record · Review · Definition · Terminology · Hierarchy · Categorisation

1 Introduction

(PHR) has been one of the main terms in eHealth research last decade due to the vast interest in developing consumer/citizen-centric healthcare systems [1–3]. The term PHR was coined back in the late 1970s [2, 4] and is used commonly in literature nowadays. However, the problem is that the term PHR itself has not gained a generally accepted definition, which has been repeatedly noted in the literature [5–12].

On the one hand, more than a decade the policymakers, academics, healthcare providers, technology firms and other health organisations have been debating, trying to define and promote the use and development of PHRs [13]. On the other hand, there also has been research findings where over half of the interviewed health professionals were not familiar with the term PHR [14]. This illustrates the problem of the term—if the professionals were not familiar with the term, it can be assumed that potential users, policymakers, etc. as well are not aware of what a PHR is.

It seems that communication about PHR is confusing - even hard to understand by professionals. Rational discourse [15] in society should be a starting point even though rational discourse may never be reached fully, we should aim at rational and

© Springer Nature Switzerland AG 2020
M. Cacace et al. (Eds.): WIS 2020, CCIS 1270, pp. 24–49, 2020.
https://doi.org/10.1007/978-3-030-57847-3_2

open discourse. One of the first steps is to come up with common agreement terms that are crucial for discourse – here the term is PHR. There is a need for clarity, truthfulness, correctness, and appropriateness as those are preconditions for rational discourse [16].

In the extant literature there seem to exist three main types (but not limited to those) of PHR: stand-alone, tethered, and interconnected (or integrated, etc.) [5, 17]. Most independent of those types is the stand-alone PHR that is not connected to other systems—such as electronic medical records (EMR) or electronic health records (EHR)—and thus can be and usually is personally maintained [5]. The second type is a tethered PHR which is an integral part or at least dependent on the host system as for example EHR/EMR provided by healthcare or other organisation [5, 17–19]. The third type, interconnected PHR, is used to describe systems that can be connected to more than one other system and it is even stated to be most sophisticated, comprehensive, and valuable [5, 20]. Alone these main types (not forgetting others) allow different approaches and viewpoints toward PHR development, which has led to a variety of PHR products differing from each other a lot [5, 21].

Thus, PHRs have been a popular topic in the field of eHealth and medical informatics. Amongst other research, many reviews have shed light on previous research about PHRs. For instance, Kim et al. [2] focused on the history of PHRs, Ennis et al. [22] on stakeholder involvement in PHR development, Bouayad et al. [23] assessed PHR data types and functionalities, and Roehrs et al. [24] focused on taxonomy and identifying challenges and open questions in literature.

Despite the vast interest on the topic, one problem remains: there does not exist a shared understanding of what is a PHR. This creates many other problems since we lack a common understanding of the topic. As it has been noted, there is a need for an update definition of eHealth because of rapid changes and different variations of using the term [25, 26]. Likewise, the situation is the same within the use of term PHR as it is part of the field of eHealth. Bird [27] note that scientific progress is based on an accumulation of knowledge and that the flimsy evidence will make scientific beliefs to come and go. As the amount of literature about PHR is wide and diverse there is a need for summarising views on what impacts of PHRs are – an issue that is not possible with a diverse use of the term. This harms all discussion about the PHRs and for instance, makes it hard to compare the results of previous researches [12] and thus prevents the evaluation of the PHR in a larger scale. Thus, what is missing is a review about definitions of personal health record (PHR) used in literature and categorisation of different kinds of PHRs

The objective of this research was to map how term personal health record is used in academic literature. Pre-study was conducted to get the first view at the situation [see 12] and based on that the need for systematic literature review for the definition of the term "personal health record" was noted. Based on findings in the pre-study we selected the following research questions:

- RQ1: What kind of definitions of PHRs are used in the scientific literature in the field of medical informatics?
- RQ2: What kind of systematic hierarchy for term PHR could facilitate coherent use of terms in the future?

To answer these questions, we conducted the systematic literature review for relevant fields. Our review is based on the review process presented by Webster and Watson [28], adjusted it with recommendations presented by Rowe [29] and check it against the demands of PRISMA [30].

In the next section, we introduce our research methodology, research questions, and processing of data. In the third section, we represent the results of this systematic literature review likewise the qualitative analysis of found definitions. In Sect. 4, we present our proposal for the term hierarchy of PHR as a structured basis for future definitions. In Sect. 5, we go through the implications of the results as well as the limitations of this review. Finally, we conclude this paper in Sect. 6.

2 Methods

Prior to a systematic review, we conducted several test searches that were conducted to a multitude of electronic databases including peer-reviewed studies about PHRs. Test searches indicated that there is an overwhelming amount of research about PHRs, which means that there is enough material for a systematic review.

In phase one, we conducted a systematic review of the peer-reviewed literature to capture as many definitions of PHRs (see Fig. 1). Our inclusion criteria required that the articles that were published in peer-reviewed sources were written in English and contained some definition or an attempt to define personal health records. The research was conducted in three major phases: data collection, applying exclusion and inclusion criteria, and data categorisation and analysis. The review process of the whole study is represented in Fig. 1.

We searched the following databases: Proquest, ScienceDirect, Pubmed, and IEE-EXplore. Proquest and ScienceDirect are multidisciplinary databases that index plenty of articles about medical informatics and health technology from different perspectives. Pubmed was included since it contains articles from a biomedical perspective and IEE-EXplore was chosen because it has a more technical perspective. Thus, those databases cover technical, medical, and multidisciplinary literature that should be included in research about personal health records.

For each database, we used the simple search term of query "personal health record" (quotation marks included/used in all searches). We choose not to include any other terms in the search query as we focused on the use of the term itself not to subject area of the articles. We wanted to keep focus in only in exact term because even it has been varying meanings and interpretations when used [see 2, 31]. For similar reasons it was decided that the search is not limited to title and abstract only but whole papers were searched. However, as PHRs have been a popular topic in research, it required us to make some limitations for our review. Thus, we narrowed our search to the time span of 2000–2017, as we wanted to focus on the use of the term, not the history of it that has been already studied [see 2].

Searches were conducted in two parts: search for articles from 2000–2016 was conducted on 24.10.2017 and articles from 2017 were searched on 8.2.2018. In figure one this is visible as numbers are present in the form of $n = X + Y$, where X = (hits from the years 2000–2016) and Y = (articles from the year 2017).

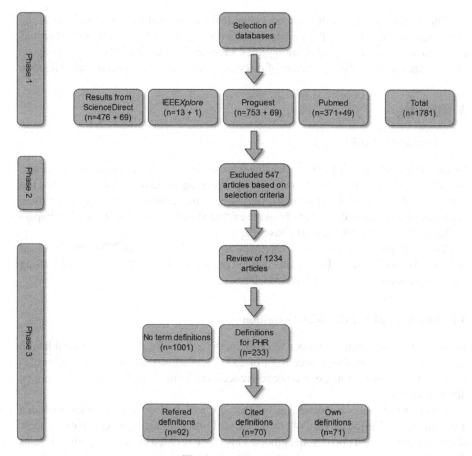

Fig. 1. Review process

In the search for Proguest database, we used additional filters limiting our search only to peer-reviewed journal articles written in English and were available with full texts. In the search for ScienceDirect, we included journal papers. In the search for Pubmed database, additional filters were also used to limit papers that are full text and written in English. In the search for IEEEXplore we did use filters that included magazines and journals.

In phase two, authors independently reviewed found articles against exclusion criteria – papers that were duplicates, conference proceedings, were not scientific articles, did not contain the term PHR, the term was only used in the reference list or was not written in English were removed. In phase three, all included papers were reviewed, analysed and categorised. The categorisation was based on how terms were used in literature and thus created during the review. The three categories were founded during the review process: 1) Terms with high abstraction level that define the idea of PHR, 2) Terms that define specific technological PHR and 3) other kind use of the term that seems not having any clear common nominator.

The Articles were read in full and systemically examined for any definition of the term "personal health record" by each author. From each article, the following data was collected: author name(s), publication year, source, and definition of PHR. Consensus on the relevance was reached by means of discussion in both inclusion and data collection

3   Results

3.1   Systematic Review

In total, we went through 1781 articles that were collected with systematic review. First, the articles that were duplicates, conference proceeding, were not scientific articles, did not contain the term PHR, the term was only used in the reference list or was not written in English were removed. 547 articles were excluded in this phase and thus 1 234 papers studies were selected for the next phase.

The total number of unique articles reviewed was 1,234 and only 233 (19%) included some kind of a definition. This means that the majority (81%) of the articles were using the term personal health record without defining it.

3.2   Overview of Articles with Definition

In this review, we found a number of different definitions for the term personal health record. Own definitions were used in 71 of 233 (31%) articles whereas 92 of 233 (40%) definitions were based on one or more references and 70 of 233 (30%) papers contained direct citations.

Papers were then categorised in two categories based on whether they included a definition. Definitions were collected in Excel and contracting interpretations were discussed and decided upon by all authors. This phase resulted in two categories: articles that did not have any definition for the term (n = 1,001) and articles that contained a definition (n = 233).

Next step was to categorise those articles that have definitions in subcategories: i) articles that refer to some other definitions (n = 92), ii) articles that cite (straight) other definitions (n = 70), and iii) articles that has authors own definition for term (n = 71), Citing articles could also include referred ones but not vice versa. The articles, that had definitions, were again screened after categorisation by both authors to ensure that both agreed on selection. Division of terms between the different categories is a fine line made by authors and hence others could come up with a somewhat different outcome. However, most articles fit quite well in some specific category and thus the outcome should be mainly similar if it be re-done with other researchers

Papers including references were taken into further analysis. To answer the RQ 1: What kind of definitions of PHRs are used in the scientific literature in the field of medical informatics? All articles that had a definition of PHR were analysed. Those 233 definitions were analysed, coded and counted. This was done by one author, but after first round, both authors participated in the approval of selections. In coding NVivo Pro 11 software was used alongside Excel.

3.3 Definitions Based on References

Definitions based on references include articles that either used references when defining the PHR or cited directly other sources. Some authors also created their definition based on referred and cited sources. These were counted also counted as referred or cited definitions. In this section, all definitions were based on references are analysed.

In further analysis of papers including references in the definition of PHR (n = 162) it was noted that 126 different references were used 280 times. There were PHR definitions in 85 articles that were cited just once, forming one-third of the used references (30%) whereas there were 19 Articles that we twice referred (n = 38, 14% of all citations) and 9 articles that were thrice referred (n = 27, 9% of all citations). Remaining 14 references that were used in four or more articles were used in total 139 times (31%). Thus, it can be stated, that references used in defining PHRs are rather scattered. However, there were few references used in definitions that emerge in literature more than others (see Table 1).

Table 1. Most used references in the articles with referred definitions.

	Reference used	Times used	Referred by articles
1	Tang et al. (2006) Personal Health Records: Definitions, Benefits, and Strategies for Overcoming Barriers to Adoption [5]	35	[18, 21, 24, 32–63]
2	Markle Foundation (2003) Personal Health Working Group – Final Report [64]	33	[5, 6, 11, 20, 65–93]
3	AHIMA (2005) e-HIM Personal Health Record Work Group Defining the Personal Health Record [94]	9	[18, 32, 43, 95–100]
4	Archer et al. (2011) Personal health records: a scoping review [17]	7	[13, 20, 51, 101–104]
5	Kahn, Aulak and Bosworth (2009) What It Takes: Characteristics of The Ideal Personal Health Record [105]	7	[1, 4, 45, 48, 106–108]
6	National Alliance for Health Information Technology (2008). Defining Key Health Information Technology Terms [109]	6	[1, 85, 105, 107, 110, 111]
7	Sittig (2002) Personal health records on the internet: a snapshot of the pioneers at the end of the 20th Century [112]	6	[32, 36, 43, 113, 114]
8	Jones et al. (2010) Characteristics of personal health records: findings of the Medical Library Association/National Library of Medicine Joint Electronic Personal Health Record Task Force [115]	5	[116–120]

(continued)

Table 1. (*continued*)

	Reference used	Times used	Referred by articles
9	National Committee on Vital and Health Statistics (2006) Personal health records and personal health record systems – a report and recommendations [121]	5	[21, 32, 51, 122, 123]
10	Pagliari et al. (2007) Potential of electronic personal health records [122]	5	[35, 48, 124–126]
11	ISO (2012) Health informatics - Personal health records – Definition, scope and context [127]	4	[24, 84, 128, 129]
12	Detmer et al. (2008) Integrated personal health records – transformative tools for consumer-centric care [130]	4	[45, 56, 114, 131]
13	Kim and Johnson (2002) Personal health records – Evaluation of functionality and utility [132]	4	[18, 51, 133, 134]

The most referred article was Tang et al. [5] with 35 references. Markle Foundation's definition [64] was the second most used reference with 33 papers referring to it directly. Interesting is that Tang et al. [5] actually do not present their own definition, but instead they refer to Markle Foundation's definition from the year 2003 [64] before considering characteristics of PHR in a wider sense.

Tang et al. [5] state that Markle Foundation has defined a PHR as "An electronic application through which individuals can access, manage and share their health information, and that of others for whom they are authorised, in a private, secure, and confidential environment" in their final report of Connecting for health [64]. It is noteworthy, that in this case a PHR is automatically seen as electronic system, although the term is also used to describe paper-based systems [see e.g. 17, 114, 135] and the term" electronic PHR" is also often used to clarify the form of a PHR [see e.g. 57, 136–138].

In addition, Markle Foundation's definition(s) can be seen as the most used reference, since also Tang et al. [5] use their definition in their article. Since Tang et al. [5] was used as reference 35 times when defining PHR, these times could be counted as second-hand references to Markle Foundation's most referred definition in the report "Connecting for health" [64]. Similarly, articles of Britto and Wimberg [69], Tenforde et al. [139], and Studeny and Coustasse [140] were used as a second-hand reference when referring to Markle Foundation's most referred definition presented above. Thus, Markle Foundations Connecting for Health report [64] is the original source used in at least 70 referred definitions, which covers one fourth (25%) of times when references were used.

In the Connecting for Health report, Markle Foundation defines PHR also as "an Internet-based set of tools that allows people to access and coordinate their lifelong health information and make appropriate parts of it available to those who need it." [64, p. 3]. The notion of PHR as a lifelong repository of health information is absent from the definition selected by Tang et al. [5], although it is repeatedly highlighted in the report [64]. Exclusion of the time span of the information from the definition is, however, a wise decision, since a PHR or even multiple PHRs rarely can cover the entire lifetime of a user. Thus, it cannot be stated that is a defining feature of a PHR. Similarly though, one could argue that also the notion of "private secure, and confidential environment" should not be a part of the definition. For instance, if an electronic PHR is hacked, is not secure anymore, but it does not decease to be a PHR. Thus, these can only be seen as desirable characteristics of a PHR.

In total 7 different documents from Markle Foundation were used 43 times as references when defining PHR in reviewed articles [see 64, 141–146]. However, the majority of these documents did not include a definition of a PHR [see 142, 144–146]. Likewise, general notions toward Markle Foundation's definition without specific references were also found in one article written by Pottas and Mostert-Phipps [147].

Another interesting note about the all the references used is, that although of all references included more scientific articles (n = 77; 61% of all references) than institutional reports and online sources (n = 49; 39% of all references), the latter were more often used in relation to their amount. When scientific articles were used as a reference in total 156 times (56%), institutional reports and online sources were used 124 times (44%). It is also noteworthy, that the majority of the institutions used in references are either based on United States (such as Markle Foundation) or are governmental institutions of the United States (such as AHIMA, HIMSS, National Alliance for HIT). These organisations seem to have a major impact on the terminology used in the field of medical informatics.

3.4   Own Definitions

Own definitions were used in 71 papers (31% of all definitions). Those definitions could be roughly divided into 3 different types (see Table 2).

Table 2. Types of own Definitions and use of those in literature

Type of definition	References	Number of occurrences
High abstraction level	[112, 135, 138, 148–155]	11
Defines specific technology or properties	[19, 24, 115, 156–186]	34
Others (Not fitting in categories above)	[7, 8, 10, 187–208]	25

First, there are the definitions that were such that they describe only aspects of personal control of information that is "health" related. Thus, these definitions could be seen to be in a higher level of abstraction of PHR that only focus on the aspect that it is a compilation of health-related information that individual control and manages. Those definitions did not consider the technology or specific attributes but merely the "idea" of PHR.

Another type of definitions was those which give a more detailed statement of what is the type of medium of PHR it is. Definitions can include the specific statement of

PHR type (e.g. it is electronic, online, etc.), which makes the difference between these definitions and Higher-level ones.

The third type rest of the definition was others that could not be categorised with a simple category. Definitions were very broad, very detailed defined, unclear, or focusing on very specific PHR solutions. Thus, those were case-specific definitions and we see that they are not reasonable to be categorised as part of any clear type of category.

4 Discussion

As our review shows, there are not commonly accepted and widely used definitions in the literature. Instead, we have quite a number of different versions that have a different level of abstraction. Furthermore, in many cases, the definitions are in contradiction with each other—which is problematic for the field. As noted, some definition focuses more on desirable features of PHRs such as secure environment or the time span of stored information [see e.g. 5, 64]. This is problematic as it indicates that if we have a system that is not safe (e.g. has critical vulnerability) or some information is missing a PHR is not a PHR any more—which most likely is not the aim of authors. There are also other too strict or specific limitations in definitions for PHRs, such as it is an online or Internet-based tool [e.g. 5, 172], it is lifelong [e.g. 5, 167], it is electronic [e.g. 156, 162], it is secure [e.g. 115, 183] etc.

The good definition for PHR needs to fulfil at least three following requirements: First, it has to be dissociated from other near terms such as EHR and EMR which means that the "personal" aspect of it should be emphasised. Secondly, it has to be technology independent to ensure its viability over time. Thirdly, it has to be flexible that it can encompass the different manifestations of PHR.

Therefore, instead of one definition for all purposes (that would be too broad) or having own individual definition in each paper we should have a suitable hierarchy for the term and its main variations to ensure that the abovementioned requirements are met. Thus, our proposal and answer for research question 2 (What kind of systematic hierarchy for term PHR could facilitate coherent use of terms in future?) is the hierarchy for the term that is based on categorisation of terms used in the literature and found types of definitions on it (see Table 2). Our proposal for the hierarchy is presented in Fig. 2. The meta-level shows that PHR is a sub-category in a larger context (of overall terminology containing related terms such as EHR, EMR, etc.) that is left out of the scope of this paper. We propose that the first level definition for PHR should be detailed but leave room for different types of PHR (compare to higher abstraction level definitions in Table 3).

Thus, our proposal for definition of PHR is following: "A personal health record (PHR) is a representation of information regarding or relevant to the health, including wellness, development, and welfare of an individual, which may be stand-alone or integrating health information from multiple sources, and for which the individual, or their authorized representative, manages and controls the PHR content and grants permissions for access by and/or sharing with other parties".

This definition is based on definition done by International Organization for Standardization (ISO) [209] with minor changes (see original: "PHR representation of information regarding or relevant to the health, including wellness, development, and welfare

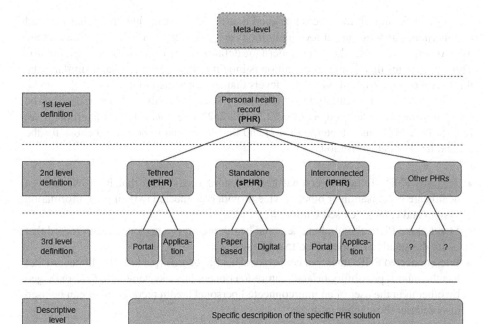

Fig. 2. Proposal for a 3-tiered PHR hierarchy

of a subject of care, which may be stand-alone or integrating health information from multiple sources, and for which the individual, or their authorized representative, manages and controls the PHR content and grants permissions for access by and/or sharing with other parties" [209]). We made the small change to definition to underline the individuals as active actors in healthcare instead of being the subject of care by replacing "a subject of care" with "the individual".

In this level of hierarchy, we do not see that the definition should contain any statements about what kind of solution or tool PHR is. If we assert too strict limitations, we may end up a situation where the definition of PHR is easily in contradiction with the idea of PHR. As example, even though Markle Foundation's definition [64] is the most used we did not see it as suitable one as it has problem of too limiting description: 'Internet-based' and 'lifelong' are too limiting as we now that there are stand-alone PHRs and lifelong is itself problematic definition as such—it seems odd that PHR would cease to be a PHR if it is not a lifelong tool – as most of nowadays PHR's are not used by today's children when they get old Thus, our proposal is more flexible and still detailed enough as it creates coherent hierarchy with different exactness in each level, instead of trying to have one term that tries to cover all different aspects within one definition. Thus, it helps to locate one's research and the context in the field but leaves the needed freedom for specific purposes when using term PHR.

For clarification, it must be underlined that Fig. 2. presents hierarchy that is based on inheritance and thus upper lever definitions are part of the lower-level definition they have a connection. Note, that terms inherit the definitions only vertically not horizontally. Thus, this means that first level definition is inbuilt in the second level and similarly the third level contains definitions of 1-2 levels that are connected to it.

The second level of definitions presents the type of PHR. This kind of type used can be found in several articles: Tethered [e.g. 17, 210–212], interconnected (or interoperative) [e.g. 5, 19, 213], stand-alone [5, 19, 87] and thus it seemed to be natural chose for the second level of categorisation:

- Tethered PHR: Tethered personal health record is a system that is provided by a healthcare organisation or other service provider, connected to their host information system and cannot be used without it.
- Stand-alone PHR: Stand-alone personal health record is a personal health record that is not designed to be connected to other systems
- Interconnected PHR: Interconnect personal health record is personal health record that has the inbuilt possibility or/and feature to connect other systems - that are managed by other than the user of an interconnected personal health record - but it can be used also without those other systems.

Tethered PHRs are the systems that are part of other systems and not work without a host system. Interconnected PHRs are a combination of stand-alone and tethered ones: Those are stand-alone in that sense that those can be used alone, but there is inbuilt interface(s) for connecting to other systems (e.g. official healthcare systems).

The third level is the level where a more detailed type is presented and can be seen in Table 3. It presents that what is the main type of PHR solution is and thus helps to differentiate those.

The descriptive level of this hierarchy is meant for a specific description of PHR at hand. In literature, this means that a specific PHR that is under the focus can be described in a level of needed accuracy. However, this level is not actually part of the hierarchy anymore but is shown as it clarifies the line that is outside of the hierarchy proposal here.

The other PHRs and subcategories for it are marked with "?" to show that there may be different kinds of PHR's that could emerge and should be included in this hierarchy.

Table 3. Structured definition of PHR

Term level 1	Term level 2	Term level 3	Definition of term	Notes
Personal health record (PHR)			PHR is a representation of information regarding or relevant to the health, including wellness, development, and welfare of an individual, which may be stand-alone or integrating health information from multiple sources, and for which the individual, or their authorized representative, manages and controls the PHR content and grants permissions for access by and/or sharing with other parties	Modified from ISO [209]
	Tethered PHR		A tethered personal health record is a system that is provided by a healthcare organization or other service provider, connected to their host information system and cannot be used without it	Inherits the definition of PHR
		Portal based tethered PHR	Portal based tethered personal health record	Inherits the definition of tethered PHR
		Application based tethered PHR	Application based tethered personal health record	Inherits the definition of tethered PHR
	Stand-alone PHR		Stand-alone personal health record is personal health record that is not designed to be connected to other systems	Inherits the definition of PHR

(*continued*)

Table 3. (*continued*)

Term level 1	Term level 2	Term level 3	Definition of term	Notes
		Paper based PHR	Paper based stand-alone personal health record	Inherits the definition of stand-alone PHR
		Digital PHR	Digitally stored stand-alone personal health record	Inherits the definition of stand-alone PHR
	Inter-connected PHR		Interconnect personal health record is personal health record, that has inbuilt possibility or/and feature to connect other systems that are managed by other than the user of interconnected personal health record - but it can be used also without those other systems	Inherits the definition of PHR
		Portal based interconnected PHR	Portal based Interconnected personal health record	Inherits the definition of interconnected PHR
		Application based interconnected PHR	Application based interconnected personal health record	Inherits the definition of interconnected PHR

5   Implications of Research and Limitations of the Review

The state of disintegrated use of terms affect how the overall picture can be achieved considering personal health records. This is case in specific fields, transdisciplinary fields and publications channels of those. If one article is using it as the extension of EMR provided by hospital, other is referring to USB-stick held by patient and third is describing the portal offered by some third party, we are not talking about same systems any more. Thus, by providing systematic categorisation of term—based on literature review—we offer way to approach PHRs with common, explicitly stated way that would be suitable for different needs for different audiences. Thus, this helps to compare different research when we can evaluate similarity/difference of those in a systematic manner.

However, we note that this research is on categorization of PHRs and others could end up with other kind of outcome with same review process, as the three are not exact lines between articles that has definition and those do not have. Likewise, the categorisation of what are own, referred or cited references are sometimes challenging and thus small changes between to which category some terms belong could occur However, our categorization gives more coherent framework that directs the more detailed and clear definitions. Therefore, categorisation offers systematic and concrete basis for term use if applied in literature, compared to the current situation where the meaning of term PHR is left open to vague interpretations.

6 Conclusions

Based on systematic literature review and analysis of term use, it seems that term PHR is used commonly but it is rarely defined or described. Even when term was defined, it was in many cases too specific and thus cutting out some systems that seem to be such they should be called as PHR. Likewise, in some cases definition was too indefinite and thus leaves too much uncertainty for reader. However, we see that biggest problem is that there are no commonly accepted definitions even there are some definitions that are more used than other definitions that were used only few times or even once. This has led to situation where we are not sure what is meant by personal health record at first place.

As response for disparity of term use, we drafted a proposal for hierarchy of PHR based categories where term is defined in different levels for different purposes. Hierarchy is based on findings of review and we see that it offers systematic proposal how terms should be used. However, our hierarchy is a proposal that should be further developed if needed to meet different needs of communication in literature and elsewhere. Thus, this article is an opening of debate that hopefully will lead to further development of term PHR and helps to clarify the discourse.

References

1. Demiris, G.: New era for the consumer health informatics research agenda. Health Syst. 1(1), 13–16 (2012). https://doi.org/10.1057/hs.2012.7
2. Kim, J., Jung, H., Bates, D.W.: History and trends of "Personal Health Record" research in PubMed. Healthc. Inform. Res. 17(1), 3–17 (2001). https://doi.org/10.4258/hir.2011.17.1.3
3. Lahtiranta, J.: Current challenges of personal health information management. J. Syst. Inf. Technol. 11(3), 230–243 (2009). https://doi.org/10.1108/13287260910983614
4. Heart, T., Ben-Assuli, O., Shabtai, I.: A review of PHR, EMR and EHR integration: a more personalized healthcare and public health policy. Health Policy Technol. 6(1), 20–25 (2017). https://doi.org/10.1016/j.hlpt.2016.08.002
5. Tang, P.C., Ash, J.S., Bates, D.W., Overhage, J.M., Sands, D.Z.: Personal health records: definitions, benefits, and strategies for overcoming barriers to adoption. J. Am. Med. Inf. Assoc. 13(2), 121–126 (2006). https://doi.org/10.1197/jamia.m2025
6. Kaelber, D.C., Jha, A.K., Johnston, D., Middleton, B., Bates, D.W.: A research agenda for personal health records (PHRs). J. Am. Med. Inf. Assoc. 15(6), 729–736 (2008). https://doi.org/10.1197/jamia.m2547
7. Reti, S.R., Feldman, H.J., Safran, C.: Governance for personal health records. J. Am. Med. Inf. Assoc. 16(1), 14–17 (2009). https://doi.org/10.1197/jamia.M2854
8. Jian, W.S., et al.: Factors influencing consumer adoption of USB-based Personal Health Records in Taiwan. BMC Health Serv. Res. 12(1) (2012). https://doi.org/10.1186/1472-6963-12-277

9. Pincirol, F., Pagliari, C.: Understanding the evolving role of the Personal Health Record. Comput. Biol. Med. **59**, 160–163 (2015). https://doi.org/10.1016/j.compbiomed.2015.02.008

10. Urbauer, P., Sauermann, S., Frohner, M., Forjan, M., Pohn, B., Mense, A.: Applicability of IHE/Continua components for PHR systems: learning from experiences. Comput. Biol. Med. **59**, 186–193 (2015). https://doi.org/10.1016/j.compbiomed.2013.12.003

11. Thompson, M.J., Reilly, J.D., Valdez, R.S.: Work system barriers to patient, provider, and caregiver use of personal health records: a systematic review. Appl. Ergon. **54**, 218–242 (2016). https://doi.org/10.1016/j.apergo.2015.10.010

12. Rantanen, M.M., Koskinen, J.: PHR, we've had a problem here. In: Kreps, D., Ess, C., Leenen, L., Kimppa, K. (eds.) HCC13 2018. IAICT, vol. 537, pp. 374–383. Springer, Cham (2018). https://doi.org/10.1007/978-3-319-99605-9_28

13. Davidson, E.J., Østerlund, C.S., Flaherty, M.G.: Drift and shift in the organizing vision career for personal health records: an investigation of innovation discourse dynamics. Inf. Organ. **25**(4), 191–221 (2015). https://doi.org/10.1016/j.infoandorg.2015.08.001

14. Huba, N., Zhang, Y.: Designing patient-centered personal health records (PHRs): health care professionals' perspective on patient-generated data. J. Med. Syst. **36**(6), 3893–3905 (2012). https://doi.org/10.1007/s10916-012-9861-z

15. Habermas, J.: Between Facts and Norms: Contributions to a Discourse Theory of Law and Democracy. MIT Press, Cambridge (1996)

16. Lyytinen, K., Hirschheim, R.: Information systems as rational discourse: an application of Habermas's theory of communicative action. Scand. J. Manage. **4**(1–2), 9–30 (1998). https://doi.org/10.1016/0956-5221(88)90013-9

17. Archer, N., Fevrier-Thomas, U., Lokker, C., et al.: Personal health records: a scoping review. J. Am. Med. Inf. Assoc. **18**(4), 515–522 (2011). https://doi.org/10.1136/amiajnl-2011-000105

18. Nazi, K.M., et al.: Embracing a health services research perspective on personal health records: lessons learned from the VA My HealtheVet system. J. Gen. Inte. Med. **25**(S1), 62–67 (2010). https://doi.org/10.1007/s11606-009-1114-6

19. Gaskin, G.L., Longhurst, C.A., Slayton, R., Das, A.K.: Sociotechnical challenges of developing an interoperable personal health record. Appl. Clin. Inf. **02**(04), 406–419 (2011). https://doi.org/10.4338/aci-2011-06-ra-0035

20. Davis, S., Roudsar, A., Raworth, R., Courtney, K.L., MacKay, L.: Shared decision-making using personal health record technology: a scoping review at the crossroads. J. Am. Med. Inf. Assoc. **24**(4), 857–866 (2017). https://doi.org/10.1093/jamia/ocw172

21. Genitsaridi, I., Kondylakis, H., Koumakis, L., Marias, K., Tsiknakis, M.: Evaluation of personal health record systems through the lenses of EC research projects. Comput. Biol. Med. **59**, 175–185 (2015). https://doi.org/10.1016/j.compbiomed.2013.11.004

22. Ennis, L., Robotham, D., Denis, M., Pandit, N., Newton, D., Rose, D., Wykes, T.: Collaborative development of an electronic Personal Health Record for people with severe and enduring mental health problems. BMC Psychiatry **14**(1) (2014). https://doi.org/10.1186/s12888-014-0305-9

23. Bouayad, L., Ialynytchev, A., Padmanabhan, B.: Patient health record systems scope and functionalities: literature review and future directions. J. Med. Internet Res. **19**(11), e388 (2017). https://doi.org/10.2196/jmir.8073

24. Roehrs, A., da Costa, C.A., Righi, R.R., de Oliveira, K.S.F.: Personal health records: a systematic literature review. J. Med. Internet Res. **19**(1), e13 (2017). https://doi.org/10.2196/jmir.5876

25. Boogerd, E., Arts, T., Engelen, L., van de Belt, T.: "What Is eHealth": time for an update? JMIR Res Protoc. **4**(1), e29 (2015). https://doi.org/10.2196/resprot.4065

26. Oh, H., Rizo, C., Enkin, M., Jadad, A.: What is eHealth (3): a systematic review of published definitions. J. Med. Internet Res. **7**(1), e1 (2005). https://doi.org/10.2196/jmir.7.1.e1
27. Bird, A.: What is scientific progress? Noûs **41**(1), 64–89 (2007)
28. Webster, J., Watson, R.T.: Analyzing the past to prepare for the future: Writing a literature review. MIS Quart., xiii-xxiii (2002). http://www.jstor.org/stable/4132319
29. Rowe, F.: What literature review is not: diversity, boundaries and recommendations. Euro. J. Inf. Syst. **23**(3), 241–255 (2014). https://doi.org/10.1057/ejis.2014.7
30. Shamseer, L., Moher, D., Clarke, M., Ghersi, D., Liberati, A., Petticrew, M., et al.: Preferred reporting items for systematic review and meta-analysis protocols (PRISMA-P) 2015: elaboration and explanation. BMJ, 350:g7647 (2015). https://doi.org/10.1136/bmj.g7647
31. Arens-Volland, A.G., Spassova, L., Bohn, T.: Promising approaches of computer-supported dietary assessment and management—current research status and available applications. Int. J. Med. Inf. **84**(12), 997–1008 (2015). https://doi.org/10.1016/j.ijmedinf.2015.08.006
32. Lee, M., Delaney, C., Moorhead, S.: Building a personal health record from a nursing perspective. Int. J. Med. Inf. **76**, S308–S316 (2007). https://doi.org/10.1016/j.ijmedinf.2007.05.010
33. Kim, E.H., et al.: Challenges to using an electronic personal health record by a low-income elderly population. J. Med. Internet Res. **11**(4), e44 (2009). https://doi.org/10.2196/jmir.1256
34. Bates, D.W., Bitton, A.: The future of health information technology in the patient-centered medical home. Health Aff. **29**(4), 614–621 (2010). https://doi.org/10.1377/hlthaff.2010.0007
35. Mitchell, B., Begoray, D.: Electronic personal health records that promote self-management in chronic illness. OJIN Online J. Issues Nurs. **15**(3), 1B–10B (2010). https://doi.org/10.3912/ojin.vol15no03ppt01
36. Wiljer, D., Leonard, K.J., Urowitz, S., Apatu, E., Massey, C., Quartey, N.K., Catton, P.: The anxious wait: assessing the impact of patient accessible EHRs for breast cancer patients. BMC Med. Inf. Decis. Making **10**(1) (2010). https://doi.org/10.1186/1472-6947-10-46
37. Steward, D.A., Hofler, R.A., Thaldorf, C., Milov, D.E.: A method for understanding some consequences of bringing patient-generated data into health care delivery. Med. Decis. Making **30**(4), E1–E13 (2010). https://doi.org/10.1177/0272989x10371829
38. Sujansky, W.V., Faus, S.A., Stone, E., Brennan, P.F.: A method to implement fine-grained access control for personal health records through standard relational database queries. J. Biomed. Inf. **43**(5), S46–S50 (2010). https://doi.org/10.1016/j.jbi.2010.08.001
39. Pearson, J.F., Brownstein, C.A., Brownstein, J.S.: Potential for electronic health records and online social networking to redefine medical research. Clin. Chem. **57**(2), 196–204 (2011). https://doi.org/10.1373/clinchem.2010.148668
40. Eccher, C., Piras, E.M., Stenico, M.: TreC - a REST-based regional PHR. Stud. Health Technol. Inf. **169**, 108–112 (2011). PMID: 21893724
41. Wibe, T., Hellesø, R., Slaughter, L., Ekstedt, M.: Lay people's experiences with reading their medical record. Soc. Sci. Med. **72**(9), 1570–1573 (2011). https://doi.org/10.1016/j.socscimed.2011.03.006
42. Sourla, E., Sioutas, S., Syrimpeis, V., Tsakalidis, A., Tzimas, G.: CardioSmart365: artificial intelligence in the service of cardiologic patients. Adv. Artif. Intell. **2012**, 1–12 (2012). https://doi.org/10.1155/2012/585072
43. Ahmadi, M., Jeddi, F.R., Gohari, M.R., Sadoughi, F.: A review of the personal health records in selected Countries and Iran. J. Med. Syst. **36**(2), 371–382 (2010). https://doi.org/10.1007/s10916-010-9482-3
44. Carrión Señor, I., Fernández-Alemán, J.L., Toval, A.: Are personal health records safe? a review of free web-accessible personal health record privacy policies. J. Med. Internet Res. **14**(4), e114 (2012). https://doi.org/10.2196/jmir.1904

45. Hilton, J.F., et al.: A cross-sectional study of barriers to personal health record use among patients attending a safety-net clinic. PLoS ONE **7**(2), e31888 (2012). https://doi.org/10.1371/journal.pone.0031888

46. Bélanger, E., Bartlett, G., Dawes, M., Rodríguez, C., Hasson-Gidoni, I.: Examining the evidence of the impact of health information technology in primary care: An argument for participatory research with health professionals and patients. Int. J. Med. Inf. **81**(10), 654–661 (2012). https://doi.org/10.1016/j.ijmedinf.2012.07.008

47. Gu, Y., Orr, M., Warren, J., Humphrey, G., Day, K., Tibby, S., Fitzpatrick, J.: Why a shared care record is an official medical record? New Zealand Med. J. (Online) **126**(1384), 109–117 (2013). PMID: 24162635

48. Chen, L., et al.: Evaluating self-management behaviors of diabetic patients in a telehealthcare program: longitudinal study over 18 months. J. Med. Internet Res. **15**(12), e266 (2013). https://doi.org/10.2196/jmir.2699

49. Gu, Y., Day, K.: Propensity of people with long-term conditions to use personal health record. Stud. Health Technol. Inf. **188**, 46–51 (2013). PMID: 23823287

50. Lau, A.Y.S., et al.: Consumers' online social network topologies and health behaviours. Stud. Health Technol. Inf. **2013**(192), 77–81 (2013). PMID:23920519

51. Nazi, K.M.: The Personal Health Record paradox: health care professionals' perspectives and the information ecology of personal health record systems in organizational and clinical settings. J. Med. Internet Res. **15**(4), e70 (2013). https://doi.org/10.2196/jmir.2443

52. Taha, J., Czaja, S.J., Sharit, J., Morrow, D.G.: Factors affecting usage of a personal health record (PHR) to manage health. Psychol. Aging **28**(4), 1124–1139 (2013). https://doi.org/10.1037/a0033911

53. Househ, M.S., Borycki, E.M., Rohrer, W.M., Kushniruk, A.W.: Developing a framework for meaningful use of personal health records (PHRs). Health Policy Technol. **3**(4), 272–280 (2014). https://doi.org/10.1016/j.hlpt.2014.08.009

54. Czaja, S.J.: Can technology empower older adults to manage their health? Generations **39**(1), 46–51 (2015)

55. Cabitza, F., Simone, C., De Michelis, G.: User-driven prioritization of features for a prospective InterPersonal Health Record: perceptions from the Italian context. Comput. Biol. Med. **59**, 202–210 (2015). https://doi.org/10.1016/j.compbiomed.2014.03.009

56. Fuji, K.T., Abbott, A.A., Galt, K.A.: A qualitative study of how patients with type 2 diabetes use an electronic stand-alone Personal Health Record. Telemed. e-Health. **21**(4), 296–300 (2015). https://doi.org/10.1089/tmj.2014.0084

57. Gartrell, K., Storr, C.L., Trinkoff, A.M., Wilson, M.L., Gurses, A.P.: Electronic personal health record use among registered nurses. Nurs. Outlook **63**(3), 278–287 (2015). https://doi.org/10.1016/j.outlook.2014.11.013

58. Ma, C.C., Kuo, K.M., Alexander, J.W.: A survey-based study of factors that motivate nurses to protect the privacy of electronic medical records. BMC Med. Inf. Decis. Making **16**(1), 1–13 (2015). https://doi.org/10.1186/s12911-016-0254-y

59. Lester, M., Boateng, S., Studeny, J., Coustasse, A.: Personal health records: beneficial or burdensome for patients and healthcare providers? Perspect. Health Inf. Manage. **13**(Spring) (2016)

60. Alsahan, A., Saddik, B.: Perceived challenges for adopting the Personal Health Record (PHR) at Ministry of National Guard Health Affairs (MNGHA) – Riyadh. Online J. Public Health Inf. **8**(3) (2016). https://doi.org/10.5210/ojphi.v8i3.6845

61. Laranjo, L., Rodolfo, I., Pereira, A.M., de Sá, A.B.: Characteristics of innovators adopting a national personal health record in portugal: cross-sectional study. JMIR Med. Inf. **5**(4), e37 (2017). https://doi.org/10.2196/medinform.7887

62. Lee, Y.S., Jung, W.M., Jang, H., Kim, S., Chung, S.Y., Chae, Y.: The dynamic relationship between emotional and physical states: an observational study of personal health records. Neuropsychiatric Dis. Treat. **13**, 411–419 (2017). https://doi.org/10.2147/ndt.s120995

63. Zhou, Y., Kankanhalli, A., Yang, Z., Lei, J.: Expectations of patient-centred care: investigating IS-related and other antecedents. Inf. Manage. **54**(5), 583–598 (2017). https://doi.org/10.1016/j.im.2016.11.009

64. Markle Foundation. The personal health working group final report (2003). https://www.markle.org/publications/1429-personal-health-working-group-final-report

65. Staroselsky, M., et al.: Improving electronic health record (EHR) accuracy and increasing compliance with health maintenance clinical guidelines through patient access and input. Int. J. Med. Inf. **75**(10–11), 693–700 (2006). https://doi.org/10.1016/j.ijmedinf.2005.10.004

66. Ball, M.J., Costin, M.Y., Lehmann, C.U.: The personal health record: consumers banking on their health. Stud. Health Technol. Inf. **134**, 35–46 (2008)

67. McDaniel, A.M., Schutte, D.L., Keller, L.O.: Consumer health informatics: From genomics to population health. Nurs. Outlook **56**(5), 216–223.e3 (2008). https://doi.org/10.1016/j.outlook.2008.06.006

68. Roblin, D.W., Houston, T.K., Allison, J.J., Joski, P.J., Becker, E.R.: Disparities in use of a personal health record in a managed care organization. J. Am. Med. Inf. Assoc. **16**(5), 683–689 (2009). https://doi.org/10.1197/jamia.m3169

69. Britto, M.T., Jimison, H.B., Munafo, J.K., Wissman, J., Rogers, M.L., Hersh, W.: Usability testing finds problems for novice users of pediatric portals. J. Am. Med. Inf. Assoc. **16**(5), 660–669 (2009). https://doi.org/10.1197/jamia.m3154

70. Nazi, K.M.: Veterans' voices: use of the American Customer Satisfaction Index (ACSI) Survey to identify My HealtheVet personal health record users' characteristics, needs, and preferences. J. Am. Med. Inf. Assoc. **17**(2), 203–211 (2010). https://doi.org/10.1136/jamia.2009.000240

71. Witry, M.J., Doucette, W.R., Daly, J.M., Levy, B.T., Chrischilles, E.A.: Family physician perceptions of personal health records. Perspect. Health Inf. Manag. **7**(Winter) (2010). PMID: 20697465

72. Bonacina, S., Marceglia, S., Bertoldi, M., Pinciroli, F.: Modelling, designing, and implementing a family-based health record prototype. Comput. Biol. Med. **40**(6), 580–590 (2010). https://doi.org/10.1016/j.compbiomed.2010.04.002

73. Chumbler, N.R., Haggstrom, D., Saleem, J.J.: Implementation of health information technology in veterans health administration to support transformational change. Med. Care **49**, S36–S42 (2011). https://doi.org/10.1097/mlr.0b013e3181d558f9

74. Haggstrom, D.A., Saleem, J.J., Russ, A.L., Jones, J., Russell, S.A., Chumbler, N.R.: Lessons learned from usability testing of the VA's personal health record. J. Am. Med. Inf. Assoc. JAMIA **18**(Suppl 1), i13–i17 (2011). https://doi.org/10.1136/amiajnl-2010-000082

75. Hogan, T.P., Wakefield, B., Nazi, K.M., Houston, T.K., Weaver, F.M.: Promoting access through complementary eHealth technologies: recommendations for VA's home telehealth and personal health record programs. J. Gen. Internal Med. **26**(S2), 628–635 (2011). https://doi.org/10.1007/s11606-011-1765-y

76. Yamin, C.K., et al.: The digital divide in adoption and use of a personal health record. Arch. Internal Med. **171**(6) (2011). https://doi.org/10.1001/archinternmed.2011.34

77. Patel, V.N., Dhopeshwarkar, R.V., Edwards, A., Barrón, Y., Sparenborg, J., Kaushal, R.: Consumer support for health information exchange and personal health records: a regional health information organization survey. J. Med. Syst. **36**(3), 1043–1052 (2010). https://doi.org/10.1007/s10916-010-9566-0

78. Chen, T.S., Liu, C.H., Chen, T.L., Chen, C.S., Bau, J.G., Lin, T.C.: Secure dynamic access control scheme of PHR in cloud computing. J. Med. Syst. **36**(6), 4005–4020 (2012). https://doi.org/10.1007/s10916-012-9873-8

79. Calvillo, J., Román, I., Roa, L.M.: Empowering citizens with access control mechanisms to their personal health resources. Int. J. Med. Inf. **82**(1), 58–72 (2013). https://doi.org/10. 1016/j.ijmedinf.2012.02.006

80. Cocosila, M., Archer, N.: Perceptions of chronically ill and healthy consumers about electronic personal health records: a comparative empirical investigation. BMJ Open **4**(7), e005304–e005304 (2014). https://doi.org/10.1136/bmjopen-2014-005304

81. Chrischilles, E.A., et al.: Personal health records: a randomized trial of effects on elder medication safety. J. Am. Med. Inf. Assoc. **21**(4), 679–686 (2013). https://doi.org/10.1136/ amiajnl-2013-002284

82. Sieverink, F., Kelders, S.M., Braakman-Jansen, L.M.A., van Gemert-Pijnen, J.E.W.C.: The added value of log file analyses of the use of a personal health record for patients with type 2 diabetes mellitus. J. Diab. Sci. Technol. **8**(2), 247–255 (2014). https://doi.org/10.1177/193 2296814525696

83. Wiesner, M., Pfeifer, D.: Health recommender systems: concepts, requirements, technical basics and challenges. Int. J. Environ. Res. Public Health **11**(3), 2580–2607 (2014). https:// doi.org/10.3390/ijerph110302580

84. Ozok, A.A., Wu, H., Garrido, M., et al.: Usability and perceived usefulness of personal health records for preventive health care: a case study focusing on patients' and primary care providers' perspectives. Appl. Ergon. **45**(3), 613–628 (2014). https://doi.org/10.1016/ j.apergo

85. Vydra, T.P., Cuaresma, E., Kretovics, M., Bose-Brill, S.: Diffusion and use of tethered personal health records in primary care. Perspect. Health Inf. Manage. **12**(Spring), 1c. Published 2015 Apr 1. PMID: 26755897 (2015)

86. Czaja, S.J., Zarcadoolas, C., Vaughon, W.L., Lee, C.C., Rockoff, M.L., Levy, J.: The usability of electronic personal health record systems for an underserved adult population. Hum. Factors J. Hum. Factors Ergon. Soc. **57**(3), 491–506 (2014). https://doi.org/10.1177/001872 0814549238

87. Demiris, G.: Consumer health informatics: past, present, and future of a rapidly evolving domain. Yearbook Med. Inf. **25**(S 01), S42–S47 (2016). https://doi.org/10.15265/iys-2016-s005

88. Kneale, L., Choi, Y., Demiris, G.: Assessing commercially available personal health records for home health. Appl. Clin. Inf. **07**(02), 355–367 (2016). https://doi.org/10.4338/aci-2015-11-ra-0156

89. Toscos, T., et al.: Impact of electronic personal health record use on engagement and intermediate health outcomes among cardiac patients: a quasi-experimental study. J. Am. Med. Inf. Assoc. **23**(1), 119–128 (2016). https://doi.org/10.1093/jamia/ocv164

90. Marsan, J., Audebran, L.K., Croteau, A.M., Magnin, G.: Healthcare service innovation based on information technology: the role of social values alignment. Systèmes D'information Management **22**(1), 97 (2017). https://doi.org/10.3917/sim.171.0097

91. Smith, M.I., et al.: Lessons learned after redesigning a personal health record. Stud. Health Technol. Inf. **245**, 216–220 (2017). https://doi.org/10.3233/978-1-61499-830-3-216

92. Assadi, V., Hassanein, K.: Consumer adoption of personal health record systems: a self-determination theory perspective. J. Med. Internet Res. **19**(7), e270 (2017). https://doi.org/ 10.2196/jmir.7721

93. Kneale, L., Demiris, G.: Lack of diversity in personal health record evaluations with older adult participants: a systematic review of literature. J. Innov. Health Inf. **23**(4), 789–798 (2017). https://doi.org/10.14236/jhi.v23i4.881

94. Burrington-Brown, J., et al.: Defining the personal health record. AHIMA releases definition, attributes of consumer health record. J. AHIMA. **76**(6), 24–25 (2005). PMID: 15986557

95. Galt, K.A., Serocca, A.B., Fuji, K.T.: Personal health record use by patients as perceived by ambulatory care physicians in Nebraska and South Dakota: a cross-sectional study. Perspect. Health Inf. Manage. / AHIMA Am. Health Inf. Manage. Assoc. **5**, 15 (2008). PMID:18927602

96. Howard, S.M., Bentley, D.R., Seol, Y.H., Sodomka, P., Wagner, P.J.: Incorporating patient perspectives into the personal health record: implications for care and caring. Perspect. Health Inf. Manage. / AHIMA Am. Health Inf. Manage. Assoc. **7**, 1e (2010)

97. Noblin, A.M., Wan, T.T.H., Fottler, M.: The impact of health literacy on a patient's decision to adopt a personal health record. Perspect. Health Inf. Manage. / AHIMA Am. Health Inf. Manage. Assoc. **9**(Fall), 1e (2012)

98. Noblin, A., Cortelyou-Ward, K., Servan, R.M.: Cloud computing and patient engagement: Leveraging available technology. J. Med. Pract. Manage. MPM **30**(2), 89–93 (2014)

99. Chen, S.W., et al.: Confidentiality protection of digital health records in cloud computing. J. Med. Syst. **40**(5) (2016). https://doi.org/10.1007/s10916-016-0484-7

100. Hsieh, H.L., Kuo, Y.M., Wang, S.R., Chuang, B.K., Tsai, C.H.: A study of personal health record user's behavioral model based on the PMT and UTAUT integrative perspective. Int. J. Environ. Res. Public Health **14**(1), 8 (2016). https://doi.org/10.3390/ijerph14010008

101. Price, M., Bellwood, P., Davies, I.: Using usability evaluation to inform Alberta's personal health record design. Stud. Health Technol. Inf. **208**, 314–318 (2015)

102. Price, M., Bellwood, P., Kitson, N., et al.: Conditions potentially sensitive to a personal health record (PHR) intervention, a systematic review. BMC Med. Inf. Decis. Making **15**(1), 32 (2015). https://doi.org/10.1186/s12911-015-0159-1

103. Ruiz, J.G., et al.: The association of graph literacy with use of and skills using an online personal health record in outpatient veterans. J. Health Commun. **21**(sup2), 83–90 (2016). https://doi.org/10.1080/10810730.2016.1193915

104. Sharit, J., et al.: Use of an online personal health record's Track Health function to promote positive lifestyle behaviors in Veterans with prediabetes. J. Health Psychol. **23**(5), 681–690 (2016). https://doi.org/10.1177/1359105316681065

105. Kahn, J.S., Aulakh, V., Bosworth, A.: What it takes: characteristics of the ideal personal health record. Health Aff. **28**(2), 369–376 (2009). https://doi.org/10.1377/hlthaff.28.2.369

106. Bonney, W.: The use of biometrics in the personal health record (PHR). Stud. Health Technol. Inf. **164**, 110–116 (2011). PMID: 21335696

107. Thompson, H., Demiris, G.: Smart homes and ambient assisted living applications: from data to knowledge empowering or overwhelming older adults? Yearb. Med. Inf. **20**(01), 51–57 (2011). https://doi.org/10.1055/s-0038-1638738

108. Fernandez, N., Copenhaver, D.J., Vawdrey, D.K., Kotchoubey, H., Stockwell, M.S.: Smartphone use among postpartum women and implications for personal health record utilization. Clin. Pediatr. **56**(4), 376–381 (2016). https://doi.org/10.1177/0009922816673438

109. National Alliance for Health Information Technology. Defining key health information technology terms (2008). http://www.himss.org/defining-key-health-information-technology-terms-onc-nahit. Accessed 16 Apr 2018

110. Thede, L.: Informatics: electronic personal health records: nursing's role. Online J. Issues Nurs. **14**(1), 1–4 (2009). https://doi.org/10.3912/ojin.vol14no1infocol01

111. Gartrell, K., Trinkoff, A.M., Storr, C.L., Wilson, M.L., Gurses, A.P.: Testing the electronic personal health record acceptance model by nurses for managing their own health: a cross-sectional survey. Appl. Clin. Inf. **6**(2), 224–247 (2015). https://doi.org/10.4338/aci-2014-11-ra-0107. Accessed 8 Apr 2015

112. Sittig, D.F.: Personal health records on the internet: a snapshot of the pioneers at the end of the 20th Century. Int. J. Med. Inf. **65**(1), 1–6 (2002). https://doi.org/10.1016/s1386-505 6(01)00215-5

113. Flores, J., Dodier, A.: HIPAA: past, present and future implications for nurses. Online J. Issues Nurs. **10**(2), 5 (2005)
114. Hoerbst, A., Kohl, C.D., Knaup, P., Ammenwerth, E.: Attitudes and behaviors related to the introduction of electronic health records among Austrian and German citizens. Int. J. Med. Inf. **79**(2), 81–89 (2010). https://doi.org/10.1016/j.ijmedinf.2009.11.002
115. Jones, D.A., Shipman, J.P., Plaut, D.A., Selden, C.R.: Characteristics of personal health records: findings of the medical library association/national library of medicine joint electronic personal health record task force. J. Med. Libr. Assoc. JMLA **98**(3), 243–249 (2010). https://doi.org/10.3163/1536-5050.98.3.013
116. Karamanlis, D.A., Tzitzis, P.M., Bratsas, C.A., Bamidis, P.D.: Personal health records in the preclinical medical curriculum: modeling student responses in a simple educational environment utilizing Google Health. BMC Med. Educ. **12**, 88 (2012). https://doi.org/10.1186/1472-6920-12-88
117. Monkman, H., Kushniruk, A.: Considerations for personal health record procurement. Stud. Health Technol. Inf. **183**, 308–313 (2013). PMID: 23388304
118. Zapata, B.C., Niñirola, A.H., Idri, A., Fernández-Alemán, J.L., Toval, A.: Mobile PHRs compliance with Android and iOS usability guidelines. J. Med. Syst. **38**(8) (2014). https://doi.org/10.1007/s10916-014-0081-6
119. Cochran, G.L., et al.: Consumer opinions of health information exchange, e-Prescribing, and personal health records. Perspect. Health Inf. Manage. **12**(Fall), 1–12 (2015). PMID: 26604874
120. Shahrabani, S., Mizrachi, Y.: Factors affecting compliance with use of online healthcare services among adults in Israel. Israel J. Health Policy Res. **5**(1) (2016). https://doi.org/10.1186/s13584-016-0073-8
121. National committee on vital and health statistics. Personal health records and personal health record systems - a report and recommendations (2006). https://www.ncvhs.hhs.gov/wp-content/uploads/2014/05/0602nhiirpt.pdf. Accessed 16th Apr 2018
122. Pagliari, C., Detmer, D., Singleton, P.: Potential of electronic personal health records. BMJ **335**(7615), 330–333 (2007). https://doi.org/10.1136/bmj.39279.482963.ad
123. Shimada, S.L., et al.: Personal health record reach in the veterans health administration: a cross-sectional analysis. J. Med. Internet Res. **16**(12), e272 (2014). https://doi.org/10.2196/jmir.3751
124. Tenforde, M., Nowacki, A., Jain, A., Hickner, J.: The association between personal health record use and diabetes quality measures. J. Gen. Internal Med. **27**(4), 420–424 (2011). https://doi.org/10.1007/s11606-011-1889-0
125. Barbarito, F., et al.: Implementing the lifelong personal health record in a regionalised health information system: the case of Lombardy, Italy. Comput. Biol. Med. **59**, 164–174 (2015). https://doi.org/10.1016/j.compbiomed.2013.10.021
126. Iljaž, R., Brodnik, A., Zrimec, T., Cukjati, I.: E-healthcare for diabetes mellitus type 2 patients – a randomised controlled trial in Slovenia. Slovenian J. Public Health **56**(3), 150–157 (2017). https://doi.org/10.1515/sjph-2017-0020
127. International Organization for Standardization. Health informatics - Personal health records - Definition, scope and context.ISO/TR 14292:2012(en). Switzerland: ISO copyright office (2012)
128. Price, M.M., Pak, R., Müller, H., Stronge, A.: Older adults' perceptions of usefulness of personal health records. Univ. Access Inf. Soc. **2**(2), 191–204 (2012). https://doi.org/10.1007/s10209-012-0275-y
129. Mense, A., Pförtner, F.H., Sauermann, S.: Security challenges in integration of a PHR-S into a standard based national EHR. Stud. Health Technol. Inf. **205**, 241–245 (2014)

130. Detmer, D., Bloomrosen, M., Raymond, B., Tang, P.: Integrated personal health records: transformative tools for consumer-centric care. BMC Med. Inf. Decis. Making **8**(1) (2008). https://doi.org/10.1186/1472-6947-8-45
131. González-Ferrer, A., Peleg, M.: Understanding requirements of clinical data standards for developing interoperable knowledge-based DSS: a case study. Comput. Stan. Interfaces **42**, 125–136 (2015). https://doi.org/10.1016/j.csi.2015.06.002
132. Kim, M.I., Johnson, K.B.: Personal health records: evaluation of functionality and utility. J. Am. Med. Inf. Assoc. **9**(2), 171–180 (2002). https://doi.org/10.1197/jamia.m0978
133. Wyne, M.F., Haider, S.N.: HIPAA compliant HIS in J2EE environment. Int. J. Healthc. Inf. Syst. Inf. **2**(4), 73–89 (2007). https://doi.org/10.4018/jhisi.2007100105
134. Wang, M., Lau, C., Matsen, F.A., Kim, Y.: Personal health information management system and its application in referral management. IEEE Trans. Inf Technol. Biomed. **8**(3), 287–297 (2004). https://doi.org/10.1109/titb.2004.834397
135. Nokes, K.M., Hughes, V., Santos, R., Bang, H.: Creating a paper-based personal health record for HIV-infected persons. J. Assoc. Nurs. AIDS Care **23**(6), 539–547 (2012). https://doi.org/10.1016/j.jana.2011.11.004
136. Webster, L., Spiro, R.F.: Health information technology: a new world for pharmacy. J. Am. Pharmacists Assoc. **50**(2), e20–e34 (2010). https://doi.org/10.1331/japha.2010.09170
137. Liu, C.F., Tsai, Y.C., Jang, F.L.: Patients' acceptance towards a web-based personal health record system: an empirical study in Taiwan. Int. J. Environ. Res. Public Health **10**(10), 5191–5208 (2013). https://doi.org/10.3390/ijerph10105191
138. Robotham, D., Mayhew, M., Rose, D., Wykes, T.: Electronic personal health records for people with severe mental illness; a feasibility study. BMC Psychiatry **15**(1) (2015). https://doi.org/10.1186/s12888-015-0558-y
139. Tenforde, M., Jain, A., Hickner, J.: The value of personal health records for chronic disease management: what do we know? Fam. Med. **43**, 351–354 (2011). PMID: 21557106
140. Studeny, J., Coustasse, A.: Personal health records: Is rapid adoption hindering interoperability? Perspect. Health Inf. Manage. **11**, 1e (2014)
141. Markle Foundation. Connecting for health. Connecting Americans to their healthcare. Final report of the working group on policies for electronic information sharing between doctors and patients (2004). https://www.markle.org/sites/default/files/CnctAmerHC_fullreport.pdf
142. Markle Foundation. Achieving electronic connectivity in healthcare. A preliminary roadmap from the nation's public and private-sector healthcare leaders. Executive summary (2004). https://www.markle.org/sites/default/files/aech_exec_summary.pdf
143. Markle Foundation. Connecting americans to their health care: a common framework for networked personal health information (2006). http://www.markle.org/sites/default/files/CF-Consumers-Full.pdf
144. Markle Foundation. Survey finds americans want electronic personal health information to improve own health care (2006). https://www.markle.org/sites/default/files/research_doc_120706.pdf
145. Markle Foundation. Americans overwhelmingly believe electronic personal health records could improve their health (2008). https://www.markle.org/sites/default/files/ResearchBrief-200806.pdf
146. Markle Foundation. PHR adoption on the rise (2011). https://www.markle.org/sites/default/files/5_PHRs.pdf
147. Pottas, C., Mostert-Phipps, N.: Citizens and personal health records - the case of Nelson Mandela Bay. Stud. Health Technol. Inf. **192**, 501–504 (2013). PMID: 23920605
148. Van Deursen, T., Koster, P., Petković, M.: Hedaquin: a Reputation-based health data quality indicator. Electron. Notes Theor. Comput. Sci. **197**(2), 159–167 (2008). https://doi.org/10.1016/j.entcs.2007.12.025

149. Council on Clinical Information Technology: Using personal health records to improve the quality of health care for children. Pediatrics **124**(1), 403–409 (2009)
150. Ahsan, M., Seldon, H.L., Sayeed, S.: Personal health records: retrieving contextual information with Google custom search. Stud. Health Technol. Inf. **182**, 10–18 (2012). PMID: 23138074
151. Simon, S.K., Seldon, H.L.: Personal health records: mobile biosensors and smartphones for developing countries. Stud. Health Technol. Inf. **2012**(182), 125–132 (2012). PMID: 23138087
152. Adler-Milstein, J., Sarma, N., Woskie, L.R., Jha, A.K.: A comparison of how four countries use health IT to support care for people with chronic conditions. Health Aff. **33**(9), 1559–1566 (2014). https://doi.org/10.1377/hlthaff.2014.0424
153. Hamdi, O., Chalouf, M.A., Ouattara, D., Krief, F.: eHealth: survey on research projects, comparative study of telemonitoring architectures and main issues. J. Netw. Comput. Appl. **46**, 100–112 (2014). https://doi.org/10.1016/j.jnca.2014.07.026
154. Laxman, K., Krishnan, S.B., Dhillon, J.S.: Barriers to adoption of consumer health informatics applications for health self-management. Health Sci. J. **9**(5), 1–7 (2015)
155. Xavier, N., Chandrasekar, V.: Cloud computing data security for personal health record by using attribute-based encryption. Int. J. Inf. Bus. Manage. **7**(1), 209–214 (2015)
156. Stead, W.W., Kelly, B.J., Kolodner, R.M.: Achievable steps toward building a national health information infrastructure in the United States. J. Am. Med. Inf. Assoc. **12**(2), 113–120 (2004). https://doi.org/10.1197/jamia.m1685
157. Bria, W.F.: Applied medical informatics for the chest physician: information you can use! Chest **129**(2), 446–451 (2006). https://doi.org/10.1378/chest.129.2.446
158. Safran, C., et al.: Toward a national framework for the secondary use of health data: an american medical informatics association white paper. J. Am. Med. Inf. Assoc. **14**(1), 1–9 (2007). https://doi.org/10.1197/jamia.m2273
159. Buettner, K., Fadem, S.Z.: The Internet as a tool for the renal community. Adv. Chronic Kidney Dis. **15**(1), 73–82 (2008). https://doi.org/10.1053/j.ackd.2007.10.002
160. Atreja, A., Gordon, S.M., Pollock, D.A., Olmsted, R.N., Brennan, P.J.: Opportunities and challenges in utilizing electronic health records for infection surveillance, prevention, and control. Am. J. Infect. Control **36**(3), S37–S46 (2008). https://doi.org/10.1016/j.ajic.2008.01.002
161. Fuji, K.T., Galt, K.A.: Pharmacists and health information technology: emerging issues in patient safety. HEC Forum **20**(3), 259–275 (2008). https://doi.org/10.1007/s10730-008-9075-4
162. Grossman, J.M., Zayas-Cabán, T., Kemper, N.: Information gap: can health insurer personal health records meet patients' and physicians' needs? Health Aff. **28**(2), 377–389 (2009). https://doi.org/10.1377/hlthaff.28.2.377
163. Kabachinski, J.: RHIO: the data saga continues. Biomed. Instrum. Technol. **43**(1), 47–51 (2009). https://doi.org/10.2345/0899-8205-43.1.47
164. Plovnick, R.M.: The progression of electronic health records and implications for psychiatry. Am. J. Psychiatry **167**(5), 498–500 (2010). https://doi.org/10.1176/appi.ajp.2009.09101473
165. Melton, G.B.: Biomedical and health informatics for surgery. Adv. Surg. **44**(1), 117–130 (2010). https://doi.org/10.1016/j.yasu.2010.05.015
166. Daniel, F., Casati, F., Silveira, P., Verga, M., Nalin, M.: Beyond health tracking: a personal health and lifestyle platform. IEEE Internet Comput. **15**(4), 14–22 (2011). https://doi.org/10.1109/mic.2011.53
167. Lafky, D.B., Horan, T.A.: Personal health records: consumer attitudes toward privacy and security of their personal health information. Health Inf. J. **17**(1), 63–71 (2011). https://doi.org/10.1177/1460458211399403

168. Springman, S.R.: Integration of the enterprise electronic health record and anesthesia information management systems. Anesthesiol. Clin. **29**(3), 455–483 (2011). https://doi.org/10.1016/j.anclin.2011.05.007

169. Kierkegaard, P.: Medical data breaches: notification delayed is notification denied. Comput. Law Secur. Rev. **28**(2), 163–183 (2012). https://doi.org/10.1016/j.clsr.2012.01.003

170. Fernández-Alemán, J.L., Seva-Llor, C.L., Toval, A., Ouhbi, S., Fernández-Luque, L.: Free web-based personal health records: an analysis of functionality. J. Med. Syst. **37**(6) (2013). https://doi.org/10.1007/s10916-013-9990-z

171. Musso, C., Aguilera, J., Otero, C., Vilas, M., Luna, D., de Quirós, F.G.B.: Informatic nephrology. Int. Urol. Nephrol. **45**(4), 1033–1038 (2012). https://doi.org/10.1007/s11255-012-0282-1

172. Li, M., Yu, S., Zheng, Y., Ren, K., Lou, W.: Scalable and secure sharing of personal health records in cloud computing using attribute-based encryption. IEEE Trans. Parallel Distrib. Syst. **24**(1), 131–143 (2013). https://doi.org/10.1109/TPDS.2012.97

173. Navaneethan, S.D., Jolly, S.E., Sharp, J., et al.: Electronic health records: a new tool to combat chronic kidney disease? Clin. Nephrol. **79**(3), 175–183 (2013). https://doi.org/10.5414/CN107757

174. Sivakumar, T.B., Geetha, S.: PHR in cloud environment using enhanced attribute based encryption and advanced encryption standard. Appl. Mech. Mater. **573**, 588–592 (2014). https://doi.org/10.4028/www.scientific.net/amm.573.588

175. Sunyaev, A.: Consumer facing health care systems. e-Serv. J. **9**(2), 1 (2014). https://doi.org/10.2979/eservicej.9.2.1

176. Knapfel, S., Plattner, B., Santo, T., Tyndall, S.: Promotion of meaningful use of a personal health record in second life. Nurs. Inf. **201**, 413–417 (2014). PMID: 24943575

177. Qian, H., Li, J., Zhang, Y., Han, J.: Privacy-preserving personal health record using multi-authority attribute-based encryption with revocation. Int. J. Inf. Secur. **14**(6), 487–497 (2014). https://doi.org/10.1007/s10207-014-0270-9

178. Ro, H.J., et al.: Establishing a personal health record system in an academic hospital: one year's experience. Korean J. Fam. Med. **36**(3), 121–127 (2015). https://doi.org/10.4082/kjfm.2015.36.3.121

179. Comandé, G., Nocco, L., Peigné, V.: An empirical study of healthcare providers and patients' perceptions of electronic health records. Comput. Biol. Med. **59**, 194–201 (2015). https://doi.org/10.1016/j.compbiomed.2014.01.011

180. Yang, J.J., Li, J., Mulder, J., Wang, Y., Chen, S., Wu, H., Wang, Q., Pan, H.: Emerging information technologies for enhanced healthcare. Comput. Ind. **69**, 3–11 (2015). https://doi.org/10.1016/j.compind.2015.01.012

181. Harper, H.:. Innovate UK: dallas. Perspect. Public Health **136**(2), 75–76 (2016). https://doi.org/10.1177/1757913915626358

182. Groenen, C.J.M., Faber, M.J., Kremer, J.A.M., Vandenbussche, F.P.H.A., van Duijnhoven, N.T.L.: Improving maternity care using a personal health record: study protocol for a stepped wedge, randomised, controlled trial. Trials **17**(1) (2016). https://doi.org/10.1186/s13063-016-1326-0

183. King, R.J., et al.: A community health record: improving health through multisector collaboration, information sharing, and technology. Prev. Chronic Dis. **13** (2016). https://doi.org/10.5888/pcd13.160101

184. Bruns, E.J., Hyde, K.L., Sather, A., Hook, A.N., Lyon, A.R.: Applying user input to the design and testing of an electronic behavioral health information system for wraparound care coordination. Adm. Policy Mental Health Mental Health Serv. Res. **43**(3), 350–368 (2015). https://doi.org/10.1007/s10488-015-0658-5

185. Walsh, L., Hemsley, B., Allan, M., et al.: The e-health literacy demands of australia's my health record: a heuristic evaluation of usability. Perspect. Health Inf. Manage. **14**(Fall), 1f (2017). Accessed 1 Oct 2017. PMID: 29118683

186. Shah, S.D., Liebovitz, D.: It takes two to tango: engaging patients and providers with portals. PM&R **9**, S85–S97 (2017). https://doi.org/10.1016/j.pmrj.2017.02.005

187. Weitz, M., et al.: In Whose Interest? Current issues in communicating personal health information: a canadian perspective. J. Law Med. Ethics **31**(2), 292–301 (2003). https://doi.org/10.1111/j.1748-720x.2003.tb00090.x

188. Hegyvary, S.T.: Working paper on grand challenges in improving global health. J. Nurs. Sch. **36**(2), 96–101 (2004). https://doi.org/10.1111/j.1547-5069.2004. 04020.x

189. Gold, J.D., Ball, M.J.: The health record banking imperative: a conceptual model. IBM Syst. J. **46**(1), 43–55 (2007). https://doi.org/10.1147/sj.461.0043

190. Loeppke, R.: The value of health and the power of prevention. Int. J. Workplace Health Manage. **1**(2), 95–108 (2008). https://doi.org/10.1108/17538350810893892

191. Frost, J., Massagli, M.: PatientsLikeMe the case for a data-centered patient community and how ALS patients use the community to inform treatment decisions and manage pulmonary health. Chronic Respir. Dis. **6**(4), 225–229 (2009). https://doi.org/10.1177/147997230934 8655

192. Pirtle, B., Chandra, A.: An overview of consumer perceptions and acceptance as well as barriers and potential of electronic personal health records. Am. J. Health Sci. (AJHS) **2**(2), 45–52 (2011). https://doi.org/10.19030/ajhs.v2i2.6627

193. Chung, J., Berkowicz, D.A., Ho, B., Jernigan, M., Chueh, H.: Creating a place for caregivers in personal health: The iHealthSpace copilot program and diabetes care. J. Diab. Sci. Technol. **5**(1), 39–46 (2011). https://doi.org/10.1177/193229681100500106

194. Emani, S., et al.: Patient perceptions of a personal health record: a test of the diffusion of innovation model. J. Med. Internet Res. **14**(6), e150 (2012). https://doi.org/10.2196/jmir. 2278

195. Kensing, F.: Personal health records. Stud. Health Technol. Inf. **180**, 9–13 (2012). PMID: 22874142

196. Otsuka, S.H., Tayal, N.H., Porter, K., Embi, P.J., Beatty, S.J.: Improving herpes zoster vaccination rates through use of a clinical pharmacist and a personal health record. Am. J. Med. **126**(9), 832.e1–832.e6 (2013). https://doi.org/10.1016/j.amjmed.2013.02.018

197. Olaronke, I., Rhoda, I., Ishaya, G., Abimbola, S.: Impacts of usability on the interoperability of electronic healthcare systems. Int. J. Innov. Appl. Stud. **8**(2), 827 (2014)

198. Danwei, C., Linling, C., Xiaowei, F., Liwen, H., Su, P., Ruoxiang, H.: Securing patient-centric personal health records sharing system in cloud computing. China Commun. **11**(13), 121–127 (2014). https://doi.org/10.1109/CC.2014.7022535

199. Kyazze, M., Wesson, J., Naude, K.: The design and implementation of a ubiquitous personal health record system for south africa. Stud. Health Technol. Inf. **206**, 29–41 (2014). PMID: 25365669

200. Bajwa, M.: Emerging 21(st) century medical technologies. Pakis. J. Med. Sci. **30**(3), 649–655 (2014). https://doi.org/10.12669/pjms.303.5211

201. Crouch, P.C.B., Rose, C.D., Johnson, M., Janson, S.L.: A pilot study to evaluate the magnitude of association of the use of electronic personal health records with patient activation and empowerment in HIV-infected veterans. PeerJ. **3**, e852 (2015). https://doi.org/10.7717/peerj.852

202. Carter, B.L., et al.: A centralized cardiovascular risk service to improve guideline adherence in private primary care offices. Contemp. Clin. Trials **43**, 25–32 (2015). https://doi.org/10.1016/j.cct.2015.04.014

203. Triantafyllopoulos, D., Korvesis, P., Mporas, I., Megalooikonomou, V.: Real-time management of multimodal streaming data for monitoring of epileptic patients. J. Med. Syst. **40**(3) (2015). https://doi.org/10.1007/s10916-015-0403-3

204. Woolfenden, S., et al.: Prevalence and factors associated with parental concerns about development detected by the parents' evaluation of developmental status (PEDS)at 6-month, 12-month and 18-month well-child checks in a birth cohort. BMJ Open **6**(9), e012144 (2016). https://doi.org/10.1136/bmjopen-2016-012144

205. Van Vugt, M., et al.: Uptake and effects of the e-vita personal health record with self-management support and coaching, for type 2 diabetes patients treated in primary care. J. Diab. Res., 1–9 (2016). https://doi.org/10.1155/2016/5027356

206. Haynes, S.: Trending now and in the future. Occup. Health Wellbeing **69**(10), 11–13 (2017)

207. Davis, S., Roudsari, A., Courtney, K.L.: Designing personal health record technology for shared decision making. Stud. Health Technol. Inf. **234**, 75–80 (2017). PMID: 28186019

208. Kao, C.K., Liebovitz, D.M.: Consumer mobile health apps: current state, barriers, and future directions. PM&R **9**, S106–S115 (2017). https://doi.org/10.1016/j.pmrj.2017.02.018

209. International Organization for Standardization. Iso/tr 14639-2:2014(en) (2014). https://www.iso.org/obp/ui/#iso:std:iso:tr:18638:ed-1:v1:en:te

210. Monsen, K.A., et al.: Developing a personal health record for community-dwelling older adults and clinicians: technology and content. J. Gerontol. Nurs. **38**(7), 21–25 (2012). https://doi.org/10.3928/00989134-20120605-03

211. Wagner, P.J., Dias, J., Howard, S., Kintziger, K.W., Hudson, M.F., Seol, Y.H., Sodomka, P.: Personal health records and hypertension control: a randomized trial. J. Am. Med. Inf. Assoc. **19**(4), 626–634 (2012)

212. Ancker, J.S., Silver, M., Kaushal, R.: Rapid growth in use of personal health records in New York, 2012–2013. J. Gen. Internal Med. **29**(6), 850–854 (2014). https://doi.org/10.1007/s11606-014-2792-2

213. Bouri, N., Ravi, S.: Going mobile: how mobile personal health records can improve health care during emergencies. JMIR Mhealth Uhealth. **2**(1), e8 (2014). https://doi.org/10.2196/mhealth.3017

Special Needs of Elderly in Using Web-Based Services

Konsta Rantakangas and Raija Halonen[✉]

M3S, University of Oulu, Oulu, Finland
posti@rantakangas.com, raija.halonen@oulu.fi

Abstract. The number of elderly is growing also in Finland. As the traditional services are decreasing and net based services are developed, also the elderly need to adapt the new services. However, the elderly have special needs compared to the younger generation, and they need to be considered when designing net services. This study responded to two research problems. First, the special needs of elderly were considered. Second, the special needs of elderly were approached from the developers' point of view. A light literature review was applied to find state-of-the-art knowledge.

Keywords: Elderly · Web-based services · Special needs

1 Introduction

In the recent past years, different web-based services enabled by information and communication technology (ICT) have become ever more significant in everyday life. However, their efficient and practical utilization is not familiar for all potential users. Elderly people are one of such users who have special needs related to web-based services, and their special needs should be considered when designing those services [1]. Especially young adults and middle-aged persons have benefited from modern Internet-based services offered by banks and public service providers. However, the elderly have noticed it more difficult when carrying their tasks because service providers have decreased their traditional ways to offer services [2, 3].

Along with ageing sight, hearing and sense of touch get worse. In addition, skills related to read, listen and understand guidelines based on trying get weaker. E.g. using mouse gets more difficult due to declined motoric ability and declined memory leads to difficulty to remember all steps when navigating in an online service process [4].

The way fonts, colour, pictures, search and navigation are tasks that can make net based services too challenging to apply by elderly [5]. On the other hand, proper planning and development allow designers to build systems with suitable usability also for elderly [6]. Checklists help web designers to ensure that their web pages are suitable also for elderly people. However, several studies have shown that the checklists do not guarantee a usable web page even if all criteria mentioned in the checklist are filled [7].

© Springer Nature Switzerland AG 2020
M. Cacace et al. (Eds.): WIS 2020, CCIS 1270, pp. 50–60, 2020.
https://doi.org/10.1007/978-3-030-57847-3_3

Most people over 65 years have experience of using ICT [4]. The living experiences of elderly have influenced their later use of web-based services and building ICT competences [7] and ever more elderly have later got familiarised with e.g. social media such as Facebook and modern ICT-based device like smart phones [8].

The current study analysed how to design different web-based services especially when regarding elderly people who have special needs as users of the services to offer information for the designers to be used in building web-based services, and that the new services would be simple and easy especially for the elderly [6, 9].

The research problem was approached with the next research questions: What kind of special needs do elderly people have as users of web-based services? How should developers design such web-based services that would support elderly with special needs?

The study was based on earlier knowledge, and it was limited to concentrate on elderly people as users of web-based services and who have special needs, which makes use of web-based services difficult or makes it impossible. Furthermore, as the study was carried out as a light literature review, it acts as a mirror of what has been reported about elderly and their potential special needs elated to using web-based services.

The paper continues as follows: First, the study applying literature review is reported. Second, the results of the study are briefly discussed. The paper ends with conclusions and proposal for a thorough study.

2 The Study

This section introduces the research approach in its first section. After that, the special needs of the elderly are described and potential special features in web-services are considered, and conclusions of the highlights of the review are presented at the end.

2.1 Research Approach

The current theoretical-based study was carried out as a light literature research. The literature for the study was searched by using Google Scholar and the background idea was to find out what is known in general from elderly people and their age-related needs as users of web-based services. To start, relevant keywords for the search were listed starting with concepts of web usability, HCI, human computer interaction, guidelines, web development. The elderly as users were searched with concepts like senior citizen, senior, older people, older adults, and elderly.

2.2 Special Needs of Elderly as Users of Web-Based Services

When talking the speed of using web-based services, elderly people are generally slower than younger adults. It also takes longer time to choose or locate points and sections in the web page such as links to next pages. This is due to weakening sight, the large amount of information on the page, and decreasing skills of cognitive skills [10]. However, even if elderly might be slower than younger adults, they do less mistakes than the younger people [11]. Even if elderly are often slower readers than younger people because they have sight issues, they also are pedantic users of web-based services [7].

Sight is a significant doer that makes it more challenging for elderly people to utilise web-based services. With ageing, sight gets weaker in many ways related to such as differing acuity and distinguishing contrasts and amount of light [5, 12]. Kantner and Rosenbaum [13] highlighted the role of own weakening seeing skill as an obstacle in using web-based services. In addition, elderly people can see lousy placement or design of push buttons too challenging. Too coloured or in general confusing colours can lead the users to get annoyed [1]. Another problem is related to the font size of the screen if users don't know how to change it, and if the fonts on the keyboard are too small, it also adds difficulties [12, 13].

Hearing issues get more serious among most people when getting old. The problems can be minimised if the tones and informative comments are loud enough and in a proper frequency rate for the elderly. Hearing issue is the most annoying problem in discussions in both face-to-face and net based discussions [1, 12].

When the **motoric skills** slowly weaken, moving pointers and choosing and pushing small buttons get more challenging than before [1, 5, 12]. In addition, rolling the mouse can be difficult for the elderly. The younger generation need significantly less time to act with pointers compared to the elderly [5]. This can lead to situations when the elderly are afraid to use the pointers because they try to avoid making mistakes with the pointers [1, 12].

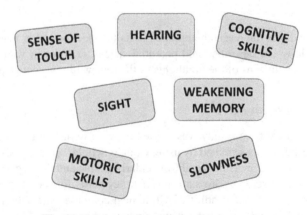

Fig. 1. Elderly special matters related to ageing.

Tsai and Lee [14] proposed that the elderly will soon use touch screens when navigating in the web-based services. However, sense of touch can be weakened due to high age, and the elderly might have unintentional double keystrokes [1]. In addition, some of the devices with touch pads do not give sufficient feedback after a successful selection of function, and the users do not know that. Therefore, the users can make additional selections in the web-based services and it can lead to such unintended choices that were not even noted during the session [1, 14].

With ageing, the skills to solve problems, remember tasks and pay attention to things. This can lead to situations when the elderly cannot learn, remember or perceive the structure of web pages of the web-based services in cases the pages are not designed keeping in mind their elderly users [5]. For example, navigating forth and back can be challenging if the user does not remember how she or he entered to the current page [1]. Along with decreasing **cognitive skills**, also **weakening memory** makes it harder to figure out navigating and structures of web pages [10]. Figure 1 illustrates the special matters that need to be understood when considering elderly people and their different competences. Studies have also shown that especially building search strings is seen challenging in general [13]. On the other hand, too much information on the web page can make the use of net service too challenging for the elderly. The elderly need more time to identify the important information among all available information and it takes more time for them [10]. Especially commercial web-based services are perceived threatening, obscuring and messy by the elderly [6].

2.3 Considering Special Needs in Web-Based Services

Elderly people with worsening sight prefer text-based net pages that utilize large fonts and that include only little graphics. The elderly perceive such pages friendlier to use than other kinds of net pages [11]. Another more pleasant feature in web-based services are simple looking net pages where the choosing buttons are large enough. Furthermore, 'back and forward' buttons should be located so that they are always easy to find. The elderly also see that popup windows cause mixing feelings because the elderly find it challenging to return to the earlier view [13]. On the other hand, the usability of web-based services does not always improve significantly if the font size is larger. However, the elderly saw it more pleasant to use web pages with larger font [7].

When the sense of touch weakens along aging the application developers face new challenges how to inform the elderly users that they have managed to choose their next action by pushing successfully the relevant button. In case the sense of touch is weak it is not reasonable to apply haptic touch because the users receive no feedback with their decreased sense of touch. This challenge can be won with a special feature called icon feedback that aims to visualise what has happened after the user touched the button [14]. In addition, including a sound signal such as a cling or honk as a mark of a successful action to the users to inform that the users can focus on a pop-up message on the screen [1].

The motoric skills should be supported by including possibilities to use both a mouse and keyboard [1]. The user interface should be designed in a way that allows the elderly users to use it without experiencing significant challenges when focusing the pointer to desired locations on the screen and thus decrease difficulties perceived by elderly when scrolling the mouse on a small object [12]. In addition, increasing the size of icons and buttons on the web pages would make it easier to use the system. Double-clicks should be replaced with one-click elements and use of mouseover should be minimised [5].

Figure 2 illustrates the consequences that emerge when the users are getting older. As verified by earlier knowledge, the elderly prefer text-based pages to graphic-based pages, the benefit from clear feedback when the icons appear or disappear, and they prefer simple outlook and axiomatic appearance of pages and contents to more sophisticated appearance.

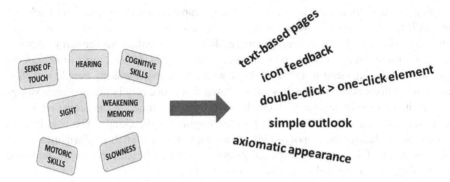

Fig. 2. Consequences of ageing.

To support versatile users in finding information they are searching, the web-based services should understand natural sentences such as 'Where can I change my password?' [1]. The extensive amount of information on a web page can make it too challenging to find and select the required choice. To reduce this challenge more practicing with navigating has been suggested, as active use of web-based services has more positive influence on learning navigation than age [15]. To avoid the extensive amount of information and its disorientating nature the web-based services should appear distinct and axiomatic, without additional elements such as graphic animations that can draw the elderly's attention. If the users experience several announcements disturbing the general information and announcements could be placed a defined section on the screen to reduce their annoying visibility [1]. In general, the developers should favour simplicity and plainness and keep the number of versatile announcements from the web service in minimum [10].

To find out the skills of future or potential users for using web-based services, the developers should perform a test that would evaluate the level of experience of the users related to the web-based services. The test can be carried out with the help of a questionnaire. Questions to ask focus on such as purposes to use the services, use experiences, needed functionalities and length of being a net service user. However, a more efficient way to analyse the skills could be to find out what the users does in the services, what they think when they use the services, and how they feel when they use the services. Chadwick-Dias et al. [16] concluded that the developers should focus more on the usage patterns and qualitative web experience of the users that would reveal how users learn using web-based services.

The developers could build a functionality into the web services that could produce a general user profile according to the user. The functionality could include a brief and easy-to-answer questionnaire to adjust the settings to fit with each user. The questionnaire could find out the state of sight, hearing, memory, and motoric skills, and it should happen quickly enough. Based on that information, the system would automatically change font-size, loud-speakers and other user features to fit that user [1].

There are guidelines to support usability especially for elderly users. The idea of guidelines is to make it easier for developers to develop web services for elderly if the developers have knowledge and checklists of requirements and features related to elderly users. Generally, the guidelines give information about navigating, explicit content expression and general output of the web services. However, the guidelines do not include information about specific sizes for fonts or pushbuttons [4, 10, 19]. Besides applying the guidelines, it is significant to invite the elderly to participate in developing the web services. In this sense, the guidelines can act as a starting point for the development and commit elderly into the development work, which makes the development more efficient [9].

Guidelines and support should offer such information that it would not contain too complicated and difficult technical terms and concepts. All technical terms should be replaced by corresponding terms that are far enough from the original terms [1]. In addition, the amount of complicated technical terms should be as small as possible to avoid extra learning load when a person is practicing using web-based services [17]. In general, positive experiences in using web-based services improves skills and motivation to learn to use other information systems and web-based services [18].

2.4 Summary of Earlier Knowledge

In all, it is important to consider the elderly people when developing services for them. They also form the population group that will grow quickly compared to other age groups. Elderly people have special needs that affect their lives and ways how they use available services. Especially in case of neglect design and development of web-based services and webpages, the elderly experience challenges to adopt and apply the offered services. Therefore, it is important to invite and commit also elderly people into the development process and projects to ensure that the products are beneficial and meet their intentions.

For the elderly, choosing desired sections or locating points on the screen takes longer time caused by weakened sight, too extensive amount of information on the page, and decreasing skills of cognitive skills [1, 5, 10, 12, 13]. However, as they understand their age-related decreased skills, the elderly pay more attention to their actions on the web pages than their younger counterparts, which makes them meticulous users of the services [7].

Earlier knowledge also revealed that the earlier experiences and skills related to ICT and web-based services encourage and help the elderly to learn to use new and different web-based services. Despite that, the number of technical concepts and terms are often perceived as confusing and adding concern among the elderly. Moreover, navigating and hyper links add challenges to use the services. Keeping this in mind, the developers should be aware of the challenges the elderly meet and use the knowledge when designing and developing new web-based solutions and services.

3 Discussion

The current study focused on two research questions: What kind of special needs do elderly people have as users of web-based services? How should developers design such web-based services that would support elderly with special needs? This section discusses the research topic from three points of view. First, a general approach is taken, that is followed by a section of special needs of the elderly as users of web-based services, and finally the special needs of elderly as users of web-based services are considered.

3.1 General Discussion

The first research question about special needs of elderly people related to web-based services could be responded with the help of earlier knowledge that the special needs of the elderly are related to slowness, sight, hearing, motoric skills, sense of touch, cognitive skills, memory, general technical skills and differing earlier experiences of using devices with information technology and web-based services. The second research question was answered by several guidelines and earlier reports how developers do consider the special needs of elderly and how they could pay more attention to the special needs.

Weakened sight can be a challenge [13] as it makes reading from different sized screens difficult especially if there are lots of text and guidelines to be understood. Other challenges are related to loss of motoric skills that affect ability to use pointers and make desired choices among several push buttons or links [1, 5, 12]. When their memories weaken, the elderly perceive difficulties to comprehend and learn the page structure and thus also navigating is difficult [5]. In addition, earlier experiences have a significant impact on the skills and readiness of the elderly to use web-based services, which suggest that special needs can and should be supported by choices made by the developers. Such choices are related to, for example, using larger fonts, stronger contrast, and non-intrusive background of text that would not impede reading [1, 5]. The weakened motoric skills could be noted by reducing need to use pointer between small items but instead, using larger push buttons and items to be pointed [12]. To reduce issues related to loss of memory, the navigating model should be clear and explicit and thus support the users whose memory and cognitive skills are weakened [5].

3.2 Special Needs of the Elderly as Users of Web-Based Services

Slowness is identified as one of the special characters of elderly as users of net that should be noted when designing services for them. The issues are emphasized especially with services that utilize timeout in the process. For example, when identifying users to register into banking services that also the elderly need it adds challenges in the use process [10]. Another concern is related to sight because a weakened sight needs to be noted and considered when designing potentially additional features into the application [13].

Besides poorly situated and unpractical push buttons, also issues with colours make the elderly feel uncomfortable to use web-based services. Small buttons and almost].

similar coloured than the background are difficult to find and identify [1, 13]. In addition, when hearing gets worse, the auditive signs get more challenging to be heard by the elderly [12]. However, not all web-based services apply auditive signs anymore. Only in case there is no visual information available, hearing should be considered with more care [1].

Along with reducing motoric skills choosing small elements on the screen comes more challenging. This can lead to making more mistakes and further cause additional problems when the elderly will not use the services due to being afraid of doing mistakes, and then, the elderly might reduce ever more usage of web-based services and will lead them not to learn and comprehend new and needed web-based services [12].

Another issue characteristic for elderly is decreased sense of touch that makes it more difficult to identify if the current touch lead to a desired function in the application, because the user can be unaware of the state of the system. Did the touch affect anything or not remains unknown. On the other hand, the number of unintended double touches increases remarkably, which also should be understood by the developers and responded in the design and implementation of the related functionalities [1].

Skills to solve problems, working memory and observing get weaker when the elderly are getting their later years of age, and that has an influence on ability to navigate and find relevant choices and buttons in the web-based services. These problems are connected with searching information with the help of building search strings and comprehending functional processes of the current service. The most evident cause for the problems is due to limited memory and cognitive skills of the elderly [13]. In addition, too much of visible information is a known problem especially in commercial web-based services [6, 10]. Figure 3 illustrates the main needs of the elderly users of web-based services as reported by earlier studies.

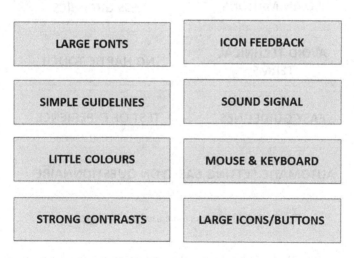

Fig. 3. Needs of the elderly.

Most elderly are familiar with personal computers but not all have experience of internet [4]. Most elderly also consider their skills to apply web-based services [13]. Also, they are afraid of making mistakes [15]. The problems emerge especially in situations when the elderly have no means to carry their tasks on site due to physical or other disabilities. In those cases, web-based services could be the best solution. However, if the elderly are afraid of using web-based services, and the dilemma can lead to expensive or difficult problems to solve. Therefore, the elderly and the challenges they perceive should be treated with care and seek for means to encourage and help them in using web-based services [7].

3.3 Supporting Special Needs in Web-Based Services

The elderly like more text-based web-based services than services that include lots of graphics [11]. Therefore the developers should consider improving web-based services that include only little additional graphics and that appear as simple as possible [13]. Text with sharp contrast and well separating background is a recommended way to ease the elderly who need the web-based services [1]. Because sense of touch and hearing get often worse as perceived by the elderly, the elderly can find it challenging to note that they already had made their choice for the next activity e.g. choosing a specific button or option in the service. This challenge was responded by applying icon feedback into the services. In practice, icon feedback utilizes visual features to inform the success of made choices [14]. Another assisting choice is to avoid applying mouseover that reduces the need to use mouse as a pointer between the push buttons. In addition, double clicks are not suitable for the elderly users [5].

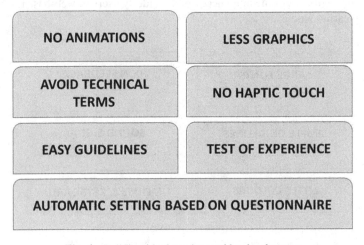

Fig. 4. Building blocks to be used by developers.

Figure 4 illustrates the building blocks to be used by developers when they design and build web-based services for elderly people. The blocks could point out such approaches and experiences that are not as familiar to developers representing younger generations than to the elderly users who will form the actual user group of the web-based services.

In addition, a special search field should be available on the pages to allow natural search strings written by the users, because if the cognitive skills are getting humbler, the users see it difficult to build search strings for themselves [1]. Earlier studies have shown that aged people form a group that is not homogenous when regarding their technological skills. This knowledge leads to suggesting that developers should offer assistance and support in a way that can be requested when using the web-based services [17]. Furthermore, the elderly should be encouraged to use and utilize different web-based services despite challenges they might experience, as only getting more practice and experiences will add praxis and knowledge, and thus reduce uncertainty and ambivalence in using the services [18]. However, a good conclusion is to remember that technology should adjust according to the users' needs and not the other way round [9].

4 Conclusion

The current research problem was related to the thought that the elderly people are not enough taken into account when designing several web-based services even if the group of elderly people forms a large user group for services, which was identified by earlier knowledge and visible also everyday lives of many of us. They cannot be included into any other user group that consists of people significantly younger than they are as ageing brings challenges that need to be considered when designing services. Earlier knowledge has revealed that most of the elderly experience similar challenges when they use the traditional services [13].

The literature review was pretty light in nature, it managed to identify several special characteristics of the elderly caused by high age or diagnosed reasons such as memory-related diseases. Similarly, the literature review revealed potential ways to mitigate the challenges the elderly face when using web-based services. This paper paid attention especially on the means and knowledge that the developers and designers of web-based services already have and could apply when building services for the elderly.

The topic of elderly people applying web-based services could be continued among elderly and focus on analysing how they experience the current available web-based services and what they expect from them. As the current knowledge has shown, the amount of elderly is increasing, and they will be applying more web-based services because they have been using them for decades – however, due to issues emerging due to ageing they will need special solutions to continue in applying them.

In addition, the future study could offer knowledge of the IT skills of the elderly and analyse if and how they have changed in time. While analysing the IT skills of the elderly, also the modern solutions could be evaluated and analysed if they develop the same pace as the skills of elderly do. Moreover, it would be interesting to know when the gap between the earlier sufficient skills and abilities is getting too large for a reasonable use of web-based services as perceived by the elderly.

References

1. Williams, D., Alam, M.A.U., Ahamed, S.I., Chu, W.: Considerations in designing human-computer interfaces for elderly people. In: 2013 13th International Conference on Quality Software, pp. 372–377 (2013)
2. Pollitt, C.: Technological Change: a central yet neglected feature of public administration. NISPAcee J. Public Adm. Policy 3(2), 31–53 (2010). https://doi.org/10.2478/v10110-010-0003-z
3. Koiranen, I., Räsänen, P., Södergård, C.: Mitä digitalisaatio on tarkoittanut kansalaisen näkökulmasta? Talous ja yhteiskunta 3(2016), 24–29 (2016)

4. Dickinson, A., Arnott, J., Prior, S.: Methods for human-computer interaction research with older people. Behav. Inf. Technol. **26**(4), 343–352 (2007)
5. Becker, S.A.: A study of web usability for older adults seeking online health resources. ACM Trans. Comput.-Hum. Interact. **11**(4), 387–406 (2004)
6. Newell, A.F.: HCI and older people. In: HCI and the Older Population (2004). 10.2638728.2641558
7. Chadwick-Dias, A., McNulty, M., Tullis, T.: Web usability and age: how design changes can improve performance. ACM SIGCAPH Comput. Phys. Handicap. **73–74**, 30–37 (2003)
8. Mikkola, K., Halonen, R.: "Nonsense?" - ICT perceived by the elderly. In: European, Mediterranean & Middle Eastern Conference on Information Systems, EMCIS 2011, Athens, Greece, 30–31 May 2011 (2011). http://emcis.eu/Emcis_archive/EMCIS/EMCIS2011/EMCISWebsite/EMCIS2011%20Proceedings/SCI1.pdf
9. Castilla, D., et al.: Process of design and usability evaluation of a telepsychology web and virtual reality system for the elderly: Butler. Int. J. Hum.-Comput. Stud. **71**(3), 350–362 (2013)
10. Hart, T.A., Chaparro, B.S., Halcomb, C.G.: Evaluating websites for older adults: adherence to 'senior-friendly' guidelines and end-user performance. Behav. Inf. Technol. **27**(3), 191–199 (2008)
11. Liao, C., Goff, L., Chaparro, A., Chaparro, B., Stumpfhauser, L.: A comparison of website usage between young adults and the elderly. Proc. Hum. Factors Ergon. Soc. Ann. Meet. **4**, 101 (2000)
12. Chen, Y.: Usability analysis on online social networks for the elderly. TKK T-110.5190 Seminar on Internetworking. Helsinki University of Technology (2009)
13. Kantner, L., Rosenbaum, S.: Usable computers for the elderly: applying coaching experiences. In: IEEE International Professional Communication Conference (2003)
14. Tsai, W.-C., Lee, C.-F.: A study on the icon feedback types of small touch screen for the elderly. In: Stephanidis, C. (ed.) UAHCI 2009. LNCS, vol. 5615, pp. 422–431. Springer, Heidelberg (2009). https://doi.org/10.1007/978-3-642-02710-9_46
15. Loos, E.: Senior citizens: digital immigrants in their own country? Observatorio (OBS*) **6**(1) (2012)
16. Chadwick-Dias, A., Tedesco, D., Tullis, T.: Older adults and web usability: is web experience the same as web expertise? In: CHI 2004 Extended Abstracts on Human Factors in Computing Systems, pp. 1391–1394 (2004)
17. Naumanen, M., Tukiainen, M.: Guiding the elderly into the use of computers and Internet-Lessons taught and learnt. In: Proceedings of Cognition and Exploratory Learning in Digital Age, pp. 19–27 (2007)
18. Czaja, S.J., Sharit, J.: Age differences in attitudes toward computers. J. Gerontol. Ser. B: Psychol. Sci. Soc. Sci. **53**(5), 329–340 (1998)
19. Hart, T.A., Chaparro, B.: Evaluation of websites for older adults: how "Senior Friendly" are they. Usability News **6**(1), 12 (2004)

Comparison of Cost and Time Effectiveness Between CT- and MRI-Based Radiotherapy Workflow for Prostate Cancer

Olli Sjöblom[1]([✉]), Sonja Turnbull-Smith[2], Heikki Minn[3], and Jani Keyriläinen[3,4]

[1] School of Economics, Information Systems Science, Turku University, Turku, Finland
oljusj@utu.fi
[2] Philips MR Therapy Oy, Vantaa, Finland
sonja.turnbull-smith@philips.com
[3] Department of Oncology and Radiotherapy, Turku University Hospital, Turku, Finland
{heikki.minn,jani.keyrilainen}@tyks.fi
[4] Department of Medical Physics, Turku University Hospital, Turku, Finland

Abstract. The real costs of health care and their economic assessment have been expressed with a great urgency in an expanding dimension. In order to consider the value-based outcomes when measuring value, very accurate knowledge about health care delivery costs is required. The allocation of the rather scarce resources within public health care is of great importance in order to better utilize the resources without lowering care quality. The approach of this paper is multidisciplinary, representing the field of health economics. The focus is in the assessment and evaluation of the costs of different simulation imaging modalities used in radiation therapy (RT) workflow. In this study, the costs of the computed tomography (CT) and the magnetic resonance imaging (MRI) are observed. In order to investigate the expenses as accurately as possible, the time-driven activity-based costing (TDABC) is applied as a research method. The specific aim of this study is to find out potential advantages of the MRI-only simulation, as this method is not very widely applied in RT. This study is a research-in-progress, presenting only the theoretical argumentation and methods, meanwhile the collection and processing of the empirical data is in progress. The research is continuing, and the empirical findings will be added to the theoretical framework in a separate paper.

Keywords: Radiotherapy treatment · Magnetic resonance imaging · Computed tomography · Value-based outcomes · Time-driven activity-based costing · Care quality

1 Introduction

Cancer mortality among both men and women has been decreasing over the last decades, due primarily to the improved diagnosis and advancement in treatment methods [1]. This trend of higher survival has been noticeable for almost all types of cancer with a few exceptions such as pancreatic cancer. The radiotherapy, i.e. radiation therapy (RT, see the Sect. 2.2) continues to play an important role in the treatment of cancer. It is estimated

M. Cacace et al. (Eds.): WIS 2020, CCIS 1270, pp. 61–72, 2020.
https://doi.org/10.1007/978-3-030-57847-3_4

that about 60% of the patients with cancer receive radiation during their lifetime as a part of their curative or palliative treatment [2].

In the RT workflow, significant improvements have been done in simulation imaging, a process for locating the cancer and its surrounding tissues and organs (see Fig. 1). This is carried out by applying either computed tomography (CT) or magnetic resonance imaging (MRI) or in most often, the combination of both. This progression has provided increasingly more accurate information in the delivery of the external beam radiation dose onto the target volume, i.e., the cancerous tissue to be irradiated, as well as the adjacent critical structures or organs at risk (OAR). As the consequence of this improvement, the superior outcome in the planning and delivery of RT as well as reduction in toxicity have been achieved, therefore providing better life quality for the cancer patients [2].

The real costs of health care and their economic assessment have been expressed with a great urgency in an expanding dimension from the point of view of allocation of scarce resources within health care systems [3, 4]. As the share of the expenditures committed in the health increase in the gross domestic product of the nations, better understanding about the costs of the health care as well as of the costs of the medical innovations is urgently needed [3, 5]. As the societies and health care organizations are moving on a larger scale towards more accountable operations, understanding the actual costs on a detailed level is unavoidable [6].

In order to improve the value of health care, the providers have focused lowering the actual costs by applying methods that do not cause adverse effects on health care quality. These efforts have essentially improved the health care reform, the focus of which is to better utilize the resources without lowering care quality. However, the real costs, including facility and equipment expenses together with more easily defined personnel and procedural costs, are rather awkwardly to be assessed. This is due to the premise of using the reimbursement about billable procedures instead of the actual utilization of the allocated resources [5, 7–9]. For working out the real costs of health care, different methods can be allocated. Several already for a quite long time used and established calculation models exist and for a special case intended models have also been developed and successfully used. Defourny et al. [3] have carried out a comprehensive search about the medical literature describing to a variable extent aspects of RT costs. In total 1344 titles were identified but after filtering duplicates etc., only 4% (n = 52) was left for in-depth analysis. The result was somewhat surprising, as only 40% of the publications employed conventional methods and only one recent of them (2%, n = 1) applied time-driven activity-based costing (TDABC) [3].

TDABC is a bottom-up costing method with granular calculations. As opposed to other methods founded on the charges billed to the payer, the calculations are based on the real consumption of the resources, like personnel, space, equipment and material [10]. This method is discussed in detail in Sect. 3.2.

Measuring the real health care costs accurately remains a challenge although the costs of producing products and services belong essentially to the management process of the business. Another considerable perspective in this context is that very often the physician practices do not possess the necessary resources to evaluate costs across services, due to which they instead focus on more easily available data like revenue or reimbursement 6. According to Defourny et al. [3], the TDABC as a method has not up to now been used very widely, which makes this approach interesting, thus providing it also with novelty value.

2 Radiation Therapy in Prostate Cancer Treatment

2.1 Prostate Cancer

Prostate cancer is the most common malignant disease among men in the industrialised countries. Almost 1.3 million new cases occurred in the year 2018, which corresponded to 7% of all cancers and 359 000 deaths due to prostate cancer worldwide [11]. In 2017, approximately 30% of all male cancers in Finland were prostate cancers, and 5 446 new cases were diagnosed according to Finnish Cancer Registry in 2017 [12]. At the same time, there were 912 deaths, the survival rate being as high as 92%. For comparison ought to be mentioned that in 2017, 34 261 new cancer cases of both sexes were detected in Finland.

RT, chemotherapy and surgery are the most common anti-cancer treatment modalities. In breast and prostate cancer endocrine treatment has an important role. The capacity of RT is based on the dose response of cells, which describes the response of the biological object for the ionizing radiation. The dose response is characteristic for different types of cells, and the difference between the response of tumour cells and the response of normal cells is the base from which all the doses for clinical treatment are chosen. In Finland, RT is given for around 17 000 cancer patients annually and almost 1 600 of them are treated at Turku University Hospital (TUH, Turku, Finland).

This research is chosen to focus on prostate cancer because at TUH's department of oncology and radiotherapy, where MRI-only workflow has been applied to RT planning of prostate cancer since 2017 [13–15].

2.2 Cancer Treatment Process

RT is defined as the use of high-energy irradiation (typically 1 MeV or greater) for eradicating proliferating cells. This is delivered in most cases by photons that are produced by a linear accelerator, but alternative possibilities are protons from a cyclotron or synchrotron as well as electrons from a linear accelerator. The duration and the total dose of the radiation treatment is dependent on its goals. For example, the RT for prostate cancer, which is the observation focus of this study, may last eight weeks, whereas a palliative RT for bone pain may take place in one individual irradiation session [16].

RT in cancer treatment is a multiphase process requiring careful planning. A schematic overview of the workflow when external beam radiation therapy (EBRT) is delivered to patient is presented in Fig. 1. In the figure, Jarrett et al. (2019) have divided the process into three different conceptual domains: diagnosis and decision support, treatment planning and treatment delivery. The domain in the middle, the planning of the RT, is the core object of this study, especially the application of different simulation imaging methods.

Simulation imaging is a process performed in order to find out the exact part of the human body for which the RT is needed. It is typically based on either CT or MRI, or both (other methods might also be necessary to apply in addition to the mentioned). In the latter case, the information is combined by image fusion i.e. image registration (see the Sect. 2.4).

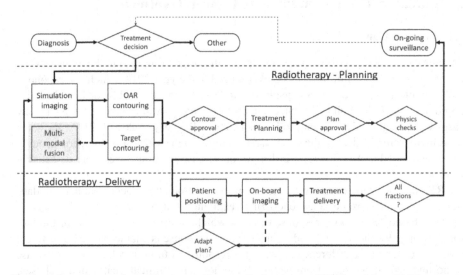

Fig. 1. Schematic overview of the external beam radiation therapy EBRT workflow (OAR: organs at risk; adopted from Jarrett *et al.* [17]).

As presented in the Fig. 1, the phase "multimodal fusion" is highlighted and connected to the process flow chart with dash a line, because it is an alternative phase, which can be avoided by applying one imaging modality only instead of a combination of several of them. This subject is discussed in detail in Sect. 2.4 and illustrated in Fig. 2.

2.3 Simulation Imaging in External Beam Radiation Therapy

CT imaging has been the most applied system and prevailing approach of simulation for as long as since the 1980s. Despite this experience with efficient development along the same time, there is still a number of areas for clinical improvement remaining although many of the challenges might be assumed to having been overcome [17]. It provides both anatomical and tissue density information for the RT planning of different sites such as prostate, rectal and gynaecological cancers when EBRT is applied as the means of treatment. Its advantages have been the availability of the machines and cost-effectiveness as well as its speed of acquisition and high spatial resolution [17]. In order to overcome the challenges and weaknesses when applying CT only, MRI is used broadly in combination with the CT imaging in RT planning for pelvic cancers.

As compared with CT, the major advantage of MRI is better soft tissue contrast. This method accurately enables e.g. the visualisation of the cancerous tissue from its surrounding soft tissues. As an additional benefit of MRI over X-ray-based imaging methods is the use of non-ionising radiation. Furthermore, as the OARs always ought to be acknowledged, the accuracy of MRI results provides the better visibility as well as their delineation, (or contouring, as called in Fig. 1). More accurate gross tumour volume and better regional lymph node characterization might also be mentioned as the advantages of the MRI over CT [13]. In addition, when an MRI-only workflow is applied, the so-called synthetic CT images can be generated, using the MRI images as the source.

By applying this method, tissues' electron density information required in the dose calculation, as well as reference images for patient position verification are provided [14]. The precise position of the patient is essential in order to focus the radiation on the cancerous tissue as accurately as possible and at the same time to avoid the non-cancerous tissue to be irradiated. However, despite all the advantages, it is worth emphasizing that on geometric accuracy MRI imposes strict requirements if used for RT planning [18]. For example, any ferromagnetic objects near the MRI suite represent external factors that may lead to changes in the geometric performance of the scanner. In case the patient has an artificial hip, this method cannot be normally applied, which matter will be discussed later in this study.

At TUH, almost 1 600 patients are treated annually with RT, and 120 RT sessions take place daily. The personnel of the RT department consist of 57 staff members: 9 oncologists, 7 physicists, 33 radiation therapists, i.e. radiation therapy technologist (RTT) and 8 supporting staff members. The department is equipped with five linear accelerators, one high dose rate after-loader as well as one CT simulator and one MRI simulator. It also has access to positron emission tomography (PET)/MRI and PET/CT devices and offers a diverse range of RT planning, calculation and dosimetry tools. The department is applying two imaging modalities in its daily RT planning, the CT and MRI.

The characteristics of CT imaging can be described as follows:

- geometrically accurate
- electron density information needed for dose calculation and reference images
- differentiates well high from low densities e.g. bone and air/soft tissue, while suffers from a quite poor soft-tissue contrast

As for MRI, the most common characteristics are:

- excellent soft-tissue contrast
- lack of electron density information necessary for accurate dose calculation and generating reference images for patient setup
- challenges in geometric accuracy with a large field of view (entire body outline)
- challenges in visualization of fiducials, bone edges and bone-air borderlines
- complex contrast formation (depends on e.g. proton density, chemical environment, water diffusion and perfusion)

In order to give some perspective about the caseload in RT, in 2018 a total of 1 542 (including five children) CT image sets for RT planning were acquired at TUH, 375 (one of them a child) of them being examinations on pelvic regions. In the same year, 1 000 simulations (including nine children) MR image sets for RT planning were done, including 388 pelvic examinations. The number of patients in 2018 represents a relevant example of the annual average, which provides a solid basis for the observations needed for the cost evaluations in this study. From the point of view of the discussion later, it is worth noticing that the number of simulations mentioned above consist of all the pelvic cancer patients, a part of which the prostate cancer patients make up.

MRI unit has been in operative use since January 2016 at TUH's department of oncology and radiotherapy. The MRI-only planning for prostate cancer has been in clinical use since March 2017. In addition, what has been written before about the comparison of CT and MRI, there have been remarkable and promising advances in the use of MRI-only RT planning and dose calculation of all pelvic cancers as well as some brain cancers. At TUH, the previous has moved to the phase III of a clinical trial in April 2020, but the latter is still in the phase I. As for the RT planning of prostate cancer, the MRI is increasingly applied for it in order to reduce the target volume delineation uncertainty [15].

2.4 Process Map of a Cancer Patient

A typical process map of a prostate patient in RT is presented in Fig. 2 as follows:

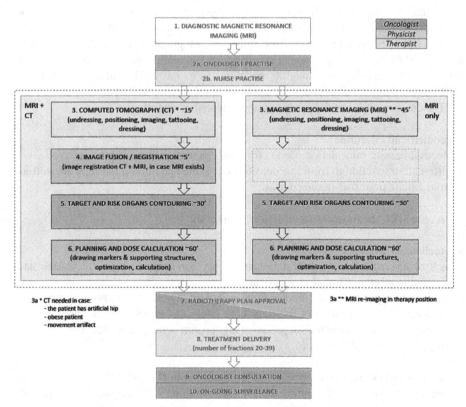

Fig. 2. A typical process map of a prostate patient at the department of radiotherapy.

An overview of the EBRT workflow was presented in Fig. 1. The core focus of this study is observing the differences between two alternative paths in RT treatment of prostate cancer patient displayed as phases 3–6 in Fig. 2. The different phases are provided with times needed to carry out the activities mentioned, including the personnel carrying out the phase. Regardless of which of two possible alternatives is chosen, a pathological cancer diagnosis has always been prepared preceding the simulation imagination processes. Also, a diagnostic MRI might have been carried out before (as presented in phase 1). Before simulation imaging, the consultations of oncologist (phase 2) and RTT (phase 3) precede the alternative imaging processes, which are the combined method applying both CT and MRI, or the alternative applying MRI only.

Imaging Applying CT and MRI. A combined method applying both CT with MRI or only CT, on the left is needed if the patient has an artificial hip, has a movement artifact or if the patient is obese (due to the limited size of the scanner's bore). The patient movement during image acquisition is a problem because the movement artifacts degrade the quality of the images, which for one, may lead to misinterpretations or cannot be used at all for anatomic delineation. Especially, in dynamic MRI scans, signal changes may be caused by the motion artifacts, which consequently may confound in a severe manner the results of rendering the statistical analysis [19]. This combination is essential to be applied (according to a rough estimate) only in 10% of the number of the patients. The CT is a relatively quick operation, carried out by an RTT taking only 15 min in average.

Tattooing in phase 3 means that tiny dots are marked on the patient's skin in order to aid in the patient positioning during an entire course of RT. These are very tiny dots made using an ink during the simulation process with the help of laser beams identical to those at the treatment units. In case any additional RT is needed later, these tattoos can be utilised as a permanent record of the treatments carried out before.

The next, a rather short phase 4 is carried out by a physicist, requiring roughly 5 min to make the registration i.e. the fusion of the images prepared with both the CT and MRI [20]. The image registration (or fusion) refers to combining the results of two different imaging methods. The goal of the RT is fully irradiating the cancerous tissue while minimising the radiation dose received by OARs, the healthy surrounding tissues [21]. The CT is mostly applied in delineating the prostate and planning the RT treatment, used especially in the three-dimensional planning of RT, due to its capability to provide the superior spatial accuracy and electron density information, which both are important for heterogeneity corrections when the dose calculations are carried out. However, a disadvantage of CT is its weak soft-tissue contrast not allowing an accurate delineation of the organs [22]. Due to this, two major drawbacks can especially be mentioned: First, the images created by CT do not provide high enough contrast between the healthy and cancerous prostate tissues; second, the delineation variability exists. Due to the poor CT soft-tissue contrast, the prostate volume tends to be overestimated, possibly leading to overexposed surrounding healthy tissues and organs [21].

MRI, on the other hand, provides a high soft-tissue contrast with rich details, considered as the reference for prostate delineation as allowing good tumour detection [21, 22]. The MRI, despite its superiority, suffers from some disadvantages. Geometric distortion at the edges of the field of view can be observed. In addition, as it does not provide the intrinsic information on electronic density, its use as the only imaging method in the treatment planning of some types of cancer is precluded. As for high-quality treatment planning, an accurate image fusion of both CT and MRI is essential. In this case, the complementary information that contained two different modalities provide a more accurate definition of the cancerous tissue [22].

Target and OAR structures are delineated (or, as called contouring in this phase) by an oncologist in the next phase 5, which takes time approximately 30 min. In phase 6, the treatment plan is created, and dose is calculated. This phase also includes the drawing of markers and/or supporting structures, as well as an optimization of treatment plan. Either a physicist or an RTT performs these tasks in an hour in average.

Drawing markers in phase 6 refers to fiducial markers or fiducials, which are gold or nickel-titanium, also known as Nitinol, seeds with the size of about a grain of rice. They, usually three of them, are placed in the tumour for helping in the image-guidance of RT. Through this procedure, applying X-rays, the tumour can be targeted precisely allowing higher radiation doses with smaller margins and thus, without causing unnecessary harm to nearby healthy tissue [23].

Imaging Applying MRI Only. According to the widely utilized practice, the co-registration of CT and MR images creates the basis for their use in RT. The MRI provides the utilization of additional anatomical details within the soft tissues, whereas the dose calculation needs the electron density information, which is available by CT.

When multi-modality imaging, i.e., the combination of CT and MRI (and perhaps other methods, too) is applied, there is a major drawback in the appearance of the registration errors during the registration of images from two or more imaging modalities [13].

As two different imaging modalities are used, additional work and time are required, which for its part raises costs. Therefore, a single imaging modality practice would be ideal. This will also reduce the number of the hospital visits of the patients, and alongside the work performed by the personnel, which together may lead to significant savings in time and costs.

Tenhunen et al. (2018) [24] carried out a study at the Comprehensive Cancer Center of Helsinki University Hospital analysing the technical planning workflow of 200 patients that were the first receiving MRI-only planned RT for localised prostate cancer. They found out that the MRI-only method was suitable technically for 92% of the patients, as the remaining 8% required supplemental CT imaging.

Consistently with this study, today at TUH the most common path used on the right side (according to a rough estimate), which is applied in more than 90% of the number of the treated prostate cancer patients, is applying MRI as only imaging method. In phase 3, about 45 min is required to allow the patient first to undress and after the whole procedure to dress again, to position the patient, to carry out the MRI and tattooing. An RTT carries out this phase. Unlike the path containing both CT and MRI, applying this method the phase 4 can be skipped, as no image fusion ought to be made. The structures are delineated by an oncologist like in the alternative path in the next phase 5 taking time almost 30 min [15]. The phase 6 is similar to that described in the Chapter "Imaging applying CT and MRI".

After either of the alternative paths chosen, finally RT plan and treatment course are approved by oncologist and physicist (phase 7). According to what has been carried out during the process before, the treatment delivery (phase 8) takes place, including 5–39 fractions. After the treatment deliveries, the consultation of oncologist (phase 9) is essential, followed by the on-going surveillance for years (phase 10).

3 Methods

3.1 Cost-Effectiveness and Radiotherapy

Essential technical advances on the RT field have been achieved since the last decade of the last century. The costs of the RT have been increasing, but it is unclear whether its clinical benefits have also improved. In order to formally evaluate the costs of the treatment in proportion the associated changes in the treatment quality, cost-effectiveness analyses and methods have been designed. Especially the RT in question, assessing its cost-effectiveness is critically important, as the costs of the oncologic care are increasing [16].

In order to consider the value-based outcomes when measuring value, essential knowledge about health care delivery costs is required. Kaplan and Porter [5, 25, 26] have suggested a framework to promote and assess value-based outcomes focusing on encouraging and increasing sustainable health care practices [5].

In Sect. 2.4 the differences in the time requirements of the different phases were presented, but like mentioned in the same context, these observations do not alone prove its cost-efficiency over applying the combination of CT and MRI. First, the cost of working time of various occupational groups, such as RTTs, physicists and oncologists, may differ significantly from each other. Second, there are several other costs and expenses to take into a consideration, as the use of equipment, premises etc. In order to formulate a reliable overall view of the real costs, an applicable model for it is needed.

Several articles concerning the calculation of RT costs have been prepared and published recently. For instance, Keel et al. [27] has carried out an extensive literature review about the challenges facing the health care today. According to them, value-based health care is proposed as a suitable strategy addressing those. The point of view in question is the care delivery value chain, which determines the value in terms of the value equation. Applying this method, the achieved health outcomes per unit cost are calculated, expending them over the whole value chain [27].

3.2 Time-Driven Activity-Based Costing

The activity-based costing (ABC) method was originally developed in the 1980s in order to respond to the rather common shortcomings in the traditional cost accounting methods. The urgent need for this arose during the era when the product complexity and size as well as volume diversification increased rapidly. When applying this method, the cost of a 'product' is calculated. In this context, the product is a course of RT, its care process activities (such as the planning of the treatment, delivery verification or dose delivery) in addition to the related resources together generating that product [28].

The TDABC was developed further based on the ABC principles using time as the unique cost driver. Each resource group, as oncologists, physicists and RTTs, is studied estimating the cost per time unit of supplying resource capacity and observing the time of these resources are committed to the specific activities. This activity-based approach is less complex to maintain than the original ABC-model, allowing as an optimized approach higher flexibility than the previously mentioned. Furthermore, this model is unique to each specific situation. According to Van Dyk et al. [28], this model allows the testing of the estimated cost of the RT need, infrastructural capabilities, operational models, expected level of complexity and economic determinants [28].

As already shortly mentioned before, the TDABC is defined as a bottom-up method, the function of which is to determine the costs step-by-step of all the resources. They include both time and other resources, e.g. equipment, facilities etc. All of them are allocated at each of the activities during the complete patient treatment process. This method enables more accurate and transparent estimates about the real expenses incurred by the providers [9].

This costing paradigm is in use among a variety of industries. Especially in the context of health care using this method, the real expense of the resources allocated actually can be calculated precisely. This can be done over the entire full cycle of the patient care. Furthermore, the breakdown of all the costs of each resource per time unit can be carried out in detail. This can be applied to both the direct costs, i.e., personnel and equipment costs as well as the indirect support expenses. One essential point in this study is that the possible inefficiency areas can be illuminated through the allocation of this method and in that case it enables to highlight the opportunities to reduce the costs in a rational way [6].

A graphic presentation is usually created in order to illustrate the workflow and consequently to find out the points where the costs rise. Such as this is displayed in Fig. 1.

TDABC method has not been applied very widely yet. The study of Schutzer et al. 10 can be mentioned as an illustrating example of why this method is worth applying. They compared the costs of the whole breast radiation therapy (WBRT) and accelerated partial breast irradiation (APBI), and found APBI to cost 30% more than WBRT. By applying this method, the researchers were able to evaluate the fundamental cost based on the real consumption of the resources instead of the charges billed to the payer [10].

4 Discussion

The study presented here is a research-in-progress, i.e., the empirical data are still missing, as it has not been possible to collect those so far. This has been due to the lack of the administrative officers that could calculate and deliver the relevant data concerning the costs of the different phases during the RT process. In order to focus on collecting and calculating the relevant data about the real costs, the theoretical framework ought to be formulated very accurately. However, as presented in Fig. 2, the required time for carrying out the different stages has been estimated on a somewhat scarce level, providing, however, some guiding for the theory framework presented here. These estimates will become more precise along with the progress of the research process. These can then be applied when targeting the costs of different treatments in order to calculate the total costs of different workflows presented in this study.

The importance of the MRI method in the prostate cancer RT is increasing. Compared with CT, its superior soft tissue contrast improves the delineation of the prostate and adjacent normal tissues, which has been known already for many years. However, despite this, the MRI has not been widely or routinely used because of several challenges when used only as the simulation method [29].

One essential target of this study is to find out, whether applying MRI-only RT planning is significantly less resource consuming method compared with applying the combination of CT and MRI at the RT process for prostate cancer. The results of the study might for its part serve as a policy maker for those radiation treatment units that consider switching to an MRI-only based RT planning.

The TDABC method has been presented before in Sect. 3.2. The chapter describes how the method can be applied in the RT process in order to figure out its real costs, especially seen from the point of view applying different imaging methods. However, despite its systematic and accurate approach, this alone does not solve the problem calculating and assessing the total costs of the process in the long run. It is more than essential mentioning in this context costs that this method does not at least straightforwardly take into account. First, investing in the equipment is a pivotal decision, as significant liquidity is required causing usually notable financing costs. The purchasing cost of an MRI-system dedicated to RT is about 1.5 M€, whereas the cost for an RT-dedicated CT scanner is only about a third of it. In order to apply the TDABC model correctly, these costs ought to be included in the operating costs of the equipment. In this context, the rate of occupancy plays an important role, as well as the estimated period of amortization.

This study will be continued by receiving accurate cost reports from the administrative department of the hospital as well as through empirical observations in order to obtain accurate time estimates for each treatment activity. Staff interviews might also be essential to carry out to elaborate the results of the observations.

References

1. Jemal, A., et al.: Annual report to the nation on the status of cancer, 1975–2014, featuring survival. J. Natl. Cancer Inst. **109** (2017)
2. Chandarana, H., Wang, H., Tijssen, R.H.N., Das, I.J.: Emerging role of MRI in radiation therapy. J. Magn. Reson. Imaging **48**, 1468–1478 (2018)
3. Defourny, N., Dunscombe, P., Perrier, L., Grau, C., Lievens, Y.: Cost evaluations of radiotherapy: what do we know? An ESTRO-HERO analysis. Radiother. Oncol. **121**, 468–474 (2016)
4. Drummond, M.F., Sculpher, M.J., Claxton, K., Stoddart, G.L., Torrance, G.W.: Methods for the Economic Evaluation of Health Care Programmes. OUP, Oxford (2015)
5. Kaplan, R.S., Porter, M.E.: How to solve the cost crisis in health care. Harv. Bus. Rev. **89**, 46–52 (2011)
6. Laviana, A.A., et al.: Utilizing time-driven activity-based costing to understand the short- and long-term costs of treating localized, low-risk prostate cancer. Cancer **122**, 447–455 (2016)
7. Teckie, S., McCloskey, S.A., Steinberg, M.L.: Value: a framework for radiation oncology. J. Clin. Oncol. **32**, 2864–2870 (2014)
8. Oklu, R., et al.: Time-driven activity-based costing in IR. J. Vasc. Interv. Radiol. **26**, 1827–1831 (2015)

9. Bauer-Nilsen, K., et al.: Evaluation of delivery costs for external beam radiation therapy and brachytherapy for locally advanced cervical cancer using time-driven activity-based costing. Int. J. Radiat. Oncol. Biol. Phys. **100**, 88–94 (2018)

10. Schutzer, M.E., Arthur, D.W., Anscher, M.S.: Time-driven activity-based costing: a comparative cost analysis of whole-breast radiotherapy versus balloon-based brachytherapy in the management of early-stage breast cancer. J. Oncol. Pract. **12**, e584–e593 (2016)

11. Ferlay, J., et al.: Global Cancer Observatory: Cancer Today. International Agency for Research on Cancer. Lyon, France (2018). https://gco.iarc.fr/today. Accessed 20 Mar 2020

12. Finnish Cancer Registry. Cancer in Finland. Statistics - Cancer in Finland (2017). https://cancerregistry.fi/statistics/cancer-in-finland/. Accessed 25 Feb 2020

13. Kemppainen, R., et al.: Magnetic resonance-only simulation and dose calculation in external beam radiation therapy: a feasibility study for pelvic cancers. Acta Oncol. (Madr) **56**, 792–798 (2017)

14. Kemppainen, R., et al.: Assessment of dosimetric and positioning accuracy of a magnetic resonance imaging-only solution for external beam radiotherapy of pelvic anatomy. Phys. Imaging Radiat. Oncol. **11**, 1–8 (2019)

15. Kuisma, A., et al.: Validation of automated magnetic resonance image segmentation for radiation therapy planning in prostate cancer. Phys. Imaging Radiat. Oncol. **13**, 14–20 (2020)

16. Sher, D.J.: Cost–effectiveness studies in radiation therapy. Expert Rev. Pharmacoecon. Outcomes Res. **10**, 567–582 (2010)

17. Jarrett, D., Stride, E., Vallis, K., Gooding, M.J.: Applications and limitations of machine learning in radiation oncology. Br. J. Radiol. **92**, 20190001 (2019)

18. Ranta, I., et al.: Quality assurance measurements of geometric accuracy for magnetic resonance imaging-based radiotherapy treatment planning. Phys. Medica **62**, 47–52 (2019)

19. Havsteen, I., et al.: Are movement artifacts in magnetic resonance imaging a real problem?-A narrative review. Front. Neurol. **8**, 232 (2017)

20. Giesel, F.L., et al.: Image fusion using CT, MRI and PET for treatment planning, navigation and follow up in percutaneous RFA. Exp. Oncol. **31**, 106–114 (2009)

21. Commandeur, F., et al.: MRI to CT prostate registration for improved targeting in cancer external beam radiotherapy. IEEE J. Biomed. Health Inform. **21**, 1015–1026 (2017)

22. Wang, X., et al.: A comparative study of three CT and MRI registration algorithms in nasopharyngeal carcinoma. J. Appl. Clin. Med. Phys. **10**, 2906 (2009)

23. van den Ende, R.P.J., et al.: MRI visibility of gold fiducial markers for image-guided radiotherapy of rectal cancer. Radiother. Oncol. J. Eur. Soc. Ther. Radiol. Oncol. **132**, 93–99 (2019)

24. Tenhunen, M., et al.: MRI-only based radiation therapy of prostate cancer: workflow and early clinical experience. Acta Oncol. (Madr) **57**, 902–907 (2018)

25. Kaplan, R.S., Anderson, S.R.: Time-driven activity-based costing. Harv. Bus. Rev. **82**, 131–138 (2004)

26. Kaplan, R.S., et al.: Using time-driven activity-based costing to identify value improvement opportunities in healthcare. J. Healthc. Manag. **59**, 399–412 (2014)

27. Keel, G., Savage, C., Rafiq, M., Mazzocato, P.: Time-driven activity-based costing in health care: a systematic review of the literature. Health Policy (New York) **121**, 755–763 (2017)

28. Van Dyk, J., Zubizarreta, E., Lievens, Y.: Cost evaluation to optimise radiation therapy implementation in different income settings: a time-driven activity-based analysis. Radiother. Oncol. **125**, 178–185 (2017)

29. Tyagi, N., et al.: Clinical workflow for MR-only simulation and planning in prostate. Radiat. Oncol. **12**, 119 (2017)

Incentivizing the Use of Quantified Self Devices: The Cases of Digital Occupational Health Programs and Data-Driven Health Insurance Plans

Stefan Stepanovic[(✉)] [iD]

Swiss Graduate School of Public Administration, University of Lausanne, Lausanne, Switzerland
stefan.stepanovic@unil.ch

Abstract. Initially designed for a use in private settings, smartwatches, activity trackers and other quantified self devices are receiving a growing attention from the organizational environment. Firms and health insurance companies, in particular, are developing digital occupational health programs and data-driven health insurance plans centered around these systems, in the hope of exploiting their potential to improve individual health management, but also to gather large quantities of data. As individual participation in such organizational programs is voluntary, organizations often rely on motivational incentives to prompt engagement. Yet, little is known about the mechanisms employed in organizational settings to incentivize the use of quantified self devices. We therefore seek, in this exploratory paper, to offer a first structured overview of this topic and identify the main motivational incentives in two emblematical cases: digital occupational health programs and data-driven health insurance plans. By doing so, we aim to specify the nature of this new dynamic around the use of quantified self devices and define some of the key lines for further investigation.

Keywords: Motivational incentives · Quantified self devices · Digital occupational health programs · Data-driven health insurance plans

1 Introduction

The use of wearable devices that allow individuals to track and monitor their personal health data is starting to become mainstream in industrialized countries [1, 2]. For purposes of individual health, fitness, or well-being [3, 4], interested parties can obtain a myriad of dedicated devices, ranging from low-cost activity trackers to wristbands, smartwatches and more complex biosensors [5]. These provide precise information about one's physical activity (e.g. calories burned, distance covered), health levels (e.g. quality of sleep, blood oxygenation) or personal performance (e.g. evolution in numbers of steps taken).

Engaging in the practice of automatically collecting personal data is generally referred to as quantified self; but also known under analogous terms such as self-tracking,

© Springer Nature Switzerland AG 2020
M. Cacace et al. (Eds.): WIS 2020, CCIS 1270, pp. 73–86, 2020.
https://doi.org/10.1007/978-3-030-57847-3_5

lifelogging or life-hacking [4, 6]. This practice builds upon the assumption that human bodies can be measured and understood through numbers [7] and that the knowledge of these numbers can enable each individual to discover, learn and act upon its attitudes and behaviors [8]. In the common understanding, quantified self practices are related to an individual use of systems in private settings: lifestyle gadgets and health products are designed for the consumer market and collected data is destined for private use only [9]. Yet, we are witnessing an emergence of third-party entities, such as government bodies, pharmaceutical industries, health insurance companies, healthcare suppliers or employers, that are integrating the relationship between the technology provider and the consumer [10–12]. They start to distribute these systems as part of their own programs; so more and more quantified self devices are embedded into medical programs supporting rehabilitation processes [13], chronic disease management [14], but also integrated into occupational health programs [15–17], or health insurance plans [10, 11, 18]. These new actors are particularly attracted by the potential of quantified self devices in terms of self-care and positive impact on behavior. But they are also interested in the massive amount of detailed data that is generated by this technology [19]. Whereas in healthcare settings, it can be argued that enabling access to such a source of personal health information may be beneficial for the community [20] – as it allows, for example, a better monitoring of diseases or further research on new therapies – in other contexts, the use of quantified self devices may raise questions among users concerning the repurposing of the collected data for commercial or organizational goals. These potential exposures may concern a categorization of habits for marketing purposes [11], an identification of high-risk profiles to determine individualized pricings health premiums [21], or an institutionalization of syndromic surveillance for work productivity [20].

In order to mitigate these concerns, organizations often use motivational incentives, such as bonuses or rewards, to motivate people to participate in programs with quantified self devices [11]. Since participation in such organizational programs relies on a voluntary basis (given that these systems gather information that is potentially sensitive), organizations distributing quantified self devices to their employees and clients seek, through the implementation of incentives, to overcome resistance and increase adoption. Yet, little is known about the procedures that are put in place by these structures, as this represents a new and developing phenomena, both within practice and research [12].

Therefore, in this paper, we present an exploratory study on the mechanisms implemented by organizations to motivate individuals to participate in programs with quantified self devices. In contrast to conclusive studies, exploratory research is typically used as an initial appraisal, to provide a direction for future research and help to elaborate study designs [22]. Concretely, after introducing motivational incentives and their use in the Information Systems (IS) field, we particularly consider two practical cases (1) digital occupational health programs and (2) data-driven health insurance plans. These record a steady increase in use of quantified self devices, as reports indicate that (1) 13 million quantified self devices have been used in occupational health programs by 2018 and that up to 27,5 million are planned to be distributed by 2020 [17, 23]; and that (2) among 221 health insurance companies in the world in 2015 [24], a majority of 60% had the intention to rapidly integrate this technology in their business plan (if not already done). For each case, we present our exploratory research design and provide the main results. We conclude by discussing these results, outlining the main learnings and proposing avenues for further research.

2 Related Papers

Since the early days of Taylorism at the beginning of the 20th century, incentives have been acknowledged as means to motivate individuals to perform tasks [25]. From the first monetary and financial remunerations, whole segments of research in psychology, organizational studies and behavioral economics have specialized into mechanisms that act on individual motivation. Most of this research builds upon the common division between intrinsic and extrinsic motivation, that refers to the nature of the motivation behind an action. Intrinsic motivation is linked to something inherently interesting or enjoyable, while extrinsic motivation refers to doing something because it leads to a separable outcome [26]. The latter has particularly led to incentive theory, which is one of the main theories of motivation [27]. It stipulates that individual behavior can be guided by external goals, such as recognition, rewards or money [28]. In the IS field, this theory has notably been apprehended through the lens of technology adoption, with Rogers [29] defining a typology of incentives that help individuals to embrace a new technology (and then eventually stick with it). He has notably classified incentives between monetary and non-monetary; immediate versus delayed (i.e. performing a task knowing that a reward will be given later) or positive or negative (i.e. praises, gratifications and rewards or, on the other end, punishments). Number of works have followed this path, with investigations on incentives applied to various fields, such as privacy and security information management (e.g. [30]), corporate performance (e.g. [31]), but also for health improvement (e.g. [32]).

Precisely, within the domain of quantified self devices, De Ridder, Kim, Jing, Khadra and Nanan [33] have conducted a systematic review of incentives for motivating people to use quantified self devices in the context of chronic disease self-management. Even though this work is rooted in a medical perspective (i.e. the user chose to use the device as part of a disease self-management), it offers a good basis for an examination of incentives offered by some types of organizations/institutions. In particular, it shows how organizations can build on the characteristics of quantified self devices (i.e. portability, connectivity, real-time reporting) to provide dialogue support to their users, i.e. evaluation of the use/performance (feedback); notice to engage with the use (reminder) or warning if there is a problematic element during the process (alert). Similarly, it associates social elements to connect users (social) as well as educational principles to provide information/training to prompt the use (education). Also, based on assumption that humans are attracted by playfulness and games in general [34], it can include fun components to make the use more enjoyable and entertaining (gamification). Finally, financial rewards can be added to provide an external source of motivation to engage in the use of quantified self devices (financial). Table 1 details these motivational incentives, as well as their general mechanisms and some concrete examples of application.

Table 1. Typology of motivational incentives for quantified self devices, derived from [33].

Motivational incentives	Incentive mechanisms	Application examples
Feedback	Informing the user about his quantified self-practice	Personalized messages, individual counselling sessions
Reminder	Systematically notifying the user to engage in the quantified self practice	SMS, push notifications
Alert	Warning the user about possible issues related to his quantified self practice	SMS, notices
Social	Connecting users between them	Forums, peer support networks, peer messages
Education	Providing the user with instructions, information and training	Online notes, leaflets, process guidelines
Gamification	Adding a fun component to the quantified self practice	Leaderboards, badges, avatars
Financial	Providing a financial remuneration for the quantified self practice	Cashback, value points, vouchers

3   Case 1: Incentives in Digital Occupational Health Programs

3.1   Research Design

Firms are considered to be very early adopters of quantified self devices in the organizational environment: they have started since the 2010s to examine the capacity of quantified self devices to tackle one of their largest cost factor, employees' health and safety, while providing an opportunity to gather information on their workforce [20]. Accordingly, we decided to look at the published academic literature to gain some insights on the current state of research. We thus conducted a scoping literature review of the incentives that are employed by firms to motivate employees to participate in programs with quantified self devices. This form of literature review serves as a preliminary assessment of the state-of-the-art, while remaining transparent, methodical and replicable [35]. The mechanisms are similar to systematic reviews, as we methodically searched academic articles in relevant electronic databases. In our case, we determined the following search string "quantified self" OR "self-tracking" OR physiolytics OR lifelogging OR wearable health device OR fitness tracker OR activity tracker AND corporat* OR work* OR organization* AND incentiv* OR motivation* OR reward and applied it to title, abstract and keywords screening in the principal databases for IS literature (AISeL), computing and information technology (ACM), as well as in one of the main cross-disciplinary databases (Web of knowledge). We specifically targeted empirical papers (journal and full conference papers) and limited our research to publications which were published in English. Finally, we excluded studies that had no direct link with quantified self devices and digital occupational health programs. By means of our database search, we identified 86 records from AISeL, 17 from ACM, and 80 from Web of knowledge. After removing duplicates, screening titles, abstracts and keywords, and applying our inclusion/exclusion criteria, we obtained a list of 12 publications which met our above-mentioned requirements (cf. Table 2).

Table 2. Selected studies for review.

Publications	Study sample and duration	Motivational incentives	Incentive mechanisms	Incentive evaluations
Chung et al. (2017) [39]	504 participants, 12 months	Feedback, Financial	Virtual points are given according to users' physical activity levels (1 step = 1 point) or if activity goals are attained in a given time (e.g. averaging 7,000 steps per day). These virtual points can be exchanged for cash rewards, gift cards or insurance discounts	Effectively motivate users in the first phases to motivate users, sustainability has to be investigated
Coffeng et al. (2017) [42]	750 participants, 30 months	Education, Feedback	Coaching feedback sessions	To be determined
Gilson et al. (2016) [43]	19 participants, 20 weeks	Feedback, Financial	Virtual points are given if physical activity goals are attained (e.g. averaging a number of steps per day). These virtual points can be transformed in vouchers	Small positive changes for a majority of users
Gomez-Carmona et al. (2017) [36]	4 participants, 1 week	Feedback, Gamification	Motivational advice related to physical performance, leaderboards	Effectively motivate users in the first phases

(*continued*)

Table 2. (*continued*)

Publications	Study sample and duration	Motivational incentives	Incentive mechanisms	Incentive evaluations
Hunter et al. (2016) [40]	853 participants, 13 months	Feedback, Financial	Virtual points are given according minutes of physical activity (1 min of activity recorded = 1 point). These virtual points can be exchanged for vouchers	Effective after 4 weeks, after 6 months no significant differences with the control group
Jelsma et al. (2019) [37]	250 participants, 12 months	Feedback, Education	Face to face sessions, individual counselling, self-help program leaflet	To be determined
Kim et al. (2016) [41]	455341 participants, 12 months	Feedback, Financial, Gamification	Various challenges regarding physical activity, rewards platform where gains can be collected	Difficult to prove the role of incentives, although participation is enhanced
Lin et al. (2006) [44]	19 participants, 14 weeks	Feedback, Gamification, Social	Daily users' steps are related to the growth of an animated virtual character	Effective as users have established new routines with positive impact on their physical activity and health levels
Lee et al. (2019) [45]	79 participants, 12 weeks	Feedback, Reminder	Daily motivational text messaging, biweekly counseling and a specifically designed workbook for 12 weeks	Counseling and tailored text messaging are effective for physically inactive users

(*continued*)

Table 2. (*continued*)

Publications	Study sample and duration	Motivational incentives	Incentive mechanisms	Incentive evaluations
Patel et al. (2016) [46]	304 participants, 26 weeks	Financial	Various challenges regarding physical activity. Individual and team performance are rewarded by cash prizes	Effective in increasing physical activity
Vyas et al. (2015) [15]	17 participants, 100 days	Feedback, Gamification	Through a step counting mechanisms, participants can unlock trophies, leaderboards	Positive results, motivation enhanced
Yu et al. (2019) [38]	1,436 participants, between 2011 and 2014	Feedback, Financial	Achieving certain health standards based on biometric screening values (e.g., Body Mass Index of 18.5–27.5) is rewarded by cash prizes	Statistically little impact

3.2 Results

One of the striking elements is the prevalence of feedback incentives in our selected studies. Arguably, due to the design of quantified self devices, a form of feedback incentive is essentially present in every program based on these systems (i.e. the user can see the data provided by the device), yet all of the identified occupational programs also propose a form of interactive feedback [e.g. 36] or individual counselling sessions [e.g. 37]. These are commonly associated with other motivational incentives, primarily with financial remuneration or gamification, but also with education (to support the communication, advices and problem-solving). In fact, out of these 12 selected studies, 6 included a form of financial incentive that provides cash rewards or vouchers (if defined goals regarding physical activity are attained). These goals generally take the form of daily objectives (e.g. averaging a certain number of steps a day) or improved biometric levels (e.g. Body Mass Index under a certain figure). Also, such incentive schemes are often associated to virtual value points, creating an intermediary currency between physical activity and its economic value. Their aim is to make it easier for participants to understand, follow and measure their progress and achievements. In terms of effectiveness, all studies reported positive results for financial incentives in promoting a participation in the beginning of the digital occupational health program, although this effect is sometimes marginal [e.g. 38]. Yet, two studies [39, 40] questioned the effects of financial incentives on the individual long-term participation (more than 6 months) as well as the durability of this approach in a digital occupational health program. Another popular motivational incentive consisted in relying on gamification, with a third of our selected publications applying such a mechanism. Virtual points also constituted a key element in the structure of these incentives: they translate users' physical activity into a metric, that is used, in this case, for leaderboards and classifications. Building on a competitive spirit of participants, these leaderboards aim to increase users' appeal to play and leverage a dynamic participation. As for incentives, gamification is found to have a positive effect on the engagement in the first phases, but there are still interrogations about the sustainability of this approach [e.g. 41]. A brief review of the retained studies can be found in Table 2.

4   Case 2: Incentives in Data-Driven Health Insurance Plans

4.1   Research Design

In liberal healthcare markets such as Germany, the Netherlands or Australia, health insurance companies have just begun to propose additional health plans that include quantified self devices [47]. Consequently, there is little academic evidence which can be assessed based on a literature analysis. Therefore, we decided to review offerings from major health insurance companies. The idea was to explore if plans with quantified self devices are proposed and if so, reference what kind of incentives are included. We decided to focus on Switzerland, as it has a liberal market with a high competition between health insurance companies: permanent residents can enroll in extra health insurance plans (such as data-driven health plans) in addition to a standard insurance plan that covers basic healthcare costs, i.e. examination and treatment of a medical condition and its consequences. There are therefore expectations with respect to choice options for the side of consumers, particularly as Swiss are often well-equipped in terms of Information Technology, financially well-off and generally early adopter of consumer technology. To review offerings, we based our research on the official directory of health insurance companies made by the Federal Office of Public Health,[1]. We concentrate on the five biggest health insurance companies (>500'000 clients), which account for two thirds of the Swiss market share and therefore offer a representative picture of what type of data-driven insurance plans individuals may obtain in Switzerland.

4.2   Results

Out of the 5 major Swiss health insurance companies (*Assura, CSS, Helsana, Swica, Concordia*), 3 offer plans with quantified self devices (i.e. CSS, Helsana, Swica). They display similar practices by offering to participants to link a quantified self device to their dedicated app and therefore open the possibility for a financial gain on healthcare costs and premiums (Table 3). Concretely, through its program *myStep*, CSS compensates with CHF 0.20 (¢20) each day when users do between 7500 steps and 9999 steps, and with

---

[1] Statistique de l'assurance maladie 2019, URL: https://www.bag.admin.ch/bag/fr/home/zahlen-und-statistiken/statistiken-zur-krankenversicherung.html.

CHF 0.40 (¢40) each day when they do more than 10000 steps [48]. Similarly, Helsana offers to consumers to connect with a Garmin or a Fitbit to their app *Helsana+* in order to collect so-called *Plus points*. A plus point is commonly obtained if users attain during the day one of the following values: 10000 steps, a pulse rate of 110 per minute for 30 min or 150 calories burned in 30 min [49]. These points may then be converted into cashback, reductions or gifts, allowing consumers to earn/save up to CHF 300 ($300) a year. Finally, Swica offers through its *Benevita* program a possibility to automatically gather quantified self data and complete an online form with health/lifestyle related questions to gather bonus points in order to save up to 15% of the premium [50]. It also proposes lifestyle challenges and fun games that users can share with other users, as well as possibilities to retrieve educational content (regarding, for instance, physical exercises or nutrition).

Table 3. Selected plans for review.

Health insurance companies	Motivational incentives	Incentive mechanisms
CSS [48]	Financial	Amount of money is credited each time a defined goal is achieved
Helsana [49]	Feedback, Financial, Gamification	Points are collected each time a defined goal/challenge is achieved. Points can be transformed into discounts or vouchers
Swica [50]	Education, Financial, Gamification, Social	Points are collected each time a defined goal/challenge is achieved. Challenges can be shared with other participants. Through the app, clients can retrieve informative leaflets on nutrition or physical activity. Points can be transformed into discounts or vouchers

5   Discussion and Key Implications for Future Research

The starting point of this explorative study is that organizations, such as firms and health insurance companies, increasingly include quantified self devices in their operations and often resort to motivational incentives to incite individuals to adopt and return to their quantified self solution [33]. Our findings show that similarities exist between digital occupational health programs and data-driven health plans in how they encourage users to participate in their respective programs. First, drawing on the design and capabilities of quantified self devices (i.e. enabling automatic flows of information about one's health levels), organizations commonly provide a feedback loop to assist participants in their tracking. This is particularly prevalent in workplace settings where firms often propose individual counselling or personalized messages as part of their digital occupational health program. This may be explained by the necessity for firms to communicate through the whole process: they need to reassure employees or clients regarding their engagement to improve their health behavior. As we have seen, quantified self devices may create a tension between leisure and work contexts as they gather, independently of context, data about one's physical activity and lifestyle [7]. So, it is essential for firms to show to their employees the added value such devices provide as well as offer help in interpreting and understanding the collected data and what is further done with it. Simultaneously, it offers to firms a way to monitor the effectiveness of the occupational program and refine the global picture regarding workforce health levels.

Our results also indicate that feedback mechanisms are commonly associated with other incentives, especially financial incentives and gamification. The extensive use of financial incentives reveals that organizations consider that existing benefits (promises that the user may improve his health levels) are still not sufficient to prompt individuals to use quantified self devices in organizational programs [11]. They therefore build their motivational strategies on external rewards, which are typically used when the barriers to adoption are perceived as high, or when the defined objectives are considered difficult to be achieved [51]. Our exploratory study suggests that, in workplace settings, financial incentives have a positive effect in the first phases of engagement with quantified self devices, although the sustainability of this approach remains questionable on the long run. This is in line with reports (e.g. [52]) that showed that financial incentives potentially reduce intrinsic motivation (even if the interest is initially high) and undermine performance once the incentive is removed or lowered. Yet, a long-term use of quantified self devices is crucial in organizational programs, both for organizations and for participants. It ensures that enough data is gathered and that this data can be used for meaningful analyses and feedback. In this way, it may raise awareness regarding health levels and potentially support an individual behavior change (which is generally a lasting process). In consequence, for digital occupational health programs, further research may focus on unveiling the long-term effectiveness of financial incentives, in order to clearly assess the scope of (positive) impact of this incentive. For data-driven health plans, the systematic use of financial incentives demonstrates the high importance given by health insurance companies to this particular mechanism. Further analysis may therefore be oriented to thoughtfully consider the ramifications of this motivational incentive: does it increase individuals' participation? If so, is there a population group that is more prone to subscribe to such plan? What are the implications in terms of participants' privacy? And, as for digital occupational health programs, do financial incentives foster a long-term engagement in data-driven health plans?

Finally, our review indicates that gamification also represents a frequent motivational incentive. This is in line with the popularity of gamification as a design approach to address motivational issues for commercial and medical purposes [34]. Its implementation in organizations mainly consists in easing the execution of actions that are associated with a positive lifestyle (e.g. points-based scheme that translate the number of steps per day) and promoting the consistent of quantified-devices (e.g. extra points if performed on consecutive days) [53]. Nonetheless, gamification, as a motivational incentive, encounters similar challenges as financial incentives: evidence shows that it may have a positive impact on the use of quantified self devices in the first weeks, but its long-term impact is still not evident. In fact, some figures and numbers suggest that gamified interactive systems for health behavior change are considered as successful in merely 50% of the cases [54]. It seems therefore important to further assess the capacity of gamification to foster long-term engagement with quantified self devices, and then consider its application in organizational environments.

In sum, quantified self devices are emerging in organizational environments and lots of opportunities for research are arising with them. Various perspectives (e.g. organizational vs. individual) and approaches (e.g. utilitarian vs. hedonic) can be adopted and developed. So, we hope that, through this explorative study, we have indicated some of the paths worth investigating; and that these paths may ultimately lead to the development of effective digital programs for organizations as well as harmonious environments for individual health.

Acknowledgements. This research has been supported by the Swiss National Science Foundation (SNSF) grant no. 172740.

References

1. Kunze, K., Iwamura, M., Kise, K., Uchida, S., Omachi, S.: Activity recognition for the mind: toward a cognitive "Quantified Self". Computer **46**(10), 105–108 (2013)
2. Starner, T.: How wearables worked their way into the mainstream. IEEE Pervasive Comput. **13**(4), 10–15 (2014)
3. Lupton, D.: Self-tracking modes: reflexive self-monitoring and data practices. In: Proceedings of the 2015 Social Life of Big Data Symposium, pp. 1–19 (2014)
4. Pfeiffer, J., von Entress-Fuersteneck, M., Urbach, N., Buchwald, A.: Quantify-me: consumer acceptance of wearable self-tracking devices. In: Proceedings of the 24th European Conference on Information Systems, pp. 1–15 (2016)
5. Patel, M.S., Asch, D.A., Volpp, K.G.: Wearable devices as facilitators, not drivers, of health behavior change. J. Am. Med. Assoc. **313**(5), 459–460 (2015)
6. Calvard, T.: Integrating social scientific perspectives on the quantified employee self. Soc. Sci. **8**(9), 1–19 (2019)
7. Whitson, J.R.: Gaming the quantified self. Surveill. Soc. **11**(1/2), 163–176 (2013)
8. Choe, E.K., Lee, N.B., Lee, B., Pratt, W., Kientz, J.A.: Understanding quantified-selfers' practices in collecting and exploring personal data. In: Proceedings of the 32nd Annual ACM Conference on Human Factors in Computing Systems, pp. 1143–1152 (2014)
9. Gabriels, K., Moerenhout, T.: Exploring entertainment medicine and professionalization of self-care: interview study among doctors on the potential effects of digital self-tracking. J. Med. Internet Res. **20**(1), 1–12 (2018)
10. Paluch, S., Tuzovic, S.: Persuaded self-tracking with wearable technology: carrot or stick? J. Serv. Mark. **33**(4), 436–448 (2019)
11. Tedesco, S., Barton, J., O'Flynn, B.: A review of activity trackers for senior citizens: research perspectives, commercial landscape and the role of the insurance industry. Sensors **17**(6), 1–39 (2017)
12. Ajana, B.: Digital health and the biopolitics of the quantified Self. Digit. Health **3**(1), 1–18 (2017)

13. Appelboom, G., et al.: Smart wearable body sensors for patient self-assessment and monitoring. Arch. Public Health **72**(28), 1–9 (2014)
14. Chiauzzi, E., Rodarte, C., DasMahapatra, P.: Patient-centered activity monitoring in the self-management of chronic health conditions. BMC Med. **13**(77), 1–6 (2015)
15. Vyas, D., Fitz-Walter, Z., Mealy, E., Soro, A., Zhang, J., Brereton, M.: Exploring physical activities in an employer-sponsored health program. In: Proceedings of the 33rd Annual ACM Conference Extended Abstracts on Human Factors in Computing Systems, pp. 1421–1426 (2015)
16. Gorm, N., Shklovski, I.: Steps, choices and moral accounting: Observations from a step-counting campaign in the workplace. In: Proceedings of the 2016 ACM Conference on Computer-Supported Cooperative Work & Social Computing, pp. 148–159 (2016)
17. Olson, P.: More Bosses Expected to Track Their Staff Through Wearables in the Next 5 Years. https://www.forbes.com/sites/parmyolson/2015/06/01/wearables-employee-tracking/
18. Mettler, T., Wulf, J.: Health promotion with physiolytics: What is driving people to subscribe in a data-driven health plan. PLoS ONE **15**(4), 1–19 (2020)
19. Silvello, A., Procaccini, A.: Connected Insurance Reshaping the Health Insurance Industry. Smart Healthcare, pp. 1–12. IntechOpen, n/d (2019)
20. Lupton, D.: The diverse domains of quantified selves: self-tracking modes and dataveillance. Econ. Soc. **45**(1), 101–122 (2016)
21. Constantiou, I.D., Kallinikos, J.: New games, new rules: big data and the changing context of strategy. J. Inf. Technol. **30**(1), 44–57 (2015)
22. Singh, K.: Quantitative Social Research Methods. Sage, New Delhi (2007)
23. Giddens, L., Gonzalez, E., Leidner, D.: I track, therefore I Am: exploring the impact of wearable fitness devices on employee identity and well-being. In: Proceedings of the 22th Americas Conference on Information Systems, pp. 1–5 (2016)
24. Accenture: Digital insurance era: Stretch your boundaries. https://www.accenture.com/_acnmedia/pdf-51/accenture-technology-vision-for-insurance-2015-full-report-pov.pdf. Accessed 01 Apr 2020
25. Harunavamwe, M., Kanengoni, H.: The impact of monetary and non-monetary rewards on motivation among lower level employees in selected retail shops. Afr. J. Bus. Manag. **7**(38), 3929 (2013)
26. Ryan, R.M., Deci, E.L.: Intrinsic and extrinsic motivations: classic definitions and new directions. Contemp. Educ. Psychol. **25**(1), 54–67 (2000)
27. Bretschneider, U., Leimeister, J.M.: Not just an ego-trip: exploring backers' motivation for funding in incentive-based crowdfunding. J. Strat. Inf. Syst. **26**(4), 246–260 (2017)
28. Hockenbury, D.H., Hockenbury, S.E.: Discovering Psychology. Macmillan, New York (2010)
29. Rogers, E.M.: Diffusion of Innovations. Simon and Schuster, New York (2010)
30. Gal-Or, E., Ghose, A.: The economic incentives for sharing security information. Inf. Syst. Res. **16**(2), 186–208 (2005)
31. O'Byrne, S., Young, D.: Top management incentives and corporate performance. J. Appl. Corp. Finance **17**(4), 105–114 (2005)
32. Doolan, D.F., Bates, D.W.: Computerized physician order entry systems in hospitals: mandates and incentives. Health Aff. **21**(4), 180–188 (2002)
33. De Ridder, M., Kim, J., Jing, Y., Khadra, M., Nanan, R.: A systematic review on incentive-driven mobile health technology: as used in diabetes management. J. Telemed. Telecare **23**(1), 26–35 (2017)
34. Hamari, J.: Transforming homo economicus into homo ludens: a field experiment on gamification in a utilitarian peer-to-peer trading service. Electron. Commer. Res. A **12**(4), 236–245 (2013)

35. Munn, Z., Peters, M.D., Stern, C., Tufanaru, C., McArthur, A., Aromataris, E.: Systematic review or scoping review? Guidance for authors when choosing between a systematic or scoping review approach. BMC Med. Res. Methodol. **18**(143), 1–7 (2018)
36. Gomez-Carmona, O., Casado-Mansilla, D.: SmiWork: an interactive smart mirror platform for workplace health promotion. In: Proceedings of the 2nd International Multidisciplinary Conference on Computer and Energy Science (SpliTech), pp. 1–6 (2017)
37. Jelsma, J.G., et al.: The Dynamic Work study: study protocol of a cluster randomized controlled trial of an occupational health intervention aimed at reducing sitting time in office workers. BMC Public Health **19**(188), 1–13 (2019). https://doi.org/10.1186/s12889-019-6467-0
38. Yu, Y., Yan, X., Zhang, X., Zhou, S.: What they gain depends on what they do: an exploratory empirical research on effective use of mobile healthcare applications. In: Proceedings of the 52nd Hawaii International Conference on System Sciences, pp. 3980–3989 (2019)
39. Chung, C.-F., Jensen, N., Shklovski, I.A., Munson, S.: Finding the right fit: understanding health tracking in workplace wellness programs. In: Proceedings of the 2017 Conference on Human Factors in Computing Systems, pp. 4875–4886 (2017)
40. Hunter, R.F., et al.: Effectiveness and cost-effectiveness of a physical activity loyalty scheme for behaviour change maintenance: a cluster randomised controlled trial. BMC Public Health **16**(1), 618 (2016)
41. Kim, J.Y., et al.: Self-monitoring utilization patterns among individuals in an incentivized program for healthy behaviors. J. Med. Internet Res. **18**(11), 1–15 (2016)
42. Coffeng, J.K., et al.: A 30-month worksite-based lifestyle program to promote cardiovascular health in middle-aged bank employees: design of the TANSNIP-PESA randomized controlled trial. Am. Heart J. **184**(1), 121–132 (2017)
43. Gilson, N.D., et al.: Chronic disease risks and use of a smartphone application during a physical activity and dietary intervention in Australian truck drivers. Aust. New Zealand J. Public Health **40**(1), 91–93 (2016)
44. Lin, J.J., Mamykina, L., Lindtner, S., Delajoux, G., Strub, H.B.: Fish'n'Steps: encouraging physical activity with an interactive computer game. In: Proceedings of the 2017 International Conference on Ubiquitous Computing, pp. 261–278 (2006)
45. Lee, S.-H., Ha, Y., Jung, M., Yang, S., Kang, W.-S.: The effects of a mobile wellness intervention with fitbit use and goal setting for workers. Telemed. e-Health **25**(11), 1115–1122 (2019)
46. Patel, M.S., et al.: Individual versus team-based financial incentives to increase physical activity: a randomized, controlled trial. J. Gen. Intern. Med. **31**(7), 746–754 (2016). https://doi.org/10.1007/s11606-016-3627-0
47. Henkel, M., Heck, T., Göretz, J.: Rewarding fitness tracking—The communication and promotion of health insurers' bonus programs and the use of self-tracking data. In: Meiselwitz, G. (ed.) SCSM 2018. LNCS, vol. 10914, pp. 28–49. Springer, Cham (2018). https://doi.org/10.1007/978-3-319-91485-5_3
48. CSS: MyStep - chaque pas compte. https://www.css.ch/fr/home/privatpersonen/kontakt_service/mycss/mystep.html. Accessed 01 Apr 2020
49. Helsana: Nous récompensons votre mode de vie sain. Avec l'app Helsana + . https://www.helsana.ch/microsite/plus/#/. Accessed 01 Apr 2020
50. Swica: Benevita. https://www.benevita.ch. Accessed 01 Apr 2020
51. Norman, G.J., Heltemes, K.J., Heck, D., Osmick, M.J.: Employee use of a wireless physical activity tracker within two incentive designs at one company. Popul. Health Manag. **19**(2), 88–94 (2016)
52. Promberger, M., Marteau, T.M.: When do financial incentives reduce intrinsic motivation? Comparing behaviors studied in psychological and economic literatures. Health Psychol. **32**(9), 950–957 (2013)

53. Alahäivälä, T., Oinas-Kukkonen, H.: Understanding persuasion contexts in health gamification: a systematic analysis of gamified health behavior change support systems literature. Int. J. Med. Inform. **96**, 62–70 (2016)
54. Hamari, J., Koivisto, J., Sarsa, H.: Does gamification work? - A literature review of empirical studies on gamification. In: Proceedings of the 47th Hawaii International Conference on System Sciences, pp. 3025–3034 (2014)

Respecting the Patients' Needs: Supporting Connected Care Using the Accountability Shared Model

Nilmini Wickramasinghe[1]([⊠]) and Rima A. Gibbings[2]

[1] Iverson Health Innovation, Swinburne University of Technology, Melbourne, Australia
nilmini.work@gmail.com
[2] Faculty of Health Sciences and Professions, University of North Georgia, Dahlonega, USA
rgibbi2@uic.edu

Abstract. Above all healthcare is charged with the "Do No Harm" adage from Hypocrites. However, in the US, more and more our healthcare systems are causing harm at multiple levels with inferior quality of services, poor access to care services, and costly treatments. Underlying this is, albeit unconscious, a lack of respect for patients. We try to address this by proffering a new model of care co-ordination to support high value patient–centered care delivery. The presented model was developed by synthesizing relevant literature and assessing this literature based on current problems and barriers in existing models of care. The following thus presents an encircled care contribution measure share model that enables patient centered value-based care to ensue. The proposed model identifies objective tracking of all clinical services by stakeholder input/feedback measures and from this inherent value and quality can be identified.

Keywords: Change-adopting healthcare systems · Patient-generated health data · Enclosed Stakeholder Share Measure Model

1 Introduction

The healthcare industry is undergoing a massive transformation as a result of multifaceted evolution that originated dynamically [1]. A substantial portion of changes in healthcare organizations is introduced via state or local regulatory agencies in the form of incentives and/or constraints [2]. These modifications are developed to enhance efficiency and improve performance while controlling cost [3]. Improved accuracy and speed in diagnosis and reporting, combined with mobile technologies and social media are collaboratively promoting care coordination and advocating new reimbursement models [4]. These payment models emphasize on the value of the care services delivered instead of rewarding providers based on volume alone [5].

Incorporating multidimensional change measures within a complex system such as the healthcare industry in the form of transformation (technology adoption) could introduce considerable challenges [6]. These challenges must be addressed at each level

© Springer Nature Switzerland AG 2020
M. Cacace et al. (Eds.): WIS 2020, CCIS 1270, pp. 87–96, 2020.
https://doi.org/10.1007/978-3-030-57847-3_6

to ensure a comprehensive reform that allows the uniform transformation of change-adopting healthcare systems [7]. To improve care quality and transform care facilities from volume-based to value-based, healthcare organizations must accurately associate performance measures to care services delivered by enhancing the use of health information technology [8].

In 2013 the U.S. healthcare expenditure consumed 17% of the national GDP with an average of $1,074 spent by residents as out-of-pocket cost [9]. Unfortunately, these numbers are not reflected in the U.S. healthcare system performance measures, especially when compared to the health outcomes in other high-income countries [10]. Higher healthcare expenditure in the U.S. is mainly attributed to the frequent use of expensive medical technologies like MRIs and not due to frequent clinical encounters [9]. To improve health outcomes, many reimbursement models have been introduced to link clinical performances to value produced and ultimately associated cost. Improving healthcare quality requires performance measures that are patient-centered, protect at-risk populations, and establish performance measuring guidelines [11].

1.1 Research Objectives

The main goal of this is to develop a new approach for care outcome evaluation. Several existing initiatives adopted by healthcare organizations and care facilities are focused on improving care quality with less emphasis on the most effective approach that could enhance care quality.

2 Literature Review

2.1 Healthcare Cost

Value-based or pay for performance models like Accountable Care Organizations (ACO), value modifiers, bundled payments, and Health Care Homes (HCH) promote care quality embedded within clinical delivery systems [12]. Quality measures must rely on several essential principles: care quality measures must include accurate and timely data, these measures must be comprehensive to consider a broad scope of clinical practice dynamics including all influencing factors (patient characteristics, external factors), and they must minimize complexity to allow easy access and reporting to clinicians [13]. To implement these guidelines accurately, the new reimbursement models emphasize on care coordination to promote cost-efficiency through shared saving programs [4]. Coordinating care between all participating stakeholders in a complex system such as the healthcare system requires monitoring the goals and (contributing) processes in all participating stakeholders [4]. Hence, a successful care performance measuring system must be capable of identifying and integrating changes from contributing stakeholders of a heterogeneous system (healthcare). Comprehensive evaluation models must promote a structure that is capable of identifying improvement and degradation areas of care processes through monitoring and reporting shared contributions of all care participants. These models can build a reliable connection between accountability measures and performance indicators and ultimately impact care quality.

2.2 Effective Healthcare Transformation

To understand effective healthcare transformation, it is first necessary to briefly examine health information history. US healthcare system is undertaking many transformational adjustments to identify value in care delivery systems and develop payment systems that are based on pay-for-performance initiatives. Recent value-based models attempt to improve care efficiency by gathering large amounts of data and from all stakeholders and developing programs that link performance to care outcomes.

2.3 Health Information History

Information systems have had a substantial role in increasing the operational and data storage capacities of different industries [14]. In the early 1960s and 1970s the healthcare field experienced a sudden transformation that allowed the gathering of patient data in the form of individual records into healthcare repositories [15]. Hardware integration into healthcare systems continued to evolve through generating online clinical orders and retrieving test results from centralized repositories that improved the connectivity of stand-alone systems [15]. In 2010, the healthcare information systems experienced rapid transformational changes in all areas of medical information [15]. These changes where in different facets of care organizations, the Health Information Systems (HIS) expanded by increasing their capacity to store larger sizes of clinical data/information and improving their interconnectivity through patient data exchange between care entities (local, state, and federal) involved in the care process [15].

As hardware and software advancements were introduced in healthcare information systems, they brought about new concerns that outlined healthcare data flow challenges [16]. In 2010, The Patient Protection and Affordable Care Act (PPACA) was signed into law to promote initiatives that could improve coverage, introduce payment reforms, and enhance clinical data exchange processes [17]. Due to the enormous size of the impacted healthcare areas by PPACA's pilot programs, ensuring the positive results of these transformational changes was both time-consuming and challenging [18]. Many of the alternative payment models introduced in PPACA were designed to improve quality and reduce cost by promoting coordinated care and efficient exchange of healthcare information [18]. The main assessment approaches for these models are in the form of establishing quality benchmarks and detecting savings that were below spending target [19].

Evaluating value-based payment models requires a clear recognition of the care activity scope and the contributions of participating stakeholders [20]. To establish such measures, a systematic approach must be created that includes a structured evaluation system [20]. The system must be capable of monitoring different facets of a value-based model simultaneously and must extend through a considerable time period to build standard measures for comparison. The time consideration is vital as it will enable the assessment process to record outcomes relevant to the process. Several evaluation frameworks have been designed and implemented that firmly emphasize on the broad evaluation of value-based initiatives in clinical settings [21]. Evaluation features must include functionality aspects, outcome measures, and cost efficiency of the proposed programs [22]. A comprehensive evaluation framework will also provide healthcare organizations with a collaborative improvement action plan that involves all stakeholders.

2.4 Effective Healthcare Transformation

Collaborative value-based evaluation programs will inherently encounter multiple challenges due to the broad scope (stakeholder diversity) of care delivery systems. Measuring the efficacy and cost-effectiveness of care services has been studied in the comparative effectiveness of competing therapies program by the Patient-Centered Outcomes Research Institute (PCORI) (established by the federal government) [23]. The goal of such comparisons is to determine program effectiveness by viewing the full outlook of the compared features including efficiency in use of healthcare resources and quality of care services delivered [23]. It is also imperative that care service delivery is not solely determined via cost analysis. Unfortunately, and due to lack of standards the U.S. healthcare system has adopted a "craft" culture where individual physician's experience with a positive outcome takes precedence over established guidelines [21]. To successfully establish clinical guidelines, healthcare organizations must promote a "complete" value analysis [21]. A comprehensive value analysis approach will consider all dimensions of value in care systems.

Transforming the healthcare industry from a volume-based industry to a value-based one requires developing a targeted care delivery system that is based on need and available resources. The most basic form of defining value in healthcare is dividing care outcomes by the cost spent to attain these outcomes [24]. To improve value, healthcare organizations must emphasize on improving (overall) outcome and reducing (overall) cost per services delivered [25]. Three main categories that must be considered while using this equation are: the scope of beneficiaries impacted by the outcome, inclusion of all stakeholder input, and the time periods estimated for the outcome and cost calculation. To capture all necessary measures included in the categories mentioned above, care facilities require the efficient implementation of information systems that are able to monitor and report on these measures, but they also require solid engagement of organizational leadership to promote transparency and adjust organizational goals emphasizing value-based methods [26].

2.5 Challenges in Applying Value-Based Models

While selecting medical services for care processes based solely on their cost is an alarming concern to patients, it is one of the determinants of value-based care. Most alternative payment models are using capitation or fixed payments for clinical services to replace fee for service with value-based models [27]. These models could potentially lead to increased wait times for physician visits as they are not including patient population needs in their clinical reward system [27]. This discrepancy could be worsened by the lack of precise and up-to-date care quality measures linked to financial incentives [28]. Alternative payment models such as the Accountable Care Organizations (ACO) emphasize on methods such as shared saving and partial capitation to align quality of care and payments [28]. Bundled payments on the other hand promote episode-based (care cycle) payments to enhance efficiency and care by designating fixed payments for certain conditions within given time windows [29]. Although both models attempt to improve care quality and control cost, they are unable to regularly include all stakeholders' contributions and input within the reimbursement system. This lack of inclusion creates measures that promote best outcomes without considering patient satisfaction or clinical resources. These measures are mainly at the population-level and they address hospital readmissions, reduction of length of stay, and minimization of expensive tests and drug use [27].

The Centers of Medicare and Medicaid Services (CMS) through the Medicare Access and CHIP Reauthorization Act (MACRA) aimed to implement value-based care in a comprehensive format. The MACRA was designed to focus on value in care by adjusting practitioners' reimbursement in the Merit-Based Incentive Payment System (MIPS) program. Through this new initiative, practitioners can select their reporting measures for the program and get evaluated by comparing their performance measures to quality benchmarks. MIPS measures are also designed to replace existing care reporting methods (Physician Quality Reporting System, Value-Based Payment Modifier, and Meaningful Use Programs) [30]. During MACRA implementation, CMS officials focused on providing practitioners with ample opportunities to lighten the adoption impact. These opportunities included a reduction in the number of the required reporting measures (3 out of 100) and exclusion of physicians who did not have a set number of Medicare patients or did not receive the threshold amount from Medicare Part B. Although these steps were taken to encourage practitioners to join value-based initiatives, in practice a large portion of the program remains unimplemented.

Comprehensive value-based models with a shared accountability perception require the integration of several components to avoid imprecise risk distribution/sharing. Fixed payments and capitation models usually group patients and/or medical services into programs that receive a fixed amount of payment/reward [27]. Patients with low health literacy, or limited access to follow-up care and support could increase the risk of their relative groups and hence introduce an undetected risk. To assess the risk incurred in each patient group or per given procedure, actuaries have been involved in processes that allocate cost of procedures based on data collected and analyzed [31, 32]. But these cost estimations potentially hold hidden risks due to the numerous changing factors such as patient biomedical needs and care accessibility factors that could unfairly apply to provider groups [27]. The main issue with the fixed payment or capitation programs is the inclusion of potential inaccuracies that might occur as a result of imprecise adjustments to reflect individual patient's health conditions included in the program [27]. Although bundled payments have proven to achieve greater savings in order of magnitude than the ACOs [27], defining the extent of care cycles included within bundled payments has been described as challenging by critics [27]. Recently developed measures in the U.S. are introducing plans to actively involve patients in their care cycle through shared decision making with the objective of improving care performance value [33]. Integrating shared decision making into clinical care routines encounters many challenges such as clinicians' hesitation in acknowledging the value of decision aid tools and lack of direct incentives that promote patient's involvement in the decision-making process [33].

2.6   Enclosed Stakeholder Contribution in Care Cycle

Research has shown that the interaction between disparate stakeholders is a required facet in developing systems [34]. As the need for healthcare services is rising significantly, it is imperative for all contributing players to actively participate in care delivery services and utilize existing resources efficiently and effectively. To engage users in the process of developing services, healthcare organizations could introduce new approaches such as "the process of tapping users" that will establish user-driven innovation pathways [35]. We recommend a comprehensive model that could incorporate stakeholder contribution and feedback using healthcare information systems. Electronic Health Records (EHR) have embedded evidence-based decision support guidelines to improve efficiency in care delivery services for chronic conditions such as asthma [36] or alerts to remind follow up visits and provide diagnostic suggestions [37]. As EHR systems are accumulating personalized information and incorporating precision medicine to enhance their efficiency in supporting clinical services [37], they could also be utilized to track patient and clinical contribution in the process of care. Furthermore EHR/EMR systems could aggregate individual care encounters' outcome with stakeholder feedback. However, establishing a standardized format within EHR/EMR systems that could translate aggregated data into actionable steps in clinical settings requires in-depth classification and analysis of massive clinical and patient-generated health data.

The **Enclosed Stakeholder Share Measure Model** (ESM) or **Accountability Shared Model** (ASM) promotes an objective of tracking all clinical services by stakeholder contribution/feedback measures. In the ESM concept, each clinical service/encounter is classified in at least one category with an identified outcome. The outcome will be identified to both clinical staff and patient groups as an objective that care processes will ideally achieve at the end of care routine. In each encounter or service, the model will quantify a stakeholder's contribution with a numeric measure that when considered with remaining participants' contributions in the care routine, it will sum up to a value of one. As encounters are considered for a given outcome the share value measure for each stakeholder could be calculated and reported as a percentage towards the considered outcome. This method potentially aims to track stakeholders' contributions to improve accountability in care processes. In practice, patient care outcomes will include a set number of encounters or care procedures. With each procedure or encounter divided into several stakeholder shares, care facilities will monitor participants contributions accurately and effectively. Determining stakeholders that require follow up or resources will improve care value by identifying and addressing these needs early in the process and also storing the data for quality improvement measure development (Fig. 1).

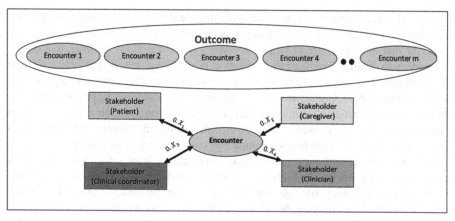

$$0.X_1 + 0.X_2 + 0.X_3 + \ldots + 0.X_n = 1$$

Fig. 1. Accountability shared model description.

3   Discussion

An essential characterization of the healthcare field is the multifaceted stakeholder engagement within services delivered. A diversified stakeholder involvement dictates a wide breadth of input data and a comprehensive application towards participating players. Healthcare data digitization (public/private) has contributed to the gathering of clinical and patient data and subsequently organizing them into actionable steps [38]. Healthcare organizations store diverse, complex, and voluminous data that are received from different participants in the care process. The data gathered often is stored in files with varying structures and formats that require big data analysis and conclude valuable insights [38]. Several important factors exist within the gathering, storing, and processing of healthcare data. The data must be monitored and reported accurately and on a timely basis, but it also must be processed in accurate context to become beneficial for predictive modeling. Healthcare data interoperability issues, provider reluctance in sharing data due to privacy and IT adoption resistance are critical factors that could impede the data gathering process [38].

The Medicare Access and CHIP Reauthorization Act (MACRA) was introduced in 2017 as a pay-for-performance initiative for Medicare providers. MACRA also offered a replacement solution for the Sustainable Growth Rate (SGR) which required annual Congress intervention. SGR was used for adjusting provider payments [39]. One of MACRA's main outcomes is the Merit-based Incentive Payment System (MIPS) [39]. The guidelines in MIPS aim to improve care performance while reducing cost and assessing care services/routines in four major categories: quality, resource use, advancing care information, and clinical practice improvement. Providers will receive a negative or a positive adjustment to their Medicare reimbursement rates depending on their performance in these categories.

The MIPS implementation process could encounter several challenges as MIPS does not allocate a substantial rate increase for the 'resource use' category. Based on the initiative regulations providers will not be motivated to minimize overall expenditure for their Medicare patients to improve reimbursement rates [39]. Another important issue that must be taken into consideration is the additional workload involved with a new layer that monitors care processes for MIPS reporting. Care facilities will accept a considerable financial obligation to develop professional teams and processes that will implement the initiative [39]. Furthermore, health disparities might expand due to MIPS implementation. Quality measures gathered from providers will be compared on a national scale with no consideration to the patient population and their socioeconomical determinants. The risk adjustment that is included in the initiative is not sufficient to capture all measures of patient contribution and collaboration in the process of care.

Improving the quality of care and controlling cost have been a main goal of big data analytics in healthcare. In this study we introduce a model that promotes accountability by allocating stakeholder share measures within the care process. To align clinical services with patient-centered care, health information systems must be able to track patient contribution and feedback accurately as part of care encounters/cycles rendered. The ESM or ASM model will assign each stakeholder (including patients) a share measure that will be tracked and reported with care outcome(s) achieved.

4   Conclusion

Above all healthcare should subscribe to the adage "Do No Harm" as per Hypocrites. However today our healthcare systems in the US too often are failing by causing harm at multiple levels due to poor quality of care or missed care, poor access to care and low value of care. Underlying this is a lack of respect to the patient, a vulnerable individual who seeks help form the system at their time of need. We recognize that new approaches to healthcare in the US designed to stem escalating costs and increasing numbers of patients presenting with chronic conditions through solutions such as bundled payments and value-based care, may be unintentionally disrespecting/disregarding some more vulnerable populations such as the elderly or lower socio-economic groups but the net results is that these vulnerable populations could be marginalized.

With an increase in the use of information systems in healthcare organizations, most patient records and clinical encounters are becoming stored in a digitized format. To meaningfully integrate the collected health data and comprehensively process all participant's contributions, innovative models must be adopted that manage data/information during the care cycle. The ESM model introduced in this study recommends a template for tracking encounters and associating them with care outcomes. To our knowledge this study is a first attempt at improving the value of care services provided by tracking all determinants that contribute to the outcome and assigns a quantifiable fixed share measure amount to the stakeholder contribution. Hence, we believe the proffered model will enable a responsible healthcare system to be created that provides high value, quality and access to all. Moreover, it enables a high level of respect to be afforded to the patient.

References

1. Burns, L.R., Pauly, M.V.: Transformation of the health care industry: curb your enthusiasm? Milbank Q. **96**, 57–109 (2018)

2. Bohmer, R.M.: The hard work of health care transformation. New Engl. J. Med. **375**, 709–711 (2016)
3. Burwell, S.M.: Setting value-based payment goals—HHS efforts to improve U.S. health care. New Engl. J. Med. **372**, 897–899 (2015)
4. Phillips, A.B., Merrill, J.A.: Innovative use of the integrative review to evaluate evidence of technology transformation in healthcare. J. Biomed. Inform. **58**, 114–121 (2015)
5. Miller, H.D.: From volume to value: better ways to pay for health care. Health Aff. **28**, 1418–1428 (2009)
6. Berg, M.: Implementing information systems in health care organizations: myths and challenges. Int. J. Med. Inform. **64**, 143–156 (2001)
7. Agarwal, R., Gao, G., DesRoches, C., Jha, A.K.: The digital transformation of healthcare: current status and the road ahead. Inf. Syst. Res. **21**, 796–809 (2010)
8. Porter, M.E.A.: Strategy for health care reform—Toward a value-based system. New Engl. J. Med. **361**, 109–112 (2009)
9. Squires, D., Anderson, C.: U.S. Health Care from a Global Perspective (2015)
10. OECD: Health at a Glance 2017: OECD Indicators. OECD (2017)
11. VanLare, J.M., Blum, J.D., Conway, P.H.: Linking performance with payment implementing the physician value-based payment modifier. JAMA, **308**, 2089–2090 (2012)
12. Pham, H.H., Cohen, M., Conway, P.H.: The pioneer accountable care organization model improving quality and lowering costs. JAMA Netw. **312**, 1635–1636 (2014)
13. Kennedy, D.M., Caselli, R.J., Berry, L.L.: A roadmap for improving healthcare service quality. J. Healthc. Manag. **56**, 385–402 (2011)
14. Porter, M.E., Miller, V.E.: How information gives you competitive advantage. Harv. Bus. Rev. (1985). http://palfreymanventures.net/porter-and-millar-1985.pdf
15. Collen, M.F., Ball, M.J.: The History of Medical Informatics in the United States. Springer, London (2015). https://doi.org/10.1007/978-1-4471-6732-7
16. Vest, J.R.: Health information exchange: persistent challenges and new strategies. JAMIA **17**, 288–294 (2010)
17. Doherty, R.B.: The certitudes and uncertainties of health care reform. Ann. Intern. Med. **152**(10), 679–682 (2010). https://www.unboundmedicine.com/medline/citation/20378676/The_certitudes_and_uncertainties_of_health_care_reform_
18. Naylor, M.D., Bowles, K.H., McCauley, K.M., Maccoy, M.C., Maislin, G., Pauly, M.V., Krakauer, R.: High-value transitional care: translation of research into practice. J. Eval. Clin. Pract. **19**, 727–733 (2011)
19. Fisher, E.S., Shortell, S.M., Kreindler, S.A., Van Citters, A.D., Larson, B.K.: A framework for evaluating the formation, implementation, and performance of accountable care organizations. Health Aff. **31**, 2368–2378 (2012)
20. Marjoua, Y.: Brief history of quality movement in US healthcare. Curr. Rev. Musculoskelet. Med. **5**, 265–273 (2012). https://doi.org/10.1007/s12178-012-9137-8
21. Leu, M.G., et al.: A framework for evaluating value of new clinical recommendations. Hosp. Pediatr. **6**, 578–586 (2016)
22. Damberg, C.L., Sorbero, M.E., Lovejoy, S.L., Martsolf, G.R., Raaen, L., Mandel, D.: Measuring success in health care value-based purchasing programs. Rand. Health Q. **4**, 9 (2014)
23. Glick, H.A., et al.: Comparative effectiveness and cost effectiveness analyses frequently agree on value. Health Aff. **34**, 805–811 (2015)
24. Weeks, W.B., Weinstein, J.N.: Caveats to consider when calculating healthcare value. Am. J. Med. **128**, 802–803 (2014)
25. Bozic, K.J.: Improving value in healthcare. Clin. Orthop. Relat. Res. **471**, 368–370 (2013). https://doi.org/10.1007/s11999-012-2712-x

26. Baxter, P.E., et al.: Leaders' experiences and perceptions implementing activity-based funding and pay-for-performance hospital funding models: a systematic review. Health Policy **119**, 1096–1110 (2015)
27. Porter, M.E., Kaplan, R.S.: How to Pay for Health Care Bundled payments will finally unleash the competition that patients want. Harv. Bus. Rev. 88–100 (2016)
28. Colla, C.H.: Swimming against the current - what might work to reduce low-value care? New Engl. J. Med. **371**, 1280 (2014)
29. Joynt, K.E., Orav, J., Zheng, J., Epstein, A.M.: Evaluation of Medicare's bundled payments initiative for medical conditions. New Engl. J. Med. **379**, 260–269 (2018)
30. Spivack, S.B., Laugesen, M.J., Oberlander, J.: The politics and policy of health reform no permanent fix: MACRA, MIPS, and politics of physician payment reform. J. Health Polit. Policy Law **43**, 1025–1040 (2018)
31. Rose, G.A.: From SGR to MACRA to MIPS: what you should know (2016). asecho.org
32. American Academy of Actuaries: An Actuarial Perspective on Accountable Care Organizations (2012)
33. Spatz, E.S., Elwyn, G., Moulton, B.W., Volk, R.J., Frosch, D.L.: Shared decision making as part of value-based care: New U.S. policies challenge our readiness (2017)
34. Bjorkquist, C., Helge, R., Kjetil, R.: User Participation and Stakeholder involvement in health care innovation - does it matter? Eur. J. Innov. Manag. **18**, 2–18 (2013)
35. Wise, E., Hogenhaven, C.: User-Driven Innovation Context and Cases in the Nordic Region. Nordic Innovation Centre (2008)
36. Kuhn, L., et al.: Planning for action: the impact of an asthma action plan decision support tool integrated into an electronic health record (EHR) at a large health care system. JABFM **28**, 382–393 (2015)
37. Castaneda, C., et al.: Clinical decision support systems for improving diagnostic accuracy and achieving precision medicine. J. Clin. Bioinform. **5**, 4 (2015)
38. Groves, P., Kayyali, B., Knott, D., Van Kuiken, S.: The 'big data' revolution in healthcare: accelerating value and Innovation. Center for US Health System Reform Business Technology Office (2013)
39. McWilliams, J.: MACRA - big fix or big problem? Ann. Intern. Med. **167**(2), 122–124 (2017)

Collecting the Fruits of Respect
in Entrepreneurship and Management
of Organizations

Utilizing Digital Tools to Enable Participation and Promote Respect

Mari Hartemo$^{(\boxtimes)}$ ⓘ and Mika Suutari

Turku University of Applied Sciences, Turku, Finland
{mari.hartemo,mika.suutari}@turkuamk.fi

Abstract. We study the terms respect, employee empowerment, participative leadership and management, and technostress by exploring the literature and previous research. We categorize the current tools of a Finnish higher education institution used for participative leadership in the IAP2 framework of public participation. Based on the categorization we analyze the current situation and create a future vision for the leaders of the organization. We create three recommendations to enable better digital participation: 1) more focus on collaboration and empowerment instead of just informing and consulting, 2) discovering the possibilities and fixing the roles of the chosen digital tools, and 3) leaders could learn from the educators. We also suggest concrete actions for how to achieve the goals.

Keywords: Higher education · Respect · Employee empowerment · Participative leadership · Technostress · Digital participation

1 Introduction

Today's organizations have a variety of digital tools to enable informing and collaborating. In this article, we argue that planning the usage of the tools well and linking them to strategical leadership is central to success of the organizations. We study the phenomena through the case of a Finnish higher education institution. At the organization, new digital tools are introduced every year and staff is suffering from technostress. Collaboration in the digital environment is the exception, not the practice. At the same time, the organization aims to be an inspiring community, whose members are empowered to co-operate. One aim of the article is to motivate the leaders of the organization to promote digital collaboration, empowerment, and respect.

The organization is a multidisciplinary higher education institution of 10,000 members. It is one of the leading universities of applied sciences in Finland. The strategy emphasizes that the organization is an inspiring community formed by the staff and students who work together in a collegial relationship and actively work for shared goals. The search for an inspiring community requires lots of respect, inclusion, and participation.

The organization does an employee engagement survey regularly. An important question dealing with the participation on the organizational level is "When decisions are made in the organization, the opinion of the people affected is usually sought." For

© Springer Nature Switzerland AG 2020
M. Cacace et al. (Eds.): WIS 2020, CCIS 1270, pp. 99–111, 2020.
https://doi.org/10.1007/978-3-030-57847-3_7

three consecutive years 2017, 2018 and 2019 the scores were not good. In 2017, 59% of the staff did not agree with the statement and in 2018 the number was even higher, 63%. In 2019, the score improved a bit and was 49%. About half of the employees are not satisfied with the current situation.

In the following chapters, we study the potential of digitalization in improving the survey results and the advantages of empowering employees in decision-making process. We study the terms respect, employee empowerment, participative leadership and management, and technostress by exploring the literature and previous research. We list the tools that are currently used at the organization for participative leadership and link and categorize them to the IAP2 framework of public participation. Based on the categorization we analyze the current situation and create a future vision for the leaders of the organization and recommendations for the actions towards the vision. The research questions of this study are:

- Why are respect, participation, and empowerment important in leadership and management?
- What digital tools are currently used at the organization for participative leadership?
- What actions are needed at the organization to enable more digital participation and promote respect in the future?

2 Literature Review

2.1 Employee Empowerment

Empowerment is a process by which people gain control over their lives [1]. It emphasizes capabilities instead of risk factors, stating that empowered persons feel more powerful and positive towards their capabilities [2]. Empowerment takes on different forms depending on whether it occurs at individual, organizational or community level [2]. Common to all forms of empowerment is that it aims to enhance wellness while it also provides people "opportunities to develop knowledge and skills and engage professionals as collaborators instead of authoritative experts" [1, 570].

In organizations, "employee empowerment" has gained interest among researchers and practitioners since 1950's [3]. It involves leadership, individual reactions, interactions between peers and the structure of work-related processes [3]. In seeking to empower employees, communication, collaboration and building trust are essential [4]. According to research, "the manager who shares information, authority, resources and accountability with employees and treats them as partners is likely to get good performance" [4, 35]. Empowered employees are more motivated and satisfied with their work, feel less job stress, and are more involved beyond the defined job, which creates a greater organizational commitment [3].

In professional organizations such as higher education, employees often expect autonomy and consultation over important decisions [5]. According to research, critical and constructive debates, open communication and collaborative decision-making processes increase creativity and innovation among employees in higher education [6]. Therefore, we assume that an empowering approach on leadership should improve performance in higher education institutes as well.

2.2 Respect from Leaders, Participative Leadership and Management, and Their Effect on Job Satisfaction

Respect is an important component of a high-performance organization [7]. James [7] lists eight ways the leaders can impart respect in everyday behavior: active listening, valuing diverse backgrounds and ideas, entrusting others with important tasks, remaining open to input, providing autonomy, affirming value to the organization, taking an interest in non-work lives, and supporting individuals in critical situations. In a study of nearly 20,000 employees around the world, Porath [8] found that when it comes to garnering commitment and engagement from employees, there's one thing that leaders need to demonstrate: respect. However, Rogers [9] states that many leaders have an incomplete understanding of what constitutes workplace respect. He divides respect in two distinct types: owed respect and earned respect. Owed respect is accorded equally to all members of an organization and earned respect recognizes individual employees who display valued qualities or behaviors.

According to the study of Porath [8], those that get respect from their leaders reported 56% better health and well-being and 89% greater enjoyment and satisfaction with their jobs. Rogers [9] also states that employees who feel respected are more satisfied with their jobs and more grateful for and loyal to their companies.

In addition to respect, participation is another concept that is linked to job satisfaction. In this paper, we define participation as "Joint consultation in decision making, goal setting, profit sharing, teamwork, and other such measures through which a firm attempts to foster or increase its employees' commitment to collective objectives" [10]. Participation has been extensively researched in academia, for example, Kim [11] studied literature and research on the relationship between participatory management and job satisfaction. The findings in Kim's literature review indicate that job satisfaction is an outcome of empowerment and that many managers, union leaders, and scholars share the belief that participative management practices have substantial positive effects on performance and satisfaction at work. Also, the literature review of Sakakibara, Ishikawa [12] and their further own study confirmed that participative climate can be an important part of creating healthy workplaces.

2.3 Technostress

The term "technostress" was made up by clinical psychologist Craig Brod in 1984. According to Brod [13] technostress is "a modern disease caused by one's inability to cope or deal with information communication technologies in a healthy manner". There are five conditions creating technostress [14]:

- "Techno-overload": work more and work faster; do more in less time
- "Techno-invasion": be reachable anywhere and anytime and feel the need to be constantly connected
- "Techno-complexity": spend time and effort learning and understanding how to use new information systems
- "Techno-insecurity": feel threatened about losing jobs to other people who have a better understanding of new technology

- "Techno-uncertainty": continuing changes and upgrades do not give a chance to develop a base of experience for a particular information system. Knowledge becomes obsolete rapidly.

Technostress can cause psychological or behavioral strains. Psychological strains are emotional reactions to stressor conditions and include, for example, dissatisfaction with the job, depression, and negative self-evaluation, whereas behavioral strains include, for example, reduced productivity, increased turnover and absenteeism, and poor task performance [15].

The case organization has explored the digital competence of staff by launching a campaign on digital skills and doing a systematic survey in which most of the staff members have participated. Based on the survey results, the leaders of the organization have been able to focus on the lacking skills and tailor some training sessions for certain units and faculties. Some of the open answers of the survey refer to symptoms of technostress and to different conditions creating it. For example "I am not good at this new stuff, and everything takes a lot of time.", "Sometimes it may be challenging to choose the right tools (digital platforms) for the certain task because there are so many options.", "I am quite energetic, almost 59 years old employee. ICT and digitalization did not exist when I was young and studying. When I started teaching in 2008, e-learning was initiated. I feel that I need update and training on my digital skills." Based on the answers, we assume that technostress symptoms exist also at the case organization.

2.4 Theoretical Framework - Spectrum of Participation

The studies focusing on the relative degree of leader and subordinate influence over the group's decisions started with Lewin's, Lippitt's and White's [16] topology of democratic, autocratic and laissez-faire leaders. The decision-making procedures used by a leader can also be ordered, for example, along the continuum ranging from high subordinate influence on complete leader influence [17].

In this article, we use the spectrum of public participation by IAP2, International Association of Public Participation, as the theoretical framework. It categorizes the continuum on more detailed level. The spectrum is used internationally, especially in many public participation plans [18], also in academic literature [see, e.g., 19, 20].

The spectrum (Fig. 1) divides the public's impact on the decision in five (5) categories: inform, consult, involve, collaborate and empower. The impact on decision increases on each step, *inform* being at the lowest end of engagement, and *empower* at the highest level. Whereas *inform* is based on one-way communication and does not seek any citizen input, *consult* and *involve* enable two-way communication. Furthermore, *collaborate* involves more deliberative communication where direct communication is facilitated and finally, *empower* places decision-making in the control of the public: "we will implement what you decide" [19].

In this article, we apply the IAP2 Spectrum of Public Participation for employees in higher education by simply replacing the term "the public" in the original framework with the term "employees" as shown in Table 1 below. By doing this, the framework helps us to analyze digital tools used in the case organization, especially their degree of support for employee engagement and participation.

Table 1. IAP2's spectrum of public participation adopted for employees in higher education. Impact on the decision increases from the left to the right.

	Inform	Consult	Involve	Collaborate	Empower
Goal	To provide the employees with balanced and objective information to assist them in understanding the problem, alternatives and/or solutions	To obtain employees feedback on analysis, alternatives and/or decision	To work directly with the employees throughout the process to ensure that employee concerns and aspirations are consistently understood and considered	To partner with the employees in each aspect of the decision including the development of alternatives and the identification of the preferred solution	To place final decision-making in the hands of the employees
Promise	We will keep you informed	We will keep you informed, listen to and acknowledge concerns and aspirations, and provide feedback on how employee input influenced the decision	We will work with you to ensure that your concerns and aspirations are directly reflected in the alternatives developed and provide feedback on how employee input influenced the decision	We will look to you for advice and innovation in formulating solutions and incorporate your advice and recommendations into the decisions to the maximum extent possible	We will implement what you decide

3 Digital Tools for Participation at the Case Organization

3.1 Current Tools

Digitalization has boosted the deployment of new software and applications at the case organization. Currently, the spectrum of digital tools at use is vast. In this chapter, we shortly present and describe the tools that are currently used for leadership purposes. The tools were selected, and initial descriptions collected from three managers of the organization in spring 2019.

Adobe Connect is a tool for video meetings and webinars. It is used for internal briefings of the whole staff and as a webinar tool in teaching. Connect includes a chat tool which is used for questions and discussion during the sessions. A screen sharing and microphones enable a deeper level participation but are not used as often as the basic chat. In Adobe Connect it is also possible to split online participants in breakout groups to enable discussions and collaboration in small groups. In the future, a system called Zoom with similar functions will replace Adobe Connect.

Digital signage displays are in use in all the campuses. These remotely manageable displays are used mainly for sharing information about current events, news and deadlines related with work or studies. At the moment, the organization is not using interactive touch displays that would enable two-way interaction in addition to the current one-way interaction.

Discendum Optima is the core digital learning environment at the university and most of the teachers and students are using it. Optima is used as the main platform in most of the courses. Due to this it is widely used for consulting purposes by teachers and students. On the other hand, it is not used for other staff members, so it is not a tool for the whole community.

The email service is Microsoft Exchange (Outlook) and its usage has spread year by year and the amount of data and information in the system has increased. The organization has also had an email marketing solution for several years, current one, Apsis, being in use since 2018. Mainly communications department uses the system. Internal email newsletters contain similar information to the digital signage displays: news, events and deadlines. Although anyone can suggest content to the newsletter, only a few people use or know about this possibility.

Organization's intranet is a SharePoint-based solution with decentralized content management. Intranet is a collection of instructions for daily work, longer-term policies and principles, definitions of internal services and tools for daily use. Intranet works as a university quality manual ensuring that everyone has the same information, instructions and tools for their work. Anyone has a possibility to update and share a piece of news, events or blog writings on the intranet, but one web editor manages the contents, structure and development of the intranet. Furthermore, anyone can give feedback by filling in one of the several feedback forms, and there are digital discussion areas, which are open to everyone, but which are not in very active use currently. Furthermore, SharePoint-based digital workspaces form one part of the intranet. These are used in smaller workgroups and can be created and managed by anyone. There are no universal rules on how to use workspaces.

The organization's public websites are targeted to external audiences but some of the contents, such as library services, are widely used by the personnel as well. Currently, these websites are mostly informative in nature.

Skype for Business can be used for video calls, video conferencing and instant messaging. It is used widely among the staff to enable remote attendance in the meetings. The desktop sharing to other participants and chatting are commonly used features during meetings. Skype for Business desktop application is installed in every employee's computer and the application window opens automatically when computer is started or unlocked. In addition to desktop application, participation in Skype for Business sessions is also possible via web browsers and the mobile application is available and used by some employees.

Another form of internal social media is Microsoft Teams that has been in use since 2018. Teams combines workplace chat, video meetings, file storage (including collaboration on files), and application integration, being more versatile and advanced tool than Yammer. In the organization, Teams has quickly gained success also among the top management and nowadays the desktop application is installed in the computer of every staff member to boost the usage. Based on Microsoft roadmap Teams will replace Skype for Business in the future and its role will therefore increase.

Webropol, Lyyti, eLomake, MessageWall and Microsoft Forms (Office 365) are the supported digital tools for polls and surveys. The tools are used for a variety of purposes, ranging from the simple polls for small teams or events to the surveys targeted for the entire staff.

Yammer, Microsoft's enterprise social networking service, was introduced in the organization in 2015. Yammer has been used for group collaboration within the university on voluntary basis, as it has never acquired an official status.

3.2   Exploring and Grading Current Tools Based on the IAP2 Spectrum

In this section we focus on the current situation and categorize the tools based on the framework of IAP2 and the ways the tools are currently used. To find out which way each digital tool is used and in which category of the framework each tool is currently positioned, we created a specific grading system and a grading tool in Microsoft Excel. The grading system is based on the categories of the framework of IAP2. Tools were given points from 0 to 2 based on five fields:

A. Facilitators (0 = none, 1 = some leaders, 2 = most of the leaders)
B. Frequency (0 = never, 1 = random, 2 = regular)
C. Goal orientation (0 = no goals, 1 = goals without connection to strategy, 2 = strategic goals)
D. Scale (0 = nobody, 1 = teams, 2 = whole organization)
E. Target groups (0 = nobody, 1 = staff, 2 = staff and students)

The maximum score for each tool is 10 in each of the framework category: inform, consult, involve, collaborate and empower. In the grading tool we used different grayscale to visualize the amount of points. The darker the cell color is the higher the score. An example of the usage of the grading tool is shown in Fig. 1.

TEAMS	Inform	Consult	Involve	Collaborate	Empower
A) Facilitators (0 = none, 1 = some leaders, 2 = most of the leaders)	2	2	2	1	0
B) Frequency (0 = never, 1 = random, 2 = regular)	2	2	2	1	0
C) Goal orientation (0 = no goals, 1 = goals without connection to strategy, 2 = strategic goals)	1	1	1	1	0
D) Scale (0 =nobody, 1 = teams, 2 = whole organization)	1	1	1	1	0
E) Target groups (0 = nobody, 1 = staff, 2 = staff and students)	2	2	2	2	0
Total points (0-10)	8	8	8	6	0

Fig. 1. An example of the usage of the grading tool. The target tool of the grading in the example is Teams.

The grading was performed by three managers at the corporate services of the case organization in April 2019. The three chosen managers have a good perspective on the usage of the digital tools throughout the organization. Each of them filled in the grading tool individually and the results were then combined and analyzed by the authors. In addition to numerical evaluation, managers were able to provide open feedback on the tools. The summary of the gradings is shown in the Table 2. The points in the summary mean the average score of three given scores.

Table 2. The summary of the grading "The Digital Tools enabling Participative Leadership". The higher the score the higher the level of usage in the specific participation category of IAP2 framework.

The Digital Tools enabling Participative Leadership

Grading Summary

	Inform	Consult	Involve	Collaborate	Empower
ADOBE CONNECT	8	8	7	4	2
BLOGS	7	2	0	0	0
DIGITAL SIGNAGE DISPLAYS	8	0	0	0	0
DISCENDUM OPTIMA	5	0	0	0	0
ELOMAKE	4	4	0	0	0
EMAIL	9	8	5	3	2
EMAIL NEWSLETTERS	7	0	0	0	0
INTRANET (incl. workspaces)	3	3	3	2	2
LYYTI	4	4	0	0	0
MESSAGEWALL	2	2	0	0	0
MICROSOFT FORMS	8	4	2	2	2
PUBLIC WEBSITE	6	2	0	0	0
SKYPE FOR BUSINESS	5	8	6	2	2
TEAMS	5	7	7	6	0
WEBROPOL	3	7	2	0	0
YAMMER	7	6	5	3	0
	91	65	37	22	10

4   Findings and Conclusions

4.1   Research Questions and Recommendations

The first research question outlined in the chapter Introduction: "Why are respect, participation and empowerment important in leadership and management?" is answered in the Literature review. The following chapter Digital tools for participation at the case organization answers to the second research question: "What digital tools are currently used at the organization for participative leadership?" Based on the grading and the literature review, we now analyze the findings and make some conclusions. By doing this, we aim to answer to the last research question: "What actions are needed at the organization to enable more digital participation and promote respect in the future?"

In the digital world of today it should be relatively easy and simple to obtain feedback on decisions and alternatives. Although there are several tools at the case organization that enable digital participation, none of the tools is systematically and widely used for empowerment purposes. There is a huge toolbox of digital systems and applications available, but it is not clear how and for what purposes they should be used. Furthermore, the open comments of the managers revealed that teachers seem to use more digital tools and participative pedagogical methods than the leaders. Therefore, we created three conclusions and recommendations as the future steps at the case organization:

1. More focus on collaboration and empowerment instead of Just informing and consulting
2. Discovering the possibilities and fixing the roles of the chosen digital tools
3. Leaders could learn from the educators

We present the conclusions in more detail in the following sections.

4.2 More Focus on Collaboration and Empowerment Instead of Just Informing and Consulting

The focus is currently in the left side of the spectrum meaning that the digital tools are used mainly for informing purposes. The consulting purpose comes next and the further right we go in the spectrum the less the tools are used for those purposes. In the future, the organization should spread the usage more evenly throughout the spectrum and place more effort on empowering and collaboration instead of informing and consulting.

Based on our literature review, focus on collaboration and empowerment would enhance wellness and good performance. Empowered employees would also be more motivated and satisfied with their work, feel less job stress, and be more involved beyond the defined job, leading to a greater organizational commitment. As the result, creativity and innovation among employees would improve. James [7] lists eight ways the leaders can impart respect in everyday behavior. Most of those, active listening, valuing diverse backgrounds and ideas, entrusting others with important tasks, remaining open to input, and providing autonomy require more than just informing. In higher education institutes, employees often expect autonomy and consultation over important decisions. We suggest that shifting the focus towards collaboration and empowerment in the usage of the digital tools would lead to higher job satisfaction, healthier workplace, and better results in the organization's employee engagement survey.

4.3 Discovering the Possibilities and Fixing the Roles of the Chosen Digital Tools

During the grading of the current digital tools at the case organization, it became clear that the organization does not have specific roles for them. Even the three managers had different opinions about how each tool is used and for which purpose. Also, the digital skills survey for the staff brought out similar challenges. In an organization of 750 employees it is, therefore, necessary to define the roles of the digital tools and communicate them consistently to the whole community. This would also reduce technostress among the employees. According to our literature review this might, for example, reduce dissatisfaction with the work and improve productivity.

Technology is indeed developing rapidly and there are constantly new digital tools available for higher education institutions. In the future, the organization could use IAP2 Spectrum to evaluate new tools and their support for collaboration, empowerment and joint decision-making. In terms of enhanced participation, tools that enable only informing or consulting should probably be avoided.

We also noticed that the organization does not use the current digital tools optimally. Therefore, our evaluation on the current situation does not do justice on all the tools. Instead, our evaluation indicates which tools might have potential for more collaborative work. In the future, the leaders of the organization should focus and guide the community how to use the collaborative features of the tools. It is also important to share best practices related to the usage of the digital tools.

4.4 Leaders Could Learn from the Educators

In the open comments of the evaluation of the tools, it was noted that the digital tools are used in learning in more collaborative and empowered manner than in leadership. The tools vary a bit but most of the tools are the same in leadership and in learning. Some teachers also use additional applications for collaboration purposes, for example Padlet, Kahoot, Socrative and Answergarden. The tools are used to activate the students and enable collaborative learning. Also, the pedagogical methods for active and participative learning seem to be more efficient than the methods leaders are using for participative leadership.

Based on the strategy the organization *"develops its communal activities both physically and virtually in shared workspaces, and with a positive, open and fair working culture, the aim is to generate an attractive community with operations to which everyone feels easy to commit"*. Even though employees work in shared workspaces and have an open working culture, the same methods and tools are not used in education and leadership, at least not the digital ones. This finding is a surprise since the question is about an educational institute where everybody is expected to understand pedagogical viewpoints.

Therefore, we state that in the management and leadership, the organization should gain more pedagogical knowledge and knowhow and share the best practices of education to the leaders. We find that the culture of digital participation and involvement should be created and use the methods and tools of digital participation on regular basis by all the leaders in facilitation of meetings, development days, training events and especially in creating strategical plans - the same way than the teachers are using participation in teaching and learning. There are not that many differences between the collaborative learning and participative leadership. The leaders are just not used to mixing them in practice.

4.5 Heading Towards Collaboration and Empowerment at the Case Organizations

Summing up the previous sections, we suggest the following actions for creating a leading culture that enables collaboration and empowerment at the case organization.

What describes the action, *why* gives reasons for the actions, and *how* suggests how to make it happen (Table 3).

Table 3. Suggested actions for creating a leading culture that enables collaboration and empowerment at the case organization

What	Why	How – preliminary plans
Defining the roles (optimal usage) of digital tools for both management and personnel	To clarify which tool to use for which purpose and to reduce technostress	Instructions, trainings, workshops
Using digital participation regularly in leadership starting from the organizational level (the top management)	To empower employees and make them feel respected, to improve the results of employee engagement survey, to make the use of digital tools of participation a daily routine	Using an existing digital tool to collaborate with issues related to the results of employee engagement survey, commenting and discussing yearly action plans on organizational level
Sharing best practices from education to management and enhance the pedagogical skills of the leaders	It should be natural for a higher education institution, to avoid spending extra time on planning methods already used by educators, to make it more natural for educators to participate	Pedagogical trainings for administrative staff, regularly sharing best practices in management meetings
Evaluating potential new digital tools with IAP2 framework and deploy them systematically	To prevent the tools to overlap too much, to reduce technostress	To define a steering group that evaluates new proposals and decides the purposes of each tool related to the framework, to stop using some overlapping tools, e.g. Yammer

4.6 Managerial Implications and Further Research

The results of this study were presented to the leaders of the case organization in September 2019 in the management forum organized on monthly basis. After the study, many actions have been taken and many development ideas implemented or under implementation. For example, in September 2019 digital participation was utilized for the preparation of the service goals discussion between the units of corporate services and the faculties of teaching and research. The evaluation process of new digital tools is also under construction. There will be a systematic process of how new interesting digital tools are proposed. Moreover, there will be a specific steering group evaluating them and deciding if the new tool is overlapping with an existing one or worth purchasing and becoming an official tool at the university. This process is meant for keeping the ecosystem of digital tools clear and preventing overlapping and useless or risky tools to be used. At the first phase, IAP2 framework is not used in the evaluation.

The suggestions listed in this study and the improvements made based on them will be interesting research topics for the near future. Will the changes made at the university be effective and will they enhance collaboration and empowerment? Will COVID-19 affect positively in the way people collaborate and empower in digital world? Will digital become as common as physical or will digital and physical even swap places, compared to the situation before COVID-19? Only time will tell.

References

1. Perkins, D.D., Zimmerman, M.A.: Empowerment theory, research, and application. Am. J. Community Psychol. **23**(5), 569–579 (1995). https://doi.org/10.1007/BF02506982
2. Zimmerman, M.A.: Empowerment theory. In: Rappaport, J., Seidman, E. (eds.) Handbook of Community Psychology, pp. 43–63. Springer, Boston (2000). https://doi.org/10.1007/978-1-4615-4193-6_2
3. Honold, L.: A review of the literature on employee empowerment. Empower. Organiz. **5**(4), 202–212 (1997)
4. Coleman, H.J.: Why employee empowerment is not just a fad. Leadersh. Org Dev. J. **17**(4), 29–36 (1996)
5. Mintzberg, H.: Covert leadership: notes on managing professionals. Knowledge workers respond to inspiration, not supervision. Harv. Bus. Rev. **76**(6), 140–147 (1998)
6. Ngcamu, B.S.: The effects of leadership traits on transformation: a case study of a South African university. J. Transdiscipl. Res. South. Afr. **13**(1) (2017)
7. James, T.: Setting the stage: Why health care needs a culture of respect, in lean forward: join the conversation on medical news. Harvard Medical School CME Online (2018). https://leanforward.hms.harvard.edu/2018/07/31/setting-the-stage-why-health-care-needs-a-culture-of-respect/
8. Porath, C.: Half of employees don't feel respected by their bosses (2014). https://hbr.org/2014/11/half-of-employees-dont-feel-respected-by-their-bosses
9. Rogers, K.: Do your employees feel respected? (2018). https://hbr.org/2018/07/do-your-emp loyees-feel-respected
10. WebFinance: Participation (2019). http://www.businessdictionary.com/definition/participa tion.html
11. Kim, S.: Participative management and job satisfaction: lessons for management leadership. Public Adm. Rev. **62**(2), 231–241 (2002)
12. Sakakibara, K., Ishikawa, H., Yamazaki, Y.: Participative climate as a key for creating healthy workplaces. In: Biron, C., Burke, R.J. (eds.) Creating Healthy Workplaces, pp. 183–204. Routledge, London (2014)
13. Brod, C.: Technostress: The Human Cost of the Computer Revolution. Addison Wesley Publishing, Reading (1984)
14. Tarafdar, M., Tu, Q., Ragu-Nathan, T.S.: Crossing to the dark side: examining creators, outcomes, and inhibitors of technostress. Commun. ACM **54**(9), 113–120 (2011)
15. Tarafdar, M., Tu, Q., Ragu-Nathan, T.S.: Impact of technostress on end-user satisfaction and performance. J. Manag. Inf. Syst. **27**(3), 303–334 (2010)
16. Lewin, K., Lippitt, R., White, R.K.: Patterns of aggressive behavior in experimentally created "social climates". J. Soc. Psychol. **10**, 271–299 (1939)
17. Yukl, G.: Toward a behavioral theory of leadership. Organiz. Behav. Hum. Perform. **6**(4), 414–440 (1971)

18. International association of public participation: core values, ethics, spectrum – the 3 pillars of public participation (2020). https://www.iap2.org/page/pillars
19. Nelimarkka, M., et al.: Comparing three online civic engagement platforms using the "Spectrum of public participation" framework. In: The Internet, Policy & Politics Conferences, Oxford 2014 (2014)
20. Guo, H., Neshkova, M.I.: Public participation and organizational performance: evidence from state agencies. J. Public Adm. Res. Theor. **22**(2), 267–288 (2011)

Comprehending User Satisfaction with Smoking-Cessation Online Health Communities: A Social Support Perspective

Chenglong Li[✉] [ID]

Turku School of Economics, University of Turku, Turku, Finland
chenglong.li@utu.fi

Abstract. This study aims to unravel the user satisfaction in smoking-cessation online health communities (OHCs). In the proposed research model, users' knowledge sharing and recommendation behaviour are motivated by user satisfaction. User satisfaction, in turn, is determined by users' confirmation of their expectations and perceived usefulness (PU) of smoking-cessation OHCs. In addition, informational support, emotional support, and esteem support are conceptualized as the determinants of PU from a social support perspective. The research model is tested by analysing online survey data (N = 173) among users of two smoking-cessation OHCs. The empirical results indicate that satisfaction affects users' knowledge sharing and recommendation behaviour positively, and both PU and confirmation determine satisfaction. PU of smoking-cessation OHCs is motivated by emotional support and esteem support. The findings extend the understanding of user satisfaction in the particular context of smoking-cessation OHCs and provide administration of smoking-cessation OHCs with practical implications.

Keywords: Social support · Smoking-Cessation · Confirmation · Online health community · Knowledge sharing · Recommendation · Satisfaction · Perceived usefulness

1 Introduction

Smoking-cessation online health communities (OHCs) like Stumppi.fi, QuitNet, and BecomeAnEx, have been increasingly utilized as a mechanism for smoking behavior change [1–3]. Unlike general Social Network Sites (SNS), such as Facebook and Twitter, smoking-cessation OHCs are intentionally designed with internet-based smoking-cessation interventions, and often consist of strangers united by a shared goal on achieving abstinence [1–3]. In such OHCs, users can ask questions about quitting, share experiences, and provide others with emotional support and companionship [1–3]. Past studies have suggested that participation in smoking-cessation OHCs might lead to positive smoking-cessation outcomes, for instance, a short-term abstinence [3].

Previous research has demonstrated that user satisfaction with Information Systems (IS) is crucial for implementing such IS successfully [4, 5]. Numerous studies have

© Springer Nature Switzerland AG 2020
M. Cacace et al. (Eds.): WIS 2020, CCIS 1270, pp. 112–127, 2020.
https://doi.org/10.1007/978-3-030-57847-3_8

uncovered several factors that influence user satisfaction in the IS field, such as information quality and system quality [6, 7]. In addition, some studies have found several positive outcomes of user satisfaction with IS, for instance, continuance intention [4]. Although these studies have offered important insights into user satisfaction with IS, there are two issues that require further research. First, there is a lack of research examining determinants of satisfaction in the particular context of smoking-cessation OHCs. Different from users of other IS, users of smoking-cessation OHCs have special needs. They are in need of social support (e.g., informational and emotional support) to help them achieve abstinence [8]. Social support is closely related to the context of smoking-cessation OHCs, and might affect user satisfaction, but largely ignored by prior research. Thus, it is necessary to investigate the antecedents of satisfaction in smoking-cessation OHCs from a social support perspective. Second, research on the consequences of satisfaction in the IS field is still limited [9]. Although user satisfaction has been found to affect users' continuance intention [4], the relationships between user satisfaction and other outcomes, such as knowledge sharing and recommendation, are not clear. Thus, further investigation is required to explore various consequences of user satisfaction with smoking-cessation OHCs.

To address above research gaps, this study purposes to investigate the antecedents and consequences of user satisfaction with smoking-cessation OHCs. Drawing upon expectation confirmation theory (ECT) [4] and social support theory [10, 11], this study advances a research model that posits: (1) users' feelings of satisfaction is determined by their confirmation of expectations and perceived usefulness (PU). (2) PU is influenced by social support obtained from smoking-cessation OHCs. (3) Satisfaction leads to users' knowledge sharing and recommendation behaviour.

The remainder of the paper is structured as follows. In Sect. 2, I review extant literature on satisfaction and social support theory. Then, I present the proposed research model and hypotheses in Sect. 3. The methodology and the results from data analysis are introduced in Sect. 4. Finally, I conclude with a discussion on the implications of my empirical findings for both theory and practice in Sect. 5.

2 Theoretical Foundation

2.1 User Satisfaction in Information Systems

User satisfaction is a dominant research stream within previous literature, and has attracted scholarly attention across multiple disciplines. In the IS field, expectation confirmation theory (ECT) is widely used to explain user satisfaction as a function of a cognitive comparison between expectations of prior IS use and its actual performance. [4]. ECT was proposed by Oliver [12], and holds that expectations and product/service performance determine customer satisfaction together. If performance exceeds users' expectations, a confirmation will manifest, and then individuals would be more satisfied with produce/service. However, if performance is below their prior expectation they would be less satisfied or even dissatisfied with product/service. ECT was then adopted in the IS field by Bhattacherjee [4]. According to Bhattacherjee [4], users' postadoption expectation is more credible because it is founded on actual IS usage. He demonstrated that confirmation of expectations from prior IS use, together with PU, determine user satisfaction. User satisfaction, in turn, affects users' continuance intention.

Beyond continuance intention, satisfaction has been found to affect other user behaviours, such as retention and word of mouth [13]. However, as Vaezi et al. [9] reported, understanding about outcomes of satisfaction is still fragmented. Thus, user satisfaction's impact on postadoption behaviours requires further investigation. In addition, previous studies have stated that user satisfaction is determined by different factors. For instance, Wixom, Todd [7] found that information quality and systems quality affect user satisfaction with data warehousing software. However, due to the uniqueness of smoking-cessation OHCs, the context-related factors has not been emphasized in prior literature. Thus, future research is needed.

2.2 Social Support Theory

Cobb [14] defined social support as information and actions that make people believe that they are "cared for and loved, esteemed and valued, as well as belong to a network of communication and mutual obligation". Social support has been found to promote many addiction treatments such as alcohol withdrawal [15] and smoking-cessation [16, 17]. Particularly, social support from strong social ties, such as partners, family members, and close friends, can enhance a smoker's cessation performance [16, 17]. In addition, prior studies have suggested that social support from weak social ties, for instance, smoking-cessation OHCs, might also lead to abstinence [3]. In other words, social support obtained from smoking-cessation OHCs might meet smokers' expectations. Such support can enhance users' perception of usefulness of OHCs, and then make them feel satisfied with such OHCs. Therefore, social support theory is appropriate to investigate the satisfaction of smoking-cessation OHCs.

Cutrona, Suhr [11] classified social support into five different types: (1) informational support, i.e., providing information on how to solve problems through suggestions or teaching. (2) Emotional support, i.e., providing comfort to reduce emotion-related stress by expressing caring or concern. (3) Esteem support, i.e., providing praise or compliment to enhance other's self-esteem. (4) Network support, i.e., providing a sense of belonging to a group. (5) Tangible support, i.e., providing goods or financial support. Previous studies have found that informational and emotional are two major types of social support shared in OHCs, followed by esteem and network support, such as OHCs related to cancer [18], and smoking-cessation [19]. However, tangible support has been reported to be rare. This might because tangible support is restricted by time and space limitations [18].

In this research, I consider three types of social support as the antecedents of the PU of smoking-cessation OHCs: informational, emotional, and esteem support. Tangible support is removed due to its rarity in OHCs [18, 20]. Network support is also be deleted in this study because it seems difficult to clearly distinguish it from companionship activities, as they are often intertwined in OHCs [20].

3 Research Model and Hypotheses

3.1 Research Model

Drawing on prior literature on satisfaction, I assume that users' knowledge sharing and recommendation behavior are determined by their satisfaction with smoking-cessation OHCs. User satisfaction, in turn, is influenced by their confirmation of expectations from prior use and PU. Further, based on social support theory, I argue that three types of social support (i.e., informational support, emotional support, and esteem support) have impacts on the PU of smoking-cessation OHCs. Table 1 presents the definitions of the constructs included in the proposed research model. Figure 1 summarizes my research model.

Table 1. List of definitions of the constructs

Construct	Definition
Emotional support (EMS)	Communicating care, empathy, encouragement, or even love in a smoking-cessation OHC [11]
Informational support (INS)	Communicating information on smoking-cessation—such as advice, success stories—in a smoking-cessation OHC [11]
Esteem support (ESS)	Communicating compliments or relief from blame in a smoking-cessation OHC [11]
Perceived usefulness (PU)	The degree to which a user believes that using a smoking-cessation OHC would enhance his or her smoking-cessation performance [21]
Knowledge sharing (KS)	The behavior of exchanging information, experience, and skills related to smoking-cessation in a smoking-cessation OHC [22]
Recommendation (REC)	The behavior to recommending the smoking-cessation OHC to others [23]
Confirmation (CON)	A user's perception of the congruence between expectations of smoking-cessation OHC use and its actual performance [4]
Satisfaction (SAT)	The degree to which a user affect with prior use of a smoking-cessation OHC [4]

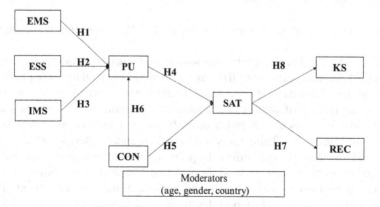

Fig. 1. The proposed research model

3.2 Research Hypotheses

Emotional support has been viewed as important to facilitate people's emotional stability through the communication of empathy, sympathy, caring, and even love [20]. For smoking quitters, they often feel distressed because of the negative emotions caused by unpleasant withdrawal symptoms, such as headache, coughing, and sore throat. They need an environment for them to release their negative energy freely and safely, and ask for emotional support from others [24]. Smoking-cessation OHCs offer such an environment. First, due to anonymity, smokers can disclose their feelings without privacy worries. Second, the majority of users are ex-smokers or current smokers who experience a similar situation and can empathize with emotional support seekers. Third, the sense of being cared from others can help users to reduce their distress, and change their personal emotions from negative to positive [19, 20]. In other words, emotional support from smoking-cessation OHCs can assist smokers to restore their emotional stability, which might help them to quit smoking habit. Hence, I assume that the more emotional support users obtain from a smoking-cessation OHC, the more useful it is perceived to be. Thus, I suggest the following hypothesis:

H1: Emotional support is positively associated with the PU of a smoking-cessation OHC.

Esteem support can help smokers to enhance their self-esteem through offering compliments and relief from blame [25, 26]. Specifically, in smoking-cessation OHCs, others' expressions of forgiveness might mitigate their self-blame with regard to relapse. In addition, others' praise or congratulations about their achievements (e.g., a week smoke-free), can help users enhance their self-belief regarding their capabilities to stop smoking. Prior literature has reported that high self-esteem is an important predictor of success in smoking-cessation [27]. In other words, esteem support from a smoking-cessation OHC can help quitters to enhance their self-esteem, which might eventually lead to abstinence. Therefore, I assume that more esteem support gained from a smoking-cessation OHC, the more useful the smoking-cessation OHC is perceived to be. The following hypothesis is suggested:

H2: Esteem support is positively associated with the PU of a smoking-cessation OHC.

Informational support can help users in solving problems by providing suggestions or teaching [20]. Smoking-cessation OHCs are an ideal information resource platform for smoking quitters. First, they can access to self-help materials, which are helpful to teach them about the benefits of quitting and enhance their intention to quit. Second, they can get other's advice on how to quit, which are useful for them to make better decisions and quitting plans [19, 28, 29]. Third, users can learn from success stories posted by others. The personal tips and experience offered by peers are suitable for meeting practical needs and enhancing quitting skills. In short, informational support from smoking-cessation OHCs may help users to prepare, plan, and act to quit their smoking habit. Thus, I assume that the informational support that from a smoking-cessation OHC will make users perceive smoking-cessation OHCs as useful. The following hypothesis is proposed:

H3: Informational support is positively associated with the PU of a smoking-cessation OHC.

According to Bhattacherjee [4], in the context of an online bank system, user satisfaction is determined by confirmation and PU together. In addition, confirmation has been found to affect PU positively. Thus, based on his findings, the following hypotheses are suggested:

H4: A user's perception of usefulness of a smoking-cessation OHC is positively related to their satisfaction with the OHC.
H5: A user's confirmation with a smoking-cessation OHC is positively related to their satisfaction with the OHC.
H6: A users' confirmation with a smoking-cessation OHC is positively associated with their perception of usefulness of the OHC.

Several studies have found that user satisfaction leads to postadoption behaviors. For instance, Morgeson [13] discovered that there is a strong relationship between user satisfaction with websites and re-use intention. Satisfaction also has been found to affect word-of-mouth recommendation directly and indirectly (through re-use intention). Based on his findings, I suppose that user satisfaction with smoking-cessation OHCs affects their recommendation behaviour. The more satisfied the users are, the higher the likelihood that they will recommend such OHCs to others beyond the OHCs. Thus, I posit:

H7: A user's satisfaction with a smoking-cessation OHC is positively associated with their recommendation behaviour.

Only a handful of studies have investigated the knowledge sharing behaviour as an outcome of user satisfaction. In the work of Cheung et al. [30], user satisfaction affects users' continuance intention of knowledge sharing in an online community of practice. Based on their finding, it is reasonable to assume that in smoking-cessation OHCs, the more satisfied the users are, the higher the likelihood that they will contribute their knowledge in the OHCs. Thus, I provide the following hypothesis:

H8: A user's satisfaction with a smoking-cessation OHC is positively associated with their knowledge sharing behaviour in them.

Prior studies have suggested to take age and gender in consideration when investigating impacts of social support on smoking cessation behaviour [17]. In addition, this study collected data from both Finland and China. Thus, in this research, age, gender, and country are considered as moderators.

4 Methodology

4.1 Development of Survey Measurements

Measurement items for constructs in the proposed theoretical model are adapted from extant literature and then reworded to fit the smoking-cessation OHC context. A five-point scale, ranging from "1 = strongly disagree" to "5 = strongly agree," is used to measure all the construct items. Specifically, the items of informational support and emotional support come from research by Liang et al. [31]. The measurements for esteem support are adopted from Oh et al. [32]. Perceived usefulness, confirmation, and satisfaction are measured with items taken from Bhattacherjee [4]. Items for knowledge sharing were adopted from the work of Hsu et al. [22]. The complete list of measurement items for constructs in the theoretical model is summarized in the Appendix.

4.2 Data Collection

This study adopts the online survey methodology for data collection. Data are gathered in two nonprofit smoking-cessation OHCs (one is Stumppi.fi in Finland; the other is smoking-cessation bar in China). I recruited participants by releasing the online questionnaire on these two smoking-cessation OHCs. Each respondent is asked to offer their background information, and to report their perception and experience of using smoking-cessation OHCs in their smoking-cessation process. Respondents received a gift for their participation. A total of 185 users agreed to join and completed the online survey (139 in China, and 46 in Finland). After deleting 12 untrustworthy responses (12 in China), I finally obtained 173 answers as a valid sample for data analysis. Table 2 presents the background information of the respondents and their smoking-cessation stage.

4.3 Data Analysis

In this study, collected data were analyzed by Partial Least Squares (PLS) 3.0 to validate the theoretical model.

The test of measurement model involved the assessment of convergent validity and discriminant validity. First, I used the factor loading for each item, composite reliability (CR), and average variance extracted (AVE) for each construct to evaluate convergent validity [33–35]. I deleted two items (EMS3 and INS1), as their factor loadings were lower than the minimum criterion. As presented in Table 3, each item's factor loadings exceeded 0.70. As shown in Table 4, the value of AVE and CR met the recommended threshold values of 0.5 and 0.7, respectively. Cronbach's alpha values also satisfied the threshold of 0.7, except informational support (0.68), suggesting acceptable convergent validity.

Table 2. Respondents' demographic data and smoking-cessation stage

Measure	Items	Frequency	Percentage (%)
Country	Finland	46	26.6
	China	127	73.4
Gender	Male	103	59.5
	Female	64	37.0
	Unwilling to disclose	6	3.5
Age	15–24	17	9.8
	25–44	117	67.6
	45–65	35	20.2
	>65	4	2.3
Smoking-cessation stage	Pre-contemplation	4	2.3
	Contemplation	45	26.0
	Preparation	19	11.0
	Action	40	23.1
	Maintenance	50	28.9
	Termination	15	8.7

Second, calculated the square root of the AVE for all constructs in the research model to test discriminant validity. Then, I made a comparison between the loadings of items for an associated construct and their cross-loadings on other constructs. As shown in Table 5, the value of the square root of the AVE for each construct was higher than its correlation with other constructs. Overall, there is strong empirical support for the discriminant validity of all constructs in my proposed model [33].

The test of the structural model included estimates of the path coefficients and the R2 values. I applied the bootstrapping procedure in PLS 3.0 to test the structural model. The overall explanatory power and estimated path coefficients are shown in Fig. 2. The model explains 59.1% of the variation in the PU of smoking-cessation OHCs, 20% of knowledge sharing, 27.3% of recommendation, and 38.3% of satisfaction. As postulated, emotional support ($\beta = 0.216$, $p < 0.05$) and esteem support ($\beta = 0.209$, $p < 0.05$) had significant positive influences on PU. Informational support was not found to affect PU significantly. PU exerted significant positive effects on satisfaction ($\beta = 0.313$, $p < 0.01$). Confirmation positively affected both PU ($\beta = 0.431$, $p < 0.001$) and satisfaction ($\beta = 0.357$, $p < 0.001$). Satisfaction determined knowledge sharing ($\beta = 0.447$, $p < 0.001$) and recommendation ($\beta = 0.522$, $p < 0.001$). Thus, H1, H2, H4, H5, H6, H7, and H8 are supported.

To test the moderating effects of age, gender, and country, a multi-group analysis was conducted. No significant deference was found between Chinese and Finnish users, nor among different age groups. A significant difference was found between female and male users with regard to the path from emotional support to PU. Emotional support significantly affected PU for female users ($\beta = 0.493$, $p < 0.001$), but not for male users.

Table 3. Loadings and cross-loadings

	EMS	ESS	IMS	KS	PU	REC	CON	SAT
EMS1	0.866							
EMS2	0.851							
EMS4	0.899							
ESS1		0.812						
ESS2		0.865						
ESS3		0.897						
IMS2			0.868					
IMS3			0.866					
KS1				0.924				
KS2				0.903				
KS3				0.923				
KS4				0.911				
PU1					0.826			
PU2					0.835			
PU3					0.796			
PU4					0.701			
REC1						0.824		
REC2						0.778		
REC3						0.838		
REC4						0.748		
CON1							0.898	
CON2							0.774	
CON3							0.881	
SAT1								0.807
SAT2								0.748
SAT3								0.809
SAT4								0.819

Table 4. Confirmatory factor analysis results

	Cronbach's alpha	Composite reliability	Average variance extracted (AVE)
EMS	0.843	0.905	0.761
ESS	0.822	0.894	0.738
IMS	0.67	0.858	0.752
KS	0.935	0.954	0.838
PU	0.799	0.87	0.626
REC	0.812	0.875	0.636
CON	0.811	0.889	0.728
SAT	0.812	0.874	0.634

Table 5. Correlation matrix and discriminant validity

	EMS	ESS	IMS	KS	PU	REC	CON	SAT
EMS	0.872							
ESS	0.74	0.859						
IMS	0.743	0.766	0.867					
KS	0.578	0.565	0.611	0.915				
PU	0.63	0.66	0.606	0.573	0.791			
REC	0.548	0.616	0.564	0.433	0.642	0.798		
CON	0.572	0.646	0.614	0.502	0.703	0.647	0.853	
SAT	0.454	0.507	0.47	0.447	0.564	0.522	0.577	0.796

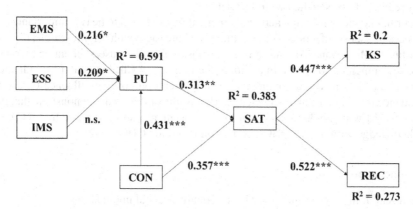

(Note: ***: p < 0.001; **: p <0.01; *: p <0.05; n.s.: not significant)

Fig. 2. The structural model

5 Discussion and Conclusions

5.1 Discussion

Building on the ECT and social support theory, this study constructs and tests a theoretical model to investigate user satisfaction in the particular context of smoking-cessation OHCs. Findings from the empirical validation of the model raise several points of interest.

First, emotional support and esteem support are found to affect the PU of smoking-cessation OHCs. This finding is consistent with prior research findings. For instance, in the research of Wu [36], social support is reported to affect the PU of general OHCs. In smoking-cessation OHCs, when users obtain emotional support and esteem support that they expect from the OHCs, they perceive such OHC as useful for facilitating their smoking-cessation outcomes. In addition, emotional support is found to be a predictor of PU for female users, but not for male users. This might because female users value emotional support more than male users, particularly in the stressful situation. When female users obtain emotional support from the OHCs, they are more likely to perceive such OHCs are useful for them to cope with stress in the process of smoking cessation.

Second, contrary to the hypothesis, informational support is not an antecedent of the PU of smoking-cessation OHCs. This finding is at odds with the prior findings. For instance, Wu [36] found that information support is a determinant of the PU of general OHCs. This might be explained by the context of smoking-cessation OHCs. According to Vaezi et al. [9], some antecedents of satisfaction are more relevant to certain contexts than others are. For smokers who intend to quit, they may get similar information support from alternative information sources, such as professional counselling and group therapy. Further investigation is required to explore these context-related factors.

Third, consistent with prior findings of Bhattacherjee [4], user satisfaction with smoking-cessation OHCs is determined by both PU and confirmation. When users confirm their expectations of using smoking-cessation OHCs in their smoking-cessation process, and perceive such OHCs are useful for helping them achieve abstinence, they are more likely to be satisfied with the OHCs.

Fourth, knowledge sharing and recommendation are found to be two important consequences of user satisfaction. These findings are consistent with prior research [13, 30]. According to Morgeson [13], user satisfaction positively affects users' intention to re-use IS and recommend it to others. In addition, the findings of Cheung et al. [30] indicated that user satisfaction with an online community exerts on positive influence on users' continuance intention to share knowledge. The results of this study demonstrate that the more satisfied with smoking-cessation OHCs, the more likely users are to contribute their knowledge within such OHCs, and recommend the OHCs to others.

5.2 Conclusions

These research findings in this study have some theoretical implications.

First, this study extends the ECT by delineating user satisfaction of smoking-cessation OHCs into social support elements. The findings on emotional and esteem support as the two important determinants of PU of smoking cessation OHCs demonstrated that PU can be explained from the social support perspective, which is closely related to the smoking cessation OHCs context. In addition, PU is positively associated with satisfaction. The satisfaction might be influenced by social support factors indirectly via PU. With these new insights, this study offers possible explanations for understating the influences of context-related factors on user satisfaction.

Second, Vaezi et al. [9] suggested to focus more on outcomes of satisfaction in IS, this study addresses this call by investigating two postadoption behaviours as consequences of satisfaction in the context of smoking-cessation OHCs. The findings indicate that users' satisfaction is a determinant for their knowledge sharing and recommendation behaviours. When users feel satisfied with smoking-cessation OHCs, the more likely they will share their own knowledge in such OHCs, as well as recommend the OHCs to others.

This study provides some practical implications for managing smoking cessation OHCs. The findings imply satisfaction determines users' knowledge sharing and recommendation behaviour, thereby offering recommendations for OHC service providers to promote knowledge sharing and recommendation by enhancing users' satisfaction with smoking-cessation OHCs. Specifically, emotional and esteem support were found to indirectly influence satisfaction via PU, suggesting that OHC service providers should focus on the strategies to promote the sharing of emotional and esteem support among users.

5.3 Limitations and Future Directions

This study has certain limitations. Firstly, the theoretical model caters exclusively to smoking-cessation OHCs and does not consider other OHCs or IS. For this reason, I speculate that the findings may not be generalizable for explaining user satisfaction in different contexts. Future research may consider collecting data from OHCs related to different health concerns. Second, in terms of antecedents, I only focus on social support elements. Other factors (e.g., information and system quality) that may affect user satisfaction in smoking-cessation OHCs could be considered in future research, in order to get a comprehensive understanding of satisfaction [9].

Acknowledgement. This research is supported by the Finnish Foundation for Economic Education (Under Grant 16-9095).

Appendix

Construct	Measurement items	Resource
Emotional support	1. When faced with difficulties, some people in the smoking-cessation OHC were on my side 2. When faced with difficulties, some people in the smoking-cessation OHC comforted and encouraged me 3. When faced with difficulties, some people in the smoking-cessation OHC listened to me talk about my private feelings 4. When faced with difficulties, some people in the smoking-cessation OHC expressed interest in and concern for my well-being	[31]
Informational support	1. Some people in the smoking-cessation OHC would offer suggestions when I needed help 2. When I encountered a problem, some people in the smoking-cessation OHC would give me information to help me overcome the problem 3. When faced with difficulties, some people in the smoking-cessation OHC would help me discover the cause and offer suggestions	
Esteem support	1. Some members of the smoking-cessation OHC showed confidence in my ability to deal with smoking 2. Some members of the smoking-cessation OHC made me feel that I was good at making decisions regarding smoking cessation 3. Some members of the smoking-cessation OHC made me feel that I was capable of handling my smoking cessation	[32]
Perceived usefulness	1. Using the smoking-cessation OHC made my smoking cessation proceed faster (productivity) 2. Using the smoking-cessation OHC made my smoking cessation proceed better (performance) 3. Using the smoking-cessation OHC helped me make better decisions regarding smoking cessation (effectiveness) 4. Overall, using the smoking-cessation OHC was useful in smoking cessation	[4]
Confirmation	1. My experience with using stumppi.fi was better than what I expected 2. The service provided by stumppi.fi was better than what I expected 3. Overall, most of my positive expectation from using stumppi.fi were confirmed	

(continued)

(*continued*)

Construct	Measurement items	Resource
Satisfaction	How do you feel about your overall experience of using this online community? 1. Very dissatisfied, dissatisfied, neutral, satisfied, very satisfied 2. Very displeased, displeased, neutral, pleased, very pleased 3. Very frustrated, frustrated, neutral, contented, very contented 4. Very terrible, terrible, neutral, delighted, very delighted	
Knowledge sharing	1. I participate frequently in knowledge-sharing activities in the smoking-cessation OHC 2. I usually spend lots of time in knowledge-sharing activities in the smoking-cessation OHC 3. I usually share information actively with others in the smoking-cessation OHC 4. I usually involve myself in discussions of various topics in the smoking-cessation OHC	[22]
Recommendation	1. I would recommend stumppi.fi to other smokers 2. I will say positive things about stumppi.fi to others 3. I would recommend stumppi.fi when someone seeks my advice on smoking cessation 4. I would recommend stumppi.fi to others via social media	[23]

References

1. Cobb, N.K., Graham, A.L., Abrams, D.B.: Social network structure of a large online community for smoking cessation. Am. J. Public Health **100**(7), 1282–1289 (2010)
2. Cobb, N.K., Graham, A.L., Byron, M.J., Niaura, R.S., Abrams, D.B., Workshop, P.: Online social networks and smoking cessation: a scientific research agenda. J. Med. Internet Res. **13**(4), e119 (2011)
3. Graham, A.L., Papandonatos, G.D., Erar, B., Stanton, C.A.: Use of an online smoking cessation community promotes abstinence: results of propensity score weighting. Health Psychol. **34**, 1286–1295 (2015)
4. Bhattacherjee, A.: Understanding information systems continuance: An expectation-confirmation model. MIS Q. **25**(3), 351–370 (2001)
5. Au, N., Ngai, E.W.T., Cheng, T.C.E.: Extending the understanding of end user information systems satisfaction formation: an equitable needs fulfillment model approach. MIS Q. **32**(1), 43–66 (2008)
6. DeLone, W.H., McLean, E.R.: Information systems success: the quest for the dependent variable. Inf. Syst. Res. **3**(1), 60–95 (1992)
7. Wixom, B.H., Todd, P.A.: A theoretical integration of user satisfaction and technology acceptance. Inf. Syst. Res. **16**(1), 85–102 (2005)
8. Mermelstein, R., Cohen, S., Lichtenstein, E., Baer, J.S., Kamarck, T.: Social support and smoking cessation and maintenance. J. Consult. Clinical Psychol. **54**(4), 447–453 (1986)

9. Vaezi, R., Mills, A., Chin, W., Zafar, H.: User satisfaction research in information systems: historical roots and approaches. Commun. Assoc. Inf. Syst. **38**(1), 501–532 (2016)

10. Cohen, S., Wills, T.A.: Stress, social support, and the buffering hypothesis. Psychol. Bull. **98**(2), 310–357 (1985)

11. Cutrona, C.E., Suhr, J.A.: Controllability of stressful events and satisfaction with spouse support behaviors. Commun. Res. **19**(2), 154–174 (1992)

12. Oliver, R.L.: A cognitive model of the antecedents and consequences of satisfaction decisions. J. Market. Res. **17**(4), 460–469 (1980)

13. Morgeson, F.V.: Comparing determinants of website satisfaction and loyalty across the e-government and e-business domains. Electron. Govern. Int. J. **8**(2–3), 164–184 (2011)

14. Cobb, S.: Social support as a moderator of life stress. Psychosomatic Med. **38**(5), 300–314 (1976)

15. Peirce, R.S., Frone, M.R., Russell, M., Cooper, M.L., Mudar, P.: A longitudinal model of social contact, social support, depression, and alcohol use. Health Psychol. **19**(1), 28–38 (2000)

16. Wagner, J., Burg, M., Sirois, B.: Social support and the transtheoretical model: Relationship of social support to smoking cessation stage, decisional balance, process use, and temptation. Addict. Behav. **29**(5), 1039–1043 (2004)

17. Westmaas, J.L., Bontemps-Jones, J., Bauer, J.E.: Social support in smoking cessation: reconciling theory and evidence. Nicotine Tob. Res. **12**(7), 695–707 (2010)

18. Wang, X., Zhao, K., Street, N.: Analyzing and predicting user participations in online health communities: a social support perspective. J. Med. Internet Res. **19**(4), e130 (2017)

19. Zhang, M., Yang, C.C.: Using content and network analysis to understand the social support exchange patterns and user behaviors of an online smoking cessation intervention program. J. Assoc. Inf. Sci. Technol. **66**(3), 564–575 (2015)

20. Huang, K.Y., Chengalur-Smith, I., Pinsonneault, A.: Sharing is caring: social support provision and companionship activities in healthcare virtual support communities. MIS Q. **43**(2), 395–423 (2019)

21. Davis, F.D.: Perceived usefulness, perceived ease of use, and user acceptance of information technology. MIS Q. **13**(3), 319–340 (1989)

22. Hsu, M.H., Ju, T.L., Yen, C.H., Chang, C.M.: Knowledge sharing behavior in virtual communities: The relationship between trust, self-efficacy, and outcome expectations. Int. J. Hum Comput Stud. **65**(2), 153–169 (2007)

23. Kim, S.S., Son, J.Y.: Out of dedication or constraint? a dual model of post-adoption phenomena and its empirical test in the context of online services. MIS Q. **33**(1), 49–70 (2009)

24. Creswell, K.G., Cheng, Y., Levine, M.D.: A test of the stress-buffering model of social support in smoking cessation: is the relationship between social support and time to relapse mediated by reduced withdrawal symptoms? Nicot. Tobacco Res. **17**(5), 566–571 (2015)

25. Deng, Z., Liu, S.: Understanding consumer health information-seeking behavior from the perspective of the risk perception attitude framework and social support in mobile social media websites. Int. J. Med. Inform. **105**, 98–109 (2017)

26. Huang, K., Chengalur-Smith, I., Ran, W.: Not just for support: companionship activities in healthcare virtual support communities. Commun. Assoc. Inf. Syst. **34**(29), 561–594 (2014)

27. Kowalski, S.D.: Self-esteem and self-efficacy as predictors of success in smoking cessation. J. Holistic Nurs. **15**(2), 128–142 (1997)

28. Granado-Font, E., Ferre-Grau, C., Rey-Renones, C., Pons-Vigues, M., Pujol, Ribera E., Berenguera, A., et al.: Coping strategies and social support in a mobile phone chat app designed to support smoking cessation: qualitative analysis. JMIR Mhealth Uhealth **6**(12), e11071 (2018)

29. Rocheleau, M., Sadasivam, R.S., Baquis, K., Stahl, H., Kinney, R.L., Pagoto, S.L., et al.: An observational study of social and emotional support in smoking cessation Twitter accounts: content analysis of tweets. J. Med. Internet Res. **17**(1), e18 (2015)
30. Cheung, C.M.K., Lee, M.K.O., Lee, Z.W.Y.: Understanding the continuance intention of knowledge sharing in online communities of practice through the post-knowledge-sharing evaluation processes. J. Am. Soc. Inf. Sci. Technol. **64**(7), 1357–1374 (2013)
31. Liang, T.P., Ho, Y.T., Li, Y.W., Turban, E.: What drives social commerce: the role of social support and relationship quality. Int. J. Electron. Commerce **16**(2), 69–90 (2011)
32. Oh, H.J., Lauckner, C., Boehmer, J., Fewins-Bliss, R., Li, K.: Facebooking for health: An examination into the solicitation and effects of health-related social support on social networking sites. Comput. Hum. Behav. **29**(5), 2072–2080 (2013)
33. Chin, W.: The partial least squares approach for structural equation modeling. In: George, A. (ed.) Modern Methods for Business Research, pp. 295–336. Lawrence Erlbaum Associates, New York (1998)
34. Hulland, J.: Use of partial least squares (PLS) in strategic management research: a review of four recent studies. Strategic Manage. J. **20**(2), 195–204 (1999)
35. Tenenhaus, M., Vinzi, V.E., Chatelin, Y.-M., Lauro, C.: PLS path modeling. Comput. Stat. Data Anal. **48**(1), 159–205 (2005)
36. Wu, B.: Patient continued use of online health care communities: web mining of patient-doctor communication. J. Med. Internet Res. **20**(4), e126 (2018)

Trust and Respect in Entrepreneurial Information Seeking Behaviours

Thao Phuong Orrensalo[(⊠)] [iD] and Shahrokh Nikou [iD]

Faculty of Social Science, Business and Economics, Åbo Akademi University, Turku, Finland
{phuong.t.le,shahrokh.nikou}@abo.fi

Abstract. Trust has been a vital research topic in entrepreneurship research. Many researchers argue that trust gives the entrepreneurs legitimacy within the market, and it is considered as a factor for information behaviours. Meanwhile, respect is also mentioned as a fundamental for trust and a necessity for building entrepreneurial networks. Despite their significance and relevance, there is still a limited study focusing on the role of trust and respect in entrepreneurs' information-seeking behaviour research. This paper, therefore, draws attention to this gap and strives to investigate how these two concepts impact entrepreneurs' information-seeking behaviour. The results show that trust and respect are two fundamental aspects that influence entrepreneurs' preference for information source selection. Furthermore, the findings show that both trust and respect act as a predominant factor for entrepreneurs to build and advance their relationships. Theoretical and practical implications and recommendations for future studies are discussed.

Keywords: Entrepreneur · Entrepreneurship · Trust · Respect · Social capital theory · Information seeking behaviour

1 Introduction

Over the past few decades, trust has gained increased attention from many researchers in entrepreneurship research due to its importance in guiding entrepreneurs in their careers. Entrepreneurs need to earn trust from others and also act as a trustor to successfully establish and grow their businesses [1]. Trust is a crucial factor for entrepreneurial activities, such as promoting the company, transferring information, enhancing customers' relationships, reducing transaction costs [2–5], and especially for nurturing entrepreneurial networks to acquire resources, opportunities, and cooperation [6–9]. Welter [10] pointed that in entrepreneurship, trust has been a well-studied subject in many academic disciplines, including human resource [9], connection with business angels, venture capitalists [11–13], banks [14], partners [15], mentors [16], and buyer-supplier relationships [17]. Many scholars consider trust to be governance factors for the globalisation of small businesses [18, 19]. While others emphasise its strategic advantage for family firms [20, 21], and especially its feature as a cost/risk deductible aspect in chaotic environments [4, 22, 23].

© Springer Nature Switzerland AG 2020
M. Cacace et al. (Eds.): WIS 2020, CCIS 1270, pp. 128–142, 2020.
https://doi.org/10.1007/978-3-030-57847-3_9

Notably, through literature of information behaviour, trust critically influences knowledge and information sharing process [24]. According to Hislop [25], individuals often refuse to share their information and knowledge once they sense the lack of trust. Connaway [26] elaborated that trust is an important factor for human information seeking and using behaviours. Moreover, Beckinsale and Theodorakopoulos [27] debated trust as an essential ingredient for enterprise-related processes of information and communication technology adoption. Micu et al. [28] illustrated the effect of e-trust in online customer experience for web entrepreneurship. Critics also highlight trust in adopting e-government [29, 30], and e-entrepreneurship [31]. The Technology Adoption Model [TAM: 32] integrates trust to define the users' perception of usefulness, perception of ease of use and favourable attitude with regards to usage of information sources [33]. So far, the importance of trust has benefited entrepreneurship research in several focused determinates. Often in those discussions, trust and its relevance to entrepreneurs' information-seeking behaviours are mentioned too. However, the effect of trust and the conditions under which trust works still face the lack of attention in entrepreneurship research, especially from entrepreneurs' information practices standpoint.

Furthermore, many authors have acknowledged the correlation between respect and trust, as well as its significance for entrepreneurs. Hakanen and Soudunsaari [34] declared that respect is a vital element of the trust-building process. Though, trust and respect have different values, they always act jointly, as a person cannot trust someone whom he/she fails to respect. According to Kuratko [35], entrepreneurs need to earn trust and respect to achieve and maintain their success in careers and businesses. In some cultures, such as South Korea, China, and Japan, respect is often mentioned as a crucial element to create a good impression; thus, trust in the business relationships [36–38]. These two phenomena have been discussed in various academic disciplines, e.g., social and organisational psychology, nursing, ethics, and education, but it has not been sufficiently addressed in the entrepreneurship research.

Considering this gap in the literature, this paper focuses on the significance and relevance of respect and trust in entrepreneurs' information-seeking behaviours and analyses it through social capital theory [34, 39–41]. The results of this paper contribute to information behaviour studies and entrepreneurship research. In particular, this research devotes its focus to an emerging and yet growing stream of research on the role of trust in the success of entrepreneurs. We contribute to the literature by providing an in-depth understanding of social networks in entrepreneurship studies [5, 10]. In doing so, we use the theory of social capital to elucidate entrepreneurial information-seeking activities [41] to examine how trust influences the information-seeking behaviours of entrepreneurs. Additionally, this paper will tackle how respect strengthens it. The following of this paper provides an overview of the relevant and core concepts, including trust, respect, social capital theory, and information-seeking behaviours. Then we present a discussion of the interplay between trust, respect and information-seeking behaviour. Finally, we provide discussion, conclusion and elaborate on the theoretical and practical implications. Recommendations for future studies will also be presented.

2 Definitions and Theoretical Background

2.1 Trust

The literature demonstrates trust as a complex construct, which has been conceptualised and defined through multiple dimensions in different scientific domains. Prominently, the definitions of trust still maintain its availability and relevance in the current research [8, 10, 13, 42–44]. Psychologists perceive trust as an individual trait, or a psychological state, in which a person possesses an attitude or tendency to accept uncertainties [45–56]. From the sociological perspective, trust is a social structure and force [47, 48], as well as a social cohesion for the nature of interpersonal relationships [49, 50]. Social psychologists examine trust as a psychological condition that a person is willing to be vulnerable [51–53] because he/she has a positive expectation in other's motives and/or conduct [54], and mutual interdependence and risk [52, 54, 55]. Sabel [56] argued that trust displays the faith and high hope in others that they will not exploit any adverse selection, moral hazard, holdup, or any other vulnerability. In other words, each member of the trustful relationship agrees to sacrifice his/her short-run and self-interest for joint goals or longer-term objectives [57]. Meanwhile, economists claim the rationale of trust, that a person calculates the possibility of an event based on its commitment to the agency theory [58, 59]. Moreover, other scholars remarked trust through various aspects such as cognitive, emotional and intentional behaviour [1, 60]. The cognitive aspect reflects the belief or an expression of it that the trustor holds towards the trustee. The emotional aspect connects to emotions such as feelings of security, both physically and psychologically [61]. Finally, the intentional behaviour aspect indicates the reliance on other people's words and actions, which is determined by the level of trust within the parties.

Furthermore, trust in business relationships shows a strong belief in only positive outcomes [62, 63]. Mohr and Spekman [64] evoked the reliance characteristics of trust in the business relationships, in which the trustor is reliant on the trustee's words to fulfil its obligation in an exchange. Additionally, Dollinger [65] presented trust as a governance factor for a business owner to overcome the uncertainty or potential risks, which always exist in the commercial transaction. Welter [10] applied trust to business owners' expectations that their partner will act on behalf of their interest, or at least consider those interests, and though they are uncertain about how satisfied they will be with the results, they still hold confidence that they will not be disappointed. Those expectations are based on the attributions that the trustor holds with regards to the trustworthiness of the trustee [52, 66].

Mayer et al. [52] recognised the trustworthiness through three characteristics, including benevolence, competence, and integrity. Benevolence implies willingness. Competence considers the ability to serve another's interests. Integrity refers to the temporal continuity, in which one's readiness and capacity to serve another's interests do not change over time. In other words, a person is trustworthy when he/she shows a consistency (integrity) in proven his/her willingness (benevolent) and ability (competent) to ethically fulfil the trustor's interests [62]. The signal of trustworthiness encourages the trustful behaviours of the entrepreneurs [10, 52]. The trustworthiness of a business partner reveals through personal characteristics, past behaviour, and emotions, such as demonstrated honesty, loyalty, sympathy and empathy [67]. Additionally, it also derives from the community or organisation, i.e., ethnic groups, professions, networks, firms, associations, or whole industries in the form of recommendations [58, 68], reputation, and image [5, 15]. Particularly, in the business world, trust is also gained from the security of political, legal or economic framework, as well as norms, values, and codes of conduct inherent within a society [5]. Often, the entrepreneurs recognise trust through personal evaluation of losses and gains in a relationship (calculative trust) [58, 69], or the social interaction (relational trust) [69, 70]. Others also inspected trust by its forms and types, cognitive-based trust and affect-based trust [71], trust, un-trust, distrust, and mistrust [72], generalised and situational trust [73–75].

2.2 The Concept of Respect

According to Regis and Porto [76], respect is one of the most basic human needs. Dillion [77] defined respect in various forms, from expressing an attitude, a feeling, to following a norm, a duty, an entitlement, a recognition, and a principle. As a centre of moral and political theory, Kant [78] draws the focus of respect on the way one treats others and him/herself. Banks and Gallagher [79] described it as a relation in which the subject properly responds to the object. It is often object-generated rather than wholly subject-generated, as the act of respect is owed to, called for, deserved, elicited, or claimed by the object [77]. This distinguishes respect from other feelings, such as fear or excitement, as they originate wholly from the subject's desires and interests. To illustrate, respect refers to "a deontic experience" [80], which makes it a must-manner in many situations [81, 82]. Moreover, Drummond [83] argued that respect is not simply a fundamental moral emotion, but also an effective response to the other as a rational agent. Respect also regards behavioural components. Through appropriate behaviours, an individual also displays his/her conduct, thought, and feelings towards others or things. Appropriate behaviours cover from engagement to restricting the response in certain ways, which considers being suitable, exemplary, or indebted to a particular object. The performance of respect can vary from supporting, complimenting, obeying, not violating or interfering, and caring [77].

Darwall [84, 85] distinguishes two kinds of respect: recognition respect and appraisal respect. Recognition respect refers to the intention to give evaluation and consideration regarding an object, thus adjust personal behaviours accordingly. The object of recognition respect often relates to laws, dangerous issues, other's feelings, social institutions, or persons in diverse contexts. Whereas, appraisal respect refers to a positive attitude towards a person due to their characteristics or achievements [85]. Langdon [86] adopted respect through four dimensions: (a) social power, (b) social rules, (c) caring and (d) equality and accepting differences.

Regarding the correlation between trust and respect, Meshanko [87] stated that when an individual feel respected, the brain will generate an increased level of neurotransmitters serotonin and oxytocin which are associated with a sense of pleasure, trust, and belongings. Ross and Parks [40] also suggested that respect will lead to the evolvement of a true caring/cared for the relationship which results in trust enhancement between the parties. Additionally, Lucian et al. [88] acknowledged respect as a core to build a safety culture, thus achieving high levels of mutual trust, collaboration, and accountability personally and institutionally. Mineo [89] further affirmed respect as one of the core values that form the foundation of trust in the workplace. The act of respect concerns supporting professional development and showing appreciation, collaboration, and caring for others as individuals with personal lives.

In the entrepreneurship study, respect is an uncommon theme. Although it regularly exists in advice for entrepreneurs that they need to show and earn respect, researchers have not paid sufficient consideration to this domain when addressing factors that influence entrepreneurial success. Literature shows that respect often appears to be crucial in cross-cultural business [36–39]. To illustrate, Jeanne and Tyree [39] emphasised that in Middle Eastern and South Asian Culture, respect is a key to successfully form a business relationship. Precisely, managers from these cultures favour doing business with those who show respect to their values. Respect, thus, support the flow of the relationship. This view is further elaborated by other researchers like [36–38] through different Asian cultures, like Japan, Korea, China. Furthermore, a culture of respect is frequently mentioned in leadership and organisational studies. It positively affects organisational performance, including the effectiveness of teamwork, cooperation communication, and job satisfaction. Every entrepreneur is a leader for their organisation and according to Hess [90], leaders need to show respect to their followers, thus motivate their contribution and commitment to the business.

2.3 Social Capital Theory

Critics concern that the centre of social capital concepts lies within the role of social relations in individual prosperity [91]. Portes [92] nominated social capital as the capacity to secure advantages through membership of social networks and other social structures. Based on Nahapiet and Ghoshal [93], social capital concerns the actual and potential resources gathered from the network of relationships held by an individual or a social unit. Some scholars defined social capital as a privilege to access rare resources apart from accessible resources [91, 94, 95]. Lin [96] further examined social capital theory based on the social network analysis, which emphasises on how the quality of social resources available within an individual social network affect his/her success and achievements. The theory of social capital is expressly rooted in the notion of trusts, norms, informal networks, which recognises social ties as valuable resources and powerful means regarding economic advancement [96]. Social resources available in personal networks stay in either tangible forms, i.e., financial capital, public spaces, private property; or intangible forms, i.e., social status, human and cultural capital, collaboration, information, reputation, credibility, access to networks, social and environmental responsibility [41, 97, 98]. Besides, Luoma-aho [99] compared social capital theory with a metaphor as an investment is required, considering the trustworthy networks and social relations that enable collaboration and reward in economic and social benefits.

Fukuyama [74] and Coleman [100] shared a statement that social capital results from the prevalence of trust in society [74, 100], which makes it a critical factor in social capital theory. Putman [101] also supported this by viewing trust as a vital driving force in the development and operation of social capital. In other words, behaviour within social networks and groups will not be very effective when the trust within is low. Trust is a base for social capital [100, 101] because, without a reasonable level of trust, the relationship, societies, partnership, and mutual commitment which characterise social capital would disappear.

In the entrepreneurship literature, trust, as a relational form of social capital, is imperative for entrepreneurs to deal with the unknown and uncertain environment, which frequently contain potential risks for the business [21–23]. Entrepreneurs often pursue ambiguous, evolving and constructive goals, and the process of entrepreneurship frequently relies on unfamiliar and dysfunctional socio-economic ties [102]. Trust, therefore, helps transform the complicated and structured transactional relations into fluid and informal relationships, as well as creates and develops social capital. To social capital theory, respect shall be considered as an emotional support, appraisal, and affirmation. This thus provides social capital for an individual while strengthening the social ties within it.

2.4 Information Seeking Behaviour

Information-seeking behaviour (ISB) explores how people search, locate and use the information to afford desired information need or fill a gap in knowledge. Specifically, it concerns the seekers' choices regarding where and how to find information, as well as the way they consider, or act based on the information they receive [103]. It examines what a person undergoes when seeking information, including actions, emotions, and attitudes [104]. According to Wilson [105], the ISB analyses human behaviour with respect to sources and channels of information in both active and passive information-seeking and information-use. Furthermore, ISB study is significant especially for the group of high-stakes and high-status occupations [104].

For entrepreneurs, information is requisite for their business to survive and grow [106, 126]. It significantly influences business strategies, operations, and evaluation of activities. Popovič et al. [107] asserted that high-quality information, which is relevant, accurate, and timely, certainly supports managerial decisions, and improve organisational performance. The information; thus, works as a strategic weapon for entrepreneurs to overcome pressure, adapt changes, survive and foster their enterprises in the complex and dynamic business world [108]. Alvarez et al. [109] emphasised the necessity of entrepreneurial continuous information learning processes to assure their competitive position [110]. To illustrate, a constant update on information related to governmental policies like taxation, the business procedure, regulations is fundamental for businesses in all stages [108, 111, 112]. Due to a non-stop increase in information needs and information landscape, entrepreneurial information-seeking behaviours happen professionally and on a daily basis. Additionally, the activities and process of entrepreneurs' information seeking may significantly impact on the outcomes of their decision and later on business success. That is why an understanding of entrepreneurs' information-seeking behaviour is essential. By studying ISB, we learn how entrepreneurs conceptualise information needs, the process of the information sources' selection and their preferences towards omnichannel of information retrieval. The results of the ISB study serve as a framework for designing and developing information packages, as well as information services that directly contribute to entrepreneurial success.

Furthermore, research has shown an inclusive reliance of entrepreneurs on their networks when seeking information [113, 114]. Social relationships serve as preferred sources for business information, while trust and trustworthiness are embedded within those. Trust positively influences the success of the relational exchange for information. Besides, due to the unstable and hazardous characteristics of the business nature and the lack of resources for making only rational choices, trust generates a sense of safety for entrepreneurs. Therefore, during their information seeking process, entrepreneurs intentionally consider the strength of their social relationships (i.e., trust) for choosing their information sources, and the selected ones are those that they trust. Meanwhile, a show of respect is vital in all behaviours as it is the basis of all relationships in society explores how people search, locate and use the information to afford desired information need or fill a gap in knowledge. Specifically, it concerns the seekers' choices regarding where and how to find information, as well as the way they consider, or act based on the information they receive [103]. It examines what a person undergoes when seeking information, including actions, emotions, and attitudes [104]. According to Wilson [105], the ISB analyses human behaviour with respect to sources and channels of information in both active and passive information-seeking and information-use. ISB study thus is significant especially for the group of high-stakes and high-status occupations [104].

3   The Interplay Between Trust, Respect and Information Seeking Behaviour Through Social Capital Theory

Based on Johnson [41], the social capital theory is necessary to provide an understanding of the structural and relational dimensions of information-seeking behaviour. The theory adoption helps us to study the effect of social structure on information access and its flow. By determining the relationship between the information seekers and information sources, including the social position of the information source, as well as concerning others within the network, the theory provides a framework for monitoring the information behaviours. For instance, the theory is employed to explain the information source preferences. People intend to seek information from those who hold strong social ties with them or those whom they have established trust and respect. Trust reflects the bonds within a social relationship. Many scholars reported that trust encourages and facilitates the sharing of business information [9, 10, 23, 25, 115].

Through social capital theory, the evaluation of social cost/risk explains the preference of information sources. People try to avoid embarrassment, loss of face, the revelation of incompetence while thriving to social benefits (e.g., making an impression, relationship building) and other factors such as willingness to share the closeness [116, 117]. In information-seeking, the information seeker chooses an information source depending on their perspective towards the sources, which trust plays as an influential factor [118]. The trustful behaviours; therefore, implies the information seekers (trustors)'s belief that the information sources (trustees) have the required information and the confidence of understandability that the information seekers shall accurately interpret the messages, and importantly, they are willing to give entire and honest information to the seekers. The degree of trust decides the level of interpersonal interactions [119]. Furthermore, with trust, people are more confident in predicting and expecting the other's actions, thus, more open to interacting in the relationship [110]. Savolainen [120] also argued that people often prefer to count on close ones as information sources because of their high trust for them. Additionally, today the information is blooming due to the development of Internet and ICT, people enter the era of "fake news" in which they are sceptical with all information that comes to them [121]. Trust then becomes an important element in nurturing and facilitating the level of participation and sharing behaviour for information in online communities as when the information seekers trust the information source, they become more confident in the information that it brings. For entrepreneurs, they habitually develop and rely on their informal networks and these are trusted sources of business information, advice, and learning [113]. Smith and Lohrke [7] clarified that people are more willing to give and receive information when trust exists and plays as an instrumental in supporting the feeling of safety while reducing uncertainty, i.e., the absence of a contract, or guarantee.

Regarding the role of respect in information-seeking behaviours, it is rather an essential manner to create trust and good harmony between the information seekers and information sources, particularly among interpersonal relationships [88, 89]. This also refers to the social cost/risk as Borgatti and Cross [116] stressed the consequence of comfortability for information seekers. Silver [122] also showed that people refuse to ask information when they sense the neglection, or in other words, being disrespected. Furthermore, conduct respect plays an essential role in entrepreneurship regarding social capital. Respect contributes to develop and maintain the social capital for an entrepreneur, which in return grants him/her a greater choice of information sources. Johnson [41] pointed out that social relationships provide an individual with a better possibility to attain the relevant and valuable information to satisfy personal information need. Additionally, an enriched social capital allows information seekers to extend their network and meet people from different social and professional backgrounds [123]. Su et al. [4] also emphasised this benefit as those who have information access to a variety of sources have a greater chance of perceiving better opportunities.

4 Implications, and Recommendations for Future Studies

In this paper, we address two important components in entrepreneurship domain, i.e., trust and respect to assess entrepreneur's information-seeking behaviour using social capital theory as a theoretical lens. The results of this paper provide an overview of the literature highlighting the importance of trust and respect in the entrepreneurs' information-seeking behaviours. The results indicate that information is vital for entrepreneurs in all stages of their careers. Therefore, the understanding of their information behaviours generally, or their information-seeking behaviours particularly will contribute to the implementation of a supportive information environment for entrepreneurship. We further contribute to the literature by showing that trust and respect are fundamental aspects that influence entrepreneurs' preference of information sources. Trust and respect act as predominant factors for entrepreneurs to build and advance various relationships. It also encourages entrepreneurs to overcome their uncertainty and their shortage of resources for making rational choices. Through the theory of social capital, we further show that the influence of trust in entrepreneurial sources selection relates to the seekers' perception of social cost/risk. Expressly, trust appears to be entrepreneurial shields from negative sequences of their social interactions. In addition, it ensures the quantity and quality of information that entrepreneurs can obtain from their information sources. Therefore, we assume that maintaining trust at any cost will naturally bring benefits to the firms and their operations.

In terms of respect, we share a discussion on a subtle and scarce domain in both entrepreneurship and information-seeking behaviour study. While explaining its concept, we also disclose respect as an instrument that nurtures trust within the relationship and fosters the extension of social capital for entrepreneurs. Noticeably, respect reduces social cost/risk when generating a supportive environment within the participants. Respect is essential for both information seekers and providers to pay attention and perform throughout their communication. Conclusively, we also recognise fundamental gaps in the extant literature, suggesting fascinating avenues for future research.

This paper profoundly reviewed prior studies that have investigated the role of trust and respect in entrepreneurs' information-seeking behaviours. From the literature, it seems that there is a lack of research regarding this topic in the field of entrepreneurship. Additionally, most of the literature only pays attention to the benefits of trust generally, including transferring information, acquiring resources, investments, promoting cooperation and substituting formal institutions. Our findings point out that information behaviour is rather a sub-concern than a mere focus of the entrepreneurship literature. Therefore, for future studies, other scholars should work on the empirical research on how trust influences the information-seeking behaviours of the entrepreneurs, i.e., their preferences towards information sources [126], their ignorance, as well as their intention to use the information sources. As entrepreneurs are also trustees and may act as the information sources, we suggest further studies to be conducted on how entrepreneurs build and maintain their trustworthiness in terms of interpersonal and virtual relationships through social media. This becomes even more critical for enterprises in the era of abundance of information where the virality of fake news in digital networks and the Internet causes the absence of trust and triggers the recovery of it. Future studies could also investigate the downside of trust in information-seeking behaviours, i.e., over-trust, mistrust, and distrust problem, the possible consequences on the business and alternative solutions on how avoid it [72, 124, 125]. Moreover, despite that digital information sources become more popular for the entrepreneurs and trust shows its importance in the adoption or resistance of these sources, this area still faces the lack of research. Therefore, future researchers would benefit from exploring how trust influences the entrepreneurial intention and usage behaviour of digital information sources. Additionally, it is essential to draw investigations on what affects trust in information-seeking behaviours, i.e., culture, personal traits, the role of security, privacy and risk perceptions.

Furthermore, entrepreneurship literature seems to neglect the study in terms of respect. It is only recognised in cross-culture study for entrepreneurship and the organisational performance, which highlight every member's conduct of respect. Besides, it is also rarely mentioned in the information behaviour literature. So far, discussion regarding respect is quite narrow and insufficient. Scholars often consider it as fundamental for building trust but fail to monitor its independent effects on relationship formation and enhancement. The absence of respect in entrepreneurship and information behaviour study hereby opens a broad scope of subjects for future research. Finally, this paper is limited to a literature discussion. The paper may also lack a rigorous approach to endogenous issues derived from the interplay between trust, respect, and entrepreneur.

References

1. Goel, S., Karri, R.: Entrepreneurs, effectual logic, and over-trust. Entrepreneurship Theory Practice, **30**(4), 477–493 (2006)
2. Kohtamäki, M., Kekäle, T., Viitala, R.: Trust and innovation: from spin-off idea to stock exchange. Creativity Innov. Manage. **13**(12), 75–88 (2004)
3. Smallbone, D., Lyon, F.: A note on trust, networks, social capital and entrepreneurial behaviour. In: Höhmann, H., Welter, F. (eds.) Entrepreneurial Strategies and Trust: Structure and Evolution of Entrepreneurial Behavioural Patterns in East and West European Environments—Concept and Considerations, pp. 19–24. Forschungsstelle Osteuropa Bremen, Arbeite papiere und Materialien, Bremen, Germany (2002)
4. Su, Y., Zahra, S., Li, R., Fan, D.: Trust, poverty, and subjective wellbeing among Chinese entrepreneurs. Entrepreneurship Regional Dev. **32**(1–2), 221–245 (2020)
5. Welter, F., Smallbone, D.: Exploring the role of trust in entrepreneurial activity. Entrepreneurship Theory Practice **30**(4), 465–475 (2006)
6. Sarasvathy, S., Venkataraman, N.D., Velamuri, R.: Three views of entrepreneurial opportunity. In: Ács, R.J., Audretsch, D.B. (eds.) Handbook of Entrepreneurship Research, 141–160. Springer, Boston (2003). https://doi.org/10.1007/978-1-4419-1191-9_4
7. Smith, D.A., Lohrke, F.T.: Entrepreneurial network development: trusting in the process. J. Bus. Res. **6**(4), 315–322 (2008)
8. Wang, S., Shang, G., Zhang, S.: Corporate governance and evolution of trust in entrepreneurial networks: a case study of NVC Lighting Holding Ltd. Chinese Manage. Stud. **13**(4), 939–966 (2019)
9. Zolin, R., Kuckertz, A., Kautonen, T.: Human resource flexibility and strong ties in entrepreneurial teams. J. Bus. Res. **64**(10), 1097–1103 (2011)
10. Welter, F.: All you need is trust? A critical review of the trust and entrepreneurship literature. Int. Small Bus. J. **30**(3), 193–212 (2012)
11. Maxwell, A.L., Lévesque, M.: Trustworthiness: a critical ingredient for entrepreneurs seeking investors. Entrepreneurship Theory Practice, **10**, 1057–1080 (2011)
12. Strätling, R., Wijbenga, F.H., Dietz, G.: The impact of contracts on trust in entrepreneur–venture capitalist relationships. Int. Small Bus. J. **55**, 81–106 (2011)
13. Xiao, L.: How lead investors build trust in the specific context of a campaign: a case study of equity crowdfunding in China. Int. J. Entrepreneurial Behav. Res. **26**(2), 203–223 (2019)
14. Howorth, C., Moro, A.: Trust within entrepreneur bank relationships: Insights from Italy. Entrepreneurship Theory Practice **30**(4), 495–517 (2006)
15. Inka, H., Orrensalo, T.: Brand image as a facilitator of relationship initiation: case studies from business practice. In: Koporcic, N., Ivanova-Gongne, M., Nyström, A.-G., Törnroos, J.-Å. (eds.) Developing Insights on Branding in the B2B Context: Case Studies from Business Practice, pp. 97–112. Emerald Publishing Limited, Bingley (2018)
16. Ben, A.K.: Business coaching for Tunisian entrepreneurs: features and success factors. Global Knowl. Memory Commun. (2020). https://doi.org/10.1108/GKMC-01-2019-0004
17. Ji, C., Chen, Q., Zhuo, N.: Enhancing consumer trust in short food supply chains: the case evidence from three agricultural e-commerce companies in China. J. Agribus. Dev. Emerg. Econ. **10**(1), 103–116 (2019)
18. Fink, M., Kessler, A.: Cooperation, trust and performance: empirical results from three countries. British J. Manage. **21**(2), 469–483 (2010)

19. Eddleston, K.A., Chrisman, J.J., Steier, L.P., Chua, J.H.: Governance and trust in family firms: an introduction. Entrepreneurship Theory Practice **34**(6), 1043–1056 (2010)

20. Fink, M.: Trust-based cooperation relationships between SMEs: are family firms any different? Int. J. Entrepreneurial Ventur. **1**(4), 382–397 (2010)

21. Shi, H., Shepherd, D., Schmidts, T.: Social capital in entrepreneurial family businesses: the role of trust. Int. J. Entrepreneurial Behav. Res. **21**(6), 814–841 (2015)

22. Manolova, T.S., Gyoshev, B.S., Manev, I.M.: The role of interpersonal trust for entrepreneurial exchange in a transition economy. Int. J. Emerg. Markets **2**(2), 107–122 (2007)

23. Puffer, S.M., McCarthy, D.J., Boisot, M.: Entrepreneurship in Russia and China: the impact of formal institutional voids. Entrepreneurship Theory Practice **34**(3), 441–467 (2010)

24. Chow, W.S., Chan, L.S.: Social network, social trust and shared goals in organizational knowledge sharing. Inf. Manage. **45**(7), 458–465 (2008)

25. Hislop, D.: Knowledge Management in Organizations: A Critical Introduction, 3rd edn. Oxford University Press, Oxford (2013)

26. Connaway, L.S.: The library in the life of the user: engaging with people where they live and learn. In: OCLC Research, Ohio. USA (2015)

27. Beckinsale, M., Ram, M., Theodorakopoulos, N.: ICT adoption and ebusiness development: Understanding ICT adoption amongst ethnic minority businesses. Int. Small Bus. J. **29**(3), 193–219 (2011)

28. Micu, A.E., Bouzaabia, O., Bouzaabia, R., Micu, A., Capatina, A.: Online customer experience in e-retailing: implications for web entrepreneurship. Int. Entrepreneurship Manage. J. **15**(2), 651–675 (2019). https://doi.org/10.1007/s11365-019-00564-x

29. Al Khattab, A., Al-Shalabi, H., Al-Rawad, M., Al-Khattab, K., Hamad, F.: The effect of trust and risk perception on citizen's intention to adopt and use e-government services in jordan. J. Serv. Sci. Manage. **8**, 279–290 (2015)

30. Mpinganjira, M.: META-RELQUAL construct validation: a South African study. African J. Econ. Manage. Stud. **6**(4), 453–465 (2014)

31. Bennani, A., Oumlil, R.: Acceptance of E-Entrepreneurship by future entrepreneurs in developing countries: case of Morocco. J. Entrepreneurship: Res. Practice **2014** (2014). Article ID 700742. https://doi.org/10.5171/2014.700742

32. Davis, F.D.: User acceptance of information systems: the technology acceptance model (TAM). Int. J. Man-Mach. Stud. **1993**(38), 475–487 (1987)

33. Kumar, A., Sikdar, P., Alam, Md.M.: E-retail adoption in emerging markets: a perspective on predictive constructs. In: Mehdi Khosrow-Pour, D.B.A. (ed.) Entrepreneurship, Collaboration, and Innovation in the Modern Business Era, Business Science Reference. IGI Global, USA (2018)

34. Hakanen, M., Soudunsaari, A.: Building trust in high-performing teams. Technol. Innov. Manage. Rev. **2**, 6 (2012)

35. Kuratko, D.F.: Entrepreneurship: Theory, Process, and Practice, 8th edn. South-Western Cengage Learning, Mason (2009)

36. Grzegorczyk, M.: The role of culture-moderated social capital in technology transfer – insights from Asia and America. Technol. Forecast. Soc. Change **143**, 132–141 (2019)

37. Khan, Y.: Tips on doing business in Japan. Global Bus. Lang. **2**(16), 187–196 (2010)

38. Mochklas, M., Fatihudin, D.: Analysis of organizational culture company South Korea in Indonesia. Int. J. Manage. (IJM) **8**(4), 66–74 (2017)

39. Jeanne, B., Tyree, M.: Research: How to Build Trust with Business Partners from Other Cultures. Harvard Business Review (2020). https://hbr.org/2020/01/research-how-to-build-trust-with-business-partners-from-other-cultures

40. Ross, D.G., Parks, M.: Mutual respect in an ethic of care: a collaborative essay on power, trust, and stereotyping. Teach. Ethics, **18**(1), 15 (2018)

41. Johnson, C.A.: Nan Lin's theory of social capital. In: Fisher, K.E., Erdelez, S., McKenie, L. (E.F.) (eds.) Theories of Information Behaviour, 323–327, Information Today Inc., Melford, New Jersey (2006)

42. Alfred, S., Wen, X.: The importance of trust in the development of entrepreneurship. Int. J. Adv. Res. Technol. **2**(12), 230–244 (2013)

43. Eddleston, K.A., Morgan, R.M.: Trust, commitment and relationships in family business: challenging conventional wisdom. J. Family Bus. Strategy **5**(3), 213–216 (2014)

44. Mickiewicz, T., Rebmann, A.: Entrepreneurship as trust. Found Trends Entrepreneurship **16**(3), 244–309 (2020)

45. Erikson, E.H.: Identity: Youth and crisis. Norton, New York (1968)

46. Rotter, J.B.: A new scale for the measurement of interpersonal trust. J. Personal. **35**, 651–665 (1967)

47. Garfinkel, H.: Studies in Ethnomethodology. Prentice-Hall, Englewood Cliffs (1967)

48. Luhmann, N.: Trust and Power. Wiley, New York (1979)

49. Granovetter, M.: Economic action and social structure: the problem of embeddedness. Am. J. Sociol. **91**, 481–510 (1985)

50. Zucker, L.G.: Production of trust: institutional sources of economic structure, 1840–1920. Res. Organ. Behav. **8**, 53–11 (1986)

51. Giddens, A.: Modernity and Self-identity: Self and Society in the Late Modern Age. Polity Press, Cambridge (1991)

52. Mayer, R.C., Davis, J.H., Schoorman, F.D.: An integrative model of organizational trust. Acad. Manage. Rev. **15**, 709–734 (1995)

53. Rousseau, D.M., Sitkin, S.B., Burt, R.S., Camerer, C.: Not so different after all: a cross-discipline view of trust. Acad. Manage. Rev. **23**(3), 393–404 (1998)

54. Das, T.K., Teng, B.S.: Between trust and control: developing confidence in partner cooperation in alliances. Acad. Manage. J. **23**, 491–512 (1998)

55. Das, T.K., Teng, B.S.: Trust, control and risk in strategic alliances: an integrated framework. Organ. Stud. **22**, 251–284 (2001)

56. Sabel, C.F.: Studied trust: building new forms of co-operation in a volatile economy. Hum. Relat. **46**(9), 1133–1170 (1993)

57. Righetti, F., Impett, E.: Sacrifice in close relationships: motives, emotions, and relationship outcomes. Soc. Personal. Psychol. Compass **11**(10), e12342 (2017). https://doi.org/10.1111/spc3.12342

58. Williamson, O.E.: Calculativeness, trust, and economic organization. J. Law Econ. **34**, 453–502 (1993)

59. Dasgupta, P.: Trust and cooperation among economic agents. Philos. Trans. R. Soc. London B Biol. Sci. **364**(1533), 3301–3309 (2009)

60. Johnson, D.S., Grayson, K.: Cognitive and affective trust in service relationships. J. Bus. Res. J. Bus. Res. **58**(4), 500–507 (2005)

61. Wicks, A.C., Berman, S.L., Jones, T.M.: The structure of optimal trust: Moral and strategic implications. Acad. Manage. Rev. **24**(1), 99–116 (1999)

62. McKnight, D.H., Cummings, L.L., Chervany, N.L.: Initial trust formation in new organizational relationships. Acad. Manage. Rev. **23**(3), 473–490 (1998)

63. Anderson, J.C., Narus, J.A.: A model of distributor firm and manufacturer firm working partnership. Marketing **54**, 48–58 (1990)

64. Mohr, J., Spekman, R.: Characteristics of partnership success: partnership attributes, communication behaviour and conflict resolution techniques. Strategic Manage. J. **15**, 135–152 (1994)

65. Dollinger, M.J.: Entrepreneurship: Strategies and Resources. Prentice Hall, Upper Saddle River (2003)

66. Pirson, M.A., Malhotra, D.: Foundations of organizational trust: what matters to different stakeholders? Organ. Sci. **22**(4), 1087–1104 (2011)
67. Nooteboom, B.: Trust: Forms, Foundations, Functions, Failures, and Figures. Edward Elgar, Cheltenham (2002)
68. Weng, J.S., Miao, C., Goh, A., Shen, Z.: Trust-based agent community for collaborative recommendation. In: Conference 5th International Joint Conference on Autonomous Agents and Multiagent Systems (AAMAS 2006), Hakodate, Japan (2006)
69. Poppo, L., Zhou, K.Z., Li, J.J.: When can you trust "Trust?" Calculative Trust, Relational Trust, and Supplier Performance. Strategic Manage. J. **1**, 15 (2014)
70. Bromiley, P., Harris, J.: Trust, transaction cost economics, and mechanisms. In: Bachmann, R., Zaheer, A. (eds.) Handbook of Trust Research, 124-143. Edward Elgar Publishing, Northampton (2006)
71. McAllister, D.J.: Affect- and cognition-based trust as foundations for interpersonal cooperation in organizations. Acad. Manage. J. **38**(1), 24–59 (1985)
72. Marsh, S., Dibben, M.R.: Trust, untrust, distrust and mistrust – an exploration of the dark(er) side. In: International Conference on Trust Management, iTrust 2005: Trust Management, pp. 17–33 (2005)
73. Ding, Z., Au, K., Chiang, F.: Social trust and angel investors' decision: a multilevel analysis across nations. J. Bus. Ventur. **30**, 307–321 (2015)
74. Fukuyama, F.: Trust: The Social Virtues and the Creation of Prosperity. The Free Press, New York (1995)
75. Kwon, S., Arenius, P.: Nations of entrepreneurs: a social capital perspective. J. Bus. Ventur. **25**(3), 315–330 (2010)
76. Regis, L., Porto, I.S.: Basic human needs of nursing professional: situations of (dis)satisfaction at work. Rev. Esc. Enferm, **45**, 2 (2011)
77. Dillion, R.S.: Respect for persons, identity, and information technology. Ethics Inf. Technol. **12**, 17–28 (2010)
78. Kant, I.: The Groundwork of Metaphysics of Moral. Harper Torchbooks, New York (1964)
79. Banks, S., Gallagher, A.: Ethics in Professional Life: Virtues for Health and Social Care. Palgrave MacMillan, New York (2009)
80. Birch, T.H.: Moral consider ability and universal consideration. Environ. Ethics **15**, 313–332 (1993)
81. Wood, A.W.: Kant's Ethical Thought. Cambridge University Press, Cambridge (1999)
82. Rawls, J.: Lectures on the history of moral philosophy. In: Herman, B. (ed.) Harvard University Press, Cambridge (2000)
83. Drummond, J.J.: Respect as a moral emotion: a phenomenological approach. Husserl Stud.s **22**, 1–27 (2006)
84. Darwall, S.: Two kinds of respect. Ethics, 88, 36–49. Reprinted in Dillon, R.S. (ed.) Dignity, Character, and Self-Respect. Routledge, New York (1977)
85. Darwall, S.: Sentiment, care, and respect. Theory Res. Educ. **8**, 153–162 (2010)
86. Langdon, S.W.: Conceptualizations of respect: qualitative and quantitative of four (five)themes. J. Psychol. **141**, 469–484 (2007)
87. Meshanko, P.: The Respect Effect: Leveraging Emotions, Culture, and Neuroscience to Build a Better Business. Dog Ear Publishing, Indianapolis (2012)
88. Lucian, L., Miles, S., Jules, D., Robert, M., Edgman-Levitan, S., Meyer, G., Healy, G.: Perspective: a culture of respect, part 2: creating a culture of respect. Acad. Med. J. Assoc. Am. Med. Colleges **87**, 853–858 (2012)
89. Mineo, D.L.: The importance of trust in leadership. Res. Manage. Rev. **20**(1), 1–6 (2014)
90. Hess, E.: Growing an Entrepreneurial Business: Concepts & Cases. Stanford University Press, Stanford, California (2011)

91. Bourdieu, P.: The forms of capital. In: Richardson, J.G. (ed.) Handbook of Theory and Research for the Sociology of Education, pp. 241–258. Greenwood, New York (1985)

92. Portes, A.: Social capital: its origins and applications in modern sociology. Ann. Rev. Sociol. **24**, 1–24 (1998)

93. Nahapiet, J., Ghoshal, S.: Social capital, intellectual capital, and the organizational advantage. Acad. Manage. Rev. **23**, 242–266 (1998)

94. Adler, P.S., Kwon, S.W.: Social capital: prospects for a new concept. Acad. Manage. Rev. **27**, 17–40 (2002)

95. Lin, N.: Social Capital: A Theory of Social Structure and Action. University Press, Cambridge (2001)

96. Bhandari, H., Yasunobu, K.: What is social capital? a comprehensive review of the concept. Asian J. Soc. Sci. **37**, 480–510 (2009)

97. Dean, A., Kretschmer, M.: Can ideas be capital? factors of production in the postindustrial economy: a review and critique. Acad. Manage. Rev. **32**(2), 573–594 (2007)

98. Luoma-aho, V., et al.: Added value of intangibles for organizational innovation. Hum. Technol. **8**(1), 7–23 (2012)

99. Luoma-aho, V.: Social capital theory. In: C. Carroll (ed.) The SAGE encyclopedia of corporate reputation, pp. 760–762. SAGE Publications Inc., Thousand Oaks (2016)

100. Coleman, J.S.: Social capital in the creation of human capital. Am. J. Sociol. **94**, S95–S120 (1988)

101. Putman, R.D.: Bowling Alone: The Collapse and Revival of American Community. Simon and Schuster, New York (2000)

102. Sarasvathy, S.D.: Causation and effectuation: toward a theoretical shift from economic inevitability to entrepreneurial contingency. Acad. Manage. Rev. **26**(2), 243–288 (2001)

103. Choo, W.C.: The Knowing Organization: How organizations use information to construct meaning, create knowledge, and make decisions. Oxford University Press (2005)

104. Case, O.D.: Looking for information: A survey of research on information seeking, needs and behaviour, 3rd edn. Emerald, UK (2012)

105. Wilson, T.D.: Human Information Behaviour. Informing Science. Special Issue on Inf. Sci. Res. **2**, 2 (2000)

106. Machado, H.: Growth of small businesses: a literature review and perspectives of studies. Gest. Prod., São Carlos, **23**(2), 419–432 (2016)

107. Popovič, A., Hackney, R., Tassabehji, R., Castelli, M.: The impact of big data analytics on firms' high value business performance. Inf. Syst. Front. **20**(2), 209–222 (2016). https://doi. org/10.1007/s10796-016-9720-4

108. Heilbrunn, S., Kushnirovich, N.: The impact of policy on immigrant entrepreneurship and businesses practice in Israel. Int. J. Public Sector Manage. **21**(7), 693–703 (2008)

109. Alvarez, G.J., Raeside, R., Jones, B.W.: The importance of analysis and planning in customer relationship marketing: Verification of the need for customer intelligence and modelling. Database Market. Customer Strategy Manage. **13**(3), 222–230 (2006)

110. Najat, B.: Importance of customer knowledge in business organizations. Int. J. Acad. Res. Bus. Soc. Sci. **7**(11), 175–187 (2017)

111. Akinso, A.: Successful Strategies for the Survival of Business Owners in Nigeria. Walden Dissertations and Doctoral Studies Collection, Walden University (2018)

112. Capella, A.: Translating ideas into action: the policy entrepreneur role at the public policy process. XXII World Congress of Political Science – Reordering Power, Shifting Boundaries, Madrid: International Political Science Association (2012)

113. Fielden, S.L., Hunt, C.: Online coaching: an alternative source of social support for female entrepreneurs during venture creation. Int. Small Bus. J. **29**(4), 345–359 (2011)

114. Greve, A., Salaff, J.W.: Social networks and entrepreneurship. Entrepreneurship: Theory and Practice, **28**(1), 1–22 (2003)

115. Welter, F., Smallbone, D.: Institutional perspectives on entrepreneurial behaviour in challenging environments. J. Small Bus. Manage. **49**(1), 107–125 (2011)
116. Borgatti, S.P., Cross, R.: A relational view of information seeking and learning in social networks. Manag. Knowl. Organ.: Creat. Retain. Transferr. Knowl. **49**(4), 432–445 (2003)
117. Kauer, S.D., Mangan, C., Sanci, L.: Do online mental health services improve help-seeking for young people? A systematic review. J. Med. Internet Res. **16**(3), 66 (2014)
118. Hertzum, M., Andersern, H., Andersen, V., Hasen, C.: Trust in information sources: seeking information from people, documents, and virtual agents. Interact. Comput. **14**(5), 575–599 (2002)
119. Borum, R.: The Science of Interpersonal Trust. Mental Health Law & Policy Faculty Publication (2010)
120. Savolainen, R.: Approaches to socio-cultural barriers to information seeking. Library Inf. Sci. Res. **38**(1), 52–59 (2016)
121. Albright, J.: Welcome to the era of fake news. Media Commun. **5**(2), 87–89 (2017)
122. Silver, M.P.: Patient perspectives on online health information and communication with doctors: a qualitative study of patients 50 years old and over. J. Med. Internet Res. **17**(1), 19 (2015)
123. Fisher, K.E., Durrance, J.C., Hinton, M.B.: Information grounds and the use of need-based services by immgrats in Queen. NY: a context-based, outcome evaluation approach. J. Am. Soc. Inf. Sci. Technol. **55**, 754–766 (2004)
124. Jukka, M., Blomqvist, K., Li, P.P., Gan, C.: Trust-distrust balance: trust ambivalence in Sino-Western B2B relationships. Cross Cult. Strategic Manage. **24**(3), 482–507 (2017)
125. Huvila, I.: Distrust, mistrust, untrust and information practices. In: Proceedings of ISIC, the Information Behaviour Conference, Zadar, Croatia, 20–23 September 2016: Part 2. Information Research vol. 22, no. 1, paper isic1617 (2017)
126. Nikou, S., Brännback, M.E., Orrensalo, T.P., Widén, G.: Social media and entrepreneurship: exploring the role of digital source selection and information literacy. In: Schjoedt, L., Brännback, M.E., Carsrud, A.L. (eds.) Understanding Social Media and Entrepreneurship. EDE, pp. 29–46. Springer, Cham (2020). https://doi.org/10.1007/978-3-030-43453-3_3

Friend or Foe: Society in the Area of Tension Between Free Data Movement and Data Protection

Blockchain Ethics: A Systematic Literature Review of Blockchain Research

Sami Hyrynsalmi[1], Sonja M. Hyrynsalmi[1(✉)], and Kai K. Kimppa[2]

[1] Department of Software Engineering, LUT University, Lahti, Finland
{sami.hyrynsalmi,sonja.hyrynsalmi}@lut.fi
[2] Turku School of Economics, University of Turku, Turku, Finland
kai.kimppa@utu.fi

Abstract. Blockchain is a recent development in technology which allows a cryptographically secured, decentralised and distributed storage of data. The technology innovation was done as a part of and became familiar through Bitcoin cryptocurrency, where it is used to openly store currency transactions among its users. Whereas a majority of recent research and development work of blockchain has been in a number of different cryptocurrency applications, the technology itself has been proposed and used in various domains ranging from open contracts to electronic voting. As the technology has potentially a remarkable power to shape the modern digital societies, its usage possesses several ethical questions. To study the state of the art in *blockchain ethics* research, this study present a systematic literature study (n = 26) on the phenomenon. The results show that the area is swiftly maturing, yet there is a call for concrete usable tools—for the practitioners and scholars—and deeper understanding of relevant ethical concerns.

Keywords: Blockchain · Ethics · Systematic literature review · eSociety

1 Introduction

The idea of blockchain, blocks that are linked using cryptography, was presented 2008 in a white paper written by an anonymous person or persons under the name Satoshi Nakamoto [21]. In that white paper, Nakamoto conceptualised the idea of cryptographically secured chain of blocks, which was presented already in 1991 by Haber and Stornetta [12]. Cryptography is a key element of any strong information security system, because it allows protection for sensitive information as decentralised and distributed storage of data. Therefore cryptography has become a critical element of international trade, investments and e-commerce [23]. The core concept of blockchain is that it uses public-key cryptography and these public keys are never tied to a real-world identity. In this kind of crypto-economy transaction, digital tokens, usually referred to as coins, are transferred using the digital signature of a hash function [22].

© Springer Nature Switzerland AG 2020
M. Cacace et al. (Eds.): WIS 2020, CCIS 1270, pp. 145–155, 2020.
https://doi.org/10.1007/978-3-030-57847-3_10

The most common example of blockchain is Bitcoin, a digital cash and decentralised peer-to-peer digital currency, which was already represented to the world in Nakamoto's white paper and created after the publication of the paper [21]. Bitcoin is the most used example of blockchain technologies and that has lead to that the terminology of blockchain and Bitcoin can sometimes be confusing— this can be interpreted as a sign that the industry is still trying to shape and establish itself and find new paths to grow [24]. Some mixing can come from that you can refer to blockchain or Bitcoin for any parts of the concept of blockchain: Blockchain 1.0., the digital payment system and currency and the protocol and technology behind cryptocurrency, Blockchain 2.0., smart contracts and financial applications using blockchain or Blockchain 3.0., other blockchain applications and implementations than just financial, for example blockchain solutions in life science and governmental actions [24].

Since the conception of blockchain as a method to implement a digital cryptocurrency a decade ago, the underlying innovation has been accepted and adapted into various different fields [cf. 13, 18]. For example, new product and service ideas involving implementation of blockchain technology has been proposed from e-voting to logistics management, and from e-commerce solutions to the digitalisation of agriculture.

It has been seen that blockchain offers a wide selection of future opportunities and the revolution of this system, which will create distributed consensus for the digital world, has just begun. Although Bitcoin is the most common example of blockchain, both financial and non-financial areas are finding blockchain technology and concepts useful. The adoption of blockchain has been rapid and even big companies such as Nasdaq and Microsoft are already using blockchain technologies in their daily operations. [6] It has been stated that now is the time to look at blockchain beyond Bitcoin, because blockchain capabilities are almost unlimited [29].

However, when technology is designed, it always has inbuilt values [28]. Most of those values are not necessarily ethical values [20], but rather other values, such as communication which is inbuilt in our mobile devices. But quite often, if not always, some of those values either are directly moral values or at least have moral consequences [28]. Technologies are not neutral—often they are not meant to be either good or evil [17], but can have such consequences none-the-less [28].

Please consider the following small example on this. Atom energy is not in theory an 'evil' technology, but atom bombs came out of it anyway, and it is hard to claim that atom bombs have toehr than two purposes: fear and destruction—fear of retribution with them, and if retribution (or first strike) is enacted, massive amounts of death and suffering. The example is of course quite drastic, but we hope it illustrates the point clearly.

Technologies such as mobile technologies are more subtle; but for example currently in the COVID-19 crisis, it has both been suggested, and also implemented that mobile devices are used for purposes they were not specifically designed for: for tracking our travel to presumably only track the spread of the virus. Suddenly it is "ok" for us to lose what little of our privacy we still have for "security". Thus, it is of utmost importance to look at the various values in technology and analyze which of them are ethically relevant and which are not, and see to it that those values which are, are taken into account in the design when possible, and either strengthened if they are positive values—or eliminated if they are morally negative.

1.1   Research Objective

The above discussion dilemma of a new technological innovation, with its underlying ethical questions, conquering the new domain areas of industries and governmental services motivates this study. That is, the aim of this paper is to shed light on the ethical considerations relating to blockchain technology. For this study, we focus purely on academic discourse concerning blockchain. Specifically, this paper focuses on the following questions:

RQ1 What is the state of the *blockchain ethics* research?
RQ2 What are the most commonly used tools, methods and frameworks for *blockchain ethics* analysis?

For this study, we define *blockchain ethics* as an ethical studies of blockchain technology, its application or moral philosophy questions in organisations, or larger entities, caused by the usage of blockchain technologies and solutions. To answer to the presented question, we employ a systematic literature review method [16] to collect the primary data for the study. We collected the primary articles from Elsevier's Scopus database (n = 26) and analyse them.

1.2   Related Studies

The current state of blockchain research overall has been fascinating researchers and there are numerous systematic literature reviews to map and find new directions for the future research. In a systematic literature review made by Yli-Huumo, Ko, Choi, Park, and Smolander [30], the researchers found out that large amount of blockchain research is focusing on the topics of privacy and security issues. The research focus has been focusing around the Bitcoin, although researchers point out that to enable the large scale implementation of blockchain for other areas, such as life science or arts, requires more detailed research about the possibilities, challenges and learnings from blockchain technologies. The lack of the critical mass of blockchain solutions has been holding the deeper research of blockchain technologies, but as the blockchain solution became more everyday in different environments, that can lead to new research directions.

Ethics of blockchain has also interested researchers but the way they have been handling the topic of ethics has varied. The most similar work for us has been published by Tang, Xiong, Becerril-Arreola, and Iyer [27]. The authors conducted a literature review and deducted a conceptual framework for blockchain ethics. The model is a three-by-three matrix, where one axis refers to level of review (micro, meso or macro) and the other axis refers to development from technologies to applications, and finally to ethical impacts of the technical choices. While the study by Tang et al. [27] is a literature review, they do not report the numbers of primary studies found, handled or included. In addition, the study does not have a section discussing inclusion and exclusion criteria for the selection of the primary studies.

The number of blockchain research has grown rapidly past few years. In the recent study of Akar and Akar [2], points out that the ethical studies of blockchain were focusing more on legal dimensions of cryptocurrencies and blockchain. The philosophical (and thus also ethical) & ontological dimensions of cryptocurrencies and blockchain technology were still underrepresented in the research, representing only 3% of all of the blockchain research. This indicates, that more deeper understanding of philosophical ethics is needed around the research of blockchains.

1.3   Structure of the Paper

The remainder of the paper starts with a presentation of the used research method and followed research process in Sect. 2. It is followed by the results and analysis (Sect. 3). Finally, a conclusion is drawn and outlook on future work is made in Sect. 4.

2   Research Method and Process

To answer to the presented research question, we utilise a literature study and analysis as a vehicle for the study. We used a systematic literature review (SLR) [16] method to collect the primary articles. As defined by Kitchenham and Charters [16, p. vi], a systematic literature review is *"a form of secondary study that uses a well-defined methodology to identify, analyse and interpret all available evidence related to a specific research question in a way that is unbiased and (to a degree) repeatable."*

For this study, we utilised a research process that is described in Fig. 1. We started with a preliminary study to verify whether there were recent existing systematic reviews and whether there was enough content for the review. In this phase after testing various alternatives, we selected the simple combination of ethic* AND (''block chain'' OR blockchain) as the search term. In addition, we decided to focus on Scopus publication database as it incorporates a large amount of different databases from various fields and organisation.

In the second phase, the search was performed and all returned items were stored. In the third phase, the inclusion and exclusion criteria were applied to the found publications. The criteria were given in Table 1. In the final phase, the articles were read through and categorised. We used thematic analysis to identify commonly repeated patterns and areas. Due to the space limitations of this report, not all selected papers will be listed and referred. The list is available upon request from the authors.

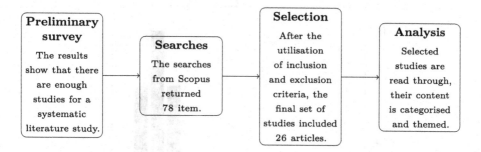

Fig. 1. The process model of this research.

Table 1. Inclusion and exclusion criteria

Inclusion criteria	Exclusion criteria
– Written in English	– Reporting language is not English
– Peer-reviewed	– Not peer-reviewed (e.g., book reviews, editorials)
– Focuses on blockchain technologies	– Blockchain is only mentioned
	– No discussion on ethics

The articles were imported from Elsevier's Scopus, a database for peer-reviewed and source-neutral research. Scopus is the one the biggest citation databases and we were searching for the state of the art articles on blockchain and ethics; especially concrete models which would present how ethics is related to issues risen by blockchain. Unfortunately not too many papers actually handled ethics of blockchain.

3   Results and Analysis

After the selection process, a total of 26 primary studies were included. The data was collected in the end of March 2020. Whereas the first white paper to describe the blockchain structure was published more than a decade ago, an academic interest on blockchain ethics has emerged during the previous three years as illustrated in Fig. 2. It is worth noting that more than half (65%) of the papers included into this study have been published during the last year.

Furthermore, while Yli-Huumo et al. [30] found over a hundred blockchain publications as recently as 2016 in their systematic mapping study, the overall number of papers touching the area of blockchain ethics still remains low. However, as Fig. 2 show, the attention to the topic has risen quickly during the years 2018–2019 and it is probable that the number of publications will still grow. In addition, as the data was collected in the end of the first quarter of the year 2020, some studies from the year 2019 and majority of the studies published in 2020 have not yet been indexed by the databases.

The papers found in the process represent various scientific areas as described by Scopus' subject area division (Fig. 3). While this was expected as the

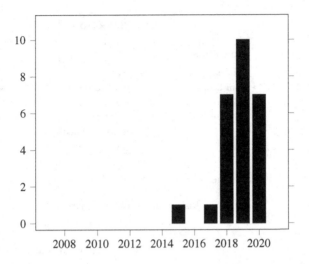

Fig. 2. Yearly number of publications discussing blockchain ethics since 2008 when Nakamoto's white paper was released.

blockchain technology is expected to have a wide range of target applications in the industry, it justified the decision to use a search engine and a publication database instead of a manual search strategy. Furthermore, this illustrates the wide range of interest having been awakened by this relatively new innovation.

The selected papers were analyzed and categorised, and the major themes rising up where identified. Surprisingly many, 11 (42%) papers out of all 26, where motivated by the lack of, and aimed to produce, an ethically justifiable blockchain solution for the problem at hand. However, while these approaches were aiming to produce an ethical solution, they were lacking an analysis of the consequences and implications of their design. Only one paper discussed the ethical concerns of the design in depth, yet the analysis was free-formatted and lacking strong ethical background.

The approaches and themes of the remaining 14 papers are variable and they do not cluster into clear areas of research. On a more general level, studies have been devoted to specific domains. For example, Adams et al. [1] discussed how blockchain can improve sustainability; Calvaresi et al. [4] analysed ethics in blockchain multi-agent systems; and Carnevale and Occhipinti [5] addressed trust in governmental blockchain solutions. Dierksmeier and Seele [7,8] discusses broadly the ethical concerns of blockchain and cryptocurrencies. Duong-Trung et al. [9], instead, proposed a solution for patient data management. Godsiff [11] was among the first to raise also ethical questions of Bitcoin and blockchain into academic debate.

Some ethical aspects or properties have generated interest among the scholars. For example, Bertino et al. [3] and Kendzierskyj et al. [15] pinpointed the importance of data transparency also in blockchain solutions; Fabiano [10] emphasise the value of personal data. Duong-Trung et al. [9] discusses pri-

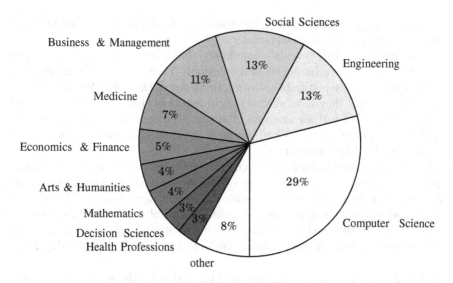

Fig. 3. Scopus documents by subject area classification of the results. Note that a single study might belong in more than one subject area. The category 'other' consists of subject areas which have less than 2% share.

vacy in a certain blockchain domain and Ishmaev [14] discussed data privacy in blockchain. In addition, Tang et al. [25,26] referred to the PAPA model, by Mason [19], as a tool for a technology level analysis of blockchain solutions.

Only a handful of studies have focused on more general ethical discussion of blockchain technologies. Kučera and Bruckner [18] presents a brief overview of two initiatives for defining ethical blockchain solutions. Tang et al. [25,26] present their three-by-three model for blockchain ethics as well as point out some future directions.

To answer the presented research questions, it can be stated that the field of blockchain ethics is emerging with various new openings and a number of recent studies published (RQ1). However, the field still remains immature and more work is needed to guide the development of the field. In our review, only a few tools, methods and frameworks were found (cf. [18,26]), yet none of those were used in any of the studied articles (RQ2). Furthermore, it remains unanswered what kind of experience and understanding of ethical analysis is needed to utilise the proposed tools.

4   Conclusion and Outlook

4.1   Key Findings

We summarise our key findings into following three points:

1. A number of designs, frameworks and architectures have been published on blockchain and motivated by claiming an ethical approach towards the subject. However, a closer look on these studies reveal that while the intention

certainly might have been good, there are no actual analyses or discussion on ethical consequences on blockchain.

On the one hand, this reveals a commonly shared concern regarding the pitfalls of blockchain technologies and solutions. That is, several scholars have defined an ethically justifiable solution to be one of the key characteristics for their system and they have shared this in report of their study. On the other hand, the lack of further analysis of actual ethicality of the proposed artefact further pinpoints the lack of common methods, tools and ethical analysis framework for blockchain ethics.

2. The blockchain technology has touched the different areas broadly. For example, there are studies devoted from various areas ranging from digitalisation of agriculture to supply chain logistics, smart contracts, sustainable development and governmental services. In addition, a number of scientific disciplines have been involved in the research. This observation emphasises the need for also ethical analysis of the proposed solutions as the technology's adaption is spreading.

3. Whereas there have been an increasing interest towards blockchain—as well as, e.g., artificial intelligence—ethics in the recent years, the ethical approach remains superficial in many of the studied articles. For example, often studies did not refer to any ethics or computer ethics sources, but instead used, e.g., GDPR as a starting point for an ethical discussion. Also, in many of the papers there might be a mention of ethics only in the topic of the paper and then only in discussion—and even there only briefly.

The findings presented in this study emphasise the need for a concrete tool or tools, framework or method to analyse the ethical aspects of different kinds of blockchain solutions. As nearly half of the primary studies included aimed to present an ethically justifiable blockchain solution for a specific problem, there is a call for easy-to-use method, tool or a framework. In addition, as it is likely that its users are not experts in computer ethics, the tool should be usable and well-guided also for non-professional users.

4.2   Avenues for Further Work

Firstly, as pointed above, further work would be required to developed an ethical apparatus for researchers and practitioners for helping to evaluate ethical considerations. A special concern should be paid to developing a concrete tool, with guidelines, which can be utilised also by practitioners without deep understanding on moral philosophical questions and schools of thought; a tool which first clarifies the questions the developers have, then the stakeholder groups and finally potential ethical answers which can solve the ethical issues in the design of blockchain solutions.

Secondly, the extant literature is lacking studies moving into higher abstraction levels from blockchain technologies. Currently, the focus has been on immediate effects generated by the technology and larger discussion on the implications is not non-existing, but still remains marginal compared to the mainstream discussions on blockchain ethics. For example, there exists calls for privacy and transparency, but hardly any other issues are addressed.

Thirdly, as research on ethics in different stages of software engineering and computer science is getting growing interest, more attention has to paid to the real meaning of ethics. Thus, researchers should acknowledge what has been done in other fields of ICT and ethics and look for some solutions from there instead of trying to reinvent the wheel. Of course, blockchain will bring its own questions as well, and these need novel solutions, but many of the more general issues have already been handled elsewhere, and these solutions can be used in relation to blockchain.

4.3   Limitations

Naturally, this study has its limitations. First, all systematic reviews with electronic search strategy are limited by the representatives of the search term. While we tested various different search terms before selecting the used one, it is still likely that we have not been able to capture studies utilizing different terms for the same phenomenon. Also, studies in languages other than English have been excluded from the study. Further work should aim to systematize the used terms and concepts.

Also, we used qualitative analysis on the selected primary studies, which is always limited to the observations and emphasis set by the researchers. Yet, this study can serve as a starting point for further literature studies in blockchain ethics.

4.4   Closing Summary

This paper presented a literature review on the recent studies relating to the ethical aspects of blockchain technologies and solutions. We used a systematic literature review method to collect the data from Scopus publication database and selected 26 primary studies to be included. We analysed the selected papers for common themes and research areas. The results show that there is an increasing attention to the theme whereas there seems to be a lack of usable ethical tools, methods and frameworks for blockchain ethics. In addition, the results show that the research domain is maturing fast and blockchain is spreading into various industrial domains. In addition, this study showed that blockchain ethics discussion remains often artificial and the study calls for further work to define and systematize the domain.

References

1. Adams, R., Kewell, B., Parry, G.: Blockchain for good? digital ledger technology and sustainable development goals. In: World Sustainability Series, pp. 127–140 (2018)

2. Akar, S., Akar, E.: Is it a new tulip mania age?: a comprehensive literature review beyond cryptocurrencies, bitcoin, and blockchain technology. J. Inf. Technol. Res. (JITR) **13**(1), 44–67 (2020)
3. Bertino, E., Kundu, A., Sura, Z.: Data transparency with blockchain and AI ethics. J. Data Inf. Qual. **11**(4), 1–8 (2019)
4. Calvaresi, D., Calbimonte, J.P., Dubovitskaya, A., Mattioli, V., Piguet, J.G., Schumacher, M.: The good, the bad, and the ethical implications of bridging blockchain and multi-agent systems. Information (Switzerland) **10**(12), 363 (2019)
5. Carnevale, A., Occhipinti, C.: Ethics and decisions in distributed technologies: a problem of trust and governance advocating substantive democracy. Adv. Intell. Syst. Comput. **1009**, 300–307 (2020). AISC
6. Crosby, M., Pattanayak, P., Verma, S., Kalyanaraman, V., et al.: Blockchain technology: beyond bitcoin. Appl. Innov. **2**(6–10), 71 (2016)
7. Dierksmeier, C., Seele, P.: Cryptocurrencies and business ethics. J. Bus. Ethics **152**(1), 1–14 (2018)
8. Dierksmeier, C., Seele, P.: Blockchain and business ethics. Bus. Ethics **29**(2), 348–359 (2020)
9. Duong-Trung, N., Son, H., Le, H., Phan, T.: Smart care: integrating blockchain technology into the design of patient-centered healthcare systems. In: ACM International Conference Proceeding Series, pp. 105–109. Association for Computing Machinery (2020)
10. Fabiano, N.: The value of personal data is the data protection and privacy preliminary condition: synthetic human profiles on the web and ethics. In: ACM International Conference Proceeding Series. Association for Computing Machinery (2020)
11. Godsiff, P.: Bitcoin: bubble or blockchain. Smart Innov. Syst. Technol. **38**, 191–203 (2015)
12. Haber, S., Stornetta, W.S.: How to time-stamp a digital document. J. Cryptol. **3**(2), 99–111 (1991). https://doi.org/10.1007/BF00196791
13. Hirsh, S., Alman, S., Lemieux, V., Meyer, E.T.: Blockchain: one emerging technology–so many applications. Proc. Assoc. Inf. Sci. Technol. **55**(1), 691–693 (2018)
14. Ishmaev, G.: The ethical limits of blockchain-enabled markets for private IoT data. In: Philosophy and Technology (2019)
15. Kendzierskyj, S., Jahankhani, H., Jamal, A., Jimenez, J.I.: The transparency of big data, data harvesting and digital twins. In: Jahankhani, H., Kendzierskyj, S., Jamal, A., Epiphaniou, G., Al-Khateeb, H. (eds.) Blockchain and Clinical Trial. ASTSA, pp. 139–148. Springer, Cham (2019). https://doi.org/10.1007/978-3-030-11289-9_6
16. Kitchenham, B.A., Charters, S.: Guidelines for performing systematic literature reviews in software engineering. version 2.3. EBSE Technical Report EBSE-2007-01, Keele University, Keele, Staffs, United Kingdom (2007)
17. Kranzberg, M.: Technology and history: "kranzberg's laws". Technol. Culture **27**(3), 544–560 (1986)
18. Kučera, J., Bruckner, T.: Blockchain and ethics: a brief overview of the emerging initiatives. CEUR Workshop Proc. **2443**, 129–139 (2019)
19. Mason, R.O.: Four ethical issues of the information age. MIS Q. **10**(1), 5–12 (1986)
20. Moor, J.H.: The nature, importance, and difficulty of machine ethics. IEEE Intell. Syst. **21**(4), 18–21 (2006)
21. Nakamoto, S.: Bitcoin: A peer-to-peer electronic cash system. Technical report (2008). https://bitcoin.org/bitcoin.pdf

22. Pilkington, M.: Blockchain technology: principles and applications. In: Research Handbook on Digital Transformations. Edward Elgar Publishing (2016)
23. Saper, N.: International cryptography regulation and the global information economy. Nw. J. Tech. & Intell. Prop. 11, xv (2012)
24. Swan, M.: Blockchain: Blueprint for a New Economy. O'Reilly Media, Inc., Newton (2015)
25. Tang, Y., Xiong, J., Becerril-Arreola, R., Iyer, L.: Blockchain ethics research: a conceptual model. In: SIGMIS-CPR 2019 - Proceedings of the 2019 Computers and People Research Conference, pp. 43–49. Association for Computing Machinery, Inc (2019)
26. Tang, Y., Xiong, J., Becerril-Arreola, R., Iyer, L.: Ethics of blockchain: a framework of technology, applications, impacts, and research directions. Inf. Technol. People 33(2), 602–632 (2019)
27. Tang, Y., Xiong, J., Becerril-Arreola, R., Iyer, L.: Ethics of blockchain. Inf. Technol. People 12, 3–4 (2019)
28. Tavani, H.T.: Ethics & Technology: Ethical Issues in an Age of Information and Communication Technology, 2nd edn. Wiley, Hoboken (2007)
29. Underwood, S.: Blockchain beyond bitcoin (2016)
30. Yli-Huumo, J., Ko, D., Choi, S., Park, S., Smolander, K.: Where is current research on blockchain technology?—a systematic review. PLoS ONE 11(10), 1–27 (2016), https://doi.org/10.1371/journal.pone.0163477

The Many Faces of Social Withdrawal in Hikikomori

Hanna Kirjavainen[1](✉) and Harri Jalonen[2]

[1] Turku University of Applied Science, Turku, Finland
hanna.kirjavainen@turkuamk.fi
[2] University of Vaasa, Vaasa, Finland
harri.jalonen@univaasa.fi

Abstract. This paper discusses socially withdrawn youths' posts on an internet forum. We explore their situation and ask what challenges are preventing them to participate into society. We use the capability approach as our viewpoint, wanting to pinpoint the youths' realized capabilities to join in and feel included, as opposed to the opportunity's society provides them. Problems with mental health, autism spectrum disorders, social anxieties and frustration towards society were identified as reasons for social withdrawal, indicating that the participants do not feel like their skills and persona is appreciated by the society.

Keywords: Social withdrawal · Social media · Youth research

1 Introduction

Within the so-called vulnerable populations, it is often so that they either use public services excessively or do not utilise them at all. Both cases consist of many dissimilar groups with nothing much in common, but the mismatch between the existing services and the needs of individuals. It is obvious that there is a need to learn more about both groups' preferences, but the methods traditionally used in involvement are not always the most effective ones. Previous research has identified that vulnerable and disadvantaged populations have difficulties to participate due to their difficult conditions or circumstances, lack of skills, poor health, economic situation, or power differentials [1, 2].

Especially challenging are the "invisible" target groups, who appear to have isolated themselves: residing outside the system, not wanting much from it, even being distrustful towards its fruits. How are the public service providers able to motivate this kind of groups to participate in society and how are the unsatisfying services developed to better match the needs of this kind of groups, if the service providers are not able to reach them and don't know much about their preferences?

One example of these kind of groups is socially withdrawn youths. It is a growing worldwide phenomenon in developed societies, consisting of young people confined in their homes, avoiding social contacts. Social withdrawal is seen as a complex hybrid of social and psychiatric issues as many, but not all, socially withdrawn suffer from

M. Cacace et al. (Eds.): WIS 2020, CCIS 1270, pp. 156–168, 2020.
https://doi.org/10.1007/978-3-030-57847-3_11

psychiatric disorders [3, 4]. There is a lack of research, which could help to understand the nature of this phenomenon and guide future research, policy, and practice [5].

Social withdrawal can be seen as a form of social exclusion and not being in education, employment or training (so called NEET youth) raises the risk to withdraw [10]. In Finland, amongst 20–24 years old, there was approximately 38.000 NEET-youths in 2018: 11.8% of the whole age group [6]. According to research, their experiences of well-being are lower than average, and they feel lonely comparatively often [7].

Technology can bring new forms of participation to public service development, so that also those citizens, who are traditionally unreachable, can access it. So far, this kind of involvement has been quite low. However, particularly social media can be seen as a context for developing the services and co-creating them together with the users. Social media empowers individuals to create and share content that the governance is not able to control [8].

This paper takes this viewpoint and approaches social media as a context from which it is possible to derive information, which would otherwise be unattainable. This paper is part of a larger research in which the aim is to find out, what are the challenges preventing socially withdrawn youths from participation and inclusion, and what would motivate them to "join in". In this paper, the focus will be on theoretical framework and initial findings.

Socially withdrawn people are not easy to research, as they try to avoid human contacts. There is a gap in the research in letting their voice to be heard, as it is not easy to find out their preferences and opinions. Social media can shed a light on socially withdrawn youths' everyday lives. This light helps to understand the situation and challenges of these youths and enriches the public service providers' knowledge about them. Thus, social media is able to make the experiences of the socially withdrawn youths visible.

2 Theoretical Framework

2.1 Social Withdrawal and the Hikikomori Syndrome

Social withdrawal is defined as permanent, solitary behaviour. Socially withdrawn people avoid social interaction and spend more time alone than the age group in general [9]. It is an issue, which can be interpreted both from the psychological and from the societal point of view. Leaning on Husu and Välimäki [10, 607], we define social withdrawal as a "complex set of relationships between self and society", as opposed to viewpoints based solely either on society or individuals' psychological and behavioural features.

The interlinkage between society and withdrawal is visible on earlier research showing that NEET youths feel lonelier than youths studying or working. This might be not only because of fewer contacts to other people, but also because lack of finances, psychological strain, and shame [12, 13]. On the other hand, the NEET status might be caused by health or mental health problems such as depression, which is linked to loneliness. Välimäki et al. [12] propose that having no friends may be even more stigmatizing than not being in employment or in education: more personal and more difficult to get over, especially as youths are expected to live a socially active life . However, studying or working does not guarantee inclusion and on the other hand, NEET youths do not necessarily suffer from social exclusion, as they might have a large social network [11, 12].

Husu and Välimäki [10] identified three different factors, which explain social withdrawal. First, there are too high expectations from the society, the impossibility of non-educated youths to attain status, income, and social capital. Second, individuals have mental health problems and they lack the social skills needed in the society. The third theme overlaps with the previous two as it consists of life-changing life events that one is not able to affect, such as a death in the family or bullying. The cause and the reason are not always clear, e.g. bullying may have a negative effect on social skills, but people with poor social skills may be an easy target for bullies [14]. In addition, parents and family structure seem to have an effect through social learning, family environment and genetics [14, 15].

One extreme representation of social withdrawal is the 'Hikikomori syndrome'. While it has originated in Japan, it seems to have grown worldwide [3], spreading with the growth of industrialization and individualism [9], as well as the constant use of technology and social media. The Japanese Ministry of Health, Labour and Welfare has a young individual who stays mostly at home, has no interest in social activities, continuation of the situation for at least six months, the person does not have a psychotic disorder or a low level of IQ and has no close friends [16]. Having said this, there is variation amongst the severity of the isolation within the group, and it has been suggested that Hikikomoris are able to have "less-demanding" friendships, such as online friends. Typically, Hikikomoris are men, the ratio being four men to one woman [15, 16].

Many, but not all of the Hikikomoris suffer from mental disorders [15]. It is not easy to analyze, when the social withdrawal is merely a symptom of some mental disorder and when it is a primary disorder itself. It has been suggested that the Hikikomori syndrome should be added to the DSM (Diagnostic and Statistical Manual of Mental Disorders) as a new psychiatric disorder [3, 4]. However, one has to bear in mind the societal impacts on the Hikikomori phenomenon, as structural marginalization is evidently linked, and even causes social marginalization [12, 13].

2.2 The Capability Approach to Social Withdrawal

The capability approach has become an important framework in relation to well-being in recent decades. Amartya Sen is one of the key developers of this framework. Sen's capability approach focuses on what people are actually able to do and to be, their "functionings", as opposed to their feelings and possessions. He sees the actual opportunities, "capabilities" individuals have, as more important than their income or other material means. "Agency" is another important concept of the capability theory. It means the ability to pursue and to realise the goals one personally wants, no matter what they consist of. The concept is thus wider than well-being; moreover, sometimes a person might even have goals, which go against his/her personal welfare [17–19].

Freedoms to "doings and beings" are dependent both on individual and contextual aspects. Surrounding society enables these functionings, both in the level of social and economic institutions and in the level of political and civil rights [20]. Sen addresses poverty as a deprivation of certain crucial capabilities: not just the physical ones, but also more elaborate social achievements, such as taking part in the community or being able to appear in public without feeling shame. This broadens the concept of wellbeing, as quality of life is more than the resources one can access. Social exclusion can be seen both as a part of capability poverty and as a cause of capability failures [17, 18, 21, see critique of Sen's work e.g. 22].

It is important to distinguish Sen's idea of freedom and individual choice from neoliberalism. The neo-liberal viewpoint individualises achievements, whereas Sen takes the diversity of people as his starting point, enhancing the significance of the surrounding society, as the interests depend on available opportunities and resources [23]. Moreover, the capability approach acknowledges the importance of societal structures and institutions [24]. The capability approach can and has been used in empirical studies in a variety of ways, covering wide range of fields. It has acted as an evaluative framework of different aspects of an individual's or group's well-being, as a tool for social cost-benefit analysis or as a viewpoint to evaluate policies [24, 25].

Implementing the capability approach to social exclusion is expedient, albeit not straightforward [26]. Hick [27], for example, states that this is due to the ambiguous and multi-dimensional nature of the social exclusion as a concept. He questions whether social exclusion is an academic concept at all but just rhetoric connected with negative associations without a shared understanding. However, Hick concludes that the capability approach is useful to connect to social exclusion, as it emphasises the multi-dimensionality of poverty, not just the resources, while acknowledging the material as a side as well. The specific framework should be adapted contextually. Peruzzi [11] states that when based on the capability deprivation approach, social exclusion can be defined as the outcome of diverse interactions between resources and constraints. This process is dynamic in nature, altering the capabilities over time.

There are different operationalizations of capabilities. Burchard and Vizard [28] list ten domains of most important capabilities in which inequality manifests itself in Britain. These domains are life, physical security, health, education and learning, standard of living, productive and valued activities, participation, social life, identity, expression and self-respect and legal security. Peruzzi [11], in turn, distinguishes seven domains for social exclusion and matches them with corresponding capabilities. These include physical health, mental well-being, enjoyment of social and family relationships, participation in political life, decent standard of living, access to social services and engagement in productive and valued activities.

3   Research Methodology

One representation of social withdrawal and the social withdrawal phenomenon is a Finnish discussion board called Ylilauta (www.ylilauta.org) and especially one of its forums, called "Hikikomero". Ylilauta is a popular forum with over 5 million visitors, approximately 2 million posts and 32 million readings per month. Ylilauta consists of different kinds of sub-boards or forums, in which the users may discuss different themes, Hikikomero being one of them. The Hikikomero forum is represented as a "peer support group for the depressed and socially excluded". The name is based on the Hikikomori syndrome, but it is also a word play; in Finnish language "hiki" means sweat and "komero" stands for a closet. The forum represents a sub-culture of its own, with a sense of community and where also a multitude of words have been developed. The participants distance themselves from the society with negative characterisations about more sociable people and use terms, which emphasize their own separation from the society [29].

According to Haasio [30], even though the name of the forum is based on the hikikomori-culture, it is not exactly the same phenomenon represented there. There are several similarities however: the life of the forum participants is focused on the computer, social contacts are formed exclusively in forums and through computer games, the virtual world presenting an escape route from dissatisfying non-virtual life. Amongst the forum writers, mental health problems seem to be quite common, and their everyday life is characterized by shyness, the fear of social situations and thus, loneliness. Many of them have been bullied in school. The feeling of otherness and isolation is a kind of self-generating downward spiral. On the other hand, the group is diverse: some of the socially isolated work or study, but still try to avoid other people as much as possible [29, 30].

The data we are using in this research are posts written to "Hikikomero" in 2018 and 2019. Since Ylilauta is an anonymous discussion board, it is difficult to gather background information about the participants. In their study, Husu & Välimäki [10] used the questionnaires the visitors themselves had generated. From these, they found that the participants were mostly male (19 out of 26) and their age was between 20 and 30, plus and minus a few years. It is of course also a possibility that the participants give false information to the forum. However, these results are in line with Haasio's and Naka's [31] research, in which they concluded that a large number or writers are between 16 and 30 and almost all of them are men.

The capability approach provides a framework to evaluate well-being. Leaning on previous studies, we hypothesize that the capability of the socially withdrawn youths is significantly lower than in the other groups and that loneliness and social anxiety are common amongst them [e.g. 10]. The process leading to social withdrawal is personal and complex, in which societal, psychological, familial, and biological factors are intertwined and interlinked [e.g. 15].

Sen suggests that the capability approach is more a framework for evaluation on individual and societal level than a complete theory. Researchers should not make preemptive lists of capabilities, as different purposes and contexts may need different capability sets. In a similar vein, he refrains from giving exhaustive lists of capabilities or prioritize them. This is partly because of the ambiguity of the terms of well-being and inequality, and partly because of the importance of context [18, 19, 32].

We deployed thematic analysis in line with our research purposes, informed with the capability approach, the previous literature about and the aspects of socially isolated. We paid attention to the challenges that may prevent socially withdrawn youth from participating in society. Particularly we were interested in decision-making, working life, or studying and different services the social sector and employment office provide. We also explored what would motivate the participants to attend and be involved in these kinds of activities. The analysis was conducted as follows.

To familiarize ourselves with the posts, we carried a search with the words "osallistua" (take part, participate, attend, engage in, be involved) and "este" (obstacle, barrier, hindrance, impediment). We found out that constraining the search only to these words excluded too many relevant posts. We learned that the posts about different services, working life and studying contained information about the hindrances and obstacles to their participation as well, so we decided to include commonly used words related to these themes. Thus, we decided to use the following search words:

- Work/job, profession, salary
- Education, study, university, university of applied sciences
- Employment promoting services, rehabilitative work activity, work experience placement, course, labour market training
- Social office, "Kela" (The Social Insurance Institution of Finland)
- Verb "osallistua" (take part, participate, attend, engage in, be involved)
- Noun "este" (obstacle, barrier, hindrance, impediment)

We went through over 2.000 posts, reading them and choosing the posts, which are relevant to our research questions, having thus found 150 compatible posts. We have collated them according to eleven preliminary categories, which were chosen according to the research questions, earlier previous research findings concerning capability sets and the social withdrawal phenomenon. Some of the codes, namely Employers and the act of seeking a job and Motivational aspects emerged from the data. The chosen preliminary categories are:

- Mental Health (14 posts)
- Social capabilities (9 posts)
- Motivational aspects (22 posts)
- Experiences from the public services (18 posts)
- Practical-level hindrances and obstacles (4 posts)
- The attitudes and responsiveness of the Society (11 posts)
- Employers and the act of seeking a job (18 posts)
- Experiences from working life (21 posts)
- Experiences from Vocational Schools and Universities (10 posts)
- Experiences from Employment promoting services (3 posts)
- Proposals and suggestions (19 posts)

Identified themes were not exclusive as in many cases problems overlapped between many categories, e.g. mental health was an issue presented in many posts. We collated the posts according to their main issue. There were several themes, which emerged from the data.

4 Findings

Our thematic analysis resonates with Peruzzi's [11] dimensions, the focus being on mental well-being and autism spectrum disorders, enjoyment of social relationships, access to not only to social but also wider public (social, health, employment, youth) services and engagement in productive and valued activities. These dimensions resonate well with the earlier research. In the following, we present our key findings with real-life examples of the posts posted to the Hikikomero forum.

Mental Well-being and Autism Spectrum Disorders

There were plenty of posts and references to mental health problems and they were present in every category. The importance of mental health does not come as a surprise, considering the close association, previous research has given with loneliness and mental health problems [see e.g. 33]. Several studies point out that loneliness and depression are interrelated with double-sided causality so that depressive symptoms predict loneliness and vice versa [e.g. 34]. This connection might be explained with several similarities between loneliness and depression: they both seem to be related to lowering of social skills, negative cognitive biases and negative experiences from past friendships [35].

In addition, autism spectrum disorders (ASD), especially Asperger and Autism, seem common amongst forum participants. Studies show that youths with Asperger or socalled High-functioning Autism (HFA) have tendency to unsuitable social behaviour and social withdrawal and their quality of life is overall lower than others [36, 37].

Mental health problems and ASDs were interpreted as an obstacle to participate in valued activities, such as working life or studying and go hand in hand with poor social capabilities and lack of motivation. They also seemed to influence how the participants are valued in society, at least their perceptions about this.

"I have fucking severe depression. I always fear that I get stigmatized and then I won't get any job or get any study place, if I go to a head doctor."

"First of all, I am not ashamed of my autism. I have not chosen to have an Asperger syndrome and ADHD linked to that. They are a part of me and connected to certain personality traits and my way of understanding reality. Because it is a neural disorder, I probably do not even understand how autistic I am, but others certainly see it more clearly and probably this fact bothers others more than me. These disorders lead to become a hikky (a noun developed in the forum, meaning a social withdrawn person) not because of shame but because social interaction feels so burdening. One might say that the mind finds peace only in solitude. To become a "hikky" is also heavily affected by that e.g. from workplaces you get fired in a probation period. No one wants to pay from a shitty outcome to an adhd-burger (burger is a noun developed in the forum, meaning a person who does not know how to behave in social situations) if the option is to hire a regular human to do the same job better."

Enjoyment of Social Relationships

Low social skills and awkwardness or anxiety in social situations were commonly exclaimed. This might be partly explained by the fact that social skill deficits character-ize autism spectrum disorders [38]. Youth with Asperger or High Functioning Autism have the wish to be social but have lacks in the knowledge of these skills or do not know how to manifest them in social situations. [39, 40].

A kind of self-preventive attitude seems also to be a quite commonly shared phe-nomenon, as low self-esteem and bad experiences from the past block the participants from trying anything anymore. Earlier research has shown that loneliness and depressive symptoms are related to lower self-esteem, as well as ASD's [41].

"(…) I was at work for a while, but I had to quit because of social problems and anxiety. Every day before work I had to take sedatives so that I could be there amongst people, but they stopped working. All the colleagues probably considered me as handicapped, but I guess I am too as I cannot have conversations or eat at the same table as others without my hands shaking and sweat flowing."

"I get many ideas and plans to get back to the course of life, but I don't get even started with any of them, at home there is nevertheless the convenient and familiar everyday life without difficulties, and what if I fail again."

Access to Public Services

The experienced exclusion and rejection from workplaces and schools and from the society in general, as well as the incomprehension and belittlement from the service providers, were seen blocking the participants' access to services altogether. Many felt that they have already tried and found that the services are not helping them. One of the explanations might be a gap in services for young people with Asperger or HFA, as they might seem highly functional with their verbal capacities and average or high IQ [40]. Another reason probably is that the Finnish service system is very focused on employment and how to improve one's employability. It does not provide many appropriate options for those with lowered capability to act [42].

"I have received nothing else from the officials, except best verses from the normal people and constant questioning of my own feeling, because nobody can really be with multiple problems, seriously excluded or a wreck with mental health problems. Any real help hasn't been given to me; I have just been pushed coldly to the deep end to learn the noble act of swimming."

"I have complained a lot that I am not capable to work. I did a rehabilitative work in library, but could not be there longer than an hour, because it was too hard. I just started to get unbearably anxious. I was ashamed to go away from there after the first hour."

Engagement in Productive and Valued Activities

Plenty of discussions revolved around participation in productive activities, as in education, employment promoting services and especially working life. The act of seeking a job was described as depressing. It was seen that employers did not appreciate the participants' skills, or they did not even get an answer to their job application. Many shared the idea that you have to have the right kind of networks or relatives in order to get a job. Moreover, many participants had several years' gaps in their curriculum vitaes, which they thought prevented them for getting a job.

"I have been trying to get a job, but nobody hires a person, who has wasted 10 years of his life in a University and not even achieved bachelor's degree. No work, no money. 10 years of life thrown away."

Overall, working life is seen as very severe, with its requirements, competitiveness and demands for social skills. Surprisingly, many seemed to have work experience, but it was mainly bad. Bullying and burnouts were mentioned in many posts. Many participants claimed that they are not able to work full hours in current working life, especially if the job is unsatisfactory or the life does not consist of positive elements to counter the work. Internationally, employment rates of those with Autism spectrum disorders seem to be significantly lower. This is unfortunate not only because from the individuals' perspective, but also because people with ASD have many strengths and capabilities useful in jobs with the need of accuracy and precision [37].

"(…) I have done grunt work for two years altogether, but you simply just cannot manage the rat race for long, as you don't have any other life besides the work. Couple of times I have also tried to "normalize" myself socially, but those efforts have not been enough, and I had to return to my closet to depress."

The employment promoting services were also a popular topic. The most shared opinion about them seemed to be that they were exploitative and not a valued activity as such. Some of the participants referred to these services as 'slavery' and voiced very pronounced opinions about them. However, some of the participants thought that services were appropriate and provided value. A literature review of customers' experiences from rehabilitative work in Finland, from which many forum participants had experiences, states that the most important development needs customers express are more meaningful tasks and better compensation. Customers' diverse needs do not seem to be considered. Very few proceed to "actual" working life, as would be the intent, which probably decreases motivation towards these kind of services [43].

"If you like that idea that someone else rakes in money from your work, who am I to judge anyone's experiences from rehabilitative work. I don't have anything against it, that with 9 euros' "salary" one drinks coffee, solves crosswords and talks crap, but if you get to do real work (even easier ones), my moral says immediately no. It is so that you have to pay decent salary from work, with its benefits and pension accruals, otherwise it is all about slavery, which distorts the appreciation of work and job opportunities e.g. in outdoor work and in the cleaning field."

There were several posts dealing with working life. Many wishes about paid jobs and adjustments of working life were raised.

"(…) That compromising is extremely stressful to an autist. In the long run, anyone tires if he tries to constantly act against his nature. In schools, there are peaceful spaces for those who need them, in workplaces there could also be. Adjusting the working life doesn't require impossibilities (…)".

This all is in line with earlier research about Finnish NEET youths' experiences, which has shown that poorly functioning job market, disappointments, and bad experiences from different kind of employment services are common [42]. Youths also wish to have a real compensation from their work. However, the service system does not have much of an impact to the labour market [42]. One option could be e.g. kind of a retirement allowance for those whose actual possibilities to find paid labour is low, and who are willing to commit long-term to some societally important task [43].

5 Conclusion

As the number of youths withdrawing to their homes continues to rise [15], there is an urgent need to understand the mindset and experiences of this group. This paper has endeavoured to increase our understanding of socially withdrawn youths' life by mapping out four dimensions, how the social exclusion and social withdrawal are manifesting themselves in the Hikikomero forum participants' life. The results show that social media provides a window to the every-day life of socially withdrawn youths in a way that can be used for enriching the knowledge base of service co-creation processes.

We identified four dimensions, i.e. mental well-being and autism spectrum disorders, enjoyment of social relationships, access to public services and engagement in productive and valued activities. These dimensions are in many ways intertwined and interacting with each other. Low social capabilities, for example, often go hand in hand with mental health problems and long-term disengagement from valued activities usually entails lower mental well-being and social skills. Frustration towards society is common as are the expressions that the participants feel like their skills and persona are worthless in the society.

Using an online forum as data raises ethical considerations, as the writers have not been able to give consent to participation. The forum is public and there is a disclaimer that the posts may be used as research material. However, some of the writers might not realize that this is the case, as the boundaries between private and public tend not to be so evident in online contexts [44]. We have respected the participants' privacy, not individualizing any writers nor providing any identifiable information about them. The text extracts are translated from Finnish into English, meaning that the data does not exist in the same format on the Internet as it does in this paper.

There are a few limitations to this research. The sample was collected from one Finnish discussion board. In addition, using internet as a data source might lead to unrepresentativeness of the target group. It is obvious that social withdrawal is such a complex phenomenon that it cannot be understood by analysing 150 social media posts. However, Hikikomero and similar social media platforms may provide a unique window into the lives of socially withdrawn youths, although one has to be careful about making adaptation assumptions to other contexts with different cultures. A qualitative research enables to explore the obstacles and motivations of the participation. More research is needed. One possible avenue for further research would be to examine how the data from social media can be used for developing public services to hard-to-reach people. In addition, it would be worthwhile to explore how artificial intelligence (e.g. unsupervised machine learning techniques) can be harnessed to analyse social media discussions.

References

1. De Freitas, C., Martin, G.: Inclusive public participation in health: policy, practice and theoretical contributions to promote the involvement of marginalized groups in healthcare. Soc. Sci. Med. **135**, 31–39 (2015)
2. Corus, C., Saatcioglu, B.: An intersectionality framework for transformative services research. Serv. Ind. J. **35**(7–8), 415–429 (2015)
3. Kato, T.A., et al.: Does the 'hikikomori' syndrome of social withdrawal exist outside Japan? A preliminary international investigation. Soc. Psychiatry Psychiatric Epidemiol. **47**, 1061–1075 (2012)
4. Teo, A.R., Gaw, A.C.: Hikikomori, a Japanese culture-bound syndrome of social withdrawal? A proposal for DSM-5. J. Nerv. Mental Dis. **198**, 444–449 (2010)
5. Li, T.M.H., Wong, P.W.C.: Editorial perspective: pathological social withdrawal during adolescence: a culture-specific or a global phenomenon? J. Child Psychol. Psychiatry **53**(10), 1039–1041 (2015)
6. Valtioneuvosto: Koulutuksen ja työn ulkopuolella olevat (NEET) nuoret, katsaus tilanteeseen ja toimenpiteisiin (2019). https://valtioneuvosto.fi/documents/1410845/4449678/Koulut uksen+ja+ty%C3%B6n+ulkopuolella+olevat+%28NEET%29+nuoret%2C+katsaus+tilant eeseen+ja+toimenpiteisiin/51231944-1fc0-ef0b-fc7a-afc6c975b010/Koulutuksen+ja+ty% C3%B6n+ulkopuolella+olevat+%28NEET%29+nuoret%2C+katsaus+tilanteeseen+ja+toi menpiteisiin.pdf. Accessed 9 April 2020
7. Aaltonen, S., Kivijärvi, A., Myllylä, M.: Työn ja koulutuksen ulkopuolella olevien nuorten aikuisten koettu hyvinvointi. Yhteiskuntapolitiikka. **84**(3), 301–311 (2019)
8. Fox, C., Jalonen, H., Baines, S., Bassi, A., Moretti, V., Willoughby, M.: Co-creation of Service Innovations in Europe (CoSIE) – White Paper. Reports from Turku University of Applied Sciences, p. 259 (2019). https://storage.googleapis.com/turku-amk/2019/06/cosie_whitepaper_2 019.pdf. Accessed 18 Feb 2020
9. Bowker, J., Rubin, K., Coplan, R.: Social Withdrawal. Encyclopaedia of Adolescence (2016)
10. Husu, H.-M., Välimäki, V.: Staying inside: social withdrawal of the young, Finnish 'Hikikomori'. J. Youth Stud. **20**(5), 605–621 (2017)
11. Peruzzi, A.: Understanding social exclusion from a longitudinal perspective: a capability-based approach. J. Hum. Dev. Capabilities **15**(4), 335–354 (2014)
12. Välimäki, V., Kivijärvi, A., Aaltonen, S.: The links between structural and social marginalisation – social relations of young Finnish adults not in employment or education. J. Youth Stud. **6**(1), 93–117 (2019)
13. Dieckhoff, M., Gash, V.: Unemployment and social participation. Int. J. Sociol. Soc. Pol. **35**(1, 2), 67 – 90 (2014)
14. Segrin, C., Nevárez, N., Arroyo, A., Harwood, J.: Family of origin environment and adolescent bullying predict young adult loneliness. J. Psychol. **146**, 119–134 (2012)
15. Li, T.M.H., Wong, P.W.C.: Youth social withdrawal behavior (hikikomori): a systematic review of qualitative and quantitative studies. Australian and New Zealand J. Psychiatry. **49**, 595–609 (2015)
16. Pozza, A., Coluccia, A., Kato, T., Gaetani, M., Ferretti, F.: The 'Hikikomori' syndrome: worldwide prevalence and co-occurring major psychiatric disorders: a systematic review and meta-analysis protocol. BMJ Open (2019)
17. Sen, A.: The living standard. Oxford Econ. Papers **36**, 74–90 (1984)
18. Sen, A.: Rights and capabilities. Resources, Values and Development. Harvard University Press, Cambridge, MA (1984b)
19. Sen, A.: Commodities and Capabilities. North Holland, Amsterdam (1985)

20. Walker, C.: Amartya sen's capability approach and education. Educ. Act. Res. **13**(1), 103–110 (2005)
21. Sen, A.: Social Exclusion: Concept, Application, and Scrutiny. Social. Development Papers No. 1, Asian Development Bank (2000)
22. Navarro, V.: Development and quality of life: a critique of amartya sen's development as freedom. Int. J. Health Serv. **30**(4), 661–674 (2000)
23. Salais, R.O., Villeneuve, R.: Introduction: Europe and the politics of capabilities. In: Salais, R., Villeneuve, R. (eds.) Europe and the Politics of Capabilities, pp. 1–18. Cambridge University Press, Cambridge (2005)
24. Robeyns, I.: The capability approach: a theoretical survey. J. Hum. Dev. **6**(1), 93–114 (2005)
25. Robeyns, I.: The capability approach in practice. J. Political Philosophy **14**(3), 351–376 (2006)
26. Alkire, S.: Why the capability approach? J. Hum. Dev. **6**(1), 115 − 135 (2007)
27. Hick, R.: The capability approach: insight for a new poverty focus. J. Soc. Policy (2005)
28. Burchardt, T., Vizard, P.: 'Operationalizing' the capability approach as a basis for equality and human rights monitoring in twenty-first-century britain. J. Hum. Dev. Capabilities **12**(1), 91–119 (2011)
29. Haasio, A.: Toiseus, tiedontarpeet ja tiedon jakaminen tietoverkon 'pienessä maailmassa': Tutkimus sosiaalisesti vetäytyneiden henkilöiden informaatiokäyttäytymisestä. Tampere University Press, Tampere (2015)
30. Haasio, A.: Hikikomorit. Avain, Helsinki (2018)
31. Haasio, A., Naka, H.: An analysis of information shared on hikikomoris discussion forums. Qual. Quantitative Mehods Libraries (QQML) **8**(4), 509–523 (2019)
32. Sen, A.: Capabilities, lists, and public reason: continuing the conversation. Feminist Econ. **10**(3), 77–80 (2004)
33. Heinrich, L.M., Gullone, E.: The clinical significance of loneliness: A literature review. Clin. Psychol. Rev. **26**, 695–718 (2006)
34. Vanhalst, J., Klimstra, T.A., Luyckx, K., Scholte, R.H., Engels, R.C., Goossens, L.: The interplay of loneliness and depressive symptoms across adolescence: exploring the role of personality traits. J. Youth Adolescence **41**, 776–787 (2012)
35. Spithoven, A.W., Lodder, G.M., Goossens, L., et al.: Adolescents' loneliness and depression associated with friendship experiences and well-being: a person-centered approach. J. Youth Adolescence **46**(2), 429–441 (2017)
36. Bauminger, N., Shulman, C., Agam, G.: Peer interaction and loneliness in high-functioning children with autism. J. Autism Dev. Disord. **33**, 489–507 (2003)
37. Scott, M., et al.: Factors impacting employment for people with autism spectrum disorder: a scoping review. Autism **23**(4), 869–901 (2019)
38. American Psychiatric Association: Diagnostic and Statistical Manual of Mental Disorders, 5th edn. American Psychiatric Association, Arlington (2013)
39. Myles, B.S., Simpson, R.L.: Asperger syndrome: an overview of characteristics. Focus Autism Other Dev. Disabilities. **17**(3), 132–137 (2002)
40. Stichter, J.P., Herzog, M.J., Visovsky, K., et al. Social competence intervention for youth with asperger syndrome and high-functioning autism: an initial investigation. J. Autism Dev. Disorders. **40**, 1067–1079 (2010)
41. Orth, U., Robins, R.W., Roberts, B.W.: Low self-esteem prospectively predicts depression in adolescence and young adulthood. J. Personal. Soc. Psychol. **95**(3), 695–708 (2008)
42. Aaltonen, S., Berg, P., Ikäheimo, S.: Nuoret luukulla. Kolme näkökulma syrjäytymiseen ja nuorten asemaan palvelujärjestelmässä. Nuorisotutkimusverkosto/Nuorisotutkimusseura. Verkkojulkaisuja **84** (2015). http://www.nuorisotutkimusseura.fi/images/julkaisuja/nuoretluu kulla.pdf. Accessed 1 June 2020

43. Sandelin, I.: Kuntouttava työtoiminta asiakkaiden kokemana. Kirjallisuuskatsaus asiakkaiden toiminnalle antamista merkityksistä. Terveyden ja Hyvinvoinnin Laitos työpaperi 8/2014. Tampere: Suomen Yliopistopaino Oy, (2014)
44. Convery, I., Cox, D.: A review of research ethics in internet-based research. Practitioner Res. Higher Educ. **6**(1), 50–57 (2012)

Understanding the Social Media Use in Tourism: An Affordance Perspective

Ting Long[1,2]([⊠]) [iD]

[1] Turku School of Economics, University of Turku, Turku, Finland
`tilong@utu.fi`
[2] National Research Center of Cultural Industries, Central China Normal University, Wuhan, China

Abstract. Social media are revolutionizing the way travelers prepare, experience, and complete the whole travel processes. Based on the technology affordance theory, this paper proposes an integrated affordance framework with the aim of understanding the functions that afford travelers' social media use behavior in tourism. The empirical results indicate there are three categories of technology affordances in whole travel stages. Information gathering and collaboration constitute the first category of affordances, and they usually exist at pre-travel and in-travel stages. Additionally, self-presentation, content sharing, visibility, interaction, and persistence affordances are second category affordances, and they often occur at in-travel and after-travel stages. Whilst the communication and triggered attending affordances are seen as third category affordances, as they occur at all travel stages. This research contributes to the literature on the affordances of social media use in the whole processes of travel and offers practical implications for managing social media in tourism.

Keywords: Social media use · Travel stages · Tourism · Technology affordance theory

1 Introduction

Social media are used worldwide, it is estimated that there are over 2.95 billion social media users globally [1]. Past decades, social media are broadly used in tourism industry, by both organizations and individuals, to facilitate the development of such industry. It is reported that 94% of travel agents in the US using Facebook for marketing [2], 57% of Finnish travelers use social media to update content about their holiday when they are traveling [3]. Nine percent of travelers from the Asia Pacific region stated that their travel was inspired by information published on social media [4]. The roles of social media in tourism have attracted a great deal of attention from IS researchers and practitioners. Prior literature has demonstrated that social media exert important impacts on tourists' behavior, for instance, the content shared via social media can affect tourists' decisions to make a travel plan or share own experience on social media [5, 6]. The influence of social media on tourists' behavior have been recognized to occur in the whole travel processes:

© Springer Nature Switzerland AG 2020
M. Cacace et al. (Eds.): WIS 2020, CCIS 1270, pp. 169–184, 2020.
https://doi.org/10.1007/978-3-030-57847-3_12

before travel, during travel, and after travel [7]. However, the understanding of social media use in the whole processes of travel is still fragmented. Prior studies focused on certain behavior that occurred at certain stages of travel, for instance, making the travel plan before travel or sharing experience after travel. At different stages of travel, tourists have different needs, and their social media use behavior might differ. It is unclear how the functions or capabilities of social media can meet tourists' needs at different travel stages. Thus, a comprehensive understanding of the relationship between social media capabilities and tourists' social media use actions in the whole travel processes is required.

To address the above research gaps, this study employs the technology affordance theory to explore the symbiotic relationship between travelers' activities and the technology capabilities of social media in the tourism context [8]. By applying the affordance perspective, the travelers' social media use behavior and the affordances of social media are considered as units of analysis, this could be helpful to gain insight into how social media afford each particular need of travelers at different travel processes correspondingly.

This study focuses specifically on the implications of social media affordances for travelers' whole travel processes, namely, pre-travel, in-travel, and after-travel. First, the features and affordances of social media were explored; nine distinctive social media affordances are identified in this study, which can support travelers' actions at different travel stages. Then, the impact of affordances at different travel processes are explored through bridging the travelers' needs and actual actions. As a result, the affordances of social media are unevenly satisfied travelers' needs at pre-travel, in-travel, and after-travel stages. Finally, three categories of social media affordances in tourism are discussed. In doing so, this research could shed light on the affordances of social media in all stages of travel. Besides, this study could facilitate the understanding of technology affordance theory in different contexts. Finally, this research could provide practical advice to tourism operators on how to enhance the social media functional design and social media adoption by travelers.

2   Theoretical Background

2.1   Social Media Use in Tourism

Social media are defined as "a group of Internet-based applications that build on the ideological and technological foundations of Web 2.0, and that allow the creation and exchange of User Generated Content" [9]. Social media have been considered as important tools for travelers to seek information, communication, present themselves, share experience, and interact with others. The previous research has highlighted the functions of social media in personal traveling. For tourists, social media have been found to be important information sources before the trip [10, 11]. Previous studies found that the decision making of travelers was influenced by online reviews [12, 13]. Furthermore, tourists also use social media to share information during the trip and to share their experience via posting photos and writing reviews after the trip [14, 15]. Recently, researchers also pay much attention to the effectiveness of social media influence in tourists' behavior [6, 16]. However, few studies have attempted to examine the affordances of social media of tourists' behavior in travel. Specifically, at pre-travel, in-travel, and after-travel stages, social media plays different roles for tourists. Thus, it is important to investigate what social media can afford for tourists from the whole processes of travel.

2.2 Technology Affordance Theory

The affordance is rooted in the work of ecological psychologist James Gibson [17], who used affordance to refer to the relationship between an animal and an environment. Then, Gaver [18] adopted the concept of affordance into Information Systems field as a new concept of technology affordance, refer "the properties of the world defined with respect to people's interaction with it". Regarding the different conceptions of technology affordance, the conception from Leonardi, Vaast [19] were employed in this study to help the understanding of the use patterns of social media in tourism as they provided a comprehensive understanding of social media affordance and emphasized on interaction between people's goals and a technology's material features.

The technology affordance has been proposed as a theoretical lens for studying social media in the IS field. For instance, at the organizational level, Treem, Leonardi [20] introduced four affordances of social media in organizations, namely, visibility, editability, persistence, and association. Majchrzak et al. [21] theorized meta-voicing, triggered attending, network-informed associating, and generative role-taking as the affordances of social media affect individuals' engagement in the knowledge conversation. Additionally, prior research has studied the technology affordances based on diverse social media platforms. For instance, DeVito et al. [22] explored six mainstream social media platforms: Facebook, Twitter, Instagram, Tumblr, LinkedIn, and Snapchat. They defined three layers and seven affordances: the self (presentation flexibility, content persistence, and identity persistence), other actor (content association, feedback directness), the audience (audience transparency, visibility control). Some researchers have tried to synergy the affordances of social media from a needs-affordances-features perspective [23]. For example, they use the affordance of self-presentation to unify similar affordances offered by other researchers: rendering [24], generative role taking [21], identity [25]. In their study, they proposed 12 different technology affordances (self-presentation, content sharing, interactivity, presence signaling, relationship formation, group management, browsing others' content, meta-voicing, communication, collaboration, competition, sourcing) from diverse social media platforms, which could be widely used to analyze the social media use behavior.

However, only a few researchers explored social media affordances in tourism context. For instance, Cabiddu et al. [26] identified the different features of high-performing and low-performing hotels to recognize three affordances, persistence engagement, customized engagement, and triggered engagement. Additionally, Gretzel [27] leveraged the social media affordances to understand the social media activism in a tourism context, she provided plenty of examples to illustrate how social media affordances facilitate the actions of tourists. In this research, the affordances of social media in the tourism context will be discussed. It is believed that the affordances of social media are diverse at different travel stages, particularly in the situation of multiple needs from tourists. In sum, the technology affordance theory as an overarching lens will be employed to uncover travelers' different social media use patterns at pre-travel, in-travel, and after-travel stages.

3 Methodology

Understanding the relationship between affordances of social media and travelers' particular travel goals demanded rich data about the travelers' actual engagement with social media platforms at different travel stages. Therefore, a qualitative research method was employed in this study.

The data were collected by interviewing users who had used social media in their travel processes and have travel experience in the last 12 months. The data were analyzed by iterating between the data and the different technology affordances provided by previous research.

3.1 Data Collection

The data was collected via semi-structured interviews, and the participants were recruited by sending interview invitations through email and WeChat (a Chinese multi-purpose messaging, social media, and mobile payment app developed by Tencent). In addition, the snowballing technique was used in this research. The interviewees could invite their friends to join in if their friends interested in this study. The interview was conducted via email or WeChat call after the respondents agreed to participate. Before the interview, the interviewees were informed of the aim of this study, the confidentiality of the collected data, privacy protection of this study, and the researcher's contact information. As the recruited interviewees were from different countries and spoke different languages, they were asked to choose the interview style (email interview or online face-to-face interview via WeChat call) and the interview language (Chinese or English). The interview was initiated by asking the interviewee to describe the types of social media they used and the use purposes. Then, the interview was proceeded by asking them if they have social media use experience for travel purposes and continued with their specific use purpose. Then, the researcher followed with the questions of social media use experience at pre-travel, in-travel, and after-travel stages. To gain details, the interviewees were encouraged to describe their purposes, and social media use behavior with examples. After the interviewees responded to the questions, further questions were asked to make sure the interviewees' meaning of specific questions. Finally, the whole record of the interview was sent to each participant to check if the document recorded their opinions correctly [28]. Additionally, each participant had received a random red packet on WeChat (from 0 to 30 RMB) or a small gift (about 3–5 EURO) as a thank-you gift.

The interviews, which conducted in Chinese, were translated into English for data analysis. Two researchers who speak both English and Chinese checked the interview text to decrease the risk of bias in the transcription.

Overall, 21 individuals participated in the interview, and all the collected data were used to analyze the social media users' behavior in travel stages. On the whole, nine participants were male and 12 were female. Six of them aged between 17 and 21 years, six aged between 22 and 26 years, nine aged between 27 and 31 years. As all the respondents were university students or researchers, the respondents represented a high education group in this study. Regarding the social media platforms, the respondents indicated that social media were widely used by them; 81% of respondents reflected they used WeChat, 52.4% of them said they used Weibo, and 42.9% of them showed they used

Facebook. Additionally, some travel-specific social media platforms were mentioned by respondents, such as Mafengwo (a Chinese social community, provides travel guide and travel-related products), Red Book (a Chinese social medium and e-commerce platform, provides diverse information about lifestyles), and Dianping (a Chinese review platform, similar with TripAdvisor). Table 1 shows the sociodemographic and descriptive characteristics of the respondents.

Table 1. Sociodemographic and descriptive characteristics of the respondents.

	Characteristics	Number (%)		Types	Number (%)
Gender	Male	9 (42.9%)	Social media	WeChat	17 (81.0%)
	Female	12 (57.1%)		Weibo	11 (52.4%)
Age	17–21	6 (28.6%)		Facebook	9 (42.9%)
	22–26	6 (28.6%)		QQ	7 (33.3%)
	27–31	9 (42.9%)		Mafengwo	7 (33.3%)
Education level	Undergraduate	7 (33.3%)		WhatsApp	6 (28.6%)
	Graduate	7 (33.3%)		Instagram	5 (23.8%)
	Postgraduate	7 (33.3%)		Red Book	4 (19.0%)
Occupation	Student	7 (33.3%)		Zhihu	3 (14.3%)
	Researcher	14 (66.7%)		Dianping	3 (14.3%)

3.2 Data Analysis

I conducted data analysis of the interviewees' descriptions intending to identify the possibilities afforded them to accomplish their goals. The analysis unit was each respondent's social media use purposes and the corresponding social media functions. The data analysis processes were divided into two steps.

Firstly, each respondent's social media use purposes or behavior were extracted from their descriptions. Then, these purposes or behavior were marked with different social media features, such as sharing, posting. Next, these features were compared with the functions described by the social media providers to crosscheck the specific functions. For instance, the respondents mentioned one of the features of Facebook was provided for them to join groups; correspondingly, the developer of Facebook described one of its functions as connect with people who share your interests with Groups. Therefore, this function was confirmed as a function of social media which could be discussed. According to the data analysis, I identified the following main social media functions from the interviews (see Table 2).

Secondly, the extracted social media functions were used to confirm social media affordances related to this study. Totally nine social media affordances were extracted from the interviews. Initially, two affordances of social media were extracted from the respondents' function descriptions. They illustrated that social media afforded them

Table 2. Social media functions described by respondents.

Social media functions	Posting contents, sharing contents, updating status/pins (PC/SC/US); Browsing, watching videos shared by others (BR/WV); Join a group/joining and creating, cooperating with other, handling activities (JG/CO/HA); Personal message, chatting, conversation, connection; (PM/CH/CON); Displaying, appealing (DIS/APPE); Pushes activities to connections, lists of "friends" or connections, visible in specific place (PATC/VP); Building, creating, participating (BU/CR/PAR); Reviewable, recordable, archival (REV/REC/ARC);

from gathering diverse information about destinations to completing travel-related tasks online. For instance, respondents were able to browse the travel information, make travel plans with their companions, or buy attraction's gate tickets on WeChat or TripAdvisor. Therefore, information gathering, and collaboration affordances could be confirmed in this study. Prior researchers, such as Halpern, Gibbs [29], Volkoff, Strong [30], Leidner et al. [31], had discussed these two affordances.

Next, five other affordances of social media were extracted from the interviews. When they described the in-travel and after-travel stages, they proposed that social media afford them to post, update, share content on those platforms, for instance, update their status during traveling. They also illustrated that social media afford them to choose to whom and (or) to which platform they share their travel-related content. Furthermore, after they shared the content, social media might provide platforms for interaction between them and their friends as well as record their travel memory. Within these social media function, five other affordances, namely, self-presentation affordance, content sharing affordance, visibility affordance, interaction affordance, and persistence affordance, were extracted [20, 24, 26, 31].

Then, two social media affordances were confirmed by the respondents' description and these two affordances occur at all stages of travel. The respondents stated that social media afford them to keep connect with their travel members or other connections. The social media also provided very appealing pictures, which trigger their travel intention or intend to visit or not visit an attraction. Based on these descriptions, communication and triggered attending were considered as another two affordances social media could provide to their users [21, 23, 26]. Table 3 shows the nine social media affordances and their descriptions.

To deepen the understanding of the data, the nine affordances of social media were scrutinized by backtracking to the respondents' descriptions again. A three layers and eight by nine matrix were made to illustrate the correspondence of functions and affordances at different travel stages. Each response was evaluated, and then both the numbers of positive responses and the total available responses were filled in the corresponding grid. For instance, eight respondents mentioned they use social media to communicate with their travel partner(s) before travel, and there are 19 available responses at this travel stage. This result was marked as 8/19 at the pre-travel stage at the Communication row and PM/CH/CON (Personal message, chatting, conversation, connection) column.

Table 3. Social media affordances and their descriptions.

Affordances	Description	References
Self-presentation	Self-presentation affordance refers to the possibilities for individuals to create and demonstrate the personal image and identity by using a variety of content formats and styles	[22, 23, 32]
Content sharing	Content sharing affordance refers to the possibilities for users to share and distribute content to others in variety of content formats and styles	[23, 25, 33]
Information gathering	Information gathering affordance refers to the possibilities for users to search, view, and filter information provided by others in a social media setting	[23, 27, 29, 31]
Communication	Communication affordance refers to the possibilities for users to communicate with other users directly in a social media setting	[22, 23, 25, 30]
Collaboration	Collaboration affordance refers to the possibilities for users to cooperate and handle interdepend activities in a social media setting	[23, 32, 34]
Triggered attending	Triggered attending affordance refers to the possibilities of instigating users' attention to other content in a social media setting	[21, 26]
Visibility	Visibility affordance refers to the possibility for users to determine what content linked to them is visible to what audiences in a social media setting	[20, 22, 32]
Interaction	Interaction affordance refers to the possibilities for users to interact with others or artefacts immediately in a social media setting	[24, 26, 31]
Persistence	Persistence affordance refers to the possibilities for users to access the original display over time in a social media setting	[20, 22, 26, 27]

4 Results

Based on the analysis of collected data, all the eight social media functions mentioned by respondents and the nine affordances of social media extracted from the interviews at different travel stages were presented in Table 4.

Table 4. An overview of social media affordance at different travel stages.

Travel stage	Affordance dimensions	Social media functions							
		PC/SC/US	BR/WV	JG/CO/HA	PM/CH/CON	DIS/APPE	PATC/VP	BU/CR/PAR	REV/REC/ARC
Pre-travel	Self-presentation								
	Content sharing								
	Information gathering		13/19						
	Communication			4/19					
	Collaboration				8/19				
	Triggered attending					3/19			
	Visibility								
	Interaction								
	Persistence								
In-travel	Self-presentation	10/19							
	Content sharing	10/19							
	Information gathering		6/19						
	Communication			5/19					
	Collaboration				3/19				
	Triggered attending					1/19			
	Visibility						3/19		
	Interaction							2/19	
	Persistence								1/19
After-travel	Self-presentation	14/18							
	Content sharing	14/18							
	Information gathering								
	Communication			1/18					
	Collaboration								
	Triggered attending					1/18			
	Visibility						6/18		
	Interaction							2/18	
	Persistence								5/18

(Notes: PC/SC/US = Posting contents, sharing contents, updating status/pins; BR/WV = Browsing, watching videos shared by others; JG/CO/HA = Join a group/joining and creating, cooperating with other, handling activities; PM/CH/CON = Personal message, chatting, conversation, connection; DIS/APPE = Displaying, appealing; PATC/VP = Pushes activities to connections, lists of "friends" or connections, visible in specific place; BU/CR/PAR = Building, creating, participating; REV/REC/ARC = Reviewable, recordable, archival.)

4.1 Affordances of Social Media at Pre-travel Stage

At pre-travel stage, information gathering, communication, collaboration, triggered attending affordances were extracted. Information gathering affordance widely existed at pre-travel stage. Most of the respondents stated they preferred to search for travel information before travel and social media were important platforms to gather the information. However, respondent 2 and respondent 19 contradicted this opinion; they argued that even though social media afford a large amount of information, the quality of information on social media platforms was questionable. Communication affordance happened when the interviewee thought it was valuable to consult others for some travel suggestions. For example, respondent 12 stated it is possible to communicate with the travel agency via WeChat directly. Collaboration affordance occurred at pre-travel stages for providing the possibilities to travelers to cooperate and deal with these travel issues on platforms. The participants reported that social media afford them to make travel plans or related decisions, and to buy cheaper gate tickets in advance. However, participant 3 and participant 21 denied the collaboration affordance of social media regarding the travel plan making, they argued instead of using social media to make a travel plan, the official website of the attraction and professional travel blog website might be more helpful. Additionally, triggered attending affordance also appeared at this stage, respondents mentioned social media might inspire them to travel by providing some initial ideas about travel (see Fig. 1).

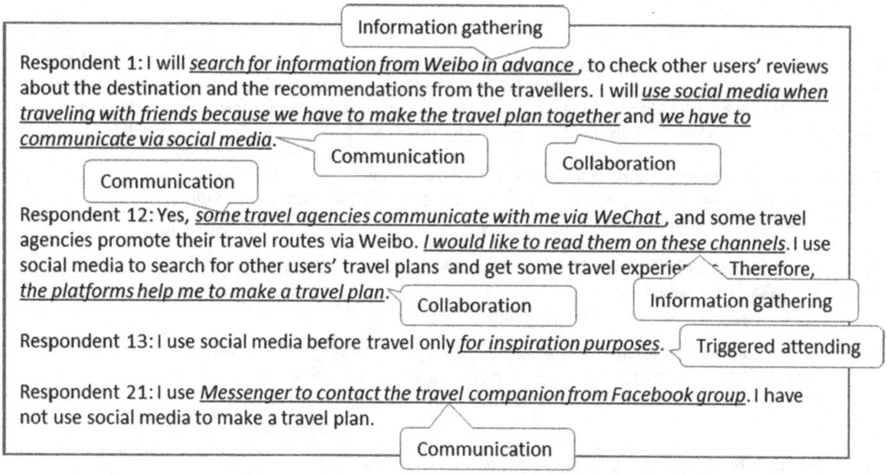

Fig. 1. Evidence of social media affordances at pre-travel stage.

4.2 Affordances of Social Media at In-travel Stage

At in-travel stage, all of the nine affordances mentioned in the data analysis section have occurred, namely, information gathering, collaboration, communication, triggered attending, content sharing, self-presentation, visibility, interaction, and persistence affordances.

At this stage, the travelers still have information searching, and collocation needs; therefore, social media also provide possibilities for them to use such platforms to actualize their needs. Self-presentation and content sharing affordances usually appear together, because when the travelers share something with others, they display themselves to others at the same time. Respondents stated social media were appropriate platforms for them to share their travel experience and feelings. However, participant 16 refused to use these two functions during the travel because he did not usually travel for leisure and he did not like posting pictures of his trip. Additionally, when participants shared content on social media, some of them also have other considerations. For example, participant 3, participant 10, and participant 20 emphasized when they shared on social media, they also considered who could read the content and to what extent.

Thus, visibility affordance occurred at this stage. Besides, interaction affordance started appeared at in-travel stage, respondents stated they use social media to participate in the activities provided by the attraction and interacted with their friends when they shared the same travel topic. Persistence affordance also occurred at this travel stage as one of the respondents reported that she would like to pin her location on WeChat to help her keep the memory easier (see Fig. 2).

Regarding the communication and triggered attending affordances, they depend on the users' perception, not depend on the travel stages change. Thus, these affordances may continuously arise when travelers have related needs and take some kind of action.

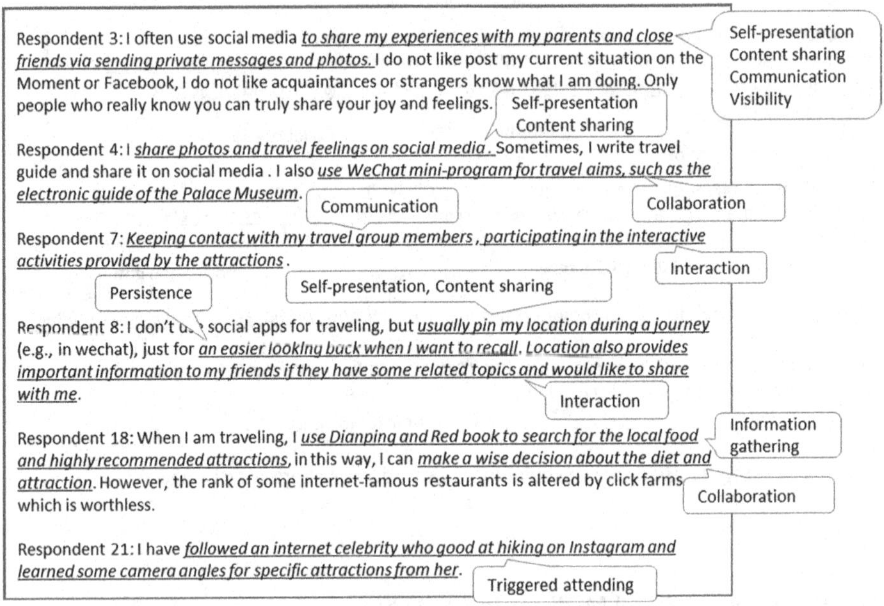

Respondent 3: I often use social media *to share my experiences with my parents and close friends via sending private messages and photos*. I do not like post my current situation on the Moment or Facebook, I do not like acquaintances or strangers know what I am doing. Only people who really know you can truly share your joy and feelings. [Self-presentation] [Content sharing] [Communication] [Visibility] [Self-presentation] [Content sharing]

Respondent 4: I *share photos and travel feelings on social media*. Sometimes, I write travel guide and share it on social media. I also *use WeChat mini-program for travel aims, such as the electronic guide of the Palace Museum*. [Communication] [Collaboration]

Respondent 7: *Keeping contact with my travel group members*, *participating in the interactive activities provided by the attractions*. [Interaction] [Persistence] [Self-presentation, Content sharing]

Respondent 8: I don't u.. social apps for traveling, but *usually pin my location during a journey* (e.g., in wechat), just for *an easier looking back when I want to recall*. *Location also provides important information to my friends if they have some related topics and would like to share with me*. [Interaction] [Information gathering]

Respondent 18: When I am traveling, I *use Dianping and Red book to search for the local food and highly recommended attractions*, in this way, I can *make a wise decision about the diet and attraction*. However, the rank of some internet-famous restaurants is altered by click farms, which is worthless. [Collaboration]

Respondent 21: I have *followed an internet celebrity who good at hiking on Instagram and learned some camera angles for specific attractions from her*. [Triggered attending]

Fig. 2. Evidence of social media affordances at in-travel stage.

4.3 Affordances of Social Media at After-Travel Stage

At after-travel stage, except information gathering and collaboration affordances, the other seven social media affordances were recognized. Information gathering and collaboration affordances only appeared at the beginning stages of travel, because the travelers needed information and would like to collaborate with others to prepare for a better travel experience. However, when the travel ended, the travelers inclined to pay more attention to self-displaying and experience sharing. For instance, travelers have a constant interest in sharing content after they finished the travel, thus self-presentation and content sharing affordances of social media could satisfy such kinds of needs. Whilst respondent 5 indicated he would not share anything more about his trip because he thought this behavior may bother his connections on social media. Compared with the in-travel stage, when completed the travel, the interviewees seemed to focus heavily on how to control the audience of their shared content and how to record their travel experience. Therefore, visibility and persistence affordances kept on occurring at this stage. Two of the respondents stated that they would like to interact with their friends concerning their experience after travel. For instance, participant 19 claimed that she wished her friends could press "like" to her post. Besides, communication and triggered attending affordances still arose. As discussed at the in-travel stage, these two affordances supported the travelers' needs for social media use attention and travel attention, not limited by time or space, but their perceptions (see Fig. 3).

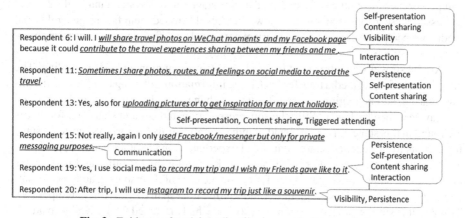

Fig. 3. Evidence of social media affordances at after-travel stage.

5   Discussion and Conclusion

The objective of this study is to achieve a comprehensive understanding of what social media functions can afford tourists' diverse needs at different travel stages. In particular, I explore nine affordances of social media at pre-travel, in-travel, after-travel stages.

5.1   Discussion

Findings reveal that tourists take advantage of a variety of social media affordances in fulfilling their travel demands in different travel stages. At pre-travel stage, travelers concentrated on searching travel information, making travel decisions, communicating with travel members or friends who have similar travel experience. These affordances of social media afford tourists to be well prepared for their upcoming travel. These findings concur with previous research information searching plays a significant role in social media to meet travelers' needs at pre-travel stage [35]. However, the results also show social media are not able to provide very effective travel information and support because of the information overloading at pre-travel stage. This finding is in line with Park, Jang [36], they also stressed this problem in their research. Regarding the triggered attending affordance of social media, there are pieces of evidence indicating tourists are easily seduced by the pictures or videos of attractions, and then plan a trip. Mariani et al. [37] showed similar research results with this.

At in-travel stage, travelers had various needs supported by social media. Self-presentation and sharing content affordances are the most frequent affordances that appear at this stage as the willingness of presentation and sharing raised from this stage. Information gathering and communication affordances are still important at this stage, as some tourists prefer to update their travel plans and keep connections with their family or friends when they are in travel. The research from Kim, Tussyadiah [38] supported these findings. Additionally, collaboration, triggered attending, visibility, interaction, and persistence affordances are occurred at this stage, though Karahanna et al. [23] had discussed these affordances as well, however, they discussed them from a general social media use perspective rather than a tourism context. These findings need more empirical research to prove.

At after-travel stage, travelers focused on self-presentation and self-recording. The affordances of social media transfer from basic information gathering to information editing, sharing, and belonging. These affordances changes by the travel stage changes and the travelers' needs change. Still, the self-presentation and content sharing affordances are found in this stage, on the one hand, it indicates after-travel stage is a significant stage for tourists to present and share their travel experience, on the other hand, it proves not all tourists are interested after-travel sharing. Regarding the visibility and persistence affordances, many tourists have been found to take care of their sharing audiences, platforms, types (texts, videos, or pictures) and sharing time span (permanent or temporary), This result is similar to Treem, Leonardi [20], they had discussed the DMOs' also attach importance to visibility and persistence affordances of social media for advertising and sales promotion. The findings also reveal the interaction affordance of social media after travel. Tourists prefer to interact with their friends in terms of the travel experience in

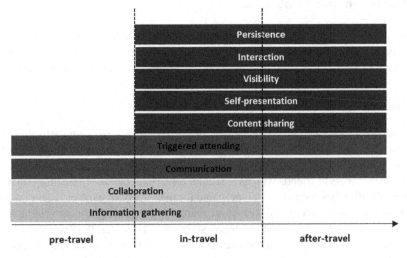

Fig. 4. Framework of social media affordances at different travel stages.

this stage, especially when they have traveled to the same attraction and have some similar travel experience. These findings contribute to the understanding of tourists' social media use in the whole travel processes and enhance the tourists' satisfaction via the facilitating of social media. Figure 4 illustrates the change of affordances at three different travel stages.

5.2 Implications

This study makes several theoretical implications. First, this work enriches social media use in tourism literature by disentangling nine different affordances of social media in tourism. The nine affordances include information gathering, collaboration, communication, triggered attending, content sharing, self-presentation, visibility, interaction, and persistence. The research findings show that technology affordance theory is a good theoretical framework to explain social media use patterns in tourism. Second, this study extends the technology affordance theory by dividing social media affordances into three categories to explain the social media use patterns in tourism. The explored affordances manifest that tourists have multiple travel needs, and their needs are diverse in different travel stages. Some affordances appear at pre-travel and in-travel stages and disappear at after-travel stages. Some affordances appear at in-travel and after-travel stages as they are sequent affordances, they only occur when the actual travel begins. These findings indicate that the affordances of social media widely exist in tourism and influence the tourists' social media use from the whole travel stages.

The research findings in this study also bear practical implications. This study explores the social media use in tourism from a comprehensive perspective, covering social media use at stages of pre-travel, in-travel, and after-travel. Thus, for many social media service providers, they could perfect their social media functional design and service provided processes to meet their users' needs accurately. Besides, practitioners should at least find a way to measure the level of affordances effectively to promote social media use for the existing and potential users.

5.3 Limitations and Future Research

There are several limitations to the current study. First, the study collected data via email and internet-call interviews instead of physical interviews, which may not offer in-depth insights on explaining the affordances of social media at all travel stages. Thus, further study may use other methods for collecting data, such as face-to-face interviews. Second, the interview groups are quite limited, such as the occupation of the respondents, the age ranges of the respondents, and the total interviewed persons. Therefore, more diverse research groups could be invited to participate in this kind of research to offer strong evidence of social media affordances in satisfying travelers' needs in tourism processes. For instance, increase the occupation diversity, enlarge the respondents' age ranges, and add the numbers of interviewees. In the future, more research could be done to focus on the geographic differences between travelers from the affordance perspective. Third, travel types were not discussed in this study. Whilst the types of trips may influence travelers' social media use, thus may be more studies that could be conducted to investigate the impact of different travel types on social media affordances in the future.

5.4 Conclusions

This study enhances our understanding of social media use in whole travel processes by introducing technology affordances perspective and explaining three categories of affordances of social media use. The empirical results show that information gathering, and collaboration are concluded as the first category of social media affordance, which only occurred at the pre-travel and in-travel stages. Content sharing, self-presentation, visibility, interaction, and persistence affordances are second category affordances, which arose only at the in-travel and after-travel stages. Additionally, communication, and triggered attending affordances are third category affordances, which occurred at all travel stages. These findings provide researchers with an improved understanding of social media use patterns in whole travel processes and the diversity of affordances. In addition, the results will be beneficial for tourism operators and social media designers, as they understand their customers' behavior from an integrated perspective.

References

1. eMarketer: Number of social network users worldwide from 2010 to 2023 (in billions) (2019). https://www.statista.com/statistics/278414/number-of-worldwide-social-network-users/. Accessed 16 Apr 2020
2. Travel Weekly: Social media platforms used by travel agents for marketing in the United States in 2016 (2016). https://www.statista.com/statistics/296230/effectiveness-of-social-media-for-travel-agents-us/. Accessed 16 Apr 2020
3. momondo.se: Do you post updates on social media when you are on holiday (e.g. Facebook, Twitter or Instagram)? (2017). https://www.statista.com/statistics/896671/social-media-usage-of-finnish-travelers/. Accessed 16 Apr 2020
4. Skyscanner: Popular trips taken by travelers in the Asia Pacific region in 2019 (2019). https://www.statista.com/statistics/1102099/apac-popular-trips-among-travelers-by-type/. Accessed 16 Apr 2020
5. Miah, S.J., Vu, H.Q., Gammack, J., McGrath, M.: A big data analytics method for tourist behaviour analysis. Inf. Manag. **54**(6), 771–785 (2017)
6. Dedeoğlu, B.B., Taheri, B., Okumus, F., Gannon, M.: Understanding the importance that consumers attach to social media sharing (ISMS): scale development and validation. Tour. Manag. **76**, 103954 (2020)
7. Hays, S., Page, S.J., Buhalis, D.: Social media as a destination marketing tool: its use by national tourism organisations. Curr. Issues Tour. **16**(3), 211–239 (2013)
8. Majchrzak, A., Markus, M.L.: Technology affordances and constraints in management information systems (MIS). In: Kessler, E. (ed.) Encyclopedia of Management Theory. Sage Publications, Thousand Oaks (2012)
9. Kaplan, A.M., Haenlein, M.: Users of the world, unite! The challenges and opportunities of social media. Bus. Horiz. **53**(1), 59–68 (2010)
10. Chung, N., Han, H., Koo, C.: Adoption of travel information in user-generated content on social media: the moderating effect of social presence. Behav. Inf. Technol. **34**(9), 902–919 (2015)
11. Kim, S.-E., Lee, K.Y., Shin, S.I., Yang, S.-B.: Effects of tourism information quality in social media on destination image formation: the case of Sina Weibo. Inf. Manag. **54**(6), 687–702 (2017)
12. Hudson, S., Thal, K.: The impact of social media on the consumer decision process: implications for tourism marketing. J. Travel Tour. Mark. **30**(1–2), 156–160 (2013)

13. Zhang, J.L., Wu, T., Fan, Z.P.: Research on precision marketing model of tourism industry based on user's mobile behavior trajectory. Mob. Inf. Syst. **2019**, 1–14 (2019)
14. Amaro, S., Duarte, P.: Social media use for travel purposes: a cross cultural comparison between Portugal and the UK. Inf. Technol. Tour. **17**(2), 161–181 (2017)
15. Fotis, J., Buhalis, D., Rossides, N.: Social Media Use and Impact During the Holiday Travel Planning Process. Springer, Vienna (2012)
16. Dolan, R., Seo, Y., Kemper, J.: Complaining practices on social media in tourism: a value co-creation and co-destruction perspective. Tour. Manag. **73**, 35–45 (2019)
17. Gibson, J.J.: The Theory of Affordances, vol. 1. Hilldale, USA (1977). no. 2
18. Gaver, W.W.: Technology affordances. In: Proceedings of the SIGCHI Conference on Human Factors in Computing Systems, pp. 7–84. Association for Computing Machinery, Louisiana (1991)
19. Leonardi, P.M., Vaast, E.: Social media and their affordances for organizing: a review and agenda for research. Acad. Manag. Ann. **11**(1), 150–188 (2017)
20. Treem, J.W., Leonardi, P.M.: Social media use in organizations: exploring the affordances of visibility, editability, persistence, and association. Ann. Int. Commun. Assoc. **36**(1), 143–189 (2013)
21. Majchrzak, A., Faraj, S., Kane, G.C., Azad, B.: The contradictory influence of social media affordances on online communal knowledge sharing. J. Comput.-Mediat. Commun. **19**(1), 38–55 (2013)
22. DeVito, M.A., Birnholtz, J., Hancock, J.T.: Platforms, people, and perception: using affordances to understand self-presentation on social media. In: Proceedings of the 2017 ACM Conference on Computer Supported Cooperative Work and Social Computing, pp. 740–54. Association for Computing Machinery, Portland (2017)
23. Karahanna, E., Xu, S.X., Xu, Y., Zhang, N.A.: The needs–affordances–features perspective for the use of social media. MIS Q. **42**(3), 737–756 (2018)
24. Davis, A., Murphy, J.D., Owens, D., Khazanchi, D., Zigurs, I.: Avatars, people, and virtual worlds: foundations for research in metaverses. J. Assoc. Inf. Syst. **10**(2), 90–117 (2009)
25. Kietzmann, J.H., Hermkens, K., McCarthy, I.P., Silvestre, B.S.: Social media? Get serious! Understanding the functional building blocks of social media. Bus. Horiz. **54**(3), 241–251 (2011)
26. Cabiddu, F., De Carlo, M., Piccoli, G.: Social media affordances: enabling customer engagement. Ann. Tour. Res. **48**, 175–192 (2014)
27. Gretzel, U.: Social media activism in tourism. J. Hosp. Tour. **15**(2), 1–14 (2017)
28. Myers, M.D., Newman, M.: The qualitative interview in IS research: examining the craft. Inf. Organ. **17**(1), 2–26 (2007)
29. Halpern, D., Gibbs, J.: Social media as a catalyst for online deliberation? Exploring the affordances of Facebook and YouTube for political expression. Comput. Hum. Behav. **29**(3), 1159–1168 (2013)
30. Volkoff, O., Strong, D.M.: Critical realism and affordances: theorizing IT-associated organizational change processes. MIS Q. **37**, 819–834 (2013)
31. Leidner, D.E., Gonzalez, E., Koch, H.: An affordance perspective of enterprise social media and organizational socialization. J. Strateg. Inf. Syst. **27**(2), 117–138 (2018)
32. Mesgari, M., Faraj, S.: Technology affordances: the case of Wikipedia. In: Proceedings of the Eighteenth Americas Conference on Information Systems, pp. 1–9. Association for Information Systems, Seattle (2012)
33. Vaast, E., Safadi, H., Lapointe, L., Negoita, B.: Social media affordances for connective action: an examination of microblogging use during the Gulf of Mexico oil spill. MIS Q. **41**(4), 1179–1205 (2017)

34. Raja-Yusof, R.-J., Norman, A.-A., Abdul-Rahman, S.-S., Mohd-Yusoff, Z.: Cyber-volunteering: social media affordances in fulfilling NGO social missions. Comput. Hum. Behav. **57**, 388–397 (2016)
35. Chung, N., Koo, C.: The use of social media in travel information search. Telemat. Inform. **32**(2), 215–229 (2015)
36. Park, J.-Y., Jang, S.S.: Confused by too many choices? Choice overload in tourism. Tour. Manag. **35**, 1–12 (2013)
37. Mariani, M.M., Di Felice, M., Mura, M.: Facebook as a destination marketing tool: evidence from Italian regional destination management organizations. Tour. Manag. **54**, 321–343 (2016)
38. Kim, J., Tussyadiah, I.P.: Social networking and social support in tourism experience: the moderating role of online self-presentation strategies. J. Travel Tour. Mark. **30**(1–2), 78–92 (2013)

Respecting the Individuals of Data Economy Ecosystems

Minna M. Rantanen$^{(\boxtimes)}$ ⓘ and Jani Koskinen ⓘ

Turku School of Economics, University of Turku, Turku, Finland
{minna.m.rantanen,jasiko}@utu.fi

Abstract. Importance of data - especially personal data - is increasing as a business asset. The role of data economy ecosystems is also growing. However, the individuals whose data are used in these systems are not respected as active members but are often seen as mere data sources. In this paper, we address the question about how the individuals could be respected through the creation of value congruence. We elaborate on the discussion about the personal values of Europeans to practices of the data economy ecosystems. Our brief analysis shows that the individuals should be respected as active members of data economy ecosystems by providing tools and information though transparent, honest and secure practices. In this, transparency seems to be the prime enabler of value congruence and thus, the basis of respecting the individuals.

Keywords: Data economy ecosystems · Personal data · Values · Respect · Individuals

1 Introduction

Data – especially personal data - have become an increasingly important asset in the modern world. This development has created a multitude of complex socio-technical systems where data are collected, stored, exchanged, analysed and used to create more value. These systems are referred to as data economy ecosystems or data economies [1, 2].

Personal data economy ecosystems rely on the cooperation of organisations and individuals. However, in current research of data economy ecosystems individuals have not been acknowledged as active parts of the data economy ecosystem but merely as data subjects. Also, data economy ecosystems are currently being orchestrated mainly by a few big tech companies, which have faced scandals due to their unethical practices concerning personal data [2, 3]. Simultaneously, individuals have been increasingly aware of the value of their data and have expressed their disappointment in the ways that data is gathered and used [4].

This development has led to a lack of trust towards the collection of personal data, which could, in the long run, undermine the promised benefits of personal data economies for all. This mistrust and its consequences can jeopardise data collection and, therefore, the whole basis of data economy [5]. Trust plays a fundamental role as a predictor of the usage of technology [6]. Thus, it is also integral to get individuals to cooperate with

© Springer Nature Switzerland AG 2020
M. Cacace et al. (Eds.): WIS 2020, CCIS 1270, pp. 185–196, 2020.
https://doi.org/10.1007/978-3-030-57847-3_13

data economies, i.e. release their personal data to the use of these ecosystems. Trust, in its essence, is an end to a process in which individuals evaluate the trustworthiness in an interaction. Trust in the case of data economy ecosystems is institutional trust, that can be defined as a specific kind of trust where the trustee places trust in the rules, roles, and norms of an institution independent of the people occupying those roles [7].

The European Union is attempting to rebuild the trust in data economies by enforcing the role of citizens as part of them with regulations such as the General data protection regulation (GDPR) [8]. Regulations like GDPR form the basis for organisational norms in Europe but leave room for different executions. Rules and norms of the organisations are complemented by corporate values that guide the actions in work [7, 9].

Value congruence has been proven to not only mediate the trust of consumers towards organisations, but it also has a strong effect on their determining their willingness to disclose personal information. In some cases, value congruence has an even more significant impact than trust [10]. Thus, aligning values of the data economy ecosystem governance with values of the individuals play an important role in personal data economy ecosystems, their trustworthiness and consequently on their viability.

Due to the infancy of the data economy ecosystems as a research field, there is still a need for justified governance models [11] as well as perspectives that focus on the individuals [2]. Consequently, there is only a little research about how orchestrators and regulators can respect the values and needs of the individuals in personal data economy ecosystems. Thus, the objective of this paper is to analyse how the needs and values of individuals could be fulfilled in the European data economy ecosystem. The research question is:

RQ: How the individuals and their needs and values could be respected in personal data economy ecosystems?

We answer this question by analysing existing knowledge about the issues that individuals value concerning the data economy [9] further in light of existing literature. This paper aims to pave the way for more human-centric practices by respecting the values and needs of the individuals. The paper will reveal the connections and gaps between theoretical knowledge and empirical evidence, thus accumulating current knowledge and revealing directions for future research and practices.

This paper is constructed as follows: the next section elaborates on the concepts of the data economy ecosystem and the role of individuals in the personal data economy ecosystems. In Sect. 3, personal values of Europeans are analysed further to discover what characteristics a fair data economy ecosystem should have. Section 4 shortly discusses the found characteristics of a fair data economy ecosystem and concludes the paper.

2 Background

2.1 Data Economy Ecosystems

Data economy ecosystems are an emerging research field. Thus, there is still a lack of consensus about the terminology. Data ecosystems are a set of actors working together on data and other shared resources [12]. In turn, a network of vendors that aim to accumulate data to create more value is called a data economy [13]. There is only a slight difference between these two. It can be argued that data ecosystems are, in some form, also data economies. We prefer the term data economy ecosystem because it incorporates both aspects. Data economy ecosystems generally mean complex socio-technical systems where data are collected, stored, exchanged and analysed to create more value. It must be noted, that in this context data are things that are known or assumed as facts that are then used as a basis of reasoning, not as mere quantities or characters. Hence, the value of data lies in their use.

In this paper, we use the following definition for the data economy ecosystem:

"Data economy ecosystem is a network, that is formed by different actors of ecosystem, that are using data as a main source or instance for business. Different actors and stakeholders are connected directly or indirectly within network and its value chains. Data economy ecosystem also incorporates the rules (official or unofficial), that direct action allowed in network." [2]

This definition suits our purpose since it highlights the plurality of actors and connections between them. Additionally, it brings forth the normative side of the data ecosystems: there are rules affecting actions in and on them. Besides legislations, companies and ecosystems have their own norms that regulate their activities within the data economy ecosystems and their governance. However, governance of digital infrastructures like data economy ecosystems is not a simple issue due to the ever-changing nature of technological ecosystems. The governance of digital infrastructures simultaneously needs to be stable and flexible. Stable enough to have an effect, but flexible enough so that it can reflect the necessary changes [14].

Challenge in the data economy ecosystem regulations – especially in regard to personal data – is finding the balance between privacy protection and benefits that can be gained through data economy. For instance, in the European Union, GDPR is an attempt to protect the privacy of the individuals by allowing them to have more control over their data [8]. However, the GDPR is not a silver bullet for more human-driven data economy ecosystems, and there are much more research and actions to be done if we truly want to respect the individuals and their needs in the data economy ecosystems.

2.2 The Need for Respecting Individuals in the Personal Data Economy

In data economies or data ecosystems, individuals are often seen as data subjects. A data subject refers to any individual person who can be identified, directly or indirectly [8]. Talking about subjects undermines the active role of the individuals in the data economy ecosystems. In academic literature, it is also typical that the research about data economies focuses on the technical or business issues of data economy ecosystems [1].

Seeing individuals as mere sources of data is either respectful or beneficial. Although personal data analytics hold great promises, it has been noted that current ways of acquiring and using them can enable a new form of digital enslavement which can endanger the autonomy of individuals and societies [15]. For example, in recent years, it has been showcased that micro-targeting of social media users has been used to influence opinions, especially in politics [16]. Thus, respecting the individuals as part of data economy ecosystems is not just a matter of preserving privacy, but also a case of societal issues.

Although movements like MyData [17] have been successfully promoting the human-driven data economies through their principles, there is still very little research about the needs of the individuals, as well as values and reasoning behind them. It has been argued that in order to understand and respect the needs of individuals, they should be acknowledged as active and productive parts of data economy ecosystems that have commonly been industry-oriented [9]. Thus, we need a way to find out what the individuals want and find a way to secure their needs through the governance of data economy ecosystems.

Respecting the individuals is by no means in contradiction to the interests of businesses operating in data economy ecosystems. Current practices of large data economy ecosystems, such as Facebook and Google, have provoked mistrust, and there have been demands for change. These modern tech giants have vast data economy ecosystems that leave little choice for customers. However, competitors will likely emerge and gain a competitive advantage through more trustworthy and fair actions [18]. Thus, respecting individuals, their need and autonomy could offer a business advantage to orchestrators and practitioners of data economy ecosystems.

Acknowledging the needs of the individuals in complex socio-technical systems such as data economy ecosystems is not a simple issue. Traditional information system development methods that consider the needs of individuals such as socio-technical design require constant and presentative participation. These requirements are impossible to meet in data economy systems since the users form a large and heterogeneous group and are not bound, for example, by organisational roles [9]. Thus, there is a need to find a way to acknowledge individuals' needs in also complex socio-technical systems.

Since needs vary a lot between individuals aiming for value congruence – aligning organisational values with individuals' values – could be a profitable way to respect the individuals. Value congruence could be used to create persistent trust towards personal data economy ecosystems. When judging the trustworthiness of an institution, people often base the trust in their interpretation of values of the institutions and how much of them share with them [4, 10]. Trust affects the willingness to disclose personal data and use technology, but it has been argued that value congruence is in some cases even more important that trust [19]. Thus, reaching for value congruence in both internal and external governance of personal data economies could be beneficial to both individuals and the practitioners of the data economy.

Thus, value congruence can help to promote trust towards data economy ecosystems and willingness to take part in them. Values of the Europeans in the context of data economy ecosystems have been mapped [9]. However, the question of how these values could be implemented in the governance of data economy ecosystems is still to be answered. In this paper, we elaborate on the previous research by analysing how these values could be respected in practice.

3   Values Behind a Trustworthy Data Economy Ecosystem

Research about human values in relation to data economy ecosystems is still scarce, but the values of the Europeans regarding fair data economy have been mapped. In her research Rantanen [9] resulted in the seven distinguished themes that people from Germany, Finland, France, and the Netherlands value in this context. These themes are:

- User's control over data and data sharing
- Transparency and being informed
- Security – Trust and fairness
- Compensation or benefits for users
- Supervision and rules
- Negative attitudes towards data collection and data economy.

It must be noted that as a sample, these four countries share fairly similar cultural values. A trusting attitude towards technology has been linked to especially to the cultural value of uncertainty avoidance [20]. Germany, Finland, France, and the Netherlands all have a high preference for avoiding uncertainty [21]. Thus, it could be assumed that incorporating these valued themes in the European data economy ecosystem would help to create trust also in the cultures that do not prefer avoiding uncertainty as much.

The last theme shows that Europeans have distrust towards data economy ecosystems. However, there are no other apparent factors behind these responses than disappointment in the current practices and cynical attitude towards change [9]. Thus, in the next subsections first six themes are further investigated.

3.1 User's Control Over Data and Data Sharing

European citizens have expressed that they would value control over the collection, use and secondary use of their data. This is a matter of dynamic and informed consent but also access to one's data and ability to supervise data collection and usage. Although only a few explicitly mentioned ownership of data personal, control over the data was seen as something that individuals should have [9].

Data have often been treated as confidential or protected, but the view that individuals have some sort of ownership on them is a reasonably new phenomenon [4]. Ownership is a problematic term when talking about data. Legally the data is often owned by the instance that owns the database [20]. However, it has been argued that for example, patients have an ethically justified right to have mastery over their data [22]. Thus, individuals should have the right to control the collection and use of their data.

Consent is one way that one's control over personal data is implemented in data economy ecosystems. Policies and regulations about getting consent have been significantly affected by the collection of genetic information, which use holds both economic and public value [4, 23]. In the European Union asking consent—or using other justified cause—is mandated by the GDPR. In GDPR, consent is considered to be valid if it is freely given, specific, informed, and the individual whose information is in the questions agrees to it [8].

However, agreeing to lengthy legal texts or accepting of cookies with a single click are hardly informed consents, since the information cannot be or is not comprehended. Thus, it can be argued that some tools for control over data are offered and mandated, but they could be better in practice. Personal data management solutions could offer a way for individuals to really gain control over their data and data sharing [24]. Alas, it should also be remembered that although people wish for more control, it is unlikely that they have the time or desire to manage and market their entire digital footprint [25]. Despite this, individuals should have at least the possibility to control their data.

3.2 Transparency and Being Informed

Control over one's data relates closely to transparency and being informed. Yet it is more specific in the sense that people highlighting it do not imply that they need to have power over data and data use. Transparency and openness were often seen as a means to gain trust. In general, people would like to be aware of the actions of the organisations of data economy ecosystems, whereby it follows that other values, such as being an active actor, can be met [9].

Transparency in this context means that organisations open their actions to public scrutiny [9]. Transparency in itself is a value that has an evolving meaning, and that can be seen as a means to ensure accountability of organisations, counter corruption and is often synonymous with open decision-making [26].

Thus, transparency requires that an organisation provides enough understandable and correct information about their actions and decision-making processes to the public. This information can then be used as a measurement of accountability, in other words, held as a promise of certain actions and decisions. Transparency from the perspective of companies is not always preferable. Transparency with low control over information by the user has a negative effect as the customers can have worries about the various potential uses of their data without any control over the situation. Thus, transparency needs to be paired with the possibility act over the information given. Transparency also helps the needs of the organisations, since prevents the spread of negative gossips, deters switching, and even suppresses adverse stock price effects [27]. This issue pinpoints the instrumental value of transparency as it is a value that reveals other issues that are not possible without it.

In the context of data economy ecosystems transparency would mean that the individuals can have information about processes involving their data. However, current ways of communicating these processes often are not understandable to non-specialists, since they rely on legal jargon or empty values that cannot be fully understood. Thus, the is no real possibility of the individuals to assess the practices or engage in the discussion.

It must be noted that due to the complex nature of data economy ecosystems, it can be hard to disclose information about the movements of data and how and why it is analysed. However, it should not be impossible because without it, we cannot reach transparency and sufficiently inform people. Consequently, failing to inform people also undermines their power over their data, since it makes the informed consent impossible. Thus, there is a need that institutions of data economy ecosystems aim to be transparent and keep the public informed.

3.3 Security

Security of the data economies, anonymisation of sensitive data and prevention of misuse of data were seen as qualities of the fair data economy. The Europeans also expressed that data should be deleted after use and that data use should be locally restricted to their home countries or Europe. Thus, security is seen as a safeguard of privacy. There were some contradictions in what constitutes a secure way of data handling. Some strongly favoured technical solutions such as artificial intelligence (AI) over humans, whereas some felt strongly that the data should be handled only by human-beings [9].

Security seems to refer to both data security and system security. Based on the contradicting notions of what constitutes as a security, it seems that people do not have a clear conception of what actually is secure and what is not. This could lead to a situation, that Hakkala [28] defines as forced trust: people have no other choice than to trust all aspects of the provided system although it is not necessarily genuinely trustworthy or secure. Forced trust should be avoided, and there should be alternatives to it.

Security is also a means for preserving the privacy of individuals. Privacy is generally highly valued, but people actively rarely protect their personal data. This phenomenon is called the "privacy paradox" since attitudes and actions are in contradiction. The privacy paradox and mechanisms behind it reveal the complex interplay of trust, people's perceptions, attitudes, and actions [29]. Demand for privacy has not gone undetected by the companies because privacy has also been tailored to a product that the consumers can purchase [10]. But how can we avoid forced trust in the context of security of data economy ecosystems? Security in itself is a complex issue that is often misunderstood. Nevertheless, it should be communicated and understood also in the context of a complex network. Thus, making security and security measurements clearer and ways for preserving privacy more usable could make a data economy ecosystem more trustworthy and perhaps create more innovative business models around privacy.

In other words, people should have more information available about the security of technology and practices from the data economy ecosystem orchestrators and practitioners. Thus, transparency could be a way to help individuals to understand the concept of security and measurements that can be made by them and others to preserve their privacy.

3.4 Trust and Fairness

Trust was seen as a quality of a fair data economy. Trust and fairness were often mentioned when describing the benevolence of the data economy. Trustworthiness was generally seen as keeping one's promises, which in this context meant that the terms and conditions agreed upon were followed and not changed. Ethical or moral actions were mentioned and sometimes described as using data for a good cause concerning moral values. Also, issues such as appropriate data management, respectful behaviour, integrity, responsibility, equality, and avoidance of harm were often mentioned [9].

This theme seems to incorporate a lot of desirable characteristics of fair data economy ecosystems, but without further descriptions. Though this theme provides insight into the Europeans conceptualisation of trustworthiness as promise-keeping, it leaves open the question about what kind of promises should be made in the first place. Terms such as ethical, moral, appropriate and respectful are unfortunately rather vague without any further explanations of how they can be actualised.

Fortunately, other themes address some of these promises and thus, provide some insight on "good promises". On the one hand, benevolence, ethicality, and moral actions tie this theme to the theme of gaining benefits. On the other hand, this theme combined with the rest of the mentioned issues can be interpreted as a need to be seen as an active actor instead of a mere resource. Also, keeping one's promises ties this theme to transparency and accountability—informing the public about the actions that are done and taking responsibility when something fails or has to be changed. Without transparency, there is a risk of gossips followed by bad reputation and lack of trust, which has a negative effect on companies [27]. Nevertheless, more empirical research about conceptions of fairness and trust is needed to understand what people mean with these terms. Only then they can be implemented into practices and governance of data economy ecosystems.

3.5 Compensation or Benefits for Users

Some of the respondents demanded compensations or more benefits in exchange for personal data. Europeans were aware of the monetary value of their data and determined that for example, personalised advertisement is not enough. Some requested that they should have monetary compensations for secondary use of their data, whereas some wanted free premiums, discounts, better personalisation or other benefits for themselves. In contrast to hedonistic demands, some stated that a fair data economy should support the common good and their data could be used to, for example, non-profit research [9].

The current distribution of benefits for increasingly valuable personal data clearly does not promote the trustworthiness of data economy ecosystems. Business benefits to companies are often discussed, and benefits for individuals are often seen merely as a means to boost business. However, it is also possible to create benefits and value for the customers directly [25].

People simply want to have something in exchange for their data, and those possible benefits predict both intention and actual disclosure of personal data [30]. However, it must be noted that the value of data is not in its sale, but how it is used. Thus, evaluating the monetary value of the personal data for the individual and consequently, monetary compensation for personal data are rather troublesome issues [10].

Often the monetary compensation is offered as free service when the personal data is the actual product of a company. Personal data is then seen as a payment for using the service, that is monetised after collection or data is used to advertisement, etc. [10]. This means, that often personal data is not collected and used for the benefit for the individuals but for the revenue of the organisations. Using somebody as merely a means to make money clearly provokes distrust - especially if the gained benefits are unclear and the data is used for something that they do not need. However, it seems that the common good is a value that is important for people, for instance when using health data outside of the healthcare for research [31]. This underlines the need for common values when using data—people are willing to give information if they see that it is something that they value even if it does not provide direct benefits for them.

It seems that also in this theme the communication is the key. Organisations should be open about how they are using the data and who benefits from it and how. However, it must be noted that this communication should be honest and not done with the intention to mislead the individuals in order to get their data. People clearly know that their data has potential value and wish to know what they could gain when releasing it. Thus, being open about beneficiaries is a characteristic of trustworthiness.

3.6 Supervision and Rules

Compliance with rules, supervision by a non-profiting institute (such as governments) and sanctions were also seen as methods of maintaining fairness and integrity of a data economy. Implicit rules that are followed were seen as a safeguard of a fair data economy [9].

This theme addresses the governance of the data economy ecosystem - the official rules that this institution should have and comply with. Governance of data ecosystems is a challenging issue since ecosystems by default cannot be strictly controlled due to their flexibility, but at the same time, it needs the common ground between stakeholders.

Data governance is an area that is not widely researched [32]. Thus, we want to clarify what kind of Governance areas should be noted and furthermore analyses to see what kind of rules we need for the data economy. Governance of data can be internal, which means that it is done by and inside of an organisation. This is the focus on traditional IT Governance where effective use of IT is a necessity for organisations that need to fulfil demands set for them by society and survive in tightening competition [33, 34].

Internal governance of data includes the norms of the organisation, guidelines and management's views and values considering data. Thus, data governance is most likely based on the values of organisations when it is possible. However, this is not always the case in networks that are based on the cooperation of a multitude of organisations. This kind of governance is called "inter-organisational IT governance" which focuses on governance between organisations [35]. Thus, values of organisations direct the rules on how data should be governed in the network. On the contrary, external governance is governance set out by outside actors of organisations and can be laws, soft laws, other regulations, standards, etc.

The governance of big data and data ecosystems is an approach that is still under development [36] and especially from the perspective of ethical governance [11]. This area of governance—data economy ecosystem governance—is an area that should incorporate all areas of governance: internal, inter-organisational, external and individual. Thus, when aiming for a trustworthy data economy ecosystem, governance models should fit the values of individuals, different organisations and society. Therefore the rules in data ecosystem should be such that they fulfil the demands of all stakeholders or the ecosystem will lose it justification from society (regulative conflict), individuals (lack of trust and thus interest to provide data [5]) or organisations as they do not see that their interest are not to be served. Hence, the need for value congruence and respecting all stakeholders is essential for data ecosystems in the long term as ecosystems that achieve this will be more compelling ones.

4   Conclusions

It seems that the characteristics of the data economy ecosystem, that truly respects the individuals could be derived from the values of the individuals. In Europe, these characteristics would be open and transparent communication and allowing people to take an active role as part of data economy ecosystems. Transparency and communication should be comprehensible to the individuals so that they can form an understanding of the practices involving their data.

Comprehensible and deliberative communication seems to be the cross-cutting theme in regard to values handled in this paper. First, individuals should have enough information to act upon in order to have control over their data and data use. Second, they need to be able to understand the practices, benefits, and rules on which data ecosystems rely so that individuals can assess the trustworthiness. Third, individuals should have tools that provide them with possibilities to act upon the information that they have accumulated.

Thus, the simple answer to our research question about how the individuals could be respected in personal data economy ecosystems is respect individuals as active members of data economy ecosystems by giving them enough information and power over their data and be transparent and honest without compromising the security.

It remains to be seen if the actors in data economy ecosystems are willing to comply with the values of individuals. Transparency and giving power to individuals could be hard for some organisations. However, in the current atmosphere, the ones that are willing to take these values as their own could gain a significant advance in the data business and business that tries to keep all control by themselves may face the significant problem by a bad reputation. Advances would follow from the value congruence, but also from regained institutional trust towards the organisation. However, these values should be extended to be a part of also external governance of the data economy ecosystems, so that the individuals can trust the entire network.

Practices in the data economy ecosystems should be examined further to find ways to acknowledge the values of individuals in data economy ecosystems. This means that we should try to find out more about the needs and values of individuals and how a value congruence could be achieved. In order to do that, we need more communication about practices of personal data economy ecosystems, more knowledge about how individuals assess the organisational values in this context and what do they really need from these systems. Thus, there is still much to know about the interplay of data economy ecosystems and individuals. Thus, more conceptual and empirical research is needed from the perspective that notes individuals as active actors in data economy ecosystems. Also, there is a need to find ways to implement these values in data economy ecosystems in practice in order to truly achieve trustworthy data economy ecosystems.

References

1. Oliveira, M.I.S., de Lima, G.F.B., Lóscio, B.F.: Investigations into data ecosystems: a systematic mapping study. KAIS **61**, 1–42 (2019)
2. Koskinen, J., Knaapi-Junnila, S., Rantanen, M.M.: What if we had fair – people-centred – data economy ecosystems? In: Proceedings of IEEE Smart World Conference 2019 (2019)
3. Koskinen, J., Rantanen, M.M., Kimppa, K.K., Hyrynsalmi, S.: Ecosystem ethics: an ethical analysis of orchestrators' ultimate power and the dilemma of ecosystem ruling. In: Suominen, A., Jud, C., Bosch, J. (eds.) IWSECO, pp. 43–54 (2017)
4. Igo, S.E.: Me and my data. Hist. Stud. Nat. Sci. **48**, 616–626 (2018)
5. Punj, G.N.: Understanding individuals' intentions to limit online personal information disclosures to protect their privacy: implications for organizations and public policy. Inf. Technol. Manag. **20**(3), 139–151 (2019)
6. Li, X., Hess, T.J., Valacich, J.S.: Why do we trust new technology? A study of initial trust formation with organizational information systems. J. Strateg. Inf. Syst. **17**, 39–71 (2008)

7. Smith, M.L.: Building institutional trust through e-government trustworthiness cues. Inf. Technol. People **23**(3), 222–246 (2010)
8. Regulation (EU) 2016/679 of the European Parliament and of the Council of 27 April 2016 on the protection of natural persons with regard to the processing of personal data and on the free movement of such data, and repealing Directive 95/46/EC (General Data Protection Regulation). Off. J. Eur. Union. L119, 1–88 (2016)
9. Rantanen, M.M.: Towards ethical guidelines for fair data economy – thematic analysis of values of Europeans. In: Proceedings of the Third Seminar on Technology Ethics 2019, CEUR-WS, pp. 43–54 (2019)
10. Elvy, S.-A.: Paying for privacy and the personal data economy. Colum. Rev. **117**, 1369 (2017)
11. Rantanen, M.M., Hyrynsalmi, S., Hyrynsalmi, S.M.: Towards ethical data ecosystems: a literature study. In: 2019 IEEE ICE/ITMC, Nice, France, pp. 1–9 (2019)
12. Oliveira, M.I.S., Lóscio, B.F.: What is a data ecosystem? In: Proceedings of the 19th Annual International Conference on Digital Government Research: Governance in the Data Age, pp. 74:1–74:9. ACM, New York (2018)
13. Communication on Building a European Data Economy. https://ec.europa.eu/digital-single-market/en/news/communication-building-european-data-economy. Accessed 20 Apr 2020
14. Tilson, D., Lyytinen, K., Sørensen, C.: Research commentary-digital infrastructures: the missing IS research agenda. Inf. Syst. Res. **21**, 748–759 (2010)
15. Chisnall, M.: Digital slavery, time for abolition? Policy Stud. 1–19 (2020)
16. Papakyriakopoulos, O., Hegelich, S., Shahrezaye, M., Serrano, J.C.M.: Social media and microtargeting: political data processing and the consequences for Germany. Big Data Soc. **5**, 1–15 (2018)
17. MyData.org – Make it happen, make it right!. https://mydata.org/. Accessed 20 Apr 2020
18. Lammi, M., Pantzar, M.: The data economy: how technological change has altered the role of the citizen-consumer. Technol. Soc. **59**, 101157 (2019)
19. Cazier, J.A., Shao, B.B., Louis, R.D.S.: Sharing information and building trust through value congruence. Inf. Syst. Front. **9**, 515–529 (2007)
20. Vance, A., Elie-Dit-Cosaque, C., Straub, D.W.: Examining trust in information technology artifacts: the effects of system quality and culture. J. Manag. Inf. Syst. **24**, 73–100 (2008)
21. Hofstede Insights: Compare Countries. https://www.hofstede-insights.com/product/compare-countries/. Accessed 20 Apr 2020
22. Koskinen, J.: Datenherrschaft–an ethically justified solution to the problem of ownership of patient information (2016)
23. Winickoff, D.: A bold experiment: Iceland's genomic venture. In: Mascalzoni, D. (ed.) Ethics, Law and Governance of Biobanking. TILELT, vol. 14, pp. 187–209. Springer, Dordrecht (2015). https://doi.org/10.1007/978-94-017-9573-9_13
24. Anciaux, N., et al.: Personal data management systems: the security and functionality standpoint. Inf. Syst. **80**, 13–35 (2019)
25. Margolis, A.: Five misconceptions about personal data: why we need a people-centred approach to "big" data. In: Ethnographic Praxis in Industry Conference Proceedings, pp. 32–43. Wiley (2013)
26. Ball, C.: What is transparency? Public Integr. **11**, 293–308 (2009)
27. Martin, K.D., Borah, A., Palmatier, R.W.: Data privacy: effects on customer and firm performance. J. Mark. **81**, 36–58 (2017)
28. Hakkala, A.: On security and privacy for networked information society: observations and solutions for security engineering and trust building in advanced societal processes (2017)
29. Gerber, N., Gerber, P., Volkamer, M.: Explaining the privacy paradox: a systematic review of literature investigating privacy attitude and behavior. Comput. Secur. **77**, 226–261 (2018)
30. Kokolakis, S.: Privacy attitudes and privacy behaviour: a review of current research on the privacy paradox phenomenon. Comput. Secur. **64**, 122–134 (2017)

31. Skovgaard, L.L., Wadmann, S., Hoeyer, K.: A review of attitudes towards the reuse of health data among people in the European Union: the primacy of purpose and the common good. Health Policy **123**, 564–571 (2019)
32. Al-Ruithe, M., Benkhelifa, E., Hameed, K.: A systematic literature review of data governance and cloud data governance. Ubiquit. Comput. **23**, 839–859 (2019)
33. Amali, L.N., Mahmuddin, M., Ahmad, M.: Information technology governance framework in the public sector organizations. Telkomnika **12**, 429 (2014)
34. Ross, J., Weill, P.: Recipe for good governance. CIO Mag. **15** (2004)
35. Helin, A.: Inter-organizational IT governance research: a literature review. IJITBAG **10**, 40–54 (2019)
36. Flyverbom, M., Deibert, R., Matten, D.: The governance of digital technology, big data, and the Internet: new roles and responsibilities for business. Bus. Soc. **58**, 3–19 (2019)

Internet of Things (IoT) Data Accessibility: Ethical Considerations

Mikko Vermanen$^{(\boxtimes)}$ ⓘ, Jani Koskinen ⓘ, and Ville Harkke ⓘ

Turku School of Economics, University of Turku, Turku, Finland
{mjverm,jasiko,ville.harkke}@utu.fi

Abstract. Internet of Things (IoT) solutions are capable of providing a vast amount of information from various entities, including technical devices, environment and individuals. The growing data collection abilities make it easier to analyse the collected data, connect it to certain individuals and use this information both for their advantage and disadvantage. Considering the fact that the accessibility of IoT data collected from individuals is strongly bound to their privacy and legal rights, it is crucial to understand how the data collection, processing and distribution can be conducted in an ethically sustainable manner. Therefore, to fulfil their obligations to follow good ethical principles, the organisations behind the IoT implementations should identify and address the potential personal risks. However, there is a lack of sufficient guidelines needed for fulfilling the ethical requirements. For this purpose, we introduce a decision tree visualising the recommended data distribution practices on a stakeholder level.

Keywords: Internet of Things · PAPA · Ethics

1 Introduction

The concept of IoT can be described as a network binding together the end-users and different monitorable or measurable entities or targets, ranging from physical objects such as buildings and vehicles [1] to immaterial interests, for instance collective traffic and consumer behaviour [2]. The link between the actors in the IoT ecosystem is the information gathered from these targets and delivered to the end-users in a comprehensible form [3]. The added value of IoT data can appear in many forms, including personal, professional and economic, and can serve a multiplicity of groups or actors, including academia, industry and government [4].

The accessibility of data in specific has been identified as a complex issue concerning a variety of personally and professionally used IoT solutions, including application areas such as home automation, healthcare, retail, industry, transportation, security and surveillance, as well as smart infrastructure [5]. Taking a deeper look at the accessibility considerations, we must understand the cumulative negative effects that can take place and keep spreading as long as no ethical rules, and eventually a social contract, has been formed. Currently, both intentional and unintentional harm towards individuals as the outcome of inaccurate data - and especially the decision-making based on this data - can

© Springer Nature Switzerland AG 2020
M. Cacace et al. (Eds.): WIS 2020, CCIS 1270, pp. 197–208, 2020.
https://doi.org/10.1007/978-3-030-57847-3_14

be critical to both their careers and personal lives [6]. Yet, even the parties causing these issues are currently not provided with sufficient tools to truly understand and address the potential risk factors. Thus, we claim that ethical guidelines for preventing these issues need to be built, as well as the tools for helping to find those possible issues.

The IoT data accessibility is strongly connected to ownership [7]. The literature related to the data ownership has proven that the property issues alone form a highly complex topic of discussion [8], and thus the potential ownership issues should also be considered while investigating accessibility. In general, we propose distributing the IoT data ownership scenarios as follows: individuals, companies, third parties or a combination of the aforementioned [7]. From this background, the practical data distribution recommendations introduced in this paper are aimed to take into account each of these parties in different data gathering and distribution settings.

Furthermore, we claim that in a commercial environment the individuals are rarely the sole owners of the collected data. This, however, is dependent on the agreement which should be conducted before the implementation of IoT solutions. Perhaps the most common arrangement is that the company or a certain section of actors inherit the ownership to the collected data, yet are obligated to follow the existing privacy regulations, whether or not they do so in reality. Thirdly, the companies may deliver the data to third parties, such as IoT service providers or business partners, etc. Finally, it is also possible to distribute the ownership between these instances. This results in a variety of ethical implications to be addressed when defining the rules for who can access the data.

To guarantee an ethically correct basis for the data collection and distribution, it should be verified that the company behind the IoT implementation is committed to following the regulative and legal boundaries. Yet, considering the vast amount of companies and organisations utilising IoT, it is difficult if not impossible to monitor their legal behaviour. Additionally, lawfulness is a necessary but not a sufficient requirement from the ethical perspective. Thus, while maybe not required by law, the companies should respect the privacy and rights of employees and other individuals in the data accessibility decision process. Likewise, the gathered data set can be such that it can contain information that may be about other legal entities if collected, for example, from public spheres or technical objects—an issue that must be acknowledged and ethically noted.

To provide holistic tools for addressing the ethical issues related to IoT use, we are building a general ethical framework for investigating the ethical issues related to IoT use, a part of which being the considerations related to the accessibility of data. The complete framework will cover the central ethical focus areas introduced in Richard O. Mason's PAPA framework [9], with added categories related to factors such as motives [10] and personal security, the latter ones' purpose being to complement the framework to thoroughly cover the specific characteristics of IoT ecosystems. While the data accessibility forms a limited part of the overall framework, it is also connected to various other focus areas, and perhaps most importantly to the privacy, property, and safety. Thus, the accessibility considerations introduced in this paper are formatted in a manner that will later allow merging them into the final framework.

The paper is structured as follows. In chapter two, we focus on presenting the PAPA model and its use in the IoT context. In chapter three, we look at the issues that should be noted while deciding who should have the accessibility to certain information in different scenarios, and as a result, we offer our conceptual decision tree-model as a promising tool helping to address the relevant considerations in practice. In chapter four, we analyse the accessibility through our model and also derive ethical insight from the deontological and consequentialist perspectives. In chapter five, we examine the practical implications of using this model. Finally, in chapter six, we end up with conclusions.

2 Background

Our investigation of the data accessibility is primarily based on the PAPA framework, originally introduced by Richard O. Mason in 1986 [9]. The PAPA framework consists of four key ethical challenges of the information age, including privacy, accuracy, property, and accessibility. Briefly explained, the privacy [11] refers to what data the individuals can keep to themselves and what data do they have to reveal to others and under what conditions. This is closely related to the privacy-related regulations such as the GDPR (General Data Protection Regulation (EU) 2016/679). However, PAPA puts more emphasis on the ethical factors compared to a purely legislative approach. For example, while the GDPR may set strict limitations to what personal data can be displayed to external parties, questions such as when the individuals can be monitored and to what extent they should be informed about the monitoring purpose and its possible role in decision-making, and whether even the legally accepted data collection is meaningful. The accuracy [9] is centred on authenticity, fidelity and accuracy of information. The accuracy of data can be especially important from the individuals' perspective in cases where personal decisions are made based on the collected data, and thus its correctness should be guaranteed. As a concrete example, the employer might monitor the location of company vehicles and make conclusions about the efficiency of employees based on this information. However, the utilised IoT device may produce inaccurate data leading to incorrect negative conclusions, thus possibly harming the employee's professional and personal position [6]. This comes down to the question of to what degree we can rely on the data produced by technology and whether the decision-making based purely on data can be considered ethically correct. The property [7] category covers the matters related to data ownership, including, but not limited to, factors such as the data owner, monetary value of data and the ownership of data transferring channels. Lastly, PAPA describes the central questions related to accessibility as "what information does a person or an organization have a right or a privilege to obtain, under what conditions and with what safeguards" [9], which we address in this paper alongside with some added ethical considerations, helping us to better fit the phenomena into the IoT context.

3 Decision Tree—Right to Access or not to Access, that is the Question

In this chapter, we examine accessibility through a Decision tree (see Fig. 1), showing that justification is a highly context- and situation-dependent matter. Firstly, we suggest considering when and with whom the access should be shared and when not.

If we want to achieve clear procedures and rules on how to grant access to the information collected via IoT, we claim that the information categories need to be determined beforehand. Personal data is nowadays largely limited by regulations, but other types of sensitive data exist as well, be it anonymous or identifiable. This covers, for example, any data gathered for professional use, which may be sensitive to the company itself. Furthermore, even if the data is not considered sensitive, we must consider whether the companies should be able to maintain decisional autonomy in terms of sharing so-called generic data or not. Furthermore, the inclusion or exclusion of external parties should be investigated separately within the context of each identified data category to provide coherent and practical guidelines. Our foundational proposal for the decision process is introduced in the following decision tree and the tasks on it to ensure a more systematic analysis of information use and ethical access to justified parties.

Decision Tree

The whole decision tree model starts with a simple question: does the receiver actually need the information and is there any potential harm in allowing access. The next issue to consider is are there any legal or contractual issues that prevent sharing the access with a receiver candidate. If there is no reason to deny access, the next issue is to clarify the type of information, as different kinds of information produce potentially distinctive kinds of issues to be looked upon.

In the light of the original PAPA definition of access, the right of an entity to obtain a piece of information depends on the nature of the information itself and the entity about to obtain it. The aim of our model is not only about limiting and safeguarding certain types of sensitive information, but also about making the whole phenomenon more visible and thus helping to understand the complexity of sharing the IoT data.

The next step in our model is to examine what is the target from which the data is gathered: a technical object, environment or a human being. While it is purposeful to examine these sources separately, we must acknowledge that in reality the information can in many cases be overlapping and we claim that those situations tend to set the tightest restrictive demands.

Technical Object

If the data is collected from a technical object, it must be ensured whether it can contain data which can be connected with an individual. If, for example, the object is used by people, it should be considered as information that is collected from individuals and the user of the decision tree should pay focus on the branches considering the targeted individual as identifiable.

If the IoT device is not collecting information about individuals, it may collect it from another legal entity or object, which may be property of some other instance. If it is a collector-owned object, the accessibility is based on the decision of the collector.

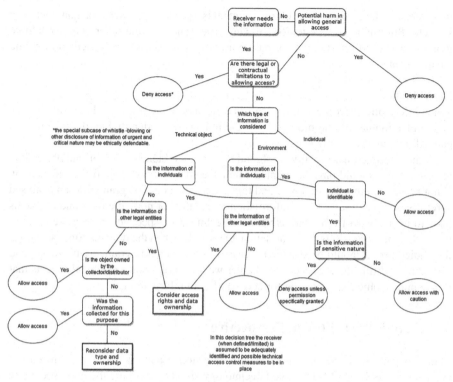

Fig. 1. Decision tree

When the object is not the collector's property, it must be ensured that there is a legal right to collect the information and that the contracts are clear and include a description of the accessibility rights.

Environment

Information can also be collected from environmental qualities with IoT. The difference between a technical object and environment is that the environmental information is not restricted to a single object, but is based on the surrounding environment and can contain more diverse information and thus must be further analysed. The first issue to take into account is again whether there is a possibility that information of individuals is collected. As an example, if an IoT device collects pictures of the environment it may end up with collecting facial information of people which can later be traced to an individual.

If information from individual is not collected it is still important to consider if there are any legal entities whose information is collected and may set restrictions for the collection of information. From an ethical perspective, it should also be considered whether the information could be defined as open access if it's collected from the public sphere. In many cases the information could be helpful for further use and thus granting access to information would serve the common good and this should be considered at the beginning of the decision tree (see potential harm in allowing general access). It is understandable that in some cases the information restriction could be needed to protect the interest of the collector—if the environment is a private one, such as a manufacturing site, etc. But this is not a situation in many cases, and thus the other choice could be granting access to information for public use, especially if it is collected from public environment.

Individual
When information involving individuals is collected, it can be divided into identifiable and unidentifiable. Furthermore, even if the individual is identifiable, the information can still be sensitive or not sensitive.

If the information is sensitive, it should be given heightened attention and protection, and the access should only be granted when specifically necessary. If the information is not sensitive, the risks are lower and thus the access could be granted when analysed carefully. In both cases—when information is sensitive or not—the risks and problems have to be analysed from legal, ethical and technical perspectives, noting the requirements that the context sets for information. Obviously, when the information is sensitive, the choice per se should be a denied access if not specifically granted with strong and transparent justification. In the next chapter we will look upon the ethical aspects that derive philosophical justification for accessibility to information.

4 Analysis from Ethical Perspective

In this chapter, we deepen the analysis of the decision tree implications from the ethical perspective. As Brey [12] has noted, technology should contribute the good society to be ethical. Computer ethics is a brand of ethics that was presented by Moor's [13] to see the impact of computers in society. The analysis of the nature and social impact of information technology to identify justified policies for the ethical use of information technology is in the heart of computer ethics.

Firstly, we need to consider whether there is a genuine need and a rational justification for distributing the data with a potential receiver. If a justified purpose doesn't exist and gaining access to this data could cause harm, we propose denying access. If the receiver either actually needs the information or if gaining access to it would not result in a harmful situation, we should clarify the possible legal or contractual limitations related to data sharing. In both cases, to follow good ethical principles, we propose denying access if either legal or contractual conflicts exist.

If no issues related to the aforementioned matters exist, we proceed to further analysis distributing our focus on three key data sources, including technical objects, environment and individuals.

4.1 Decision Tree Considerations

Technical Object
One of the most common approaches is to gather IoT data from technical objects. In cases where the data is not and cannot be connected to individuals, we should investigate if the information concerns other legal entities, such as organizations or cities. If not,

and the data collector/distributor owns the observed object, there are no apparent ethical issues related to sharing the collected information. Accordingly, if the individuals are anyhow involved with the data, we propose examining the individuals' position described in detail later in this chapter. If the collector/distributor does not own the object, we propose considering in cooperation with the object owner whether the data serves the original purpose and if there are any concerns that the use of data could negatively affect either party. As an example, if a company collects new data or utilizes readily collected IoT data from objects owned by the public sector, it should ensure that the owner party approves further information distribution. Furthermore, the collectors may even be obligated to share this information among external parties based on regulations and/or motives of the owner. If no issues are identified, there are no ethical limitations restricting the data distribution. Additionally, if the data was not originally collected for the intended purpose, we recommend reconsidering the type of leveraged data in addition to the possible ownership matters affecting the suitability of the data.

Environment

Next, we examine the situations where IoT data is not directly collected from separable objects or individuals, but the surrounding environment. Regardless of the fact that the motives of data gathering may not involve individuals on purpose, human-related data may be gathered as a side-product, even if this is unintentional. For example, IoT-based traffic monitoring may produce identifiable information as a side-product and can enable personal identification and monitoring based on, for instance, face-recognition. This brings up an ethical conflict that can be difficult to avoid. To protect personal privacy, the collectors should be capable of hiding the identities of the involved individuals. In some cases, this may not even be possible from a technical perspective and would thus disable the monitoring as a whole in order to follow ethically correct principles. In situations where traffic cameras display recognizable graphics, even its distribution with authorities cannot automatically be considered ethical, unless the individuals have been informed about the procedure and thus given the opportunity to avoid the chance of being under surveillance and identified. Numerous cases of such settings can be found throughout the internet, where traffic cameras provide publicly available photos and/or videos where both the drivers and vehicles can be identified based on facial characteristics or vehicle IDs. Thus, when collecting information form the environment (especially if it is a public sphere) the potential risks should be analysed before starting data collection likewise periodically afterward to find new emerging ethical issues. If, however, it is possible to guarantee that the data has no personal relation and is not connected to other legal entities, the distribution of data can be considered justified from the ethical perspective. If the data is in fact connected to other legal entities, we propose considering the access rights and data ownership. However, we limit our analysis in this point as if the target is a legal entity and the legislative and contract issues are the main focus areas in this kind of situation. The legal entity itself does not have a moral actor ship—even people behind it may have and action of legal entity has consequences. Nevertheless, this is a complex issue to be further analysed by some other place and time.

Individual

Thirdly, and often connected to both of the earlier described data sources, we examine the intentional and unintentional collection of individual data. If it is impossible to identify the involved individual, the distribution of data can, in principle, be considered ethically justified. However, we emphasize that ensuring complete anonymity is often difficult and the possibility of unpredictable personal connections can exist, the data collector/owner should always proceed to data distribution with extreme caution.

This said, if the individuals are identifiable in any form, the principles introduced in the context of technical objects apply (see "Is the information of individuals" in the branch 'Technical object'). Furthermore, in cases where the individuals are identifiable, we suggest investigating the situation from two perspectives: personally sensitive and personally insensitive information. When the collected and potentially shared data is both identifiable and sensitive, particular attention should be given to who is allowed to access the data and whether its collection is ethically acceptable and/or justifiable in general. Even though these situations are already strictly controlled by regulations such as the GDPR, the legal obligations may not take into account the ethical matters to a sufficient degree. Thus, in addition to following the regulatory obligations, the data collectors and distributors, as well as the receiving parties, should take responsibility to thoroughly clarify the possible ethical conflicts related to the individuals' rights, even when the grounds for data collection and/or distribution are found to be just. Even in these exceptional cases, the data collectors and distributors are strongly suggested to examine the possible solutions to hide the personal factors behind the data after it has been collected by, for example, post-manipulation methods such as masking. However, if the collection and/or distribution of sensitive data is mandatory, the distribution should be limited to only the truly mandatory parties. Additionally, such data should be stored responsibly and disposed as early as possible. Even more importantly, the individuals should always be given the opportunity to refuse from sensitive data collection, except extreme situations, such as legal obligations. Even if the information is not sensitive, the same factors should be investigated thoroughly and risks avoided, especially as the seemingly insensitive or even anonymous data can unpredictably end up as identifiable if, for example, it can be connected to other data collected from the same individuals.

4.2 Consequential and Deontological Analysis

In this chapter, we outline the ethical conflicts related to the key categories introduced in the decision tree from consequential and deontological perspectives. Moor notes the importance of general ethics for computer ethics, since it provides categories and procedures of what is ethically relevant and it also prompts us to rethink our values and the nature of information technology [13]. Like Moor later noted, there is a need for unifying the view of those ethical perspectives to find stronger ethical bases [14]. However, we do not try to unify those theories - instead we see that we could use both approaches to see possible ethical problems and issues that rise in the context of IoT collected information accessibility.

From *consequential* perspective, the position of individuals, and especially the outcomes related to involving them and their personal information into the data gathering and distribution processes, should be addressed and considered before implementing an

IoT solution which they will actively or passively interact with. It is primarily not encouraged to apply a purely utilitarian approach in the IoT context, as the individuals' privacy and general ethical position are likely not given enough emphasis when the focus is strongly directed towards the end result. Furthermore, whether or not the consequences of data distribution are seen to outweigh the value of protecting a single individual's position is ultimately based on a subjective opinion. This calls for balancing measures, and for that purpose, we see deontology as a suitable alternative or supplementary theory.

The *deontological* perspective also provides fruitful ethical foundations for the data collectors and distributors to follow, as its principles can be rather fluently applied in the IoT context as well. Especially together with the consequentialist perspective it creates stronger basis for our analysis—as they take different issues and principles under consideration.

In accordance with deontology, we claim that it is not ethically justified to demand individuals' consent for gratuitous collection and distribution of data, especially when their privacy is at stake. Thus, as a positive duty, is it encouraged to primarily aim for common benefit, thus creating an environment into which the individuals are motivated to contribute, rather than being solely obligated to do so.

Meanwhile, the fulfilment of negative duty can, in theory, be considered to be partially guaranteed by obligatory legislations and regulations such as the GDPR. However, the data collectors' and distributors' actual compliance with the regulations is difficult or impossible to verify. Additionally, the regulations in themselves likely do not thoroughly address the ethical requirements, whose fulfilment should thus be further supported, especially as the current lack of ethical consensus can lead to various unintentional conflicts with the position of individuals. Thus, again, there is a clear need for ethical guidelines to provide organisations with currently lacking tools necessary to understand and address these issues.

Immanuel Kant and his deontological view in his work Groundwork of the Metaphysic of Morals [15] needs to be addressed here as it is maybe the most influential philosopher in the area of deontological ethics. For Kant, rational agents and autonomy of those actors are preconditions for whether an actor's acts can be held to be moral or not. People need to have free will and the possibility to choose their actions, otherwise no moral action exists because forced actions are not the moral will of people. Thus, we need people to make decisions on how information is used, and this underlines the need for companies to devote focus and people to it. Another issue that we want to rise is the second formulation of Categorical Imperative:

"Act in such a way as to treat humanity, whether in our own person or in that of anyone else, always as an end and never merely as a means." [15]

We may collect and use information from people, but we also need to respect and treat people such a way that they are not seen mere information sources but active actors that have rights. Benefits and harms to individuals when collecting information should be always considered and the aim should be good for all parties.

Conclusively, in IoT context, we suggest biasing the ethical focus towards fulfilling the deontological principles, which we claim to better serve the common good and reduce the risk of personal discrimination, even while it may reduce the acquired functional benefits. However, strict compliance with a specific ethical theory may still set unnecessary and artificial boundaries which, while not actually enhancing the position of the individuals, could reduce the practical benefits acquired by the utilisation of IoT without a rational reason. This leads us to an intersection where a satisfactory balance between the individuals' and organisations' benefits and needs have to be achieved. Thus, a disciplinary trade-off between deontology and consequentialism could still be justified in cases where the position of individuals is provenly not compromised or when the outcomes are guaranteed to serve a significantly larger or more critical purpose, for example when the distribution of personal data could help reducing or to avoid the spreading of an epidemic illness.

5   Practical Implications

While this paper mainly focuses on the accessibility of personally identifiable data, we should also acknowledge that seemingly anonymous data can still be connected to individuals in some circumstances, as previously described. In a business context, the full comprehension of these issues requires a deeper understanding of the specific company setting, including the number of employees, their responsibility areas, characteristics and various other factors that make it possible to connect the information to certain individuals. Thus, the ethical considerations introduced in this paper are strongly advised to be applied also in settings where the data collected from individuals is seemingly anonymous. Furthermore, this claim is supported by the fact that no exact definitions setting boundaries to personal and non-personal currently exist, thus making the ethical background and requirements of any setting worth investigation.

One of the central topics to be investigated when considering the position of individuals is personal autonomy [16]. Whether or not the employees are able to take part in the decision-making related to what data is collected from them, can be accessed by any other actor can be considered as an indicator of the companies' ethical standards. Again, the autonomy implications should be taken into account in each presented phase of the IoT data life-cycle. In practice, this requires a carefully formed agreement, based on which the employees are capable of providing their informed consent. Whether the possible denial of the contract terms can lead to weakened professional position or even termination of employment, should be regulated from both legal and ethical perspectives. This said, following solely the regulative boundaries set by the GDPR for instance, does not guarantee ethical correctness. Likewise, the rights of other legal entities should be noted, being one of the potential future research areas. Furthermore, as it is currently difficult if not impossible to observe and confirm that companies do follow these regulations, we encourage enhancing the situation through enhanced mutual trust and respect, which would likely be positively affected by clear procedural guidelines. Companies should commit to following ethical principles by implementing ethical analysis as an integral part of a business process and thus support more ethical business in the information society.

6 Conclusion

To thoroughly address the ethical implications related to the accessibility of IoT data, it is crucial to widen our perspectives from purely regulatory foundations. While the regulations do protect the rights of individuals from the legal perspective, various ethical implications remain unaddressed without further consideration. Thus, we consider the distributor of data to be ethically responsible for taking into account the position of and the possible harm towards individuals even if the utilised data-sharing approach is legally correct.

However, we must simultaneously acknowledge that the consequences of heightened privacy protection may not be solely positive [17], as the benefits of IoT solutions rely upon the collected data and its availability, which emphasises the importance of finding a balanced way to apply ethical principles without hindering technical development.

From the philosophical perspective, our ethical conclusions are based on a combination of consequentialism and deontology, which we claim as a realistic and constructive approach in the IoT context. While the consequential principles provide justification for the use of personal data on a fundamental level, the deontological norms balance the situation by taking into account the position of individuals through both positive and negative duties.

On practical level, even when data are collected from instances that are not directly related to individuals, such as technical devices or environment, personal information may get collected and distributed as a side-product, either intentionally or unintentionally. This puts the data distributors into an ethically challenging situation, where the potential risks can be difficult to identify in- dependently. Thus, these actors need to be provided with sufficient knowledge and clear guidelines to properly address the ethical issues. For that purpose, we introduced a decision tree (Fig. 1) covering the data distribution considerations related to three central data sources: technical objects, environment and individuals.

References

1. Miorandi, D., Sicari, S., De Pellegrini, F., Chlamtac, I.: Internet of Things: vision, applications and research challenges. Ad Hoc Netw. **10**(7), 1497–1516 (2012)
2. Gubbi, J., Buyya, R., Marusic, S., Palaniswami, M.: Internet of Things (IoT): a vision, architectural elements, and future directions. Future Gener. Comput. Syst. **29**(7), 1645–1660 (2013)
3. Jin, J., Gubbi, J., Marusic, S., Palaniswami, M.: An information framework for creating a smart city through Internet of Things. IEEE Internet Things J. **1**(2), 112–121 (2014)
4. Khan, R., Khan, S.U., Zaheer, R., Khan, S.: Future internet: the Internet of Things architecture, possible applications and key challenges. In: 2012 10th International Conference on Frontiers of Information Technology, pp. 257–260. IEEE (2012)
5. Sayana, L.S., Joshi, B.K.: Security issues in Internet of Things. In: UGC Sponsored National Conference on Global Challenges – Role of Sciences & Technology in Imparting their Solutions (GCRSTS 2016) 23–24 April, 2016. TIT&S Bhiwani, Haryana (2016)
6. Vermanen, M, Rantanen, M.M., Harkke, V.: Ethical challenges of IoT utilization in SMEs from an individual employee's perspective. In: Proceedings of the 27th European Conference on Information Systems (ECIS), Stockholm & Uppsala, Sweden (2019)

7. Vermanen, M., Koskinen, J., Harkke, V.: Securing the Internet of Things (IoT) data ownership: a meta-data approach (Forthcoming)
8. Jane˘cek, V.: Ownership of personal data on the Internet of Things. Comput. Law Secur. Rev. **34**(5), 1039–1052 (2018)
9. Mason, R.O.: Four ethical issues of the information age. MIS Q. **10**(1), 5–12 (1986)
10. Conger, S., Loch, K.D., Helft, B.L.: Ethics and information technology use: a factor analysis of attitudes to computer use. Inf. Syst. J. **5**(3), 161–183 (1995)
11. Vermanen, M., Rantanen Minna, M.: Privacy issues in IoT ecosystems from an individual employee's perspective. In: Third Annual Seminar on Technology Ethics, Turku, Finland (2019)
12. Brey, P.: The strategic role of technology in a good society. Technol. Soc. **52**, 39–45 (2018)
13. Moor, J.H.: What is computer ethics? Metaphilosophy **16**(4), 266–275 (1985)
14. Moor, J.H.: Just consequentialism and computing. Ethics Inf. Technol. **1**(1), 61–65 (1999)
15. Kant, I.: Groundwork for the metaphysics of morals. Translated by Jonathan Bennett (2008). https://www.earlymoderntexts.com/assets/pdfs/kant1785.pdf
16. Winter, J.S.: Surveillance in ubiquitous network societies: normative conflicts related to the consumer in-store supermarket experience in the context of the Internet of Things. Ethics Inf. Technol. **16**(1), 27–41 (2014)
17. Lee, I., Lee, K.: The Internet of Things (IoT): applications, investments, and challenges for enterprises. Bus. Horiz. **58**(4), 431–440 (2015)

Bridging the Digital Divide: Strengthening (Health-) Literacy and Supporting Trainings in Information Society

Challenging the Concept of Digital Nativeness – Through the Assessment of Information Literacy and Digital Literacy

Milla Aavakare(✉) ⓘ and Shahrokh Nikou ⓘ

Åbo Akademi University, Turku, Finland
{milla.aavakare,shahrokh.nikou}@abo.fi

Abstract. New opportunities for learning and teaching are introduced as the aftermath of the emergence of new digital technologies. Concurrently, change is taking place within the concept of literacy, as different dimensions of literacy have emerged. Information- and digital literacy are prominent examples of this, as their significance in the 21st century has received an array of scholarly attention. However, dimensions of literacy and technology acceptance within the educational context have been extensively bound to the discussion of digital natives and digital immigrants based on their age factor. A generalisation of this nature disregards diversity within the suggested groups, as differences can appear in other influencing factors. Hence, this study aims to look beyond age as a divider of digital nativeness, and instead takes a focus on other possible boundaries of characterisation. The results show that both information and digital literacy are important factors, and that literacy is a competence that depends on the access, frequency of use and the ability to use digital technologies. As such, the interactions of individuals with digital technologies should be used to classify individuals as digital native and digital immigrants.

Keywords: Digitalisation · Digital immigrants · Digital literacy · Digital natives · Digital tools · Educational institutions · Information literacy

1 Introduction

Two decades ago, Prensky [1] characterised the group of individuals born after 1980 as digital natives growing up with, and thereby relying on, technology. These digital natives, in contrast to their digital immigrant counterparts born before 1980, were said to live their lives surrounded by technologies and digital tools [1]. The claims made by Prensky generated discussion and debate, as some commentators [2–4] have questioned the claim of this generational change and the lack of empirical evidence. As mentioned by Bennett et al. [3], the discussion over the concept of digital natives' rests on two central claims, the first of which is the existence of a distinct generation of digital natives. The second claim is that the nature of education needs to change and accommodate to the needs of this new distinct generation. Yet, calling for such grand change during the absence of an empirical basis can be viewed as problematic. A generalisation of this

© Springer Nature Switzerland AG 2020
M. Cacace et al. (Eds.): WIS 2020, CCIS 1270, pp. 211–225, 2020.
https://doi.org/10.1007/978-3-030-57847-3_15

nature disregards diversity within the suggested group of digital natives, as very real differences can derive from other factors, e.g., access to digital technologies, frequency of use of digital technologies, as well as self-reported levels of proficiency when it comes to the utilisation of digital technologies.

This paper aims to look beyond age as a divider of digital nativeness, and instead takes a focus on other possible boundaries of characterisation through the assessment of the following research questions *"to what extent do digital literacy and information literacy explain the intention to use digital technologies in a learning environment,* and *"what role does access, frequency of use and proficiency with digital technology play?"*. To answer the research questions, based on an extensive literature review, we set out to build a conceptual model and examine the model through an empirical study using a novel methodological approach. We employ fuzzy-set Qualitative Comparative Analysis (fsQCA) to provide unique and complementary insights to the phenomenon under investigation.

2   Background

As stated by Nikou et al. [5], literacy refers to the condition of an individual being literate. Traditionally, this concept of literacy has been associated with the abilities of reading and writing. With time, however, the literacy concept has evolved to encompass abilities reaching far beyond the original perception. In the information-based society, literacy can be understood as "a means of identification, understanding, interpretation, creation, and communication in an increasingly digital, text-mediated, information-rich and fast-changing world" [6]. The evolution of this concept is understandable when considering the technological progress and digitalisation of the past decades. As such, a multitude of new literacy dimensions such as information literacy [7, 8] and digital literacy [9, 10] have emerged. Abilities related to use of ICT for information evaluation have reached a new state of significance as they have developed in to a "survival skill" [9]. As suggested by Eshet-Alkalai [9], some of the underlying causes to this include the changes which have occurred in the rate of exposure to information, as well as the fact that information is easily manipulated to its nature. In consideration of these changes, it is not difficult to comprehend the importance of information- and digital literacy and therefore the concerns related to these abilities, especially in the context of utilisation of digital technologies. The usage of digital technologies can consist of versatile use of hardware and software for varying purposes, as digital technology is extensively present within contemporary activities. This prominent presence calls for the need of digital literacy skills, defined as "the multiplicity of literacies associated with the use of digital technologies" [10, p. 1066].

The significance of information- and digital literacy matter particularly in the context of education. Possibilities enabled by data and analytics have facilitated new ways of monitoring progress, predictive ways of harnessing information of learning trajectories, as well as new opportunities for targeted and personalised learning [11]. Moreover, additional educational possibilities enabled by digital technologies have been researched in the context of 5G technology [12], social media [13] and telecommunications [14]. The development of digital technologies can therefore have a profound effect on both formal and informal learning environments. However, in order to obtain the advantages of digital technologies in education, the technologies must first be accepted by students and teachers. Thus far, research has been conducted on technology acceptance within classrooms, as e.g., Gu et al. [15] have set out to assess differences in technology acceptance and utilisation among digital immigrant teachers and digital native students. The findings indicate that there are, indeed, differences between digital immigrant teachers and digital native students when it comes to their interpretation of the importance of technology utilisation [15].

However, as mentioned by Bennett et al. [3], research evidence tends to focus on highly technologically adept young people while simultaneously somewhat neglecting to incorporate young people who do not have resembling access to technology or resembling technology skills. In fact, Bennett et al. [3] suggest that "with this [generalisation] comes the danger that those less interested and less able will be neglected, and that the potential impact of socio-economic and cultural factors will be overlooked. It may be that there is as much variation within the digital native generation as between the generations" (p. 779). The conclusion being that although technology might be embedded in the lives of young people, it does not mean that young people's utilisation and skills are uniform or superior than their counterpart generation. Hence, further research regarding the concept of digital nativeness should commence before inaugurating major fundamental changes within education in order to accommodate to a generalised perception of digital natives.

3 Theoretical Background

This section discusses factors that are assumed to have impact on the intention to use technology and the development of a theory-based conceptual model. The aim is to connect dimensions of literacy with intention to use technology while examining the moderating, if any, effects of access, frequency of use and proficiency with digital technology.

3.1 Alternative Boundaries of Characterisation

According to the American Library Association [16], information literacy (IL) can be defined as a collection of abilities which bring about an individual's ability to "recognize when information is needed and have the ability to locate, evaluate, and use effectively the needed information" (p. 2). Prior research [5, 18] has revealed that information literacy has a significant effect on the attitude towards the use of digital technologies, while in turn, attitude has been shown to have a significant effect on intention to use said technologies [18]. In addition to information literacy, digital literacy (DL) has also been found to affect the intention to use technology [18, 19]. Differing partially from IL, DL is defined by the American Library Association [17] as "the ability to use information and communication technologies to find, understand, evaluate, create, and communicate digital information" (p. 2). Although IL is occasionally presented as a component of DL, a distinction is made between the two in this paper, as IL refers here to the cognitive skills which are used to evaluate information in an educated and effective way [9], whereas DL refers to the ability to understand and use information in multiple formats from an array of digitally available sources [20]. Both IL and DL related skills can be seen as vital in the contemporary society, especially due to their connection to education and the fact that learning today can occur through the utilisation of digital technologies. Thus, the effects of IL and DL on the intention to use digital technologies for learning are inevitable.

This paper intends to challenge the concept of age as a divider of digital nativeness, and instead focus on other possible boundaries of characterisation. Therefore, in addition to IL and DL, three other factors of possible impact will be explored: access (ACC), frequency of use (FRE) and proficiency (PRO). Access refers here to the individuals' access to digital technologies, FRE refers to the frequency at which they use said technologies, and PRO refers to the individuals self-reported proficiency of using digital technologies. The suggested factors can impact an individual's intention to use digital technologies for various purposes, including learning. We also believe that using these factors would enable to characterise and categorise individuals better than relying merely to their age. Moreover, access to digital technologies or proficiency with said technologies enable to assess more profoundly individual's literacy competency.

3.2   Intention to Use Digital Technologies for Teaching and Learning

In this paper, intention to use technology (INT) refers to an individual's intention to use digital technologies for teaching and learning purposes. The INT construct was selected as the observed outcome, as the aim of this research is to explore how the intention to use digital technologies can be influenced by information- and digital literacy when simultaneously taking access, frequency and proficiency into account. The construct of intention to use has been widely studied as an outcome variable in the research of future technology use [21–25].

4   Research Methodology

Prior studies of the subject matter have been conducted with extensive use of Structural Equation Modelling [19, 36–38], which has provided insights that need further research. Therefore, fuzzy-set Qualitative Comparative Analysis (fsQCA) can provide new knowledge of the subject matter and will thus be used for this study.

4.1   Data Collection

After an extensive literature review, a survey questionnaire was devised to obtain the opinions of the potential respondents (university students and university staff), after which it was utilised to gain deeper insight to their intention to use digital technology in learning and teaching environments. The questionnaires consisted of questions assessing background information, respondents' access to digital technologies, frequency of use of digital technology, and self-reported levels of proficiency with digital technology, being all related to the educational context and learning purposes. This was followed by questions designed to measure the respondents' perception regarding their own information- and digital literacy. The information literacy items were adapted from Kurbanoglu et al.

[26], while the digital literacy items were adapted from Ng [10]. Questions regarding information- and digital literacy were measured on a 7-point Likert scale, ranging from 1 – Strongly disagree to 7 – Strongly agree. Meanwhile, access and frequency were answered as categorical variables. In the question regarding access, respondents were asked about their access to mobile smart phones, tablets, desktop computers, laptop computers, game consoles and wearable devices. In the questions regarding frequency and proficiency, respondents were asked about word processors (e.g., Word, Pages), spreadsheets (e.g., Excel, Numbers), presentations (e.g., PowerPoint, Keynote), file sharing (e.g., Google Drive, Dropbox), photo editing (e.g., Photoshop, PhotoScape), website management tools (e.g., WordPress, Squarespace), mobile device organisers (e.g., address book, calendar), email services (e.g., Outlook, Gmail) and social media (e.g., Facebook, Instagram). Proficiency was measured on a 7-point Likert scale, ranging from 1 – Not proficient at all to 7 – Very proficient. The devised online questionnaire was then distributed through multiple channels digitally. In addition, flyers were circulated at four university campuses in Finland.

5 Descriptive Data Analysis

The dataset for students comprised of 157 students, where 100 were females, 55 were males, and 2 identified as other. Meanwhile, the dataset for non-students, i.e., university staff (teachers and researchers), administrative and service personnel consisted of 100 employees, where 51 were females, 48 were males, and 1 identified as other. The average age of the students is 25.3 and for the non-students group the average is 42.3. Naturally, the student group included also older individuals just at the non-student group included younger individuals. However, the average age of the groups aligns well with the traditional concept of age as a divider for digital nativeness, a concept debated by e.g., Nikou et al. [38]. Additional information regarding the demographic information of the respondents and the results with respect to access to digital technology (Table 1), frequency of software use (Table 2) and self-report rating of proficiency with digital technology can be seen in Table 3.

Table 1. Access to digital technology.

Digital tools	1	2	3	4	5	Mean
Mobile (smart) phone	.06% [0%]	.06% [1%]	0% [0%]	1.3% [1%]	97.5% [98%]	4.94 [4.96]
Tablet	57.3% [43%]	21.7% [20%]	8.3% [10%]	7.6% [7%]	5.1% [20%]	1.81 [2.41]
Desktop computer	31.2% [22%]	28.7% [12%]	11.5% [8%]	5.7% [5%]	22.9% [53%]	2.6 [3.55]

(*continued*)

Table 1. (*continued*)

Digital tools	1	2	3	4	5	Mean
Laptop computer	.06% [2%]	8.9% [3%]	18.5% [6%]	21.7% [11%]	50.3% [78%]	4.12 [4.6]
Game console	54.8% [71%]	25.5% [21%]	14.6% [6%]	2.5% [2%]	2.5% [0%]	1.72 [1.39]
Wearable device (e.g., smartwatch, fitbit)	80.3% [75%]	3.8% [4%]	1.3% [2%]	3.8% [4%]	10.8% [15%]	1.61 [1.8]

Note: 1 = I do not use; 2 = A few times a month or less; 3 = A few times a week; 4 = About once a day; 5 = Several times each day. Values within the brackets represent data for non-students.

As shown in the tables above, differences between students and non-students can be identified within all variables. In Table 1, non-students scored a higher mean regarding access to mobile smart phones, tablets, desktop computers, laptop computers, and wearable devices. Meanwhile, students scored a higher mean only in regard to game consoles.

Table 2. Frequency of software use.

Digital tools	1	2	3	4	5	Mean
Word processor	0% [0%]	15.3% [7%]	47.1% [12%]	15.9% [10%]	21.7% [71%]	3.43 [4.45]
Spreadsheet	11.5% [2%]	39.5% [19%]	29.9% [31%]	9.6% [13%]	9.6% [35%]	2.66 [3.61]
Presentation	3.2% [2%]	69.4% [23%]	24.2% [37%]	.06% [20%]	2.5% [18%]	2.29 [3.29]
File sharing	2.5% [1%]	24.8% [28%]	38.9% [27%]	18.5% [19%]	15.3% [25%]	3.19 [3.39]
Photo/image editing	39.5% [28%]	40.8% [44%]	14.6% [20%]	2.5% [3%]	2.5% [5%]	1.87 [2.13]
Website management	70.7% [52%]	19.7% [39%]	4.5% [5%]	2.5% [4%]	2.5% [0%]	1.46 [1.61]
Mobile device organiser	8.3% [16%]	14% [17%]	26.1% [12%]	20.4% [24%]	31.2% [31%]	3.52 [3.37]
Email services	0% [0%]	.06% [0%]	3.8% [1%]	23.6% [6%]	72% [93%]	4.66 [4.92]
Social media	.06% [7%]	2.5% [3%]	2.5% [6%]	12.1% [18%]	82.2% [66%]	4.72 [4.33]

Note: 1 = I do not use; 2 = A few times a month or less; 3 = A few times a week; 4 = About once a day; 5 = Several times each day. Values within the brackets represent data for non-students.

In Table 2, non-students scored a higher mean regarding the usage frequency of word processors, spreadsheets, presentations, file sharing, photo editing, website management, and email services. Meanwhile, students scored a higher mean in regard to mobile devices organisers and social media.

Table 3. Self-report rating of proficiency.

Digital tools	1	2	3	4	5	6	7	Mean
Word processor	0% [0%]	0% [0%]	0% [3%]	7% [6%]	31.2% [13%]	37.6% [35%]	24.2% [43%]	5.78 [6.1]
Spreadsheet	3.8% [2%]	10.8% [6%]	19.7% [14%]	24.2% [17%]	19.1% [23%]	14% [20%]	8.3% [18%]	4.19 [4.85]
Presentation	0% [1%]	1.3% [0%]	7.6% [2%]	22.9% [14%]	31.2% [28%]	24.2% [26%]	12.7% [29%]	5.07 [5.62]
File sharing	0% [2%]	3.2% [7%]	7% [7%]	9.6% [15%]	26.1% [23%]	29.9% [21%]	24.2% [25%]	5.45 [5.13]
Photo/image editing	21.7% [21%]	16.6% [19%]	22.3% [11%]	17.8% [18%]	12.1% [11%]	7% [15%]	2.5% [5%]	3.13 [3.44]
Website management	43.3% [38%]	14% [14%]	15.3% [18%]	16.6% [13%]	3.2% [10%]	3.2% [5%]	4.5% [2%]	2.49 [2.66]
Mobile device organiser	1.3% [9%]	2.5% [9%]	6.4% [9%]	14% [13%]	18.5% [20%]	25.5% [22%]	31.8% [18%]	5.49 [4.64]
Email services	.06% [0%]	0% [0%]	0% [0%]	7% [5%]	15.3% [16%]	36.9% [38%]	40.1% [41%]	6.07 [6.15]
Social media	.06% [8%]	1.9% [2%]	3.2% [7%]	10.2% [7%]	17.2% [26%]	33.1% [26%]	33.8% [24%]	5.75 [5.15]

Note: 1 (Not proficient at all) and 7 (Very proficient). Values within the brackets represent data for non-students.

In Table 3, non-students scored a higher mean regarding the self-reported rating of proficiency in the use of word processors, spreadsheets, presentations, photo editing, website management, and email services. Meanwhile, students scored a higher mean in regard to file sharing, mobile devices organisers, and social media. Overall, non-students (i.e., university staff, the "digital immigrants") scored higher at various instances when compared to the students (i.e., the "digital natives"). This counteracts the traditional line of division drawn using age as a divider when it comes to digital nativeness and the perceived capabilities that come with said assumption.

5.1 Measurement Model

In this section, we present the statistical results of the measurement model. A confirmatory factor analysis (CFA) was run for all the constructs in order to examine internal consistency and discriminant validity. The results show that all items were loaded into their respective constructs. The internal consistency was examined through the Cronbach's alpha, composite reliability and average variance extracted (AVE). Cronbach's alpha (α) values were all above the threshold of .70 (min $=$ .854; max $=$ .918). The values of AVE ranged from .599 to .637, CR values ranged from .897 to .931, all well above the recommended minimums of .50 and .70 respectively [28]. The standardised item loadings for each construct exceeded the recommended value of .70; some items with lower loadings were excluded from the further analysis. Discriminant validity was examined in order to evaluate if each construct's AVE square root was greater than its highest correlation with any other construct, and the results showed no discriminant validity issues (see Table 4).

Table 4. Discriminant validity (diagonal values show AVE square root).

	DL	IL	INT
Digital literacy	**0.785**		
Information literacy	0.621	**0.774**	
Intention to use	0.420	0.409	**0.798**

In addition to all the validity tests explained above, the common method bias was examined through a two-step approach. First, Harman's single factor test was conducted, and the test result showed that the majority of variance could not be attributed to one factor. The first factor accounts for 42% of the variance [29]. In the second step, all items were modelled as the indicators of a factor, as recommended by Malhotra et al. [30]. The test results showed poor model fit, thus, it can be assumed that the CMB was not an issue in this study. Next, we examined our data using fuzzy-set Qualitative Comparative Analysis [27], a method which has attracted attention from many researchers in various research disciplines.

6 Fuzzy-Set Qualitative Comparative Analysis

Fuzzy-set Qualitative Comparative Analysis (fsQCA) introduced by Ragin [27] has been utilised by scholars conducting research within several different fields [39, 41, 42]. As stated by Nikou et al. [5], "this method [fsQCA] provides a means to overcome some of the limitations of conventional statistical methods, such as regression-based analysis. It enables to account for the complex interdependencies, conjunctive paths, and the causal relationships between variables which might better inform the factors influencing the outcome variables" [5, p. 9]. Through the use of Boolean algebra, fsQCA provides logical comparisons, while presenting dependent and independent variables on a scale rather than as binary values. This enables the possibility to identify patterns of elements behind the outcome of study [5].

6.1 fsQCA Necessity Analysis

The necessity analysis enables to assess if there are any variables (conditions, in term of the fsQCA approach) that can be identified as necessary for intention [31]. Necessary refers to a situation where a condition must be present for the outcome of interest to occur, and sufficient if it can produce an outcome by itself. If the consistency value exceeds .90, then it can be assumed that considerable relationships exist [32]. The necessity analysis results showed that none of the conditions (variables) used in the analysis (i.e., digital literacy, information literacy) were seen as necessary conditions for intention to use digital technologies for learning. Although, this cannot be confirmed without running the main part of fsQCA, that is sufficiency analysis. There are several steps and phases in fsQCA that should be sequentially followed. First, all the variables (conditions) measured on a continuous scale have to be converted into fuzzy sets between 0 to 1, a practice which is called calibration. A value of 0 indicates fully out or no set membership and a value of 1 indicates fully in or full set membership [33]. According to Ragin [33], three anchors can be defined to determine the degree of membership for each condition (variable). These anchors indicate for full membership a fuzzy score $= .95$, for full nonmembership a fuzzy score $= .05$, and for cross-over point a fuzzy score $= .50$. After all values were calibrated into fuzzy sets, a truth table of 2^k rows was constructed, where k is the number of predictor variables (conditions), and each row represent a possible combination [34].

Regarding the consistency threshold, Ragin [33] suggested to set the level to $>.75$. Consistency measures the degree to which a subset relation has been approximated and it is similar to significance in correlational methods [32]. When constructing the truth table and reviewing the configurations, those that do not comply to this rule can be deleted. The solution coverage is used to assess the empirical relevance of a consistent subset, similar to the explained variance (R^2) value in regression analysis [35]. The fsQCA analysis produces three different solution sets: (a) parsimonious, (b) intermediate, and (c) complex. Ragin [33] suggested to use the intermediate solutions to articulate the results. The interpretation of the intermediate solutions is tricky, and the domain knowledge of the researcher is highly important [33]. The following notations will be used when fsQCA results are discussed. Black circles (●) indicate the presence of a condition and blank circles (○) indicate its absence. Blank spaces indicate "do not care," in other words, the causal condition may be either absent or present [31]. Three control variables were included in the analysis, access to digital technologies, frequency of use of digital technologies and proficiency with digital technologies. They have been presented in the form of crisp variables. Thus, black circles (●) indicate "high (access, frequency and proficiency)" and blank circles (○) denote high (access, frequency and proficiency). For the gender, black circles (●) were used to indicate males and blank circles (○) to indicate females.

6.2 fsQCA Results

In this section the fsQCA results are presented and discussed. The results are identified based on the casual configuration of five conditions (variables), namely, digital literacy (DL), information literacy (IL), access to digital technologies (ACC), frequency of use of digital technologies (FRE) and proficiency with digital technologies (PRO) leading to the occurrence of the outcome, i.e., intention to use digital technologies for learning. Two different analysis were conducted, one for university students and one for non-students (i.e., university staff). The fsQCA results for the student sample without including gender as a control variable are presented in Table 5. As shown, five configurations of conditions were obtained. The overall consistency is .864 and the overall solution coverage value is .768, indicating that these five solutions cover 77% of the cases (respondents). *Solution 1* indicates that the presence of both ACC and IL and the absence of PRO are sufficient conditions for the outcome of interest (intention to use digital technologies for learning) to occur. *Solution 2* indicates that the presence of ACC and the absence of IL lead to the outcome of interest. *Solution 3* indicates that the presence of ACC and the presence of DL lead to the outcome of interest. *Solution 4* indicates that the presence of FRE and presence of DL combined with the absence of PRO lead to the outcome of interest. *Solution 5* indicates that the presence of FRE, presence of IL and presence of DL lead to the outcome of interest.

Table 5. Intermediate solution for intention to use digital technology (student sample)

Solution	ACC	FRE	PRO	IL	DL	Raw coverage	Unique coverage	Consistency
1	●		○	●		0.135	0.041	0.744
2	●			○		0.132	0.007	0.988
3	●				●	0.170	0.031	0.991
4		●	○		●	0.067	0.020	0.985
5		●		●	●	0.111	0.026	0.999

The fsQCA results for the student sample with gender included as a control variable is presented in Table 6. As shown by the table, eight configurations of conditions were obtained. The overall consistency is .942 and the overall solution coverage value is .407, indicating that these eight solutions cover 41% of the cases (respondents). *Solution 1* indicates that the presence of FRE and the absence of PRO are sufficient conditions for the outcome of interest (intention to use digital technologies for learning) to occur. This is the only solution where gender does not play a role. *Solution 2* indicates that the presence of DL and IL lead to the outcome of interest, although it should be noted that this solution applies only to male respondents. *Solution 3* indicates that the presence of ACC and the presence of IL combined with the absence of PRO lead to the outcome of interest, although it should be noted that this solution applies only to female respondents. *Solution 4* indicates that the presence of PRO and IL combined with the absence of ACC and DL lead to the outcome of interest, although it should be noted that this solution applies only to female respondents. Solution 5 indicates that the presence of ACC combined with the absence of FRE and IL lead to the outcome of interest, a solution which applies only to female respondents. Solution 6 indicates that the presence of ACC and PRO combined with the absence of DL lead to the outcome of interest, a solution which applies only to female respondents. Solution 7 indicates that the presence of ACC, PRO and DL combined with the absence of FRE lead to the outcome of interest, a solution which applies only to male respondents. Solution 8 indicates that the presence of RPO, IL and DL combined with the absence of ACC and FRE lead to the outcome of interest, a solution which applies only to female respondents.

Table 6. Intermediate solution for intention to use digital technology (student sample + gender)

Solution	Gen	ACC	FRE	PRO	IL	DL	Raw coverage	Unique coverage	Consistency
1			●	○			0.097	0.057	0.801
2	●				●	●	0.117	0.092	1.000
3	○	●		○	●		0.055	0.021	0.995
4	○	○		●	●	○	0.038	0.018	1.000
5	○	●	○			○	0.043	0.016	1.000
6	○	●		●		○	0.035	0.027	1.000
7	●	●	○	●		●	0.038	0.025	0.988
8	○	○	○	●	●	●	0.071	0.071	0.998

The fsQCA results for non-students (i.e., university staff) without including gender as a control variable are presented in Table 7. As shown, four configurations of conditions were obtained. The overall consistency is .932 and the overall solution coverage value is .608, indicating that these four solutions cover 61% of the cases (respondents). *Solution 1* indicates that the presence of ACC and the absence of DL are sufficient conditions for the outcome of interest to occur. *Solution 2* indicates that the presence of PRO and IL combined with the absence of FRE lead to the outcome of interest. *Solution 3* indicates that the presence of FRE and IL combined with the absence of PRO lead to the outcome of interest. *Solution 4* indicates that the presence of FRE and IL f combined with the absence of ACC lead to the outcome of interest.

Table 7. Intermediate solution for intention to use digital technology (staff sample)

Solution	ACC	FRE	PRO	IL	DL	Raw coverage	Unique coverage	Consistency
1	●				○	0.135	0.041	0.744
2		○	●	●		0.132	0.007	0.988
3		●	○	●		0.170	0.031	0.991
4	○	●		●		0.111	0.026	0.999

The fsQCA results for non-students with their gender included in the fsQCA analysis are presented in Table 8. As shown, five configurations of conditions were obtained. The overall consistency is .910 and the overall solution coverage value is .671, indicating that these five solutions cover 67% of the cases (respondents). *Solution 1* indicates that the presence of ACC and DL are sufficient conditions for the outcome of interest (intention to use digital technologies for learning) to occur. It should be noted in this solution gender of the respondents does not play a role. *Solution 2* indicates that the presence of ACC and IL lead to the outcome of interest, a solution which applies only to male respondents. *Solution 3* indicates that the presence of PRO and IL combined with the absence of FRE lead to the outcome of interest, a solution which gender of the respondents does not play a role and this solution. *Solution 4* indicates that the presence of FRE and IL combined with the absence of PRO lead to the outcome of interest. It should be noted that this solution is applicable only to females. *Solution 5* indicates that the presence of FRE, IL and DL combined with the absence of ACC lead to the outcome of interest, a solution which applies only to female respondents.

Table 8. Intermediate solution for intention to use digital technology (staff sample + gender)

Solution	Gen	ACC	FRE	PRO	IL	DL	Raw coverage	Unique coverage	Consistency
1		●				●	0.310	0.086	0.981
2	●	●			●		0.294	0.096	0.838
3			○	●	●		0.062	0.043	0.932
4	○		●	○	●		0.227	0.102	0.827
5	○	○	●		●	●	0.178	0.028	1.000

7 Conclusion

The application of information literacy, digital literacy, access to digital technologies, frequency of use of digital technologies and proficiency with digital technologies has been examined and evaluated. This paper examines their impact on the intention to use digital technology in teaching and learning environments among university students and university staff. The fuzzy-set Qualitative Comparative Analysis (fsQCA) has been employed and the findings indicate that for university students, digital literacy, frequency of use and access to digital technology are determinal factors influencing the intention to use digital technology. As for the university staff sample, the results indicate that frequency and information literacy are important factors. When taking gender into account, some variations can be found within the result. For both groups, the majority of solutions only apply for female respondents.

In this paper, university students and university staff consisted of both traditionally perceived "digital natives" and "digital immigrants", with disregard to their age. Classifying individual as digital native and digital immigrant has been debated by many authors such as Nikou et al. [38]. Therefore, access, frequency and proficiency were instead suggested as possible boundaries of characterisation. When looking at these suggestions, differences between students and non-students were identified within all these factors (i.e., access, frequency and proficiency). In fact, non-students (i.e., university staff, the "digital immigrants") scored higher at various instances when compared to the students (i.e., the "digital natives"). Overall, the university staff had more access to digital tools, had a higher frequency of software use, and even a higher self-report rating of proficiency. This challenges the traditional point of division utilising age [1] as a divider when it comes to digital nativeness.

The utilisation of fsQCA in this paper has provided complementary insights to prior research using the SEM method [19, 36, 37, 39, 40] through different configurations of conditions which lead to the outcome of interest. Regarding the sample of students, the most frequently appearing conditions (variables) within the solutions were access and digital literacy. Meanwhile, for the university staff sample, the most frequently appearing condition was information literacy. When taking gender into account, the most prominent conditions within the solutions for the student sample were access, proficiency and information literacy. With the non-student group, the most prominent condition was information literacy. Concludingly, the concept of digital nativeness can be perceived as more complex than a line of division drawn between those born before and after 1980. Other boundaries of characterisation should not be left overlooked while exploring individual's intention to use digital technologies for teaching and learning, as factors such as digital literacy, information literacy, access to digital tools, usage frequency, and individuals trust in their own proficiency can impact said intention.

Naturally, this research possesses some limitations. Due to the data collection method being a self-completion survey, the limitations include inability to control the quality of the respondents. Furthermore, the outcomes of the answers provided by the respondents are limited due to closed-ended questions. Future research could build upon the findings of this paper while simultaneously suggesting new factors for boundaries of characterisation. The direction of future research could additionally incorporate qualitative efforts in order to gain more dimension within the subject matter.

Acknowledgement. This work was supported by Academy of Finland, project The Impact of Information Literacy in the Digital Workplace [grant number 295743].

References

1. Prensky, M.: Digital natives, digital immigrants, part 1. Horizon **9**(5), 1–6 (2001)
2. Benini, S., Murray, L.: Challenging Prensky's characterization of digital natives and digital immigrants in a real-world classroom setting. Digit. Lit. Foreign Second Lang. Educ. **69–85**, 70 (2014)
3. Bennett, S., Maton, K., Kervin, L.: The 'digital natives' debate: a critical review of the evidence. Br. J. Educ. Technol. **39**(5), 775–786 (2008)
4. Bennett, S., Maton, K.: Beyond the 'digital natives' debate: towards a more nuanced understanding of students' technology experiences. J. Comput. Assist. Learn. **26**(5), 321–331 (2010)
5. Nikou, S., Brännback, M., Widén, G.: The impact of digitalization on literacy: digital immigrants vs. digital natives. In: Proceedings of the 27th European Conference on Information Systems (ECIS), Stockholm and Uppsala, Sweden (2019)

6. UNESCO: Literacy. https://en.unesco.org/themes/literacy. Accessed 31 Mar 2019
7. Eisenberg, M.B.: Information literacy: essential skills for the information age. DESIDOC J. Libr. Inf. Technol. **28**(2), 39–47 (2008)
8. Lloyd, A.: Information literacy landscapes: an emerging picture. J. Doc. **62**(5), 570–583 (2006)
9. Eshet-Alkalai, Y.: Digital literacy: a conceptual framework for survival skills in the digital era. J. Educ. Multimed. Hypermedia **13**(1), 93–106 (2004)
10. Ng, W.: Can we teach digital natives digital literacy? Comput. Educ. **59**(3), 1065–1078 (2012)
11. Lodge, J.M., Kennedy, G., Lockyer, L.: Digital learning environments, the science of learning and the relationship between the teacher and the learner. In: Carroll, A., Cunnington, R., Nugent, A. (eds.) Learning Under the Lens: Applying Findings from the Science of Learning to the Classroom. CRC Press, Abingdon (2019)
12. Baratè, A., Haus, G., Ludovico, L.A., Pagani, E., Scarabottolo, N.: 5G Technology for Augmented and Virtual Reality in Education. In: Proceedings of the International Conference on Education and New Developments 2019 (END 2019), pp. 512–516 (2019)
13. Piotrowski, C.: Emerging research on social media use in education: a study of dissertations. Res. High. Educ. J. **27** (2015)
14. Uskov, V., Uskova, M.: Applications of telecommunications in education: national science foundation projects on advanced technological and online education in information engineering technology. In: 10th International Conference on Telecommunications, 2003, ICT 2003, vol. 2, pp. 1701–1708. IEEE (2003)
15. Gu, X., Zhu, Y., Guo, X.: Meeting the "digital natives": understanding the acceptance of technology in classrooms. J. Educ. Technol. Soc. **16**(1), 392–402 (2013)
16. American Library Association (ALA): Information literacy competency standards for higher education (2002)
17. American Library Association (ALA): Digital literacy task force. digital literacy, libraries, and public policy. https://www.districtdispatch.org/wp-content/uploads/2013/01/2012_OITP_dig ilitreport_1_22_13.pdf. Accessed 7 Feb 2013
18. Nikou, S., Brännback, M., Widén, G.: The impact of multidimensionality of literacy on the use of digital technology: digital immigrants and digital natives. In: Li, H., Pálsdóttir, Á., Trill, R., Suomi, R., Amelina, Y. (eds.) WIS 2018. CCIS, vol. 907, pp. 117–133. Springer, Cham (2018). https://doi.org/10.1007/978-3-319-97931-1_10
19. Aavakare, M.: The impact of digital literacy and information literacy on the intention to use digital technologies for learning: a quantitative study utilizing the unified theory of acceptance and use of technology. Master thesis (2019). https://www.doria.fi/handle/10024/173070. Accessed 11 June 2020
20. Gilster, P.: Digital Literacy. Wiley, New York (1997)
21. Ajzen, I.: From intentions to actions: a theory of planned behavior. In: Kuhl, J., Beckmann, J. (eds.) Action Control. SSSSP, pp. 11–39. Springer, Heidelberg (1985). https://doi.org/10. 1007/978-3-642-69746-3_2
22. Davis, F.D.: Perceived usefulness, perceived ease of use, and user acceptance of information technology. MIS Q. **13**, 319–340 (1989)
23. Fishbein, M., Ajzen, I.: Belief, Attitude, Intention, and Behaviour: An Introduction to Theory and Research. Addison-Wesley, Reading (1975)
24. Venkatesh, V., Morris, M.G., Davis, G.B., Davis, F.D.: User acceptance of information technology: toward a unified view. MIS Q. **27**, 425–478 (2003)
25. Venkatesh, V., Thong, J.Y., Xu, X.: Consumer acceptance and use of information technology: extending the unified theory of acceptance and use of technology. MIS Q. **36**(1), 157–178 (2012)
26. Kurbanoglu, S.S., Akkoyunlu, B., Umay, A.: Developing the information literacy self-efficacy scale. J. Doc. **62**(6), 730–743 (2006)

27. Ragin, C.C.: The Comparative Method: Moving Beyond Qualitative and Quantitative Strategies. University of California Press, Berkeley (1987)
28. Bagozzi, R.P., Yi, Y.: On the evaluation of structural equation models. J. Acad. Mark. Sci. **16**(1), 74–94 (1988)
29. Podsakoff, P.M., MacKenzie, S.B., Lee, J.Y., Podsakoff, N.P.: Common method biases in behavioural research: a critical review of the literature and recommended remedies. J. Appl. Psychol. **88**(5), 879–903 (2003)
30. Malhotra, N.K., Kim, S.S., Patil, A.: Common method variance in IS research: a comparison of alternative approaches and a reanalysis of past research. Manag. Sci. **52**(12), 1865–1883 (2006)
31. Ragin, C.C., Fiss, P.C.: Net effects analysis versus configurational analysis: an empirical demonstration. In: Ragin, C.C. (ed.) Redesigning Social Inquiry: Fuzzy Sets and Beyond, pp. 190–212. University of Chicago Press, Chicago (2008)
32. Schneider, C.Q., Wagemann, C.: Standards of good practice in qualitative comparative analysis (QCA) and fuzzy-sets. Comp. Sociol. **9**(3), 397–418 (2010)
33. Ragin, C.C.: Redesigning Social Inquiry: Fuzzy Sets and Beyond. Chicago University Press, Chicago (2008)
34. Mikalef, P., Pateli, A.: Information technology-enabled dynamic capabilities and their indirect effect on competitive performance: findings from PLS-SEM and fsQCA. J. Bus. Res. **70**, 1–16 (2017)
35. Mendel, J.M., Korjani, M.M.: Charles Ragin's fuzzy set qualitative comparative analysis (fsQCA) used for linguistic summarizations. Inf. Sci. **202**(2012), 1–23 (2012)
36. Mohammadyari, S., Singh, H.: Understanding the effect of e-learning on individual performance: the role of digital literacy. Comput. Educ. **82**, 11–25 (2015)
37. Wongvilaisakul, W., Lekcharoen, S.: The acceptance of e-learning using SEM approach: a case of IT literacy development for PIM students. In: 12th International Conference on Electrical Engineering/Electronics, Computer, Telecommunications and Information Technology (ECTI-CON), pp. 1–6. IEEE (2015)
38. Nikou, S., Cavalheiro, S., Widén, G.: Digital natives and digital immigrants in the creative economy. In: Sundqvist, A., Berget, G., Nolin, J., Skjerdingstad, K.I. (eds.) iConference 2020. LNCS, vol. 12051, pp. 343–362. Springer, Cham (2020). https://doi.org/10.1007/978-3-030-43687-2_27
39. Bouwman, H., Nikou, S., Molina-Castillo, F.J., de Reuver, M.: The impact of digitalization on business models. Digit. Policy Regul. Gov. **20**(2), 05–124 (2018)
40. Nikou, S.: Factors driving the adoption of smart home technology: an empirical assessment. Telemat. Inform. **45**, 101283 (2019). https://doi.org/10.1016/j.tele.2019.101283
41. Nikou, S., Brännback, M., Carsrud, A.L., Brush, C.G.: Entrepreneurial intentions and gender: pathways to start-up. Int. J. Gend. Entrep. **11**(3), 348–372 (2019)
42. Mezei, J., Nikou, S.: On the use of configurational analysis in entrepreneurial research. In: A Research Agenda for Entrepreneurial Cognition and Intention. Edward Elgar Publishing, pp. 142–160. https://doi.org/10.4337/9781784716813.00012 (2019)

The Adoption of New Health Information and Communication Technology: Perception of the Abilities to Use New Technology and Possibilities to Get Help at it

Ágústa Pálsdóttir[✉]

Information Science, University of Iceland, Oddi v/Sæmundargötu, 101 Reykjavík, Iceland
agustap@hi.is

Abstract. The paper examines the adoption of new health information and communications technologies (ICT) among different groups of Icelanders, as well as how they perceive their abilities to use new ICT and their possibilities to receive help at it. Data was collected by a survey. Differences across age, sex, and education were examined. The results revealed that new ICT had only been adopted to a limited extent. In addition, the possibilities to do so were not regarded to be good, as the participants found it difficult both to start using new ICT and to get help at using technology when they needed it. The study concludes that for people to be ready to accept new health ICT and take it into use they need support through training as well as technical support.

Keywords: Health information · Technology adoption · Technological support

1 Introduction

People's potential for lifelong learning and informed decisions making about their health is a crucial issue. The enhancement of media and information literacy [1] is important in this regard, as it has been generally recognized as important factor for lifelong learning about health. In the past years there have been great advancements in the way that information can be communicated and accessed. Health information is increasingly being disseminated digitally and people are constantly required to adjust to and learn about recent advances in their information environment.

Given the growing amount of information that can be gathered from digital sources it is essential to recognize how people accept new technology and make use of it to gather information about their health history and healthy lifestyle. The current paper will examine the adoption of new information and communications technologies (ICTs) for health information among different groups of Icelanders.

Advances in digital technology and the growing amount of digital health information has brought new possibilities for people to manage their own health, practice better self-care and improve their health behaviour. Norman and Skinner [2] have introduced the concept of eHealth literacy and defined it as "the ability to seek, find, understand, and

© Springer Nature Switzerland AG 2020
M. Cacace et al. (Eds.): WIS 2020, CCIS 1270, pp. 226–237, 2020.
https://doi.org/10.1007/978-3-030-57847-3_16

appraise health information from electronic sources and apply the knowledge gained to addressing or solving a health problem" (p. 69). Thus, to be able to benefit from digital health information demands that people possess the media and informational competence which is required to take advantage of the digital information environment [1].

It has been suggested that the employment of devices and programs using digital technology will create increasing opportunities for people to practice health care management [3, 4]. However, several barriers at using them have also been identified. This includes for example limitations regarding internet access, memory available to download new apps, and available data or minutes, for the use of health apps in smartphones [5]. The issue of data protection has been also been discussed and concerns raised about personal data safety risk and the need to improve the user privacy [6, 7].

The significance of the quality of information has, furthermore, been pointed out. This relates not only to the content of the information, that must be relevant to the needs of end user, but also to the quantity of it, which should not be overwhelming [8]. There are, indeed, indications that people prefer to get support from health professionals to identify reliable health information that suit them [9]. It is therefore vital to guide them as to where they can access quality digital health information, that they can trust. Otherwise, they may be cut off from using it to make rational decisions about their health-related behaviour.

Moreover, it has been stressed how important it is that technology is not complicated and difficult to use. There are indications that health apps need to be simple and intuitive to use, with an easy input of health data, as well as possessing features that save time over current methods [10]. In fact, both the perceived usefulness of adopting technology and the ease of using it, have been incorporated in theoretical models as significant motivational factors that affect the acceptance of new information technology, such as the Technology Acceptance Model (TAM) and the extension of the model TAM2 [11, 12], as well as a motivational model of microcomputer usage [13].

Studies that have that explore how socio-demographic factors relate to internet access and the use of digital health information have continually demonstrate that certain groups within society are more at disadvantage than others. Education has been found to be a strong predictor, with those who have a higher level of education being more likely to seek digital health information than those with less education [14–16]. In addition, younger people and women have been reported to seek digital health information more than those who are older and men [14, 16, 17]. The older people are, the more likely they are to be in need of help at taking new technology into use [18].

For people to be able to benefit from digital health information it must be provided in a way that meets their needs. Knowledge about who are in a position to make use of new health ICT, and who are less able to benefit from it, is necessary in order to provide support as needed.

Access to the internet is widespread in Iceland. In 2014 a total of 95% of the population was reported to connect to the internet at least ones a week [19]. Thus, the conditions for obtaining digital health information can be considered excellent in that regard. It must, however, to be kept in mind that access to the internet does not necessarily translate into the use of digital health information [15]. It is therefore necessary to consider other aspects in relation to digital health information as well. Nevertheless, steps have been taken to improve access to health information in Iceland. A new legal framework was set in 2009 to ensure people access to their health history through their health records, however many of the files are not yet in a digital form [20]. The latest initiative is the development of the ICT system 'Heilsuvera' which is supposed to provide people with a better and more direct access to information about their own health. The system allows people, for example, to book appointments, view drug prescriptions, and to communicate with doctors or other health professionals to get various health information tailored to their own needs. Some parts of people's health history are already being recorded into the system on a daily basis, while other types of access are still under development. This includes for example health records made during doctors' appointments, which are not accessible yet through it. In addition to this, the system provides access to various reliable information about healthy lifestyle [21].

1.1 Aim and Research Questions

The aim of the study is to explore how Icelanders who are 18 years or older take health ICT into use, how they perceive their abilities to use new technology, as well as their possibilities to receive help at it. To do so, answers to the following questions will be sought: 1) How do different groups of Icelanders' use recently available ICT to access information about their health history and healthy lifestyle? 2) How do they evaluate their capabilities to start using new ICT? 3) How do they perceive their possibilities to receive help at using ICT?

The purpose of addressing this issue is to understand better the opportunities and/or challenges faced by different groups of people at gaining knowledge about their health by using new health ICT. An improved awareness of the issue may help to increase the efficiency of disseminating health information and, thereby, enhance people's abilities to adopting healthier lifestyle.

2 Methods

Data for the study were gathered in from November 2018 to January 2019 from two random samples using an internet and a telephone survey. For the telephone survey, a sample of 300 people aged 60 years and older from the whole country, randomly selected from the National Register of Persons in Iceland, was used. For the internet survey a random sample of 1500 people at the age of 18 to 59 years, from the Social Science Research Institute at the University of Iceland net panel, was used. The net panel consists of people aged 18 years or older from the whole country. The choice of participants in the net panel follows strict methodological rules to avoid convenience sampling. The net panel is updated regularly to ensure that it corresponds with the distribution in the population, regarding sex, age and residence. Both datasets were merged, allowing answers from all individuals belonging to each set of data. The total response rate was 39%. Because of the response rate, the data were weighed by gender, age, place of residence and education, so that it corresponds with the distribution in the population. Information about the distribution in the population were collected from Statistics Iceland.

2.1 Measurements and Data Analysis

In addition to the socio-demographic information, which included the background variables education, sex and age, the measurements consisted of four sets of questions:

1. Motivation towards healthy lifestyle was examined by two questions: 1) How interested the participants were in information about health and lifestyle; 2) How often they discussed the topic with others. A five-point response scale was used (Very interested/often – Very low interest/Never).
2. One question examined how important it was for the participants to have full access to their health history through electronic health records. A five-point response scale was used (Very important – Very unimportant).
3. Use of health information and communication technology was examined by four questions: 1) The use of the health ICT system 'Heilsuvera' to communicate with doctors or to get information about their health, for example to book appointments, view drug prescriptions, or send messages to their doctor; 2) The use of 'Heilsuvera' to seek information about healthy lifestyle, such as nutrition or exercise; 3) The use of apps in smartphones or smartwatches to monitor or record health information; 4) The use of a blood pressure monitor to record their health information. A five-point response scale was used (Very often – Never).
4. Possibilities of taking new health information and communication technology in use was examined by two questions: 1) How difficult it is to begin to use new technology; 2) How easy it is to get help at using technology when needed. A five-point response scale was used (Strongly agree – Strongly disagree).

All analysis is based on weighed data. Differences across age, sex, and education were examined and chi-squared test was used to measure if they were statistically significant.

3   Results

The chapter starts by presenting results about the participants motivation towards health and lifestyle information and the importance of having access to health records. This will be followed by results about the use of the information and communication system 'Heilsuvera', the use of smartphones/smartwatches, and blood pressure monitors. Finally, results about the experience of taking new ICT in use and the participants possibilities of getting help at it will be introduced.

When asked about interest in information about health and lifestyle, a total of 62% of all participants replied that they were either very or rather interested. Furthermore, 52% of all participants claimed that they talked about the topic with others either very or rather often. The difference by groups is presented in Fig. 1.

As can be seen in Fig. 1, interest in information about health and lifestyle varies by groups of participants, with a significant difference found by age and sex. The oldest group was more interested than those who are younger, and women were considerably more interested than men. Furthermore, a significant difference was found by all groups when the participants were asked how often they talked with others about health and lifestyle. Women talked considerably more often about this topic than men. In addition,

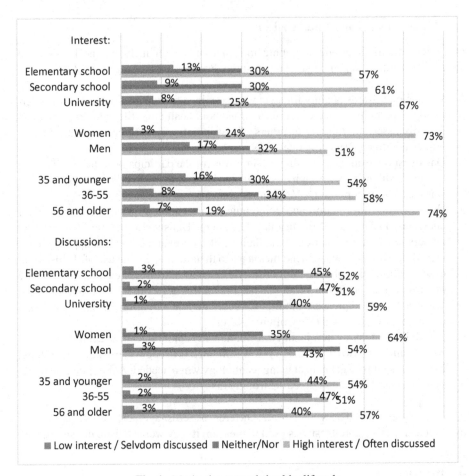

Fig. 1. Motivation towards healthy lifestyle

participants with university education and those who are 56 years and older discussed it more often than the those who have less education and belong to the younger groups.

When asked how important it is to have full access to health history through electronic health records, a total of 78% all participants replied that it is either very or rather important. Men and those who are 56 years or older were least in favour of this, with 70% and 71% retrospectively considering it to be very or rather important. Women, on the other hand, were most in favour, with a total of 86% of them considering this very or rather important.

Results about the use of the health system 'Heilsuvera' show that 58% of all participants had never used it to communicate with their doctors, or to get information about their health. In addition, 80% of all participants had never used the system to seek information about healthy lifestyle. Results about different groups of participants are presented in Fig. 2.

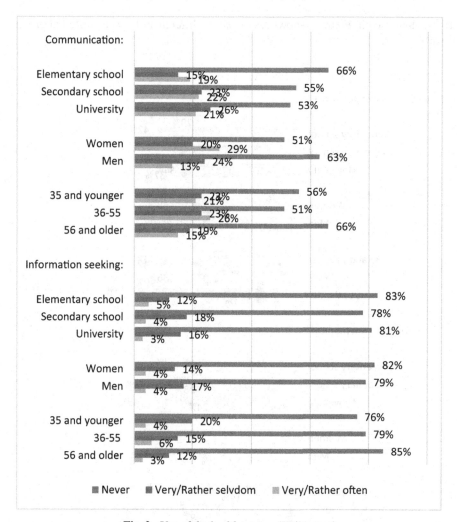

Fig. 2. Use of the health system 'Heilsuvera'

Figure 2 shows some differences across groups of participants for the use of the health system to communicate with doctors, However, the only significant results are by sex, with women using the system more often than men do. In addition, results about the use of the system for seeking information about healthy lifestyle revealed no significant differences across groups and that the participants had rarely sought information in it. Only between 3% to 5% of them had sought information very or rather often, while between 76% to 85% had never used to the system for information seeking.

An examination of the use of health apps in smartphones or smartwatches revealed that half of all the participants had either never (38%) or very seldom (12%) used them to monitor and/or record their health information. The results about the use of blood pressure monitors to record health information were similar, as 31% had never and 22%

very seldom used it. Figure 3 shows results about differences between different groups of participants.

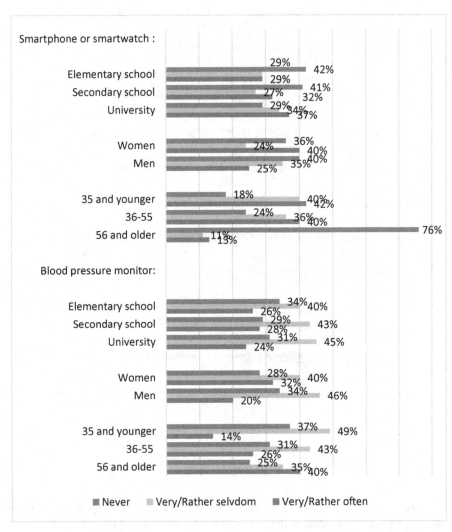

Fig. 3. Use of health apps in smartphones/smartwatches – use of blood pressure monitors

Significant differences were revealed between all groups of participants for the use of health apps in smartphones or smartwatches. Figure 3 shows that the more educated people are, the more likely they were to have used the apps. However, the results also show that almost the same rate of people with elementary and secondary education have never used them. More women had used health apps than men. And, the older people are, the less likely they were to have done so, with a total of 76% of people 56 year and older reporting that they had never used health apps.

Figure 3 also shows that the difference between the age groups is reversed when people were asked about the use of blood pressure monitors to record health information, as the older people are the more likely they were to have use it. Again, there is a difference by sex, with women being likely to have used blood pressure monitors than men.

When asked if they found it difficult to begin to use new ICT, a total of 62% of all participants agreed with it. The results also show that only 11% of all participants found it easy to get help at using ICT if they needed it. Results about differences between groups are presented in Fig. 4.

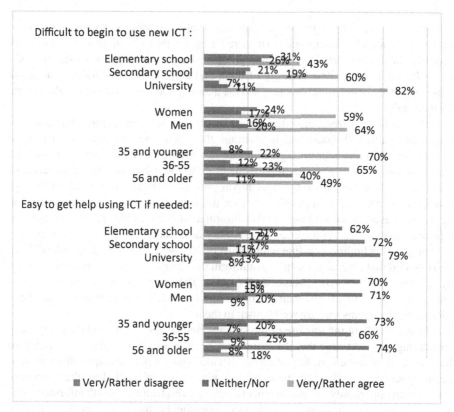

Fig. 4. Difficulties at taking new ICT into use – possibilities at getting help

As Fig. 4 shows, the participants varied in their opinion of how difficult it is to begin to use new ICT, the analysis revealed significant differences between all groups. The results show that the more educated people are and the younger they are, the more difficult they found this. Furthermore, men found this more difficult than women. In addition, analysis of the question about how easy it is to receive help at using ICT revealed significant differences between all groups. The more educated people are, the more difficult they found it to get help. Although the difference by sex is small, women claimed to get help more easily than men. And the oldest group found it easier to get help than those who are younger.

4 Discussion

The ability to adopt new health technology has become essential as health information is increasingly made available in a digital form. The current study examined the use of health ICT among different groups of Icelanders, as well as how they perceived their abilities to use new technology and their possibilities to receive help at it.

The key elements of both eHealth literacy and media and information literacy is that people possess the motivation and the personal skills that allow them to acquire information about healthy living and draw knowledge from it, for their own advantage [1, 2].

The study revealed that the participants were motivated towards getting health information and considered it important to have full access to their own health history through electronic health records. They had though only to a limited extent accepted new ICT for health information. The majority of them had either never or seldom used health apps in smartphones or smartwatches, and the majority had never used the health system 'Heilsuvera'.

There were, however, some differences by groups, as women were more likely to have used health ICT than men. In addition, those who are less educated and those who are 56 and older tend to lag behind those who are more educated and younger. This corresponds with previous reports about differences by sex, education, and age [14, 16, 17]. However, for the use of blood pressure monitors results about the age difference were reversed, as people got older, the more likely they were to have used it. Hence, well established means to gather information, which older people are familiar with and have grown accustomed to use, may have more value for them than new technology. This finding is in line with results by Rosales and Fernández-Ardèvol [22], who reported that older adult´s choice of information channels is based on their "values, style, habits and long-term perspective" (p. 63). They, furthermore, claim that this is among the reasons that limits their use of smartphones and leads them instead to gather information by means that are well known to them.

The results about the low use of the system 'Heilsuvera' are perhaps not surprising considering the short time that the system has been in use. It may always be expected that it takes time and effort, first of all to introduce and get people acquainted with new technology, and secondly to get them engaged with using it. Nevertheless, the system can be seen as an opportunity for improvement in access to high quality health information, as well as for people to communicate with doctors or other health professionals and receive various tailored information about their health. The value of the information itself is essential. The possibility to receive health information that are tailored to people's own needs has been found to be a motivator that encourages people to make an effort at using digital solutions [23, 24]. Thus, given time for people to become knowledgeable about the possibilities that 'Heilsuvera' offers, and provided that they will also be offered support at taking it into use, it can be concluded that the system makes promising possibilities for the future.

Furthermore, the participants found it difficult to take new ICT into use and claimed that it is not easy for them to get help at using technology when they needed it. These are factors that can have a bearing on whether or not people are ready to make the effort of starting to use new technology. Previous studies have for example pointed out that the ease of using new technology is of importance [10–13].

As before, there was a difference by sex, with women considering it both less difficult to begin to use new ICT and easier to get help at it then men did. The finding that, the more educated and the younger people are, the more difficult they found it to take new ICT in to use and less easy to receive help at it, was however unexpected. Anderson and Perrin [18] have for example reported that the older people are, the more likely they are to need help at using new technology. It seems also logical that those who have more education consider their possibilities of using new ICT to be better than those who are less educated. Competency theory, however, may offer some explanation to this. The theory argues that people with low skills or knowledge also lack the ability to recognize it, therefore they tend to overestimate their capabilities. Highly qualified people, on the other hand, are inclined to underestimate their abilities. Even though they have fairly good judgement of their absolute performance, they have a tendency to overestimate how well others are doing. As a result, their evaluation of how well they perform compared to others is biased [25]. Although it is interesting to compare the study results with the theory it, nevertheless, needs to be taken into account that it was not tested in the study. But these results are interesting and give reasons to study further people's perceptions of their informational and technological competence and how they can be supported at taking new ICT in use.

The overall study is limited by a total response rate of 39%. Although his may be considered satisfactory in a survey it raises the question whether or not those who answered the survey are giving a biased picture of those who did not respond. In order to compensate for this bias the data were weighed by gender, age, place of residence and education, so that it corresponds with the distribution in the population, as reported by Statistics Iceland. The findings may, therefore, provide valuable information about the adoption, acceptance, and use of new ICT.

5   Conclusion

The study sought to recognize Icelanders use of recently available ICT to gather information about their health history and about healthy lifestyle, as well as how they evaluate their capabilities to start using new ICT and perceive their possibilities to receive help at using it. The results revealed, despite some differences by education, sex and age, that new ICT for health information had only been adopted to a limited extent. In addition, the possibilities of it were not regarded to be good, as the participants found it difficult to start using new ICT and to get help at using technology when they needed it. Thus, the conclusion of the study is that for people to be ready to accept new technology and take it into use, they need training and technical support.

The results from the study help to shed a light on how peoples potentials to benefit from development in ICT, and to identify their needs for support at using health ICT. There is, however, a great deal more to learn about the topic. The results from the study help to shed a light on people's potentials to benefit from development in ICT, and to identify their needs for support at using health ICT. There is, however, a great deal more to learn about the topic. More analyses of the results could be done, for example cross analysis among age, sex, and education. The effect of people's health status on the relationship between age and interest in using health ICT is also worth considering in future studies. Furthermore, the study is limited by the use of quantitative research methods and further research using more varied methods is needed. Especially, qualitative studies, that can explore more deeply why people do not use new technology and what kind of support they need and prefer to receive. This is important because ICT develops rapidly, which is a progress that can be expected to continue in the coming years.

References

1. UNESCO: Media and information literacy (2014). http://www.unesco.org/new/en/commun ication-and-information/media-development/media-literacy/mil-as-composite-concept/
2. Norman, C., Skinner, H.: EHealth literacy: essential skills for consumer health in a networked world. J. Med. Internet Res. **8**(2), e9 (2006). https://doi.org/10.2196/jmir.8.2.e9
3. Mendiola, M.F., Kalnicki, M., Lindenauer, S.: Valuable features in mobile health apps for patients and consumers: content analysis of apps and user ratings. JMIR Mhealth Uhealth **3**(2), e40 (2015). https://www.ncbi.nlm.nih.gov/pmc/articles/PMC4446515/
4. Michie, S., Yardley, L., West, R., Patrick, K., Greaves, F.: Developing and evaluating digital interventions to promote behavior change in health and health care: recommendations resulting from an international workshop. J. Med. Internet Res. **19**(6), e232 (2017). http://www.jmir.org/2017/6/e232/
5. Real, F.J., DeBlasio, D., Rounce, C., Henize, A.W., Beck, A.F., Klein, M.D.: Opportunities for and barriers to using smartphones for health education among families at an urban primary care clinic. Clin. Pediatr. **57**(11), 1281–1285 (2018)
6. Bondaronek, P., Alkhaldi, G., Slee, A., Hamilton, F.L., Murray, E.: Quality of publicly available physical activity apps: review and content analysis. JMIR Mhealth Uhealth **6**(3), e53 (2018). https://doi.org/10.2196/mhealth.9069
7. Huckvale, K., Prieto, J.T., Tilney, M., Benghzi, P., Car, J.: Unaddressed privacy risks in accredited health and wellness apps: a cross-sectional systematic assessment. BMC Med. **13**(1), 214 (2015). https://doi.org/10.1186/s12916-015-0444-y
8. Aji, M., et al.: Exploring user needs and preferences for mobile apps for sleep disturbance: mixed methods study. JMIR Ment. Health **6**(5), e13895 (2019). https://doi.org/10.2196/13895
9. Lee, K., Hoti, K., Hughes, J.D., Emmerton, L.: Dr Google is here to stay but health care professionals are still valued: an analysis of health care consumers' internet navigation support preferences. J. Med. Internet Res. **9**(6), e210 (2017). https://doi.org/10.2196/jmir.7489
10. Tsai, H.S., Taiwan, H., Shillair, R., Cotton, S.R., Winstead, V., Yost, E.: Getting grandma online: are tablets the answer for increasing digital inclusion for older adults in the U.S.? Educ. Gerontol. **41**, 695–709 (2015)
11. Davis, F.D.: Perceived usefulness, perceived ease of use, and user acceptance of information technology. MIS Q. **13**(3), 319–340 (1989)
12. Viswanath, V., Davis, F.D.: A theoretical extension of the technology acceptance model: four longitudinal field studies. Manag. Sci. **46**(2), 186–204 (2000)
13. Igbaria, M., Parasuraman, S., Baroudi, J.J.: A motivational model of microcomputer usage. J. Manag. Inf. Syst. **13**(1), 127–143 (1996)
14. Din, H.N., McDaniels-Davidson, C., Nodora, J., Madanat, H.: Profiles of a health information–seeking population and the current digital divide: cross-sectional analysis of the 2015–2016 California health interview survey. J. Med. Internet Res. **21**(5), e11931 (2019). https://www.jmir.org/2019/5/e11931/

15. Ono, H., Zavodny, M.: Digital inequality: a five-country comparison using microdata. Soc. Sci. Res. **36**(3), 1135–1155 (2007)
16. Pálsdóttir, Á.: Seeking information about health and lifestyle on the Internet. Inf. Res. **14**(1) (2009). paper 389. http://informationr.net/ir/14-1/paper389.html
17. Robinson, L., et al.: Digital inequalities and why they matter. Inf. Commun. Soc. **18**(5), 569–582 (2015). https://doi.org/10.1080/1369118X.2015.1012532
18. Anderson, M., Perrin, A.: Tech adoption climbs among older adults: roughly two-thirds of those ages 65 and older go online and a record share now own smartphones: although many seniors remain relatively divorced from digital life. Pew Research Centre (2017). https://www.pewinternet.org/2017/05/17/tech-adoption-climbs-among-older-adults/
19. Statistics Iceland: Computer and Internet usage in Iceland and other European countries 2013. Stat. Ser.: Tour. Transp. IT **99**(1) (2014). https://hagstofa.is/lisalib/getfile.aspx?ItemID=14251
20. Health Records Act nr. 55 April 27, 2009. https://www.government.is/media/velferdarraduneyti-media/media/acrobat-enskar_sidur/Health-Records-Act-No-55-2009-as-amended-2016.pdf
21. Directory of Health: Heilsuvera: mínar heilbrigðisupplýsingar (2016). https://www.landlaeknir.is/gaedi-og-eftirlit/heilbrigdisthjonusta/rafraen-sjukraskra/heilsuvera-minar-heilbrigdisupplysingar/
22. Rosales, A., Fernández-Ardèvol, M.: Smartphone usage diversity among older people. In: Sayago, S. (ed.) Perspectives on Human-Computer Interaction Research with Older People. HIS, pp. 51–66. Springer, Cham (2019). https://doi.org/10.1007/978-3-030-06076-3_4
23. Jimison, H., et al.: Barriers and drivers of health information technology use for the elderly, chronically ill, and underserved. Evidence Report/Technology Assessment No. 175. AHRQ Publication No. 09-E004. Agency for Healthcare Research and Quality, Rockville (2008)
24. Loos, E.: Senior citizens: digital immigrants in their own country? Observatories **6**(1), 1–23 (2012)
25. Kruger, J., Dunning, D.: Unskilled and unaware of it: how difficulties in recognizing one's own incompetence lead to inflated self-assessment. J. Pers. Soc. Psychol. **77**(6), 1121–1134 (1999)

Youth Attitudes Towards Immigrants in Southern Ostrobothnia, Finland

Saaga Somerkoski[⊠]

Faculty of Education, University of Turku, Turku, Finland
saaga.s.somerkoski@utu.fi

Abstract. The aim of this study is to compare the attitudes towards immigrants among Finnish second grade students. The study was carried out in Southern Ostrobothnia region where the number of immigrants is the lowest in Finland. During the next decades, immigrants will be an important source of labor, since the population in our country is getting older - faster than in any other European country. The data (n = 275) was collected during spring 2018 from colleges and upper secondary schools. The youths' attitudes varied towards different immigration groups and nationalities. Attitudes towards the immigration of children and workers for example, were more positive than attitudes towards unemployed migrants and refugees. In terms of nationalities, Western immigrants were more positively welcomed than immigrants from war zones and areas with the crisis were. In the open answers, the attitudes towards immigration were particularly concerned with refugees and the policy of immigration. Open answers included both racist and negative statements as well as statements to helping refugees.

Keywords: Youth · Attitudes · Immigrants · Multiculturalism · Southern Ostrobothnia

1 Introduction

The Finnish immigration population has increased substantially during the last three decades. In 2018, the percentage of immigrants in Finland was 7% which means 402 619 individuals [1]. Based on the estimations, the number of immigrants in Finland will increase to one million until the year 2050 [2].

Immigration provokes more and more public discussion in Finland and abroad [3]. To be able to live and work in the productive way, it is essential to understand, collaborate and respect individuals from other cultures, especially in Finland where the population is aging rapidly. Furthermore, during the prospective years Finland needs new workers desperately for the labor market. The increase in immigrant labor requires cooperation and cultural tolerance. Students are future workers. This is why it is essential to understand young peoples' perceptions toward immigrants among future workers in Finland.

The aim of this study is to analyze the attitudes towards immigrants among Finnish second grade students. We wanted to understand how the attitudes of Finnish youth vary

© Springer Nature Switzerland AG 2020
M. Cacace et al. (Eds.): WIS 2020, CCIS 1270, pp. 238–250, 2020.
https://doi.org/10.1007/978-3-030-57847-3_17

between the groups and nationalities of immigrants. Secondly, we wanted to research the youth perceptions by researching how the Finnish youth speak about immigrants and immigration, if they have a free possibility for that.

The study is placed in South Ostrobothnia region for several reasons. To begin with, the absolute number of the immigrants is the smallest in the country. Secondly, the level of education in the study area of the South Ostrobothnia region is the lowest in Finnish provinces. The third fact is that the balance of recourses (labor and pensioners) in the South Ostrobothnia region is the worst in Finland. During the next decades, immigrants will be an important source of labor, since the population in our country is getting older - faster than in any other European country [2, 4, 5].

For these reasons, it is probable that the number of the immigrants will increase in South Ostrobothnia region and, the workers who are now used to work or study with Finns must in near future get used to working with the people who come from other cultures.

2 The Global, National and Local State of Immigration

This study investigates attitudes. Attitudes can be determined as "Learned, comparably permanent, positive or negative position toward a person, object or environment." Attitudes have an effect on our daily actions and participate in the control of behavior and interpret of the environment. Attitudes also have an effect on how we behave in social interaction [6, 7].

2.1 Global State of Attitudes Towards Immigration

In the past, global events have kept media climate and global news in a state, which is not sympathetic toward immigration, for instance President Donald Trump's attempt to prevent illegal immigration with the wall in the borders of Mexico, Britain leaving the EU partially to control immigration and numerous terror attacks and asylum seekers arrival to Europe. [8–10]

When xenophobia in Europe has become more common, the support of national parties that are against immigration increases [5]. According to 2018 local report of Polis [11] xenophobia and the racist crimes have become common also in Finland. Critical attitudes towards immigration have become more common and strengthened towards non-European people in Europe. Furthermore, negative attitudes towards the non-European immigrants will increase when the amount of immigrants increases [12].

It has to be noted that men's attitudes are on average more negative than women's [1]. Among gender other factors such as age, education, the residence of place, political conviction and the amount of individual's amount of immigrant connections have an effect on attitudes towards immigrants. In addition, prevalent social environment and atmosphere (such as economic depression and unemployment rates) have an effect on attitudes [1].

2.2 National State of Attitudes Towards Immigration

The terrorist stabbing in 2017 hit in the middle of a Finnish affluent society. After that extremism, racism and negative attitudes became more common in the local media and the public discussion became more critical towards immigrants. Moreover, asylum-seekers in Finland were related to sex offence crimes, which made the local news even more critical towards immigration. Nationally, we have come to a point where the nationalistic Finnish Party has become the most popular party in Finland (over 20% support) [13].

The youth studies have been criticized from the fact that the studies are mainly located in the urban settings. Countryside often plays a smaller role in the studies about youth [14]. The South Ostrobothnia region can be considered as an area, which is mostly agriculture dominated countryside with small cities, communities and villages [15]. Most of the studies overall in Finland focus on University cities and big cities and countryside is left out. In addition, the young people in the remote areas may not be as much in touch with multicultural issues and with individuals from other countries as in the bigger cities [16, 17].

Immigrants in Finland are centred in bigger cities where the services are easily available. The difference for immigrants in different areas in Finland is big. Furthermore, the range of immigrants in Southern Ostrobothnia area is different in comparison with our national immigration population. The amount of immigrants in Southern Ostrobothnia is above 4000 people, it is 2.3% of the local population. The comparable amount in Southwest Finland is 33 506 people (7.4%) [1] Culturally, immigrants from further cultures such as Somalian immigrants, are one of the biggest immigration nationalities in Finland but non-existent in South Ostrobothnia. Immigration population in South Ostrobothnia is more likely to come from the neighbour countries of Finland instead of humanitarian countries [17, 18], Table 1.

Table 1. The percentages of foreign people in some of the regions in Finland 2017 [17, 18]. (Statistics Finland 2018)

Area	N	%
Finland	384 123	7
South Ostrobothnia	4 193	2,2
Ostrobothnia	12 681	7
Helsinki metropolitan	213 290	13
Southwest Finland	33 506	7

Previous studies have shown that Finnish youth has more positive attitudes towards the immigration of the labor compared with the immigration of refugees [2]. We also know that young adults are standing more positively on the immigration of people from Western countries, people with higher education and people with better positions in work [2]. In addition, we have to remember that integrating into another society, economically, socially, politically and culturally is a long and slow process. Negative attitudes make it more difficult to integrate and get employed. For instance, Karmela Liebkind states that getting a job is often considered the most important factor for immigrant's integration to the society [19]. Further on, Liebkind considers work as an environment that helps individual to create social contacts and engaging with the society as an equal citizen. Additionally, younger immigrants have their difficulties in integration and survival as social exclusion and school bullying are alarming problems among Finnish youth. It is easy to see that the experiences of discrimination are affecting on the well-being of many minority group members [19]. While the number of Finnish immigration population is getting bigger, we should focus on the two-way process of integration. This means both the local citizen's and immigrant's adaptation to the changing situation [19].

2.3 Local State of Attitudes Towards Immigration

Like in previous studies, also in the quantitative part of this study women's attitudes towards immigration were more positive than men were. Other factors such as level of education and parents' level of education (especially mothers') were linked to attitudes according to the quantitative analyses of this research. Personal experiences or connections to multiculturalism had a positive effect on respondent's attitudes towards immigration. In this article, we will only be focusing on the qualitative data of this research.

Based on the YATI quantitative results [20] it seems that Finnish speaking young women's attitudes towards immigration were more positive than young men's. Other factors, such as level of education and parents' level of education (especially mothers') were linked to the attitudes toward immigration and immigrants. Children of highly educated mothers had more positive attitudes toward immigrants and immigration than those children, whose mothers did not have high education. In addition, based on YATI quantitative data, it also seemed that personal experiences or connections to multiculturalism had a positive effect on respondent's attitudes.

3 Methods and Analysis

This study discusses the youth attitudes towards immigrants. Based in the earlier Finnish studies of youth attitudes we designed a questionnaire Youth Attitudes Towards Immigrants (YATI) [2, 21–24] The data was collected with Webropol software during the spring term 2018 (n = 275). The central results from the quantitative part of the survey are presented in the end of Sect. 2 in this paper. To understand the quantitative results of the questionnaire, we decided to analyze the open-ended question separately.

Overall, 16 schools were engaged in this study. Of the respondents 69% were Upper Secondary School students and 24% secondary school 9th grade students (15 years). Additionally, 7% of the participants were students from other second grade educational institutions. 58% of the respondents were women (n = 159) and 41% men (n = 111). About 1.5% of the respondents reported their gender to be other than men or women. The age distribution of respondents was from 15 to 20 years. The demographic background regarding the nationality of the respondents was very homogeneous as 99% of the respondents were Finnish-speaking Finns.

The YATI questionnaire consisted of three parts. In the first part, we collected the demographic information such as age, gender, and connections to other cultures, parent's education or native language. In the second part, there were 50 statements about immigrants and immigration. The statements were 5-scale Likert (I agree – I disagree). In Part III (also Likert-scale) questions we asked how willingly the respondent would accept immigrants concerning the immigrants' background, nationality or moving reason.

At the end of the questionnaire, there was one open-ended question: Regarding this questionnaire or immigrants or immigration, is there something else, you would like to say? The respondents could express themselves here anonymous and freely. The answers were analysed with the content analysis. Overall, 39 people (n = 39) responded to the open-ended question. From them, 21 answers were included in this analysis. Out of those, nine were women and 13 men. Based on the analysis four main categories were formulated. The categories were 1. Immigrants as victims, 2. Immigrants as threat, 3. Immigrants as the wasters or producers of resources (benefit or disappear), 4. Immigration in media. These will be explained in detail in Sect. 4.

4   Results

Based on the analysis, we found four groups of the open-ended answers that explained the attitudes toward immigrants and immigration in this study. Firstly, in the Results section of this paper we will present the YATI quantitative results and secondly the YAT qualitative results to get a holistic picture of the research topic.

4.1   Attitudes Towards Different Immigration Groups and Nationalities

The attitudes towards different immigration groups varied. Youth attitudes towards the immigration of children, marriage immigrants and workers were positive. Attitudes towards unemployed and refugees were negative, Figure 1.

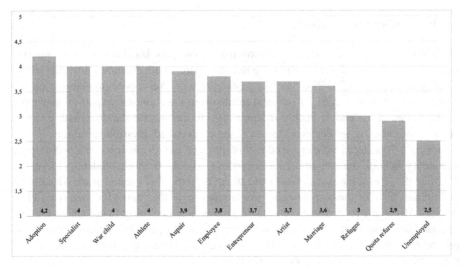

Fig. 1. Attitudes towards different immigration groups

When comparing attitudes towards different nationalities of immigrants, the comparison showed that youths attitudes towards immigrants from Western countries were positive; vice versa, negative towards immigrants from war and crisis areas. In this study, youth attitudes were the most negative towards immigrants who moved from areas with humanitarian crises or war area such as Iran, Syria, Afghanistan or Somalia. Youth attitudes were the most positive towards immigrants from Britain, the USA, Sweden or Germany. Based on the results of this study, it seems that youths' attitudes were more positive towards people who come from similar culture to their own, Figure 2.

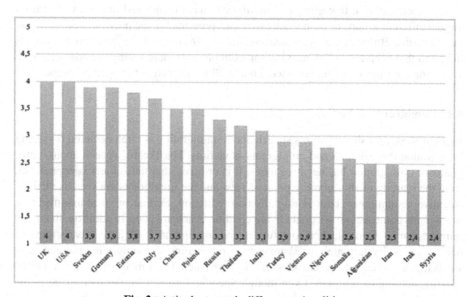

Fig. 2. Attitudes towards different nationalities

This result was supported by some of the answers in the YATI qualitative analysis. For example, the gender of the respondent marked the type of answer. In both the quantitative and qualitative results, men's attitudes were toward immigration were more critical than women's. From 13 answers of men, 11 included criticism or negative attitudes towards immigration. Yet both women's and men's answers included criticism towards immigration.

"I don't care where a person comes from or what is he's occupation"
Woman, 20, Vocational School

"I don't want to be a racist but my prejudices have not came from only what I've heard but also what I have experienced"
Man, 20, Vocational School

In addition, the difference between attitudes towards refugees and labour could be found in many answers. Overall, the speech about immigration could be considered as sorting by separating and mentioning different groups of people, culture and immigrants. 80% (n = 17) of the answers included some kind of mention of specific group of immigrants.

> *"I would only take children or people with family but not men alone. If they want to live here, they should learn the Finnish culture and go to services supporting employment"*
> **Woman, 16, Upper Secondary School**

In general, only a few groups of immigrants were mentioned in the answers even though different groups of immigrants were just presented in the previous section of the questionnaire. Based on the open answers, moving from humanitarian areas and effects linked to that such as asylum seeking for example were dominating the answers. Vice versa, some groups of immigrants were not at all mentioned in the open answers.

4.2 Immigrants as Victims

As Finnish studies show, youth's speech about immigration is often centered on seeing immigration through lack and immigrants as victims. The Youths' speech about immigrants or immigration has negative tones. It is ordinary that the subject is approached from the scarcity or shortcoming point of view and the immigrants are seen as victims. Negative assumptions about immigration are common. Further on, it is assumed that immigrants come from inadequate living conditions and are poor. In addition, in media, immigration is often attached to refugees and immigrants have a negative stigma of being victims. Even though the share of refugees in Finnish immigration population is small [23, 25]. Half of the answers in this study included a mention of humanitarian moving, helping or refugees. Even though Specific groups were not mentioned in the speech, the respondents reported their assumptions of the inadequate living conditions of immigrants as well as Finland as a helper.

> *"I think it is important to help those who are in need, but todays refugees have left their country only because they don't think it has a future. They see Finland as a Country, which rose from bad conditions to a welfare state. They think Finland has a future unlike their one country, which has always been on war."*
> **Man, 18, Upper Secondary School**

The respondent mentions "Those who need help" but still he questions their need for asylum. He mentions the war but later on he assumes that people want to move to Finland only to rise their standards of living.

> *"It's started to feel like most of the immigrants are not willing to respect Finnish people and culture and are only here as economic refugees"*
> **Man, 20, Vocational School**

The results of the qualitative study seem to strengthen the quantitative results as the young people described unemployed immigrants and refugees the most negatively.

4.3 Immigrants as Wasters or Producers of National Recourses (Benefit or Disappear)

While some of the respondents saw the immigrants through refugee status, the others were willing to provide help for the immigrants' survival in their new home country. The respondents did not provide this attitude pro bono, but accepting the refugee type immigrants to stay in Finland only under certain conditions. In this group, the respondents saw the immigrants either *the users or wasters of national recourses* (n = 6). The condition respondents provided was the idea of *to benefit Finnish society or to disappear.* If one does not benefit the nation, he or she should disappear from the country.

The other condition was that if the immigrant wanted to stay in Finland, he or she should create social relations, adopt the society and start benefitting the Finnish nation. Correspondingly, the respondents wrote more respectively about immigrants who were working, learning Finnish culture and obeying laws and norms. These same topics are on the table of the media conversation around multiculturalism and immigration.

> *"I don't mind if you come here for work. However if you come here to benefit from our recourses you can disappear"*
>
> **Man, 16, Upper Secondary School**

This type of answers described that immigrants should earn their place in the Finnish society by being productive, by working and by paying taxes. This aspect is supported by the quantitative analyzes were attitudes were more positive towards engineers, specialists and students.

> *"I welcome you to Finland if your aim is to learn Finnish culture, laws, norms and language and getting a job or education. It is Ok for me as long as immigrants are not given any privileges and are treated the same way as Finns – In good and in bad. People in working age and ability to work as soon as possible to pay taxes, but no more mouths to feed"*
>
> **Woman, 16, Upper Secondary School**

Concern about resources can be picked from the answers. The immigrants are principally welcome to Finland, but the condition is that we *should not give the immigrants more than we give to our own citizens.* It is hard for an immigrant to be employed in Finland because of the negative attitudes and also the assumption or reality of the lack of language skills. Some even have a theory of competition of recourses, were the competition about recourses between groups induces prejudices and fear [26–28].

4.4 Immigrants as Threat

One third of the answers (n = 7) was connected with security and safety. Immigrants could be considered in some answers as a threat to national safety and immigrants as threatening or dangerous. In addition, concerns about crime and willingness to follow Finnish laws and cultural norms rose from the answers.

"A more precise back ground check should be done for people who move from conflict areas. Also their integration should be taking care of and look after their mental health to avoid radicalization"

Woman, 16, Upper Secondary School

Some of the respondents mentioned the mental health of immigrants. The respondents were also reporting about their own prejudices and the risk they assumed immigrants would cause. In addition, the immigrants as a group were claimed with doing more crimes than the Finnish-speaking Finns who live permanently in Finland

"I am the most willing to take children and woman. I have more negative attitudes towards older man who move alone because of the negative impression I have got"

Woman, 17, Upper Secondary School

"You did not ask anything about the causes of extremism of Islam. Islamisation causes security risks, terrorist and no-go areas."

Man, 18, Upper Secondary School

Some of the answers contained the extremism and the hate speech. These respondents gave antagonistic, racist of nationalistic statements about immigrants and immigration.

"Finland belongs to Finns. When all of our own problems are solved, we can consider on helping others. We do not need any towelheads here raging with knives or blowing anybody up. Russkies can also stay on their side of the border"

Man, 18, Upper Secondary School

"CLOSE THE BORDERS!!!"

Man, 16, Secondary School

"On behalf of The White Finland!"

Man, 16, Secondary School

The Finnish Social media and protest marchers are widely using this type of foregoing statements about immigrants and immigration. It is possible that a 16-years old teen does not understand what he is saying. In the answers, negative criticism was often directed to specific groups such as "unemployed", nationalities "Ruskkies", religion – Islam and gender and status "lonely men". In addition, expression "White Finland" has a reference to skin color. As we know racism does not only include racist statements or discrimination on the grounds of race but also multicultural framing or discriminating [29–31].

4.5 Media's Impressions About Immigration

Media was mentioned in (n = 5) answers from different aspects. Media pictures only selected parts of immigration; some of the themes are highlighted and some are not.

Positive and neutral events are rarely newsworthy, so the negative publishing gets more attention. Culturally different cultures are more distinguishable both in the media and in the street scene and more likely to produce emotions, conversation and attention. Culturally similar cultures to ours disappear in the masses and do not pay attention. In addition, youth in this study talked about cultural differences and learning Finnish laws, norms and cultural confusion.

"I don't know so much about immigration so I hope we would talk about it in school. I think media gives rather negative image about immigration"
Man, 16, Upper Secondary School

"It is hard to get rid of immigrant resistance while media is exaggerating. In Facebook there are a lot of writings against immigrants"
Woman, 17, Upper Secondary School

"National media has become politicized and informs about events unilaterally and untruthfully. For example, the disadvantages of immigration are being understated. Power elite only accepts tolerance towards different cultures. Nowadays patriotism has become racism and criticism is considered as hate speech."
Man, 18, Upper Secondary School

It is significant that youth have considered the influence of media on their attitudes and on the image of immigration. While the impact of media is constantly growing, it is demanding to teach people source criticism and ability to read media.

5 Conclusions

This paper investigated the attitudes towards immigrants among Finnish second grade students. The study was carried out in Southern Ostrobothnia region where the number of immigrants is the lowest in Finland. During the next decades, immigrants will be an important source of labor, since the population in our country is getting older - faster than in any other European country [2, 4, 5].

The data (n = 275) was collected during spring 2018 from colleges and upper secondary schools in Southern Ostrobothnia region. The attitudes varied toward different immigration groups and nationalities. Attitudes towards the immigration of children and workers were more positive than attitudes towards unemployed, migrants and refugees. In terms of nationalities, Western culture representatives, for instance immigrants from Europe or Scandinavia were more positively welcomed than immigrants from war zones and areas with the crisis were. We found these results in both analysis YATI quantitative and qualitative.

The attitudes towards immigration were particularly concerned with refugees and the policy of immigration. Open answers included both racist and negative statements as well as statements to helping refugees. Based on the content analysis four main categories were formulated. The categories were immigrants as victims; immigrants as threat; immigrants as wasters or producer of resources ("benefit or disappear") and immigration in the media. The qualitative results of this study showed that youth portrayed immigration from one position. The respondents accepted immigration if it was beneficial for the responding country and executing immigration was welcomed positively. However, humanitarian immigration, for instance refugees, that do not include element of benefitting the Finnish society, arouse negative attitudes and criticism. On the other hand, some of the respondents reported the idea of providing help for the immigrants. Based on the findings of this study, the immigration discourse was somewhat one-sided: the respondents made comments on immigrants with labor or refugee status, but for instance, student immigrants were not mentioned at all. The media might have its influence on this.

Seeing Islam as a threat has become a more common view in the conversation about immigration. This may be one reason for more negative attitudes towards Islamic immigrants and nationalities. In addition, the familiarity of Western culture tradition, such as European or Scandinavian culture may have been the reason for more positive attitudes towards immigrants coming from those countries. In addition, the idea of cultural distance and the negative attitudes seem to accumulate in the certain immigration groups and these groups are reflected as victims, threat or resource users.

When analyzing the answers, it is worthwhile consider, what were the themes the respondents did not report on. Interestingly, no one of the respondents reported about immigration purely as a positive phenomenon. The image of donating Finnish resources "free to the others" seems to be in connection with the negative attitudes. We did not find any comments such as "It is nice to get to know people from different cultures" or "I think immigration enriches our culture". Based on this result, we conclude that the respondents presented a somewhat stereotypic image of the immigration.

Finally, during the reviewing process the immigration phenomenon has become state-of-the-art. Even under the state of a global emergency, during the time when COVID-19 pandemic spread spring 2020, multicultural questions have been a highly topical matter. Like other countries, Finnish government decided to close the borders of the country to slow down by the spreading of COVID-19. The position of refugees is even more complex than before. The idea of giving refugees a privilege to cross the borders in a state when no one can move anywhere can increase negative reactions. In addition, it is possible that the attitudes towards immigrants get more negative during an economic depression. Now when we have faced one of the hardest economic depressions of our time, it is possible that we will face a situation where the negative attitudes towards immigrants will get stronger than before. Recent occurrences concerning the killing of George Floyd and the protest against racism have resurfaced the themes of attitudes towards multiculturalism.

Acknowledgements. The author wants to thank the South Ostrobothnia Regional Fund for partial funding of this study.

References

1. Statistics Finland: Immigrants (2018). https://www.stat.fi/tup/maahanmuutto/maahanmuutta jat-vaestossa.html

2. Sjöblom-Immala, H.: Tervetuloa Suomeen? Korkeakouluopiskelijoiden asenteita mittaava Etnobarometri. Siirtolaisinstituutti, Turku (2013)

3. Horsti, K.: Vierauden rajat. Monikulttuurisuus ja turvapaikanhakijat journalismissa. Tampereen Yliopistopaino, Tampere (2005)

4. Södering, I.: Suomen väestökysymys ja maahanmuutto. In: Fågel, S. (ed.) Olemme muuttaneet. Näkökulmia maahanmuuttoon, perheiden kotoutumiseen ja ammatillisen työn käytäntöihin. Väestöliitto, Helsinki (2005)

5. Hatton, T.: Immigration, public opinion and the recession in Europe. Econ. Policy 31(86), 205–246 (2016). https://academic.oup.com/economicpolicy/article/31/86/205/2392431

6. Kalliopuska, M.: Psykologian sanasto. Otava, Helsinki (2005)

7. Erwin, P.: Asenteet ja niihin vaikuttaminen. WSOY, Helsinki (2001)

8. Kokkonen, Y., Parkkinen, S.: Trump: Meksikon muuri tarvitaan kansallisen turvallisuuden takaamiseksi. Presidentti Donald Trump puhui Valkoisessa talossa parhaaseen katseluaikaan ja kertoi laittomien siirtolaisten tekemistä rikoksista. Yle Uutiset 8.1.2019, Helsinki (2019). https://yle.fi/uutiset/3-10587211

9. Sipilä, A.: Miksi britit äänestivät itsensä ulos EU:sta? HS listaa 10 syytä Brexit-leirin voitolle. Helsingin Sanomat 25.6.2016, Helsinki (2016). https://www.hs.fi/ulkomaat/art-200000290 7911.html

10. Helsingin Sanomat: Brexitin peruminen olisi voitto Euroopan unionille – myös britit tietävät nyt paremmin, mitä EU-ero tarkoittaisi. Helsingin Sanomat 11.1.2019, Helsinki (2019). https://www.hs.fi/paakirjoitukset/art-2000005962594.html

11. Rauta, J.: Poliisin tietoon tullut viharikollisuus Suomessa 2017. Poliisiammattikorkeakoulun raportteja 131. Poliisiammattikorkeakoulu, Tampere (2018). http://www.theseus.fi/bitstream/ handle/10024/154780/POLAMK_Rap131_web.pdf?sequence=1&isAllowed=y

12. Gorodzeisky, A., Semyonov, M.: Not only competitive threat but also racial prejudice: sources of anti-immigrant attitudes in European societies. Int. J. Public Opin. Res. 28(3), 331–354 (2016). https://academic.oup.com/ijpor/article/28/3/331/1750622

13. Yle. Ylen kannatusmittaus: Keskustan kannatus sukeltaa jälleen, vihreiden suosio kasvaa ja perussuomalaisten kannatushuippu takana, 6 February 2020. https://yle.fi/uutiset/3-11193715

14. Farrugia, D.: Towards a spatialised youth sociology: the rural and the urban in times of change. J. Youth Stud. 17(3), 293–307 (2014). https://www.tandfonline.com/doi/pdf/10.1080/ 13676261.2013.830700?needAccess=true

15. Jäske, P.: Asuminen Etelä-Pohjanmaalla. Julkaisu B:31. Etelä-Pohjanmaan liitto, Seinäjoki (2008)

16. Avonius, M., Kestilä-Kekkonen, E.: Suomalaisten maltilliset ja kirjavat maahanmuuttoasenteet. Yhteiskuntapolitiikan julkaisuja 83(1) (2018). http://www.julkari.fi/bitstream/handle/ 10024/136481/YP1801_Avonius%26Kestila-Kekkonen.pdf?sequence=1&isAllowed=y

17. Häkkinen, A., Mattila, M.: Etelä-Pohjanmaan maahanmuuttajat. Siirtolaisuusinstituutti, Seinäjoki (2011)

18. Saarteenoja, A., Träsk, M., Tantarinmäki, S., Mattila, M.: Maaseudun maahanmuuttajat: Kokemuksia työperäisestä maahanmuutosta Etelä-Pohjanmaan ja Varsinais-Suomen maaseudulla. Raportteja 41. Ruralia-instituutti, Seinäjoki (2009). http://www.helsinki.fi/rur alia/julkaisut/pdf/Raportteja41.pdf

19. Liebkind, K.: Kun kulttuurit kohtaavat. In: Liebkind, K. (ed.) Monikulttuurinen Suomi. Etniset suhteet tutkimuksen valossa. Gaudeamus, Helsinki, 2. Painos, pp. 13–27 (2001)

20. Somerkoski, S.: Lukiolaisten ja 9.-luokkalaisten asenteet maahanmuuttoa kohtaan Etelä-Pohjanmaalla. Master thesis. University of Turku, Turku (2020)

21. Söderling, I.: Suomalaisten suhtautuminen ulkomaalaisiin [electronic data]. Versio 1.0 (2002-01-23). Yhteiskuntatieteellinen tietoarkisto (1996). http://urn.fi/urn:nbn:fi:fsd:T-FSD1111

22. Myllyniemi, S.: Puolustuskannalla. Nuorisobarometri 2010. Nuorisotutkimusverkoston/Nuorisotutkimusseuran julkaisuja 107 & Nuorisoasiain neuvottelukunnan julkaisuja 43. Opetus-ja kulttuuriministeriö, Nuorisotutkimusseura & Valtion nuorisoasiain neuvottelukunta, Helsinki (2010)

23. Myllyniemi, S.: Ihmisarvoinen nuoruus. Nuorisobarometri 2014. Nuorisotutkimusseuran julkaisuja 159. Opetus- ja kulttuuriministeriö, Nuorisoasiain neuvottelukunta & Nuorisotutkimusverkosto, Helsinki (2014)

24. Räty, H.: Asennetutkimuksen unohdettu historia. Teoreettis-metodologinen tarkastelu asenteesta sosiaalipsykologisen tiedon kategoriana. Joensuun korkeakoulu & Joensuun korkeakoulun kirjasto, Joensuu (1982)

25. Suurpää, L.: Erilaisuuden hierarkiat: suomalaisia käsityksiä maahanmuuttajista, suvaitsevaisuudesta ja rasismista. Julkaisuja. Nuorisotutkimusverkosto, Nuorisotutkimusseura, 28. Nuorisotutkimusseura, Helsinki (2002)

26. Björklund, K.: Haluun koulutusta, haluun työtä ja elämän Suomessa. Yksin tulleiden pakolaisten kotoutuminen Varsinais-Suomessa. Siirtolaisuusinstituutti, Turku (2014)

27. Bobo, L., Hutchings, V.L.: Perceptions of racial group competition: extending Blumer's theory of group position to a multiracial social context. Am. Sociol. Rev. 61, 951–972 (1996). https://www.jstor.org/stable/2096302?origin=crossref&seq=1#metadata_info_tab_contents

28. Solares, E., Liebkind, K.: Ryhmien väliset ennakkoluulot ja niihin vaikuttaminen. In: Steiner, T., Vainionpää, J., Huttunen, R. (eds.) Samalta viivalta 9. PS-kustannus, Jyväskylä, pp. 13–38 (2015)

29. Sinokki, J.: Rasismin määritelmä. In: Sinokki, J. (ed.) Rasismi ja filosofia. Eetos, Turku (2017). https://www.academia.edu/32062931/Rasismin_määritelmä_kirjassa_Rasismi_ja_fil osofia_?auto=download

30. Kivijärvi, A., Honkasalo, V.: Monikulttuuristen nuorten ja nuorisotyöntekijöiden tulkintoja rasismista. In: Martikainen, M., Haikkola, L. (eds.) Maahanmuutto ja sukupolvet. Suomalaisen kirjallisuuden seura, Helsinki, pp. 257–272 (2010)

31. Puuronen, V.: Rasistinen Suomi. Gaudeamus, Helsinki (2011)

Practical Training in Teacher Education: Reflecting Physical and Psychological Learning Environment

Brita Somerkoski$^{(\boxtimes)}$ (iD), Paivi Granö, and Teija Koskela

University of Turku, Department of Teacher Education, Rauma, Finland
`brita.somerkoski@utu.fi`

Abstract. This study investigated how international students were reflecting the learning environment and in particular, the physical and psychological dimensions of it. During the practical training in their homeland in Southern Africa area the student teachers used multiple learner-centered strategies, such as self-reporting, discussions in groups, learning cafés and teamwork. Based on the data, the trainees were managing these well. In addition, if their teaching methods were not working, they used meta-reflection strategies and critical thinking to find solutions for providing pupils better learning experiences. Regarding the physical learning environment, in their homeland schools, the trainees were reporting about the scarcity of materials, such as textbooks and furniture, but especially the technical devices, such as laptops, projectors or tablets. Some of the trainees reported finding replacement for this type of learning by using other than digital learning material, for instance crayons, posters or stones outside the classroom.

Keywords: Learning environment · Teacher student · Meta-reflection · Portfolio

1 Introduction

The teaching profession is born within historical and cultural contexts. On the other hand, schools provide the knowledge and skills that families are not able to teach to their children. Teachers in their profession are between the identities of their pupils and the learning environment [1]. In this study, our intention is to research the group of international teacher trainee students and how they reflect the educational content in their practical training portfolios.

The number of international students is increasing around the world and the internationalisation of curriculum, is a global effect of internationalisation [2]. Internationalised curriculum, like here, shapes students by certain actions and ways of being. Teaching in an international context involves the elements of comparison [3]. However, the aim of this study is not on comparisons between any countries, their resources or on their education systems. Instead, we want to respect other cultures and to understand the possibilities of transferring the central educational ideas to another culture. Furthermore, the results of this study provide us with valuable information when designing and implementing educational programs for international students. With this study, we want to describe

© Springer Nature Switzerland AG 2020
M. Cacace et al. (Eds.): WIS 2020, CCIS 1270, pp. 251–264, 2020.
https://doi.org/10.1007/978-3-030-57847-3_18

what kind of teaching strategies the teacher trainees apply for their final practical training period in their home country in Southern Africa area. These strategies and solutions are carried out towards the end of their 3-year Bachelor of Education studies carried out in Finland.

The respect of diverse background of students is a prerequisite for professionals in higher education [4]. Understanding the culture of 'the others' by learning to implement educational ideas is not a clear concept. It is possible that student mobility processes, instead of learning or respecting, increase the hegemony of Western cultural values or global capitalism [5, 6]. Although some of the African countries have adopted the idea of learner-centred pedagogy or participatory teaching, Larsen [7] and Vavrus [8] state that these positive reforms can lead to epistemological blindness. To address the research aim of this study, two research questions we raised as follows: What were chosen for the teaching strategies during the final practical training period? How do the international trainees reflect and construct the physical and psychological dimensions of the learning environment in their home country?

2 Student Teacher as a Learner

Teacher reflection can be seen as an analysis of need, conclusions, problems or changes. These are parts of professional development including cognitions of improved practices [9]. The student teachers, here called trainees, learn at university from their reflections and experiences and through dialogues. All this is an essential part of their professional development [10, 11]. Britzman sees a teacher from three distinguished domains: teacher identity; the teacher as the controller of the learning environment and teacher as an expert of delivering the knowledge [12]. The aim of Finnish teacher education is to create reflective teachers who are free and able to use research when designing learning environments and pedagogic solutions. They have the professional autonomy to choose the best teaching methods and learning environment [13].

In Finnish schools, the learner-centred approach is used, and some activities are even designed together with the pupils [14]. The idea of the learner as an active participant who constructs his or her own learning is called constructivism. In his cultural-historical theory about cognitive development, Vygotsky [15] states that the interaction between young children and their caretakers is crucial for the cognitive development. The theory is usually called social constructivism or sociocultural theory. This idea is shared in many Western culture countries, for instance in the teacher education as the students write essays and create portfolios to reflect their experiences and to construct their learning [16]. Vygotsky's theory provides multiple applications to general and special education. One of these is the Zone of Proximal Development (ZPD). The theory contains the idea of scaffolding. Scaffolding means that although person is not able to manage the task, he or she can manage, if he or she gets support from an expert nearby. Soon the learner will be able to carry out the task on his or her own [17].

If we consider that the universities are implementing the educational concept of constructivism, we have to take into consideration that firstly, when teaching educational subjects to the international students, we do not start from the zero. Each of the student has lived about 20 years through interpersonal relationships, a shared sense of identity, a shared understanding as well as shared norms, values, trust, cooperation, and reciprocity. These shared resources are called social capital [18]. Further, every one of us is a member of a micro culture with the ethnic backgrounds, family and personal resources. We are also members of a social macro culture with values, policies and sanctions [19]. Schools are an essential part of this macro culture, a continuation of the family, as they are places where knowledge, values, respect and morality are learned and constructed. From earlier studies we know, that minority ethnic students, including those who are high science achievers are less likely to aspire with scientific careers. In particular, this concerns girls in ethnic or racial minority [20]. Nevertheless, in Africa, recent discussions have emphasized that young people there, are raising increasing interest, as their aspirations are a resource that may lead the continent to economic growth. Young men and women are involved with international aid, advocacy organizations, media, popular culture, churches and mosques. Their aspiration is in creating knowledge as well as shaping public opinion [21].

Atjonen, Korkeakoski and Mehtäläinen posit that the teaching profession focuses on learning environments, individual needs and competencies. The researchers state that teaching in the Finnish universities has become more learner-centered, yet teachers see themselves as multi skilled experts in the field of education [22]. The integration of theory and practice is built in the Finnish teacher education. The practical nature of teacher job builds upon deeper understanding: it provides the students with capabilities for acting independently as a teacher, instructor and evaluator. Furthermore, guided teaching practice involves the giving of lessons, guidance discussions and familiarisation of responsibilities related to various issues raising in the everyday life of schools [23]. In this research, the international students have carried out two of their bachelor level practical training periods in Finland. The final period is carried out in their home country in the area of Southern Africa.

3   The Concept of Learning Environment in This Study

It is critical to have a definition of the *learning environment* in this study. Yet the researchers agree that it includes *other* meanings *than the physical space* where the learning happens. Generally, in the educational context, the concept is quite broad and it refers to educational cultures, values and approaches. The concept of learning environment describes the goals for teaching and learning [24] as well as activities, places, communities, or modes of action that support learning. The learning environment is pedagogically planned and it is sharpened with perspectives, for instance physical [24] social [25] and psychological [26] dimensions. Sometimes pedagogic [27] dimension is presented, yet the pedagogic is included in the concept of *learning*. The new generation pedagogic learning environment is open and shared [28], but in general the definition includes the pedagogic solutions, design situations and theories used in teaching [29]. Physical learning environment refers to concrete spaces, materials, technical solutions or tools; the social learning environment is focused on interaction between individuals and on the group dynamics, and the pedagogic learning environment gets its shape form the pedagogical phenomena, such as the learner-based approach or the problem based learning. [27] The physical learning environment includes libraries, laboratories, playground, machinery, decorative objects, lighting and fittings. The researchers state that physical environment is an agent of intellectual stimulation that enables effective learning. The researchers state also that effective learning is not possible if the classroom is overpopulated [30].

The teacher has multiple roles in all the perspectives or dimensions of learning environments, but especially in the psychological dimension of the learning as this includes all the cognitive processes [31, 32]. Correspondingly, the learning environment and the process of learning itself can never be separated. They support each other and are connected through the learner [33]. Sometimes also, a concept of *digital learning environment* is used. Tightly connected with the digital learning environment is the concept of *digital divide*. A digital divide understood as uneven distribution of Information and Communication Technologies (ICT). In general, ICT is expensive and therefore the adoption and utilization of it is highly uneven. It is generally agreed that poverty is one of the main causes of digital divide, but also gender disparities or unwillingness to use ICT may cause digital divide [34, 35]. In this paper, we include the digital or eLearning environment in the physical dimension. In addition, in the research literature, also concepts, such as virtual learning environment is used [36]. It is obvious that the attitudes, skills and behaviors that a pupil brings into the classroom are important, as do the types of learning activities, participation, engagement and motivation. The prevailing culture of a classroom formed by its members and their life histories and broader school climate and safety do explain at least a part the motivation and the learning [37].

The definition of learning environment in this study is two-fold: firstly, in the trainee portfolios the teacher student reflects the learning environment at school they are carrying out their practical training. Secondly, the practical training is a learning environment for the international students as part of their university studies. Therefore, it is essential to describe the content where the data was gathered. The practical training was a study course *Teaching practice, Competence and expertise. Planning, implementation and evaluation projects (10 ECTS)*. This bachelor of education course consists of planning, observing, the teaching period, seminars and the portfolio. "With this course, students achieve the competence in teaching by organizing the learning environment, planning the research-based curricula for a group or class including teaching and the learning methods and assessments of the pupils as well as their own development as a teacher. This teaching practice will be completed in the country of question in cooperation with the school authorities".

4 Methods, Data and Analysis

The goal is that students can independently produce teaching periods in different subjects in accordance with the pupil group and it's unique features; students can study learning within the period and evaluate the meaning of pedagogical means and their impact on learning; students understand the meaning and possibilities of the environment for learning and can build suitable environments [38]."

During this course, the students produce a 20-h long learning period within 2–3 subjects based on problem and research-based learning, which are not restricted in subjects but mixed in progressive ways. They use learning theory as the base of the teaching period and problem and research based learning as the approach. The trainees, 8 male and 12 female students, aged 19–28 years (mean age 22 years), chose the school where they wanted to carry out the teaching practice in. With the permission of the headmaster, the school staff pointed out a pupil group the trainee would teach. The pupil group came from grades 1–7. The allocated teaching time was 20 lessons within 2–4 weeks' time. According to the curriculum of the target group, the headmaster and the teacher in charge approved the topic or theme for teaching. The trainees observed a certain amount of lessons in the school where they were carrying out the practical training as well as planned the learning theme and contents independently based on the curriculum. The student would plan independently the material he or she will use, where the learning will take place, how the learning is organized and what kinds of tasks or homework will be given. In the end, the trainee would provide data on each pupil and their learning progress. Finally, the trainee proceeds the portfolio reflecting the practical training period.

In this study, the data consisted of practical training portfolios (n = 20) of the trainees. The practical training was carried out during the 5th semester, spring 2019. The portfolios included the description of the school, the class and the staff, the lesson plans, the training experiences reflections and pupil evaluations.

We read carefully through the material several times. From the text, those passages where the teacher trainee reflects learning environments or teaching methods were chosen as data. In the thematic content analysis, we abstracted the data by choosing the most essential words or word clusters from the text. Our focus was in the descriptions of the learning environments. We organized the data into a matrix for the analysis and abstracted the text passages; categorized and connected them into the main category - the four types of learning environment: physical (phy), psychological (psy), social (soc) and pedagogical (ped) as presented in Table 1. Due to the limited space, we present only two of those dimensions: physical and psychological. Additionally, we decided to exclude the geographic descriptions, lesson plans, photos, evaluation procedures as well as possible feedback parts of the portfolios. We did not distinguish the genders in the data, as we saw that the gender difference would not be at focus in this study.

Table 1. Examples of the portfolio text analysis in this study. Learning environment dimension as main category: physical (phy), psychological (psy), social (soc) or pedagogic (ped)

Text passage	Lower category	Upper category	Main category
The **unavailability of computers**, ipads and internet at the school **made it a hindrance to the period.** — The availability of posters, textbooks, notebooks, newspapers, stones, open space, pens and pencils **made everything possible**	scarcity of technical devices, finding alternative working methods	digital divide	phy, ped

(*continued*)

Table 1. (*continued*)

Text passage	Lower category	Upper category	Main category
The school is located on a mountainous area where there are **stones outside the classroom.** These stones are a **good learning material in an activity** about comparing and ordering. — They are tasked to collect 3 stones per group of different sizes. Questions by the teacher were as follow: which stone is the biggest, smallest, and are there stones of the same size? After that they start arranging the stones from the biggest to smallest and vice-versa	outside learning environment, hands on	experimental learning	phy, ped, psy
The learning process was well **activated** using **role plays** and **presentations about the functions** of body pans using flashcards. Good to use **group work. Self-assessment** helps determine if pupils have learned or not	interactive learning environment, group work, self-assessment, metacognition	experiental learning, interaction	phy, ped, soc, psy
In many lessons observed the teachers **did most of the work,** while the pupils were listening or noting down what was being taught Pupils **were not engaged** in the lessons — to **try to involve all the pupils in my lessons. Engagement** is very vital in **the learning process,** the **teacher must interact** and be engaged with all the pupils in class —	student engagement, teacher involvement	engagement, interaction	psy, soc

5 Results

The results are based on the qualitative thematic content analysis. No frequencies are reported. The total amount of texts we chose to represent the study data was 133 (n = 133) text passages reflecting the learning environment of the practical training. The researchers have organized the results based on a theory-driven understanding of learning environment containing physical, psychological, social and pedagogical dimensions (see Sect. 3), but the analysis itself was content analysis without any theory as a base.

Physical learning Environment. Here the physical learning environment refers to the building and structures, objects (such as books) or spaces. We present the results concerning digital learning environment [36] as a part of physical learning environment, yet in the research literature, the digital learning environment is presented as an independent dimension and research area. The latest Finnish Core Curriculum [39] enhances and lets learners more than before, move freely in the school building, to use new kinds of furniture or to use outdoor possibilities. In the research data (the portfolios), the physical learning environment seemed to be meaningful to the trainees. For instance, they reported about the seat and desk arrangements in the classroom.

"I arranged pupils' desks in groups when we were doing the human body systems, and when we were doing activities, I arranged them in pairs." (R15C)

How the seats were arranged in the classroom seemed important for the trainees as they reported that during the time the class was learning with their permanent teacher, the pupils were used to sitting in "the traditional setting" in the rows. The trainee made the arrangements when he or she wanted to carry out a group work or hands-on exercises for experiential learning. The trainees made notes that some of the pupils were seated so that they *"they couldn't clearly see what was being presented on the blackboard"* (R17A) or that some of the furniture such as chairs were broken (R14A) and therefore there were two pupils sitting on one chair. It is possible that the "traditional setting" with the classroom furniture was due to the amount of the pupils in the same classroom. Some of the trainees reported that the classrooms were too full of people: *"46 pupils which mean it is overcrowded. This is quite a challenge–"* (R14C). This has caused situations that affect the pedagogic or didactic solutions the trainee is choosing to use during the lesson.

"The spaces between pupils sits were too tight that I could not easily walk past each learner during lessons, it also meant that during teaching I was forced to minimize my movement as I would waste time trying to squeeze in through tight paths to my wish and understanding, it helps when the teachers is able to reach all corners of the classroom without struggle, this makes it easy to help pupils individually." (R3A)

Also, due to the big number of students in the classroom, the trainees wanted to organize outside classroom lessons, *"the majority of the trainee's lessons could be and were done outside"* (R12D). Sometimes the outdoor classrooms were not possible due to school regulations *"– not allowed to have outdoor lessons unless it was for an arts lesson"* (R8A). The trainees stated that the outside classroom lessons would be necessary, because they *"stimulate the student's senses and to encourage a sense of intrinsic motivation in their learning progress"* (R13J). Yet some of the trainees stated that in the beginning, the outdoor learning environment was not such a success *"when the pupils went outside was a disaster and disruptive as some pupils started running and playing"* (R6C). Some of the trainees reflected their development as teacher by trying another method:

"- - and then I gave instructions to go back into the classroom and pupils would go into pairs and had five minutes to come back to class and this was more effective". (R6C)

Providing students an alternative learning environment shows that the trainee is able to reflect her or his actions in the classroom critically. This kind of ability to reflect the learning environment is an essential part of professional growth and development. Based on the picture material in the portfolios (we will not present the pictures here due to the GDPR in EU), there seems to be a resource disparity between the schools. This affects the physical learning environment significantly. Some of the trainees reported that there was scarcity of materials, textbooks, tables and chairs in the school in their home country. The scarcity and a remarkable difference compared to Finland was not just from the daily products, but also from the technical devices, such as laptops, computer laboratories or projectors.

"- -no electronic gadgets, few textbooks and the library were mostly closed because they do not have enough books and someone running it--" (R15F)

When possible, the trainees chose the digital learning environment, such as showing pictures with a projector, playing games, or using online learning platforms. The trainees reported that this type of training was both entertaining and motivating.

"Most of my lessons included the use of technology and online learning platforms as I wanted to create a flexible yet engaging learning environment." (R13B)

In some of the schools, the technical devices, such as computers, laptops, iPads or cell phones were not used for the scarcity, but the fact that they were not allowed at all. In these cases, the trainee had to create a survival agenda for the digital divide. Although the lack of teaching materials in the physical learning environment affected tremendously the didactic solutions and the lesson plans the trainees were carrying out during their practical training, some of them could see positive development in the situation:

"Sharing resources yields better understanding as the pupils get to tackle the activities together and share information. The learners would be more engaged and focused when working in pairs." (R20A)

If the trainee was not able to use the digital devices or there was scarcity of the printed learning material, the availability of posters, notebooks, newspapers, stones, open space, blackboard, crayons and pencils made the learning possible creating an alternative learning environment.

Psychological Learning Environment. This dimension of the learning environment refers to the thinking schemas, memorizing, implementing and constructing the knowledge, skills and attitudes to achieve the competence [26]. In the data, the psychological learning environment was mainly based on the idea of constructivism [17]. The constructive approach is based on the meta-analysis of the learners' abilities. The trainees stated that the learner constructs her or his "knowledge and took initiative to learn" (R13D) this was done to internalize the information. The constructive approach would not be possible if the learner did not analyze his or her learning and abilities. This was done for instance with the self-evaluation provided by the trainee. With the help of self-evaluation, the trainee got the essential information not just about the abilities but also the learning content that still needed support and scaffolding from the teacher. In the constructive approach, the pupil is directing his or her learning by asking questions based on their individual needs. Furthermore, communication enables, informs and creates an information channel that both parties can understand and convey the teaching and learning in the classroom. The psychological dimension of the learning environment is connected with the social dimension, especially when it comes to the teacher pupil relationship. For instance, during the practical training period one of the pupils gave feedback to the teacher trainee. The feedback was about speaking too fast:

"During the lessons for example, some pupils indicated that they did not understand some of the concepts because I was too fast in my explanations. Based on this feedback, I was able to re-adjust my methods to accommodate everyone." (R4D)

The leading point of view in the data was turning the perspective from teacher-centered to learner-centered. This was done by enhancing the communication both from teacher to pupils and vice versa. The trainees stated that increased communication would enable better learning. In this process teacher - by choosing the didactic method - enhances the engagement and the responsibility of the learning. The trainees stated in the data that this was transforming the role of teacher from the active distributor of information to more supporter.

"The idea was not to spoon-feed but to guide. This enables them to do their own research and present it their own way. By doing this, I was able to see their abilities and explore how to help and guide them to do better." (R15G)

For the constructive approach, the learning is seen more as a process where pupils need problem-solving skills and collaboration with others. This could sometimes lead to the change of physical learning environment:

"Whenever I had planned for classroom discussions, I would use circular seating in order to have a flow of ideas and for no one to feel left out." (R16C)

The problem-solving skills did not always solve theoretical problems, as the trainees reported on the data that they used experiential learning methods to familiarize pupils with the concept of "learning by doing", with hands-on activities and with exploring the features of the materials, such as leaves, newspapers, sand or flowers. Some of the trainees reported that their relationship to creativity was not obvious; the pupils were not used to produce and try innovative learning and design. The trainees wanted to give positive feedback to the pupils so they would keep up with the motivation and have confidence in their learning. Also, some of the trainees reflected that the pupils were not motivated to participate in art lessons of any kind and did not value them too much.

"It encourages the student to have first-hand experiences with the materials, rather than learning through someone else's experiences in textbook or lecture." (R17A)

The trainees reported on the data about experiential and situational learning. They stated that situational learning is an adequate gateway to enhance critical thinking. Giving children the opportunity to explore and formulate their own thinking into constructive concepts will boost their senses of self-awareness. The trainees understood the importance of the visual aids, such as photos, pictures and presentations and they stated that using visual aids would ease the understanding about the concepts and definitions better. Some of these images were artifacts that promoted and developed pupils' imagination. Pupils need their experiential learning when developing their 21st century competence. This state-of-the-art competence consists of teamwork, information literacy, cultural awareness, creativity and innovation. The trainees carried out varying teaching methods to enhance the cognitive skills, for instance debating game or the inquiry-based approach (problem-based learning). This would help pupils to broaden their perspectives and perceptions. The pupils would think critically, investigate and find solutions to answer the questions asked by the trainee, such as: "How would we look like without bones?"

"This kind of learning theory did not only allow for critical thinking but allowed pupils to look at the different perspectives, criticize them and find out which one is the best choice, also known as multi-perspectivity." (R8C)

Based on the data, the teacher trainee portfolios of the practical training period in their home country the most of the trainees, thou carrying out their training period autonomously, shared the idea of learner-centered learning as well as constructive approach and teamwork. The open learning environments, widely used in Finland, were mostly new to the trainees and they were eager to implement the idea of studying outdoors or re-organizing the class furniture to enhance the communication. In general, the communication and social relationships were focused during the practical training. The trainees stated that the free communication would enhance pupils' abilities to work independently. The schools where the trainees carried out their practical training were neither homogenous when it comes to the economic and material resources nor when it comes to the demographic background of the pupils. Nevertheless, the most of the trainees reported about the scarcity and lack of the resources. This seemed to affect the didactic solutions they were able to make in their practical training period.

6 Discussion

This study was based on a qualitative research design that investigated how international students were reflecting the learning environment and in particular, the physical and psychological dimensions of it. We wanted to investigate the teaching strategies used and how the trainees constructed the physical and psychological dimensions of the learning environment in their home country. The practical training portfolios provided a unique data for the study as the goal of this study was to describe those learning environments and educational principles the teacher trainees are choosing and applying.

The research data was the training portfolios (n = 20). We analyzed the data by uniting the text passages of the portfolios (n = 133) into one matrix. Therefore, it was not possible to analyze the individual differences of the trainees, but getting a holistic picture of the data. The most of the trainees reported that they wanted to implement Vygotsky's theory of the constructivist approach. This led the trainees for several measures, such as re-organizing the classroom furniture to enhance the pupils' abilities for group work, communication and learning; having outdoor lessons; applying hands-on activities and with visual aids as well as experiential and situational learning principles.

During their practical training period the trainees used many kinds of communication strategies with the learners, such as self-reporting, discussions in groups, learning cafés and teamwork. Based on the data, the trainees were managing these well. In addition, they were able to reflect if a strategy they were using was or was not working as well as finding reasons for this. Some of the trainees reported about the professional failures that they later on were able to correct, for instance guiding the pupils in a different way or organizing activities in groups instead of teaching pupils individually. These situations are promising signs of professional growth and development.

Regarding the physical learning environment, the trainees were reflecting the scarcity of materials in their homeland schools, such as textbooks and furniture, but in particular technical devices, such as laptops, projectors or tablets. Some of the trainees reported finding replacement for this type of learning by using other than digital learning material, for instance crayons, posters or stones outside the classroom. Correspondingly, many of the classrooms were overcrowded, with more than 40 pupils. When designing the curriculum for the international university students, we should consider focusing more on how to apply effective learning environment in situations of this kind. This could be carried out for instance by uniting two Finnish classes during a practical training in Finland. The setting needs more research as the crowded classroom in the training school affected the widely used strategy of scaffolding and individual teaching as well as the possibilities to carry out teamwork and discussions.

Limitations. Finnish research-based teacher education is connected with the practical training in schools and, the theoretical educational thinking has strong focus in linking theory into practice. Over the 5-year teacher education program, three periods of practical training are carried out. During their studies, the Finnish trainees observe lessons by experienced teachers and during the practical training sessions they are guided by the supervisory teachers, professors and lecturers. Training experience comprise about 15–20% of the trainees preparation time. The most of this practical training is completed within Teacher Training Schools that are governed by the universities and have specialized in the educational programs and research. The supervisory teachers guide the trainees during the practical training periods in peer dialogues and individual meetings. In this study, the trainees did have guidance from the faculty members during their practical training periods in Finland. The final practical training, that comprised the data in this study, was carried out in the trainees' homeland in Southern Africa. The supervisory teacher represented the home country of the trainee and it is probable that he or she as an African pedagogical expert did not share the pedagogic principles, theories or measures of the Finnish education. Also, the cultural differences between Finland and the home country of the trainee, may have affected the possibilities and solutions to develop and implement a practical training period [40, 41]. However, the learning portfolio produced at the transition phase between the end of the studies and at the beginning of the career, would provide rich and valuable research data also for the future studies about qualitative learning outcomes or cultural differences.

Acknowledgements. The writers would like to thank The Finnish Cultural Foundation Satakunta Regional Fund for funding this study partially.

References

1. Smulyan, L.: Constructing teaching identities. In: Christine, S., Francis, B., Smulyan, L. (eds.) Handbook of Gender and Education, pp. 469–483. Sage, London (2009)
2. Gordon, G.: Global contexts. In: Gordon, G., Whitchurch, C. (eds.) Academic and Professional Identities in Higher Education: The Challenges of a Diversifying Workforce, pp. 13–35. Routledge, New York (2010)
3. Abdi, A., Kapoor, D.: Global perspectives on adult education: an introduction. In: Abdi, A., Kapoor, D. (eds.) Global Perspectives on Adult Education, pp. 1–16. Palgrave Macmillan, New York (2009)
4. Sambell, K., Brown, S., Graham, L.: Professionalism in practice. In: Sambell, K., Brown, S., Graham, L. (eds.) Professionalism in Practice. Palgrave Macmillan, Cham (2017)
5. Dei, G.: Indigenizing the curriculum: the case of the African university. In: Dei, G. (ed.) African Indigenous Knowledge and the Disciplines, pp. 165–180. Springer, Netherlands (2014)
6. Shizha, E., Abdi, A.: Globalization and adult education in the South. In: Ali Abdi, A., Kapoor, D. (eds.) Global Perspectives on Adult Education, pp. 1–16. Palgrave Macmillan, New York (2009)
7. Larsen; M.: Internationalisation of Higher Education: An Analysis Through Spatial, Network and Mobilities Theorie, pp. 113–120. Palgrave Macmillan, New York (2016)
8. Vavrus, F.: Ensuring Quality by Attending to Inquiry: Learner-Centred Pedagogy in Sub-Saharan Africa. NESCO-International Institute for Capacity Building in Africa, Addis Ababa (2011)
9. Avalos, B.: Teacher professional development in Teacher Education. Teach. Teach. Educ. **27**(1), 10–20 (2011)
10. Calvo de Mora, J., Wood, K.: Practical Knowledge in Teacher Education: Approaches to Teacher Internship Programmes. Routledge, London (2014)
11. Somerkoski, B.: Chasing professional Phronesis in safety and well-being: teacher education curriculum as a case. In: Li, H., Pálsdóttir, Á., Trill, R., Suomi, R., Amelina, Y. (eds.) WIS 2018. CCIS, vol. 907, pp. 148–161. Springer, Cham (2018). https://doi.org/10.1007/978-3-319-97931-1_12
12. Fenimore-Smith, K.: Democratic practices and dialogic frameworks: efforts toward transcending the cultural myths of teaching. J. Teach. Educ. **55**(3), 227–239 (2004)
13. Sahlberg, P.: Educational Change in Finland. International Handbook of Educational Change. Kluwer Academic Publishers, Dordrecht, Netherlands (2009)
14. Somerkoski, B., Granö, P.: Concepts of Finnish Education: African student teacher reflections at the cultural cross-roads. In: Jutila, M. (ed.) Education Curriculum Development: Perspectives, Challenges and Future Directions. Nova Science Publishers, New York (2020)
15. Vygotsky, L.: Educational Psychology, 2nd edn. St. Lucie Press, Florida (1997)
16. Kaasila, R.: Bridging the mathematics education course and teaching practice: a Finnish example of how to construct and conduct a research-based teacher education. In: Calvo de Mora, J., Wood, K. (eds.) Practical Knowledge in Teacher Education: Approaches to Teacher Internship Programs, pp. 1 – 17. Routledge, Hoboken, New Jersey (2014)
17. de Florio, I.: Effective Teaching and Successful Learning. Bridging the Gap between Research and Practice. Cambridge University Press, New York (2016)

18. Huang, J.: Education and Social Capital. Empirical Evidence from Micro Analytic Analyses. Tinberger Institute Research Series, Rozenberg (2010)
19. Nurmi, K., Kontiainen, S.: A framework for adult learning in cultural context: mediating cultural encounters. In: Kauppi, A., Kontiainen, S., Tuomisto, J., Vaherva, T. (eds.) Adult learning in a cultural context, pp. 65–71. Adult Education Research Society, Helsinki (1995)
20. Frederiksen, B., Munive, J.: Young men and women in Africa Conflicts, enterprise and aspiration. Nordic J. Youth Res. **18**(3), 249–258 (2010). Danish Institute for International Studies, Denmark. https://journals.sagepub.com/doi/pdf/10.1177/110330881001800301
21. Archer, L., Dewitt, J., Osborne, J.: Is science for us? Black students' and parents' views of science and science careers. Sci. Educ. **99**(2), 199–237 (2015). https://doi.org/10.1002/sce.21146
22. Atjonen, P., Korkeakoski, E., Mehtäläinen, J.: Key pedagogical principles and their major obstacles as perceived by comprehensive school teachers. Teach. Teach. Theor. Pract. **17**(3), 273–288 (2011)
23. Ministry of Education and Culture: Teacher Education in Finland. 1/2014. Jyväskylä, University of Jyväskylä (2014) https://www.jyu.fi/edupsy/fi/laitokset/okl/en/curriculum/curriculum%20pdf. Accessed 11 Apr 2020
24. Felani, M., Ahmad, S.: Physical learning environment: impact on children school readiness in Malaysian. Soc. Behav. Sci. **222**(23), 9–18 (2016)
25. Castro, C., António, A.: Teaching chemistry in a social learning environment: facing drivers and barriers. In: Proceedings of ICERI2011 Conference, Madrid, Spain, 14th–16th November, pp. 3377–3385 (2011)
26. Aghamolaei, T., Fazel, I.: Medical students' perceptions of the educational environment at an Iranian medical sciences university. BMC Med. Educ. **87**(10) (2010)
27. Amar, B.: Designing pedagogical learning environment. Int. J. Adv. Sci. Technol. **6**, 1–14 (2009)
28. Bradbeer, C.: Working together in the space between. In: Pedagogy, Learning Environment and Teacher Collaboration, Evaluating Learning Environments, Snapshots of Emerging Issues, Methods and Knowledge, vol. 8, pp. 75–90 (2016)
29. Piispanen, M.: Hyvä oppimisympäristö. Oppilaiden, vanhempien ja opettajien hyvyyskäsitysten kohtaaminen peruskoulussa. Jyväskylän yliopisto, Kokkola (2008)
30. Asiyai, R.: Students' perception of the condition of their classroom physical learning environment and its impact on their learning and motivation. Coll. Stud. J. **48**(4), 716–726 (2014)
31. Lan-Ying, H., Xue-Mei, D.: An empirical study of learner-based teaching in EFL. Sino-US Engl. Teach. **9**(4), 1061–1064 (2012)
32. Jones, C.: Entrepreneurship education: Revisiting our role and its purpose. J. Small Bus. Enterp. Develop. **17**(4), 500–513 (2010)
33. Rogoff, B.: Apprenticeship in Thinking. Cognitive Development. Oxford University Press, Oxford (1990)
34. Mubaraq, F.: Rethinking the digital divide: emerging challenges in the new global economy. Dissertation study. University of Turku, Finland. E/28 (2018)
35. Tuikka, A-M., Vesala, H., Teittinen, A.: Digital disability divide in Finland. In: Li, H., Pálsdóttir, A., Trill, R., Suomi, R., Yegeniya, A. (eds.) Well-Being in the Information Society. Fighting Inequalities. Communications in Computer and Information Science, vol. 907, pp. 162–173, 7th International Conference, WIS 2018, Turku, Finland, 27–29 August 2018
36. Ding, J., Xiong, C., Liu, H.: Construction of a digital learning environment based on cloud computing. Br. J. Educ. Technol. **46**(6), 1367–1377 (2015)

37. Middleton, M., Perks, K.: New metaphor for motivation understanding student motivation. In: Classroom Insights from Educational Psychology: Motivation to learn. Transforming classroom culture to support student achievement. Corwin, Thousand Oaks, CA, pp. 1–12 (2014). https://sk.sagepub.com/books/motivation-to-learn/d8.xml
38. Curriculum of Bachelor of Education. University of Turku, Turku (2017)
39. National core curriculum for Basic Education 2014. Finnish National Board of Education. Helsinki (2014)
40. Darling-Hammond, L., Rothman, R.: Teaching in the Flat World: Learning from High-Performing Systems. Teachers College Press, New York (2015). http://ebookcentral.proquest. com/lib/kutu/detail.action?docID=3545037
41. Niemi, H., Jakku-Sihvonen, R.: Research-based teacher education. In: Jakku- Sihvonen, R., Niemi, H. (eds.) Research-Based Teacher Education in Finland: Reflections by Finnish Teacher Educators. Finnish Educational Research Association, Turku (2006)

Digitizing Basic Occupational Health and Safety Knowledge for Ebola Virus Disease Missions – Reaching Frontline Responders Through an Online Course

Heini Utunen[1,2](✉)

[1] World Health Organization, Geneva, Switzerland
utunenh@who.int
[2] Tampere University, Tampere, Finland

Abstract. This paper investigates the World Health Organization's (WHO) ePROTECT course, an occupational health and safety online briefing for Ebola Virus Disease (Ebola) that has become a key resource for responders battling Ebola on the frontline across different professional roles in various organizations, mainly in the Democratic Republic of Congo (DRC) and its neighbouring countries. It is a basis of the WHO's duty of care and has been made mandatory for its own personnel before deploying into Ebola missions. This study looks at the use case of the course. User patterns, locations, backgrounds and affiliations were analyzed. Additionally, a user survey was sent to all active course users to understand their motivation for taking the course. Significant user figures beyond WHO staff suggest the online course is a critical resource, transferring life-saving knowledge to responders at the Ebola frontline much beyond WHO. United Nations personnel make up the biggest user group. Completion rate in the English course is at a very high level; 90.8% of users completed the course. According to the user survey, the DRC and neighboring countries represent 2 in 3 of all course participants, suggesting the course is used in countries of active outbreak or immediate vicinity and majority of the users had worked in the Ebola themselves. Compulsory course requirement and keenness to gain more knowledge on the disease were the main motivations for course enrolment.

Keywords: Online learning · Digitized learning · Frontline response · Health emergencies · Ebola virus disease · WHO · OpenWHO · Information society

1 Introduction

Two of the latest Ebola outbreaks emerged in the Democratic Republic of the Congo (DRC) in 2018. The first one, 9th on record in the DRC, centred in the Équateur province. It was declared on the 8th of May 2018 and ended on the 24th of July 2018 [1]. The following outbreak, 10th on record in the DRC, was declared just a week after the 1st of August 2018 by the Ministry of Health on the other side of the vast county, in the province of North Kivu, where the disease had never been seen before [2]. The latter

© Springer Nature Switzerland AG 2020
M. Cacace et al. (Eds.): WIS 2020, CCIS 1270, pp. 265–282, 2020.
https://doi.org/10.1007/978-3-030-57847-3_19

North Kivu outbreak has continued through the beginning of 2020, making it the longest Ebola epidemic in the DRC in more than 40 years since the disease was first identified in 1976, close to the Ebola river in the northern DRC [3] as seen in Fig. 1.

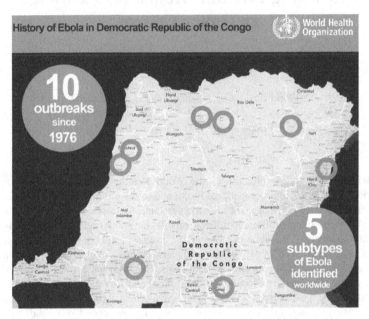

Fig. 1. History of Ebola in Democratic Republic of the Congo [3].

Informed by the May 2018 outbreak, a need for an online learning resource for deploying occupational health and safety personnel was identified jointly by the WHO Africa Region and the Learning Unit of the WHO Health Emergencies Programme (WHE). A course would require an open-source, online, low-bandwidth adjusted learning environment. In 2017 WHE launched such a platform, OpenWHO.org, to transfer WHO's technical knowledge to the frontlines of any health emergency response in low resourced settings, such as the Ebola outbreaks [4].

ePROTECT Ebola, a health and safety briefing in a self-paced Massive Open Online Course (MOOC) format, was published on OpenWHO the 6th of June 2018 and made a mandatory requirement for WHO deployments [5]. The learning resource was readily available as the 2018 North Kivu Ebola outbreak started in August 2018.

The course covers basic information needed to protect oneself when deploying to countries with Ebola virus disease. All WHO personnel responding to Ebola outbreaks are expected to complete the course as it aims to help protect personnel and prevent further spread of Ebola. Those who work on specialized tasks, such as working in direct contact with sick people, will need more advanced-level training and coaching. The learning objectives of the ePROTECT Ebola course are to: a) describe the signs, symptoms and transmission of Ebola virus disease and list prevention and control measures; b) use appropriate infection prevention and control precautions to protect yourself against Ebola virus and remain healthy during your mission; c) protect your health before, during and after deployment; d) describe the procedure to follow in case of sickness (related to Ebola virus disease or not, and/or accidental exposure to Ebola virus) and list the principles of medical evacuation and follow-up care; and e) recognize and manage stress.

The course along with other Ebola-related materials has witnessed a dramatic and sustained spike in the use on the platform, particularly in Sub-Saharan African countries. The course is available in both English and French, and provides basic information needed to prepare health emergency responders to stay safe and healthy for deployment to an Ebola-affected area. The course is generic and does not provide function-specific resources, for which there are other courses available on the OpenWHO. In total, five Ebola learning resources are hosted on OpenWHO as per Fig. 2 below [6].

Fig. 2. Ebola learning resources including different languages on OpenWHO.org

Some learning resources have been translated into local languages following a language mapping for the outbreak specific courses targeting health care workers and clinicians. The outbreaks of 2018 required translation into Lingala (spoken in Équateur province) and Congolese Swahili (spoken in both Équateur and North Kivu, along with French and English). ePROTECT Ebola was only produced in English and French due to the initial target audience of WHO personnel being deployed to DRC who speak either one or both of these languages.

This article examines and provides a description of the course use. The research questions in this study are as follows:

- What are the user metrics following the first 15 months of the course launch?
- Where are the users located?
- What are the course users' motivations to take the course and how did the course users hear about the course and access it?
- What are the top affiliations and demographics of the course users?
- How do the use case for the English and French language course versions compare?

1.1 Online Learning in Low Resourced Settings for Health Professionals

Currently, Massive Open Online Courses (MOOCs) present average completion rates of only 5–10% globally [7–12] and mostly remain in the domain of high-income countries [7, 8]. Veletsianos and Shepherdson (2016) highlight that MOOC learners spread over 194 countries with most users in North America and Europe, the majority of whom are males 20–40 years old, who already possess a college degree or higher [12, 13]. Despite this general trend, the literature notes several programs that defy this.

One prominent success was an online course in nursing leadership in the Americas, reported by Ortega and colleagues, with a 74–84% completion rate and a mean score of 90% on the final exam [14]. An online course in laboratory leadership and management in the Middle East and North Africa reported similar performance [15], as did a virtual campus in Mexico [16], and a cultural sensitivity training for rural Australia [17]. Online journal clubs [18] also proved successful. Murugesan and colleagues saw a completion rate of five times the average in a MOOC with majority low and middle-income country participation [7] and Laurillard reported a MOOC reaching 27 of the 47 most educationally-challenged countries, and in particular the disadvantaged groups [19].

Learning is defined in Business English as "the process of getting an understanding of something by studying it or by experience" in Cambridge Dictionary 2019 [20]. Cordell et al. (1998) stated that as the healthcare field is heavily information-oriented, well-managed "portable" information is crucial for every stakeholder involved, from frontline workers to policymakers [21]. Pakenham-Walsh and Bukachi (2009) established that information needs vary among health professionals, especially in developing countries [22]. Many factors influence continuous information needs. These factors can be related to profession, home institution, culture and usual infrastructure. Because of the complexity of these interrelated factors, there is no single method which allows a clear evaluation of health professionals' information needs. Every health professional has specific information needs, which may vary over time, clinical caseload and place.

Researchers Liyanagunawardena and Aboshady, as well as Murugesan et al. have studied the specific requirements of creating MOOCs for lower- and middle-income countries (LMIC) and recommended either excluding video and other high-bandwidth formats, or ensuring content accessibility offline, for example either creating an offline archive or offering downloadable material for later use [7, 23].

Other obvious obstacles include: lack of infrastructure, technical failures, structural barriers such as lack of IT gear and training, lack of time to access information on the ground, lack of communication of information from higher levels, and management of the information which is key, as introduced by Rutland and Smith [24, 25]. With limited access to internet in many rural facilities in developing countries (e.g. in Botswana), Park et al. noted in 2016 that healthcare workers struggle to get the right information in a timely manner due to possible discrepancies or outdated information, which complicates their work and may result in a lower trust from patients [26].

Knowledge transfer is key for professionals in health emergencies as important practical information about an agency's emergency response procedures may only be known by an experienced administrator or someone who has been working for the organization for a long time. In such a situation, there is a need to update information among the health professionals working in emergencies. Gebbie and Merrill noted that public health organizations and individuals of the public health workforce themselves expect an adequate emergency preparedness to make sure the response is both relevant and timely [27].

2   Research Methods

Statistical data of the two identical courses, English and French, totalling more than 16,000 users was generated in September 2019, 15 months after the English course launch and 12 months after the French course launch. The data was collected from the online courses' statistical data and metrics reporting system on the OpenWHO platform. User patterns and locations were analyzed based on Google Analytics. The OpenWHO platform's own statistics capabilities and data sets were overlaid.

Parallel to this, a user survey was sent to all active course users through a platform course announcement. The survey received 706 (606 in English, 100 in French) responses on user motivation, learning needs and level of comprehension, and were further analyzed to understand the use case and how the course was perceived by the users. The generic user sentiments were collected through their feedback in the open comments of the user survey. The most popular words used were extracted and analyzed with BigML and clustered by the lead word and most frequent words to review what type of topics were repeated in the answers. The user survey posed the following questions:

1. What was your motivation for taking this course?
2. How did you hear about this course?
3. Are you currently working or have you previously worked in an Ebola response?
4. Are you currently based in the Democratic Republic of Congo or bordering countries (South Sudan, Uganda, etc.)?
5. How did this course meet your learning needs?
6. Was the language used in the learning materials easy to understand?
7. Could you easily navigate the learning content on the website?
8. Would you recommend this course to others?
9. Are there any comments or suggestions you would like to share with us?

3   Global Use Case Examined

3.1   User Metrics and Completion Rates

The results show that as of September 2019, the English version of ePROTECT Ebola had 14,023 registered users, and 12,743 certificates of completion awarded with 90.8% completion rate. The French course had 2,307 registrations with 859 course certificates amounting to 37.2% completion rate. The English course completion rate of more than 90% is beyond industry standards [8, 10] and confirms the course is of a real need and completed diligently by the majority of the users. Also, the French course completion rate of 37% is very high against general completion rates (Table 1).

Table 1. ePROTECT Ebola overall courrse use (English and French) as of September 2019.

Course	Launch date	Total enrolments	Certificates issued	Completion rate
ePROTECT Ebola (English)	5 June 2018	14,023	12,743	90.8%
ePROTECT Ebola (French)	6 June 2018	2,307	859	37.2%

Since the course launch early June 2018, as illustrated in Fig. 3, both course enrolments and new user registrations swelled significantly in the months immediately following two outbreak declarations in the DRC in 2018. A very sharp spike was seen in October 2018, soon after two key events: firstly, in September 2018, WHO declared the risk of the spread of Ebola from the DRC to be "very high" at the regional level [2] and secondly, in October 2018, the UN and the Ministry of Health of South Sudan urged personnel to refresh their knowledge of Ebola and recommended the course. South Sudan's 1,000 enrolments made the country reach the third highest gross number of all enrolled users on the course at the end of 2018.

The increases in course enrolments and user registrations that had been sustained throughout 2018 also continued into 2019 and increased again as the Director-General of WHO declared the North Kivu outbreak to be a Public Health Emergency of International Concern on the 17th of July 2019 [2].

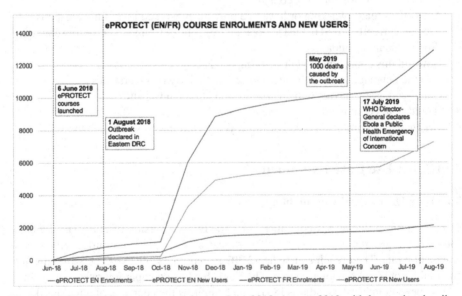

Fig. 3. ePROTECT Ebola course enrolments June 2018–August 2019 with key outbreak milestones. The new users graphs show the proportion of new learners brought by the course to the OpenWHO platform.

As mentioned in the Introduction, ePROTECT is one of the five Ebola resources on OpenWHO.org. Other Ebola courses also had an increase in interest when the first DRC outbreak was declared in May 2018 (Fig. 4). All Ebola courses attracted hundreds of users and reached thousands of users as the second outbreak surged from August 2018 onward. ePROTECT is the most popular Ebola-related course by registrations and was the second most popular course on OpenWHO after the Antimicrobial Resistance (AMR) course in 2019. Only when the 2019 novel coronavirus disease (COVID-19) emerged did COVID-19 resources become more popular than ePROTECT Ebola and AMR.

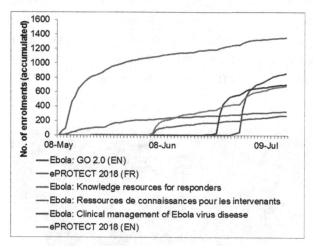

Fig. 4. Use of OpenWHO knowledge resources during first Ebola outbreak of 2018.

3.2 Course Use Geographically

When examining the global use figures of the ePROTECT Ebola course, the northern hemisphere is in the lead for the top ten countries with English language course use (Table 2a). The top ten countries for the French language (Table 2b) course use is similar, with the top two countries' registered users being the same in both languages. This user pattern is very similar to MOOC statistics reported globally [7, 8]. African countries which have had Ebola outbreaks within or near their borders constitute a significant use case for ePROTECT Ebola. The use is very centralized in total, the top five user countries constituting 41% of all ePROTECT Ebola users across the two-course languages.

By September 2019, the countries with the most users in the southern hemisphere were South Sudan, India, Nigeria and DRC, as shown in Table 2. To halt the spread of Ebola, two of these, South Sudan and DRC are listed as Priority 1 countries for Ebola operational readiness by the WHO (Fig. 5). South Sudan alone accounts for almost 2,000 users of the course.

Table 2. Top 10 countries by registrations, English course (2a) and French course (2b).

2a English course	Learners	2b French course	Learners
United States	5,096 (34.91%)	United States	374 (15.45%)
United Kingdom	3,490 (23.91%)	United Kingdom	343 (14.17%)
South Sudan	1,654 (11.33%)	DRC	315 (13.02%)
Netherlands	761 (5.21%)	South Sudan	131 (5.41%)
Italy	447 (3.06%)	France	87 (3.60%)
Denmark	341 (2.34%)	Netherlands	77 (3.18%)
India	320 (2.19%)	Rwanda	59 (2.44%)
Nigeria	303 (2.08%)	Guinea	43 (1.78%)
Kenya	252 (1.73%)	Cameroon	38 (1.57%)
France	251 (1.72%)	Switzerland	38 (1.57%)

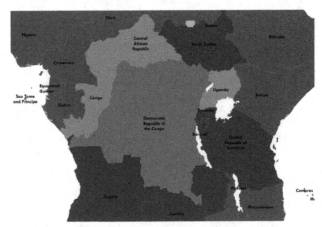

Fig. 5. WHO Regional Strategic Ebola Virus Disease Readiness Preparedness Plan June 2018–February 2019, WHO AFRO [28].

One reason for the proportionally high northern hemisphere enrolments could be that the course was requested to be completed by the international deployees to the Ebola response and therefore a group of the users are naturally from outside DRC and neighbouring countries. This also explains the fairly low user number in the DRC itself; the local responders are not requested to complete the course. First hand evidence from having worked with some of the Congolese Ebola responders personally, they also have experience from previous Ebola outbreaks in the country and thus would possess necessary knowledge.

3.3 User Motivation and How Users Heard About the Course and Accessed it

To understand the course user motivation, possible Ebola work context and the user experience should be considered. The course had 16,000 enrolments and the survey was sent out as an email announcement. Fewer than 7,000 users opened the announcement and 706 users filled it in. The user survey shows the motivation for the respondents (Fig. 6). They are divided by compulsory requirement, personal protection related motivations, those with interest in the disease itself, those who wish to strengthen their own knowledge, as well as those who wish to strengthen their CV or qualifications.

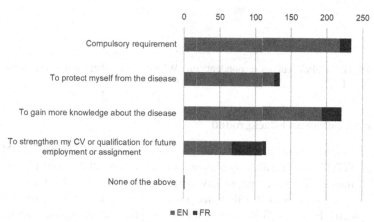

Fig. 6. ePROTECT Ebola survey respondents on "What was your motivation for taking this course?" n = 706 (EN 606, FR 100)

Similarly, when asked how the survey respondents heard about the course (Fig. 7), more than half of the English course users indicated their employer and approximately one third had found it on the internet themselves. One in ten had heard about it from a colleague or friend. For the French course, half of the respondents found it themselves through the internet, and one in four through colleagues, while even fewer found it through their employer. The French course user profile therefore aligns with a different motivation: that of self-interest and self-searched user.

An evaluation of channels through which users were brought to both the English and French courses demonstrates these are somewhat different. The English course is found mainly through Google, WHO Ebola websites and thirdly by UN National Library of Medicine, the latter being the main site for the French course users to find the course. Social media such as Facebook is much less important for both language courses but still brings traffic to the platform. A larger survey of the whole of OpenWHO platform traffic analysis showed similar differences between English and French site users [29]. Some sample user feedbacks are provided in the Annex 1.

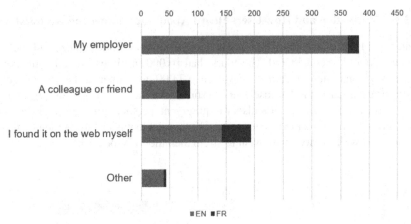

Fig. 7. ePROTECT Ebola survey respondents on "Where did you hear about this course?" n = 706 (EN 606, FR 100)

3.4 User Affiliation and Background

The most common professional affiliation of users enrolled in the course is "UN country team (UNCT)", which makes up almost half (44.8%) of all the course's registered users and confirms the course's popularity at the country-level (Fig. 8). The second and third most popular professional affiliations of users are "international organization" and "NGO" respectively. Of the WHO staff, a total of 677 had enrolled in the course. WHO has deployed approximately that amount of international staff during the first year of

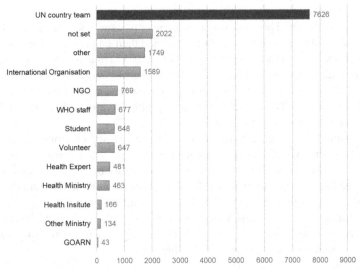

Fig. 8. ePROTECT Ebola English and French course users' professional affiliation. *Not set means the course participant has not wanted to reveal the professional background. *Other means their affiliation is not in the 12 affiliation options offered.

response and it corresponds to the figures being a compulsory requirement. Similarly, "UN country team" is the most popular professional affiliation of users based in South Sudan, Sudan and Kenya as detailed later in this article.

Further investigation of user demographics in Ebola readiness and preparedness countries of the WHO African region was made (Fig. 5). These nine countries are surrounding DRC, namely Rwanda, Burundi, Uganda, South Sudan, Tanzania, Central African Republic, Republic of the Congo, Zambia, and Angola. All Ebola-related courses on the OpenWHO platform in general, and the ePROTECT in particular has witnessed a spike in enrolments from the DRC and neighbouring countries where 2 in 3 of user survey respondents are based at. Further, according to the user survey, 2 in 3 users of the English course and 1 in 3 users of the French course have worked in Ebola response.

Between the 9th of October and the 25th of October 2018, the platform successfully welcomed 500–600 new users per day from the priority countries for Ebola preparedness activities, with a record of nearly 1,000 enrolments from South Sudan, after a successful UNCT campaign to recommend the course to the personnel. These countries contributed to approximately 900 new course enrolments a day across the English and French versions of the ePROTECT Ebola course at the end of 2019, during heavy transmission of the second DRC Ebola outbreak. Sudan belongs to the WHO Eastern Mediterranean region and is therefore not in the African Regional Readiness and Preparedness Plan but counts for a significant use case.

Looking at the largest use in the Global South by countries (Fig. 9), there is variety among the personnel registered, with South Sudan and Kenya UN country team being the biggest groups. In the countries with no Ebola outbreaks, such as India and Nigeria, the students and volunteers are the leading user groups by numbers. The same pattern is seen throughout the OpenWHO course use.

	South Sudan	India	Nigeria	DRC
Number of users	3224	342	241	300
Top user affiliation	UN country team (1976)	Student (206)	Volunteer (47)	UN country team (49)
2nd most common user affiliation	International organizations (326)	Other (29)	Health Ministries (44)	International organizations (46)
3rd most common user affiliation	Other (315)	Health Expert (24)	Other (35)	NGO (41)

Fig. 9. Top 4 countries in the Global South and top user affiliation for all Ebola resources.

3.5 User Demographics

When examining the age and gender distribution across the ePROTECT courses (Fig. 10), the largest user group for both languages is aged 30–39 years, with younger and older cohorts being less represented. The 50–59 are already a significantly smaller group and 60–69 very small user groups. Of those users who marked their gender, the clear majority are men, in the French course the male proportion being even higher than in the English course. This speaks to Veletsianos and Shepherdson's findings [12] on the MOOC learners in the northern hemisphere, the majority being male 20–40 years of age. What we do not know of OpenWHO users is whether they already possess a college degree or higher. Typically, OpenWHO provides topic and outbreak-related additional training for professionals in their domains. This is the case of the WHO and UN deployees to health emergencies: they are mandatorily experts of their own domains already.

The open-end comments provided word clusters as in Fig. 11. A high proportion of the respondents, 97.8%, would recommend the course to others.

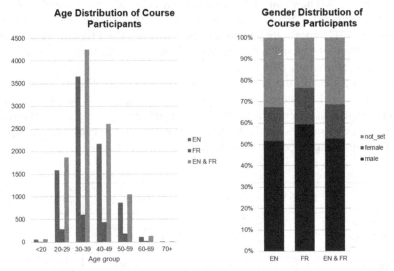

Fig. 10. Age and gender distribution of the ePROTECT participants who disclosed the information.

■ helpful (13.83%): helpful, ebola, prevention, content, material, online, experience, provided, protect.

■ people (11.65%): people, information, video, disease, helpful, management, add, themselves, daily.

■ ebola (12.16%): ebola, awareness, disease, information, improve, staff, consider, study, risk.

■ country (13.22%): country, knowledge, disease, protect, organization, emergency, control, drc, lot.

■ community (11.94%): community, continue, virus, person, appreciate, ebola, preparedness, type, self.

■ certificate (13.13%): certificate, practice, health, questions, protect, update, please, available, recommend.

▣ understand (11.88%): understand, access, completion, outbreak, care, request, staff, encourage, un.

■ learning (12.19%): learning, internet, opportunity, vaccine, currently, employers, provided, capacity, recommend.

Fig. 11. User survey's most popular words from the open comments analyzed using BigML and clustered by the lead word and most frequent words.

4 Discussion

This study surveyed general use case findings of the online course ePROTECT Ebola to understand the users, their locations, motivations, affiliations and background.

The course enables knowledge transfer for the most complex settings and makes critical protective information available with ease, thus providing unlimited equity and access to any interested learner. The user enrolments, increasing trend of the course use and the significantly high completion rates suggest the course has met its objectives. The course is formatted in an online package suited for low-income settings, thus mitigating barriers to access of information on the frontline of the response. The significant difference to global MOOC trends are the very high completion rates of this course.

The reach and accessibility of ePROTECT Ebola is evident, as it is hosted on an open-source online platform adjusted for low-bandwidths. Importantly, this online course demonstrates reach, access and use case in low resourced settings, which are often less represented in the domains of MOOCs as referenced by the literature. Interestingly, the discussion spaces on the course seem to create a microcosm that enables online information sharing across national borders among peers.

Emphasis was given to the course use, especially in the two Ebola outbreak hotspots in the DRC and the neighboring countries. These are locations where physical access is restricted due to security-compromised, distant, and hard to reach areas. The online dissemination in suitable formats for these contexts is crucial to close the gap for equitable access to information.

The English course users indicated the course had been made compulsory or they wanted to gain more knowledge and protect themselves. The biggest motivation for the French course users was the strengthening of the CV or qualification for future assignments, which was the smallest number of responses to the motivation question by the English course users. This indicates that the French course was likely performed by personnel for whom it was not mandatory, but rather an investment in learning and career. These could be personnel from the DRC or other countries in the vicinity. The lower course completion rate of the French course could be explained by this factor too.

Several users also stated that after completing the course, they decided not to seek deployment to Ebola missions. This indicates that the course can provide essential information early and function as and "reality check" for staff, allowing them to reflect on whether they are willing to take risks related to deployment. These risks include the direct threat of contracting Ebola virus disease, one of the deadliest infectious diseases, as well as environmental risks in which the response is operating, including severe physical risks of other infectious diseases, armed conflict, violence, active volcanoes as well as the methane filled lake in North Kivu. User testimonials also stated that the course had boosted their confidence before deployment, provided adequate information to protect them and helped their families understand the dangers they could face.

While the course was initially targeted to WHO personnel, it has expanded to be a resource recommended by other parts of the UN and employers. The high number of UNCT and international organization registrations suggests that the course is a WHO service of a specialized agency in health to the rest of the UN. The references made by UNCTs such as in South Sudan and the US National Library for Medicine are important channels in bringing learners to the course. Therefore, getting the course recommended by trusted organizations can make it even more popular. The user feedback gives a positive testimony of the course suitability in familiarizing and preparing for Ebola response mission.

The global use case of ePROTECT Ebola is very diverse due to the Ebola response community globally, either in the countries with Ebola outbreaks, or personnel working or interested in working in the response. The users largely represent the same phenomena as the MOOCs globally, by age, gender and geo-location [8–12]. The MOOC popularity globally is lower in the Global South. With the topic related to the outbreak mainly present in the Sub-Saharan Africa, the use in the countries with a history of Ebola outbreaks is expected and thus the use in the Global South is also present.

At the time of submitting this article in June 2020, a new Ebola outbreak was officially declared by The Ministry of Health of the DRC in Équateur Province on 1 June 2020 [30]. The outbreak that started in 2018 in North Kivu and Ituri provinces is still ongoing [31]. The need for ePROTECT Ebola thus continues.

Meanwhile, WHO as a whole and the OpenWHO team are in full response to the ongoing COVID-19 pandemic. Earlier health emergency and outbreak specific online course materials have enabled the platform to grow into a central learning hub for health experts worldwide. OpenWHO currently hosts more than 3 million course enrolments, the majority of which have resulted from COVID-19 course content. The ePROTECT Ebola course paved the way and got a continuation through the course ePROTECT Respiratory Infections, launched in February 2020 for COVID-19 occupational health and safety knowledge transfer.

4.1 Limitations and Suggestions for Further Future Research

The research examined the users, their motivation and use case of the OpenWHO ePRO-TECT Ebola course through available data. Course statistical data has some limitations as some users may have registered for the course in one country and accessed it in another. Also, if a foreign VPN is used for internet routing, the real use location is not captured. Given the data set includes more than 16,000 users, the general use case is still clear.

The user survey has its limitations, as only about 4% of the users responded to it, but proportionally the same share responded of the English users (4.32%) and French users (4.31%). The Ebola responders and the UN staff in the emergency domain may be some of the busiest people in the world, fighting diseases in complex contexts. Therefore, the response rate is explained by the responders being so busy. Repeated user surveys upon repatriation from a mission could be considered, as well as in-depth user interviews which might bring more clarity on the course's usefulness.

WHO personnel in countries are also considered part of the UN country team, but as only one affiliation could be chosen, most likely all WHO personnel have chosen WHO, though they could be UNCT members too. Further research would be necessary to understand user backgrounds, their employment going forward and after deployment, as well as review of the usefulness of the material.

Given the languages in potential Ebola contexts and the readiness of countries, Arabic and Portuguese course necessity could be assessed. Some service design research would benefit the different language courses, given that more than 25% of French users said that navigation in the learning content was not easy. Only 2% of the English users felt the same.

Additional research could include information acquisition on related online learning platforms and better understanding of the users' information behaviours, such as how the real time information dissemination between responders in the collaborative and discussion groups could be better utilized. Online information literacy research could also inform the differences among the various language users and help target resources to different audiences. For future consideration, during the time of this article's submission WHO has made available ePROTECT Respiratory Infections in response to the emergence of COVID-19. Need for ePROTECTs for other transmission modes and vectors could be examined among the responders.

5   Conclusion

The course acts as a primary introduction to Ebola deployment and is a core resource used by thousands of current and future frontline Ebola responders, thus fulfilling the duty of care for WHO and similar organizations which are deploying personnel into outbreak responses of one of the deadliest diseases known. The course users are from all around the world. The course would form a readily available knowledge base if the Ebola outbreak were to flare up in other countries.

The related fields of study benefit from this research as it provides user findings from a global platform. The research could also set a precedent for other organizations operating in the similar environments and mandated in information dissemination and capacity building.

This research provides evidence on the power of online learning in emergencies and how it can benefit organizations deploying and planning to deploy personnel to demanding missions. The real time production of resources for personnel in easily accessible formats is the 21st century solution for geographically dispersed organizations, offering learners access to the same source of trusted information.

Acknowledgements.   **Academic supervisors of the doctoral dissertation studies**
Associate Professor, J. Tuomas Harviainen, Tampere University
University lecturer, Heidi Enwald, University of Oulu
WHO colleagues in Learning and Capacity Development
Supervisor, Head of Unit, Dr Gaya Manori Gamhewage
OpenWHO team Ursula Yu Zhao, Ngouille Ndiaye, Corentin Piroux, Paula Christen, Melissa Attias and Michael Reza Farzi.

Annex 1. Survey Respondents Open Comment Feedbacks Sample

Good course, especially for all people that will going to country suspected a disease.

The course is very useful not only to those countries which are affected but it provides vast knowledge to an individual on how to react when encounters such challenges. I suggest that may this course be available even on hard copies to enable the larger community which may not be able to access internet or computers. If possible be availed in all countries regardless of the outbreaks and in local languages. I believe information is power and for warned is for armed. If people are prior prepared and better informed it will assist in reducing the spread of infectious deadly diseases.

Looking forward for to learn about other emerging diseases like Nipah virus disease etc.

Course material was good and the presenters were clear and well spoken so easy to follow. The course could do with some additional information aimed at people who will not be front line respondent's but will be in support roles and also information on how to protect your self and your family would be good.

I think there should be more information about the local situation and method.

I would recommend that this course be made compulsory for all the UN, NGOs, and Government workers who are working within the Ebola affected countries and the neighboring countries.

Thank you for providing this information in a very simple manner.

The course really brings out issues Ebola transmission and prevention.

I learn a lot, now I can protect myself from Ebola disease Thanks to all.

Expand learning time, time is too limited, provide some of video about Infection Prevention and Control process in for visual training.

This course is very important to everyone to acquire Knowledge and learn how to prevent our self from contacting the disease.

This course should be extended as far as for the all community of South Sudan so that they can also be saved from this Ebola thank you.

The course is very informative and has given me full knowledge of the EVD and the precautions to take to protect myself as well as stop the spread of the virus. My thanks goes to those who developed the course and for my employer for making a requirement for all the staff to do the course.

Please provide details of the Ebola Virus. Examples such as; How long will it live outside the body for instance, a contaminated door handle or even a toilet seat? Can a person be infected by buying fruit or vegetables in a market which were touched by a sick/infected person?

I recommended for community mobilizer.

I have almost participated in all course of openwho.org offers and gain a lot of knowledge and perspective on different title and subjects of emergency. however, i never encounter course focusing on Traveler's Health service and ways and documents that raise capacity of such matters. I am hoping to see related course on the future.

References

1. World Health Organization, Ebola situation reports 12 May 2018 and 25 July 2018 https://www.who.int/ebola/situation-reports/drc-2018/en/. Accessed 28 Aug 2020
2. World Health Organization, Disease outbreak news 4 August 2018. https://www.who.int/csr/don/4-August-2018-ebola-drc/en. Accessed 03 Jan 2020
3. World Health Organization, History of Ebola in the Democratic Republic of the Congo. https://www.who.int/ebola/historical-outbreaks-drc/en/. Accessed 03 Jan 2020
4. WHO Health Emergencies Learning platform. https://OpenWHO.org. Accessed 02 Jan 2020

5. ePROTECT Ebola - occupational health and safety online learning course. https://openwho. org/courses/e-protect. Accessed 03 Mar 2020
6. Utunen, H., Christen, P., Gamhewage, G., Zhao, U., Attias, M.: Knowledge transfer for Ebola outbreak – production and use of OpenWHO.org online learning resources. In: 14th International Conference on Wireless and Mobile Computing, Networking and Communications (WiMob), Limassol, pp. 20–27 (2018)
7. Murugesan, R., Nobes, A., Wild, J.: A MOOC approach for training researchers in developing countries. Open Praxis **9**, 45–57 (2017). https://doi.org/10.5944/openpraxis.9.1.476
8. Liyanagunawardena, T.R., Adams, A.A., Williams, S.A.: MOOCs: a systematic study of the published literature 2008–2012. Int. Rev. Res. Open Distrib. Learn. **14**, 202–227 (2013). http://doi.org/10.19173/irrodl.v14i3.1455
9. Jordan, K.: Initial trends in enrolment and completion of massive open online courses. Int. Rev. Res. Open Distrib. Learn. **15**(1) (2014). https://doi.org/10.19173/irrodl.v15i1.1651
10. Hew, K.F., Cheung, W.S.: Students' and instructors' use of massive open online courses (MOOCs). Motivations and challenges. Educ. Res. Rev. **12**, 45–58 (2014). https://doi.org/10. 1016/j.edurev.2014.05.001
11. Sneddon, J., Barlow, G., Bradley, S., Brink, A., Chandy, S.J., Nathwani, D.: Development and impact of a massive open online course (MOOC) for antimicrobial stewardship. J. Antimicrob. Chemother. **73**, 1091–1097 (2018). http://doi.org/10.1093/jac/dkx493
12. Veletsianos, G., Shepherdson, P.: A systematic analysis and synthesis of the empirical MOOC literature published in 2013–2015. Int. Rev. Res. Open Distrib. Learn. **17**, 198–221 (2016). https://doi.org/10.19173/irrodl.v17i2.2448
13. Liyanagunawardena, T.R., Williams, S.A.: Massive open online courses on health and medicine: review. J. Med. Internet Res. **16**, e191 (2014). https://doi.org/10.2196/jmir.3439
14. Ortega, J., Hooshmand, M., Foronda, C., Padron, M., Simon, D., Waters, M., et al.: Developing nurse leaders across the Americas: evaluation of an online nursing leadership course. Rev. Panam. Salud Publica **42**, 1–8 (2018). https://doi.org/10.26633/RPSP.2018.152
15. Perrone, L.A., Confer, D., Scott, E., Livingston, L., Bradburn, C., McGee, A. et al: Implementation of a mentored professional development programme in laboratory leadership and management in the Middle East and North Africa. EMHJ-Eastern Mediterranean Health Journal, **22**, 832–839 (2016). https://doi.org/10.26719/2016.22.11.832
16. Ramos Herrera, I., Alfaro Alfaro, N., Fonseca León, J., García Sandoval, C., González Castañeda, M., López Zermeño, Md.C., et al.: Virtual campus of public health: six years of human resources education in Mexico. Revista Panamericana de Salud Publica **36**, 342–347 (2014). http://doi.org/S1020-49892014001000009
17. Lau, M., Woodward-Kron, R., Livesay, K., Elliott, K., Nicholson, P.: Cultural respect encompassing simulation training: being heard about health through broadband. J. Public Health Res. **5**, 36–42 (2016). https://doi.org/10.4081/jphr.2016.657
18. Palan, J., Roberts, V., Bloch, B., Kulkarni, A., Bhowal, B., Dias, J.: The use of a virtual learning environment in promoting virtual journal clubs and case-based discussions in trauma and orthopaedic postgraduate medical education: the Leicester experience. J. Bone Joint Surg. Br. **94**, 1170–1175 (2012). http://doi.org/10.1302/0301-620X.94B9.28780
19. Laurillard, D.: The educational problem that MOOCs could solve: professional development for teachers of disadvantaged students. Research in Learning Technology, 24 (2016). https:// doi.org/10.3402/rlt.v24.29369
20. Cambridge Dictionary https://dictionary.cambridge.org/dictionary/english/learning
21. Cordell, W., Overhage, J., Waeckerle, J.: Strategies for improving information management in emergency medicine to meet clinical, research, and administrative needs. Ann. Emergency Med. **31**(2), 172–178 (1998). https://doi.org/10.1111/j.1553-271

22. Pakenham-Walsh, N., Bukachi, F.: Information needs of health care workers in developing countries: a literature review with a focus on Africa. Hum. Res. Health **7**, 1 (2009). https://doi.org/10.1186/1478-4491-7-30

23. Liyanagunawardena, T.R., Aboshady, O.A.: Massive open online courses: a resource for health education in developing countries. Glob Health Promotion **25**, 74–76 (2018). http://doi.org/10.1177/1757975916680970

24. Hew, K.F., Cheung, W.S.: Students' and instructors' use of massive open online courses (MOOCs): Motivations and challenges. Educ. Res. Rev. **12**, 45–58 (2014). https://doi.org/10.1016/j.edurev.2014.05.001

25. Rutland, J., Smith, A.: Information needs of the 'frontline' public health workforce. Public Health **124**(11), 659–663 (2010). https://doi.org/10.1016/j.puhe.2010.06.002

26. Park, E.: Information needs of Botswana health care workers and perceptions of Wikipedia. Int. J. Med. Inform. **95**, 8–16 (2016). https://doi.org/10.1016/j.ijmedinf.2016.07.013

27. Gebbie, K., Merrill, J.: Public health worker competencies for emergency response. J. Public Health Manage. Practice, **8**, 73–81 (2002). http://doi.org/10.1097/01.ACM.0000242573.713 14.74

28. WHO Regional Strategic Ebola Virus Disease Readiness Preparedness Plan June 2018 – February 2019, WHO AFRO. https://www.who.int/csr/resources/publications/ebola/strate gic-plan-for-evd/en/

29. Zhao, U., George R., Utunen H., Gamhewage G.: OpenWHO traffic analysis: can we predict non-profit course reach by dissemination channel? (2019). http://ceur-ws.org/Vol-2356/bus iness_short5.pdf

30. WHO Newsroom. Ebola outbreak detected in northwest Democratic Republic of the Congo. https://www.who.int/news-room/detail/01-06-2020-new-ebola-outbreak-detected-in-northw est-democratic-republic-of-the-congo-who-surge-team-supporting-the-response. Accessed 26 June 2020

31. Ebola virus disease Democratic Republic of Congo: external situation report 95/ 2020. https://www.who.int/publications/i/item/10665-332254. Accessed 26 June 2020

Author Index

Printed in the United States
by Baker & Taylor Publisher Services